Communities and Crisis

The Medieval Mediterranean

Peoples, Economies and Cultures, 400–1500

VOLUME 83

Communities and Crisis

Bologna during the Black Death

By

Shona Kelly Wray

BRILL

LEIDEN • BOSTON
2009

Cover illustration: Archivio di Stato, Demaniale, 340/5083, doc. 21 (4 July, 1348)
Testament of Darius Farolfini

This book is printed on acid-free paper.

Library of Congress Cataloging-in-Publication Data

Kelly Wray, Shona.
Communities and crisis : Bologna during the Black Death / by Shona Kelly Wray.
p. cm. — (The medieval Mediterranean : peoples, economies, and cultures, 400–1500, ISSN 0928-5520 ; v. 83)
Includes bibliographical references and index.
ISBN 978-90-04-17634-8 (hbk. : alk. paper) 1. Black Death—Social aspects—Italy—Bologna—History. 2. Black Death—Social aspects—Italy—Bologna—History—Sources. 3. Notaries—Italy—Bologna—History—To 1500. 4. Wills—Italy—Bologna—History—To 1500. 5. City and town life—Italy—Bologna—History—To 1500. 6. Community life—Italy—Bologna—History—To 1500. 7. Parishes—Italy—Bologna—History—To 1500. 8. Bologna (Italy)—History—To 1506. 9. Bologna (Italy)—Social conditions. 10. Bologna (Italy)—Economic conditions. I. Title. II. Series.

RC178.I82B659 2009
614.5'7320945411—dc22

2009012906

ISSN 0928-5520
ISBN 978 90 04 17634 8

PRINTED IN THE NETHERLANDS

CONTENTS

ACKNOWLEDGEMENTS

This book has been a long time in coming. While I have thoroughly enjoyed talking about my findings at conferences and seminars, returning to the archives, and exploring topics spurred by new readings in the notarial records and discussions at meetings, my choices to extend the process have sorely tried the patience of editors at Brill, colleagues in my department, and my family at home. I owe to them first of all a deep debt of gratitude for their support.

Scholarship is nourished and enriched by participation in communities that sustain research and communication. I was fortunate to spend time in one such wonderful community of scholars and artists at the American Academy in Rome. I thank especially Lester Little and Michelle Mulcahey and members of the Medieval Studies discussion group at the AAR for their insightful communications. My colleagues at UMKC have formed another strong supporting community for me, of which I am lucky to have so many excellent medievalists as partners in research and teaching. Of my colleagues I thank especially Jim Falls, who read through the manuscript at an earlier stage, and Linda Voigts, who provided me with exciting opportunities early on to discuss my findings on the Black Death. The students in my undergraduate course on the Black Death and graduate students in various seminars have also been a stimulating force in my work and thinking. I also wish to thank the Miller Nichols Library staff and especially the office of Inter-Library Loan. In addition to the Rome Prize, the research for this book was supported by a University of Missouri Research Board Grant and a Faculty Research Grant.

Over the years I have been able to hone my ideas on testaments and notarial records, on women's inheritance, and on the Black Death with many exceptional individuals at conferences and seminars in the US and overseas. I have grown and my work has benefited from their suggestions, but all errors and shortcomings remain, of course, my own. I have learned from and thank Martin Bertram, Isabelle Chabot, Sam Cohn, William Connell, George Dameron, Steven A. Epstein, Monica Green, Linda Guzzetti, Shennon Hutton, Sherri Johnston, Bill Jordan, Julius Kirshner, Glenn Kumhera, Trish Skinner, Carol Lansing, Christine

Meek, Andreas Meyer, Paul Oldfield, Duane Osheim, Dan Smail, and Jutta Sperling. Sarah Blanshei read several chapters and has given me invaluable advice from her immense knowledge of the sources. Special thanks also go to Roisin Cossar and Elena Brizio who read through the entire manuscript with care. The work has also benefited from the comments of two anonymous readers for Brill.

In the Archivio di Stato of Bologna, Massimo Giansante has always been extremely generous with his great knowledge of the archives. Giorgio Tamba as director of the ASB was also very supportive of my project. Their scholarship and archival expertise have been important guides for me. The staff of the ASB make it a pleasurable place to work. At the University of Bologna, Tiziana Lazzari, Paolo Pirillo, and Rosella Rinaldi provided a forum for fruitful discussions of my research. I am privileged to have known two masters: Gianfranco Orlandelli, with whom I studied paleography, and Antonio Ivan Pini, who offered me advice when I was a graduate student mining the depths of the *Memoriali*. It should be obvious that the prolific writings of Antonio Ivan Pini inform large parts of this monograph. His untimely death was a loss to all students of medieval Bologna. I offer this book in dedication to his memory.

My sister, Maggi Kelly, generously gave her time and expertise to produce the maps. I dedicate this book also to her and the rest of my family.

Parts of Chapters Three, Four, and Six appeared in earlier versions and different form in the following articles: "*Speculum et Exemplar*: The Notaries of Bologna during the Black Death," *Quellen und Forschungen aus italienischen Archiven und Bibliotheken* 81 (2001): 200–227; "Women, Family, and Inheritance in Bologna during the Black Death," in *Love, Marriage, and Family Ties in the Middle Ages*, eds. Miriam Muller and Isabel Davis (Belgium: Brepols, 2003), 205-215; "Boccaccio and the Doctors: Medicine and Compassion in the Face of Plague," *Journal of Medieval History* 30 (2004): 301–322; "Tracking Families and Flight in Bologna during the Black Death," *Medieval Prosopograpy: History and Collective Biography* 25 (2004, published 2008): 145–160.

LIST OF TABLES, FIGURES, AND MAPS

Tables

Figures

Maps

A NOTE ON CURRENCY, NAMES, AND TITLES

The monetary sums noted in the documents are monies of account involving the standard values of *denari*, *soldi*, and *lire*. Twelve *denari* equaled a *soldo*, and twenty *soldi* equaled a *lire*. The money that was coined and circulated in Bologna during 1191 to 1464 were the Bolognini, appearing as *grosso* or *picciolo* (worth one twelfth of a *grosso*), which are not listed in the documents or this study. Some bequests from the Bolognese testaments were indicated in values of the Venetian ducat and Florentine florin. Calculations to convert these currencies to the Bolognese *soldi* and *denari* can be done by means of Peter Spufford, *A Handbook of Medieval Exchange* (London, 1986), pp. 72–77.

Names have been left in the original Latin, except for those individuals who are well known, such as the law professors of the university of Bologna or religious figures. I have also used the Italianized names when referring to the elite families of Bologna. In the text and tables I have retained the Latin names through out, including use of fq for *filius quondam* or *filia quondam*. I have followed exactly the records in the spelling of names, which was not standardized: there was frequent doubling of letters (e.g., Pepolis and Peppolis, Galuciis and Galluciis); the letters *h* and *p* were often added (e.g., Blanchuciis/Blancuciis, Bonacaptis/Bonacatis, Bolognittus/Bologniptus, and in the case of the priestly title *dopnus* for *dominus*); and several letters were used interchangeably such as *ch*, *c*, and *g* (e.g., Panichalis/Panicalis/Panigallis), *u* and *o* (e.g., Bertulucius/Bertolucius), *s* and *x* (e.g., Basacomatribus/Baxacomatribus), *c* and *t* (e.g., Galutiis/Galuciis). However, because notaries switched back and forth between *ç*/*Ç* and *z*/*Z* (e.g., Bonzaminus or Bonçaminus, Zambechariis or Çambechariis), I have for ease and simplicity in searching names used *z*/*Z*. I am loath to impose upon the notarial records a sort of standardization that was not present. The retention of the Latin spelling is not intended to confuse, but instead aid scholars in further research of this material.

Titles in late medieval Italy varied according to local usage. In fourteenth-century Bologna the use of *dominus* and *domina* was standard for married people and does not appear to have indicated any difference in social status. Thus I have omitted it and retained only those titles which did differentiate the holder from others either in terms of wealth or social prominence, such as *nobilis* or *providus*, or profession, such as *magister* or *ser*. It should be noted that, according to the written evidence in the notarial records, the notaries of Bologna did not regularly use the title *ser*. The priests of Bologna were distinguished by the title *dopnus*, which I have retained.

INTRODUCTION

> ... considering that during this year there was in all the world and especially in Bologna an infinite mortality the likes of which has never been seen on earth ...*
>
> From a petition for tax relief to lords of Bologna, Giovanni and Giacomo Pepoli, 20 August 1348

This book is about society under stress, about people's actions in the face of disease. A frightening, new pestilence entered the ports of Sicily and northern Italy at the end of 1347 and spread inland in the spring of 1348. It moved throughout Europe in the following three years, killing over one third of the entire population. Italy was the first place in Europe to suffer, and the devastation was particularly heavy, with some towns losing over half of their populations. Whether the Black Death was an epidemic of bubonic plague due to the bacterium, *Yersinia pestis*, or of a viral hemorrhagic fever or was the result of concurrent, multiple epidemics is not the subject of this book.[1] Instead, the subject is the populace of the late medieval town of Bologna. The Black Death serves as a lens to examine a social world. What is uncovered from the documents about the actions of individuals during the epidemic may also be useful to researchers of the disease, but it would be inaccurate to predict how the epidemic should have unfolded based on modern plague studies. Diseases mutate over time and, thus, the context for discussion of the experience of the Black Death cannot be bubonic plague. Instead, this study of the epidemic starts with the evidence that

* Archivio di Stato di Bologna, Provigioni cartacee, Signoria Pepoli, reg. 36, fol. 133v: "Considerantes in toto munde et maxime in civitate Bononie divinitum et destinatum anno presenti maximum infinite mortalitatis iudicium quod numquam in terris simile visum fuit..."

[1] I use the term "plague" to refer to a non-specific disease and the historical label of the "Black Death" to connote the first epidemic of 1347–1351, not the disease nor the recurrent later epidemics. On the debate on the epidemiology of the Black Death see Susan Scott and Christopher J. Duncan, *Biology of Plagues: Evidence from Historical Populations* (Cambridge, 2001) and Samuel Kline Cohn, Jr., *The Black Death Transformed: Disease and Culture in Early Renaissance Europe* (New York, 2002) and his critique of Scott and Duncan in Cohn and Guido Alfani, "Households and Plague in Early Modern Italy," *Journal of Interdisciplinary History* 38 (2007): 177–205.

remains and makes no assumptions about what may or may not have happened based on the characteristics of the disease.

The social communities of late medieval urban Italy are the context for this study. During the last three decades there has been a spate of studies on the social communities and networks that shaped and informed life in medieval and Renaissance Italy. The bonds of family, work, religion, and neighborhood were interwoven through all social interactions. Much of our knowledge of the social life of the medieval populace comes from studies of Renaissance Florence and Venice.[2] This book explores these themes in an earlier period, which is often harder to investigate because of the lack of appropriate sources, and in a city, which has not received adequate attention from English-language scholars despite the fame of its university and wealth of archival material. As a town of approximately 50,000 at the end of the thirteenth and perhaps 45,000 before the Black Death, Bologna is more representative than heavily-examined Florence and Venice. Its political history of turning from a communal government to a *signoria* before mid fourteenth century, instead of an enduring republic, also makes Bologna's history more typical.

In contrast to the paucity of studies on medieval Bologna, the topic of the Black Death has been the subject of intense historical scrutiny.[3] The debates surrounding the medieval epidemic of 1347–1349 appear unending. Despite the mountains of published material, there is a strong need for further investigation for Bologna and beyond.[4] This book goes beyond any previous study of the Black Death by examining the

---

[2] See references in footnote 1 of Chapter Five.

[3] The bibliography is enormous, especially for England, and can best be approached by recent document collections, such as Rosemary Horrox, *The Black Death* (Manchester, 1994) and John Aberth, *The Black Death 1348–1350: A Brief History with Documents* (Boston, 2005), and general works such Colin Platt, *King Death* (Toronto, 1997), William Naphy and Andrew Spicer, *The Black Death and the History of Plagues 1345–1730* (Stroud, Gloucestershire, 2000), and Philip Ziegler, *The Black Death* (1970; repr. London, 1997), which remains a useful survey. For northern Europe, see Ole Benedictow, *The Black Death 1346–1353: The Complete History* (Rochester, NY, 2004). For Italy, see *La peste nera: Dati di una realtà ed elementi di una interpretazione* (Spoleto, 1994) and Cohn, *Black Death Transformed*.

[4] Antonio Ivan Pini has done the most in furthering our understanding of the impact of plague on Bologna, but he did not, however, produce a study of Bologna during the epidemic. Antonio Ivan Pini, "Forme di conduzione, rendita fondiaria e rese cerealicole nel Bolognese dopo la peste del 1348: L'azienda del convento di San Domenico," in *Medioevo rurale: Sulle tracce della civiltà contadina*, eds. Vito Fumagalli and Gabriella Rossetti (Bologna, 1980), 259–297.

immediate experience of the epidemic. Historians of medieval Italy have relied on chroniclers and literary authors such as Giovanni Boccaccio, Agnolo di Tura del Grasso, and Gabriele de' Mussis to understand what it must have been like to live through the unbelievably frightening experience of massive mortality brought on by an unknown, infectious disease on an epidemic scale. Chroniclers expressed their horror of the experience of plague in intensely dramatic descriptions, and the Black Death is everywhere told and retold today with their emphasis on shock, horror, and upheaval. College textbooks for Western and World history survey courses repeat medieval chroniclers's portrayals of the epidemic, emphasizing the breakdown of normal human relations. Responding to an unabated appetite for studies of the Black Death, the popular press continues to print new books that rehash the same medieval stories adding to the mix new additions of scientific findings on modern diseases.[5] My work does not rely on literary accounts, but presents new medieval evidence of actual behaviors during the epidemic using an under-utilized source: the testament. Micro-historical studies based on the reconstruction of families are difficult, if not impossible, for most of the medieval period, but the many testaments produced in Bologna during the months when the plague struck has allowed for such an analysis. The information found in the notarial registers of Bologna, known as the *Libri Memoriali*, and the testaments of the suppressed religious houses, known as the *Demaniale*, is unmatched. By means of the paper trail of the contract-based, notarial culture of medieval Bologna, we can construct an accurate portrait of life during the crisis.

Notarial culture was fundamental, penetrating all sectors of medieval life, and thus notarial sources provide evidence for the activities of people at all levels of society. In addition to uncovering material on historical subjects that are often lost to history such as women and members of the non-elite classes, notarial records also reveal important new information about the historical figures who have traditionally garnered the limelight. For Bologna, political historians have studied the decrees and legislation of the ruling Pepoli family, but the acts and testaments of the *Memoriali* at mid fourteenth century shed new light on their piety and place within the civic communities. Similarly, the

---

[5] John Kelly, *The Great Mortality: An Intimate History of the Black Death, the Most Devastating Plague of All Time* (New York, 2005).

professors of the *Studium* were famous in their day and their treatises have long been the focus of study by historians of education and the law. Their wills as discussed in this book provide information on the marriage and inheritance strategies of this powerful and prestigious intellectual class. But the clients of notaries were not simply the rich and famous. As the wills of artisanal families discussed in this book reveal, many of the commoner classes made choices that were significantly different from the elites on whom most studies have been based. Also offered in this book is new information on notaries that goes beyond the usual discussion of the notariate and notarial law. Their registers illuminate not only the ways that the notariate functioned as an institution permeating almost all aspects of governmental, commercial, and social interactions in town, but also the social role of the notary in civic life, especially in the neighborhoods. Thus this book is not merely an investigation of the immediate experience of the Black Death, it is also a demonstration of the fundamental nature of notarial culture in medieval civic life. Notarial records provide a roadmap to understand the experience of the epidemic, and plague promoted an abundance of records in a short time that allow us to chart the extent to which notarial culture informed daily life.

Most examinations of reaction to plague that reach the detailed level of this book come from the early modern period when the disease repeatedly cycled back through Europe. Historians tell the story of attitudes to plague in the early modern period in terms of the determined management of disease by professionals. The administrations of Renaissance Italian cities organized boards of health to oversee activity during recurring outbreaks. Urban health officials of the fifteenth and sixteenth centuries developed ordinances with strict measures and penalties for dealing with public health during times of plague. Cities imposed quarantines on people exposed to contagion. Whole families were isolated, while the infected were removed to pesthouses. Under official direction, the bedding and belongings of victims of plague were burned, and their houses were fumigated with smoke and cleansed with vinegar. Boards of health organized burials outside the city following detailed regulations concerning the location of graves and disposal of corpses.[6] If they did not already have one, cities paid for communal

[6] For the management of plague in Renaissance Italy, see the works of Carlo Cipolla on plague ordinances and legislation in seventeenth-century Italy: *Faith, Reason and*

doctors or *medici condotti*, who provided free services to the poor and charged wealthier patients on a sliding scale.[7] Physicians wrote tract after tract on the prevention of and remedies against plague. With the invention of the printing press, these tractates were made widely available.[8] And for those who were too poor to procure the more expensive ingredients, public health officials circulated recipes for the "easy medicines" recommended by board-sponsored physicians.

While much less evidence exists to study the management of the disease in 1348, what remains also supports the view that people of all social ranks sought to manage their responses to the epidemic. The well-known physicians and professors of medicine in Italy, Gentile da Foligno and Giovanni della Penna, also produced *consilia* against plague. They were addressed to civic officials and physicians in order that immediate action be taken to prevent and treat the disease. As Anna Campbell, Dominick Palazzotto, and Jon Arrizibalaga have demonstrated, their advice is very similar to later plague tractates.[9] The magistrates of some Italian cities immediately passed legislation to prevent the spread of disease. The most famous example and fullest extant civic plague ordinances of 1348 come from Pistoia.[10] As will be discussed in Chapter Four, the intention of the ordinances was to keep Pistoia free from the infection that was raging in the nearby towns of Pisa and Lucca: mobility was restricted, infected clothing or bedding

---

the Plague in Seventeenth-Century Tuscany (New York, 1979); *Fighting the Plague in Seventeenth-Century Italy* (Madison, Wisconsin, 1981); "A Plague Doctor," in *The Medieval City*, eds. Harry A. Miskimmin, David Herlihy, and A.L. Udovitch (New Haven, 1977), 65–72.

[7] Katherine Park, *Doctors and Medicine in Early Renaissance Florence* (Princeton, 1985), pp. 90–91.

[8] See Darrel W. Amundsen, "Medical Deontology and Pestilential Disease in the Late Middle Ages," in his *Medicine, Society, and Faith in the Ancient and Medieval Worlds* (Baltimore, 1996), 289–309. Cohn, *Black Death Transformed* pp. 274–279 lists the plague tracts published by Sudhoff in the *Archiv fur Geschichte der Medezin* between the years 1910 and 1925.

[9] Cohn argues that there is a difference between the tracts of 1348–1349 and those of the later fourteenth century in *Black Death Transformed*. See, however, the works of Anna Montgomery Campbell, *The Black Death and Men of Learning* (New York, 1931); Dominick Palazzotto, "The Black Death and Medicine: A Report and Analysis of the Tractates written between 1348 and 1350" (PhD diss., University of Kansas, 1973); and Jon Arrizabalaga, "Facing the Black Death: Perceptions and Reactions of University Medical Practitioners," in *Practical Medicine from Salerno to the Black Death* (Cambridge, 1994), 237–88.

[10] Alberto Chiappelli, "Gli ordinamenti sanitari del comune di Pistoia contro la pestilenza del 1348," *Archivio Storico Italiano* ser. 4, 20 (1887), 3–21.

was burned, burials were regulated, and deaths were reported to the commune. Regulations of butchers and tanners were implemented to preserve public health by reducing miasma or corrupt air. All of these measures were in line with later plague legislation.

In other towns in Italy less evidence remains, but the same general trend to manage the disease can be found. Florence, where plague had entered earlier in March, passed similar regulations in April concerning travel and the belongings of infected persons. A commission was appointed to regulate matters of public health, and the city paid for the autopsies of bodies of several plague victims "in order to know their illness more clearly".[11] The government of Perugia asked physicians to dissect the cadavers of plague victims.[12] The government of Venice passed plague legislation in 1348 that prohibited movement and regulated burials.[13]

In Bologna, no plague legislation has remained. However, as will be demonstrated in Chapter Four, the government did not disband. The *signori* or lords of Bologna continued their normal executive function of receiving citizens's petitions during the summer when plague was raging. The introductory quote is taken from one of these petitions. The voice of Bolognese citizens expressing their shock at the onset of the epidemic is almost impossible to find among the legal records. Indeed, in the testaments written during the epidemic there is no mention of plague. Nevertheless, the huge numbers of these documents are eloquent testimony to the very real and frightening presence of massive death. It is in the mundane and highly formulaic notarial records that we find the most vivid evidence for the management of life during a time of overwhelming death. This book tries to redress the imbalance in current scholarship that privileges the Renaissance actions of the social management of disease and dismisses similar previous medieval attempts.

After plague entered Bologna thousands of individuals and families were faced with the prospect of widespread illness and death. Unlike natural disasters, such as fire or earthquake, disease did give one time

---

[11] Park, *Doctors and Medicine*, p. 4.

[12] John Henderson, "The Black Death in Florence: Medical and communal responses," in *Death in Towns: Urban Responses to the Dying and Dead, 100–1600*, ed. Steven Bassett (Leicester, 1992), p. 146.

[13] See discussion in Chapter Four and articles in *Venezia e la peste 1348/1797* (Venice, 1979) and Mario Brunetti, "Venezia durante la peste del 1348," *Ateneo Veneto* 22, n. 1 (1909), 290–311 and 22, n. 2 (1909), 5–42.

to put one's affairs in order. Mothers and fathers had to arrange for the future of their children and their loved ones. The most important arrangement to make was to complete one's testament, since this document provided for both immediate and future, temporal and spiritual concerns. Men and women, as we will see, put aside their daily tasks of commercial exchange and made their wills. Because of the sheer number of testaments that were drawn up, they are the best guide to the experience of this crisis. Through them we can see the efforts of individuals trying to deal with the effects of epidemic disease on their daily life.

Testaments are a particularly rich and complex type of historical document. At the making of a will the testator was immersed in a moment of great decision. Present, past, and future were merged as the testator assessed his or her current personal financial situation and decided how best to fulfill hopes and concerns for the memorialization of the soul and the future of the family. The testator had to look ahead and prepare for the passage of his or her soul, while also recalling the past events of his or her life and the people that had filled it. This moment represented the confluence of many circumstances and relationships, of both spiritual and secular concerns.[14] Debts could be settled, marriages provided for, the material comfort of one's spouse and children secured, business and neighborhood ties recognized and rewarded. At the same time, the testator prepared for the life of the soul after death. As Jacques Chiffoleau aptly pointed out, the making of a will marked an act of continuity, of concern for the perpetuation of the family in the future and the journey of the soul to the next life.[15]

This work tracks the social experience of the Black Death through the evidence of notarial acts and testaments from two years: the year of the epidemic of 1348 and a comparative year, 1337, when Bologna was relatively free of disease, famine, or major war. From the normal year there remain in the *Memoriali* 315 copies of testaments redacted in the city, whereas for the plague year are preserved 1147 last wills and codicils that were copied into the *Memoriali* registers and a further

---

[14] James Banker looks at wills in a similar fashion, since he emphasizes that the testator balances future needs of his family with his longing for eternal life and wider social remembrance. See James Banker, *Death in the Community: Memorialization and Confraternities in an Italian Commune in the Late Middle Ages* (Athens, 1988), p. 1.

[15] Jacques Chiffoleau, *La comptabilité de l'au-delà: Les hommes, la mort et la religion dans la région d'Avignon à la fin due moyen âge (vers 1320–vers 1480)* (Rome, 1980).

85 original parchment wills that were deposited in the Franciscan and Dominican houses and can be found today in the papers of the suppressed religious houses, the *Demaniale*.[16] Although the numbers may justify it, this book does not offer a statistical analysis of the testaments. Such an analysis is apt to disregard the richly complicated nature of the testament. As Martin Bertram has emphasized, despite its strongly formulaic aspect, a testament is "by its nature an individual and complex document whose contents cannot be as easily schematized as those of leases or tax rolls."[17] Conclusions are not based on statistical tests, but rather the qualitative analysis of a large number of data. The analysis begins with the particulars, the bits of information revealed in the wills, that are inserted as tessarae in a mosaic which, it is hoped, presents a nuanced and detailed picture of late medieval urban life. Or, to use another analogy, much as an archeologist has to piece together a building from small fragments, this book uses the historical sources as the guide to understanding social life. The assemblage of the narrative is not without consideration of a realistic structure to the building or a composition for the patterns of the mosaic. In other words, the information gathered is not considered to have been randomly produced nor should it be arbitrarily organized and analyzed. The core is provided by the studies of social interactions of Renaissance Italian cities mentioned above: the importance of "family, friends, and neighbors" is recognized as paradigm of urban life, which was affected by gender and class. However, none of these concepts is utilized independently of the data. The categories of analysis and conclusions of this book are intimately linked, in other words, grounded, in the data.[18]

---

[16] Except where noted in Chapter Three, the research for this book covers those contracts noted as redacted in Bologna and not in the *contado* or surrounding district.

[17] Martin Bertram, "'Renaissance Mentality' in Italian Testaments?" review article in *Journal of Modern History* 67 (1995), 358–369.

[18] The process of research and analysis I am describing is similar to the methodology of developing theories in the "grounded theory" approach of Post-Keynesian economics. See Frederic S. Lee, "Theory foundation and the methodological foundations of Post Keynesian economics," in *Applied Economics and the Critical Realist Critique*, ed. Paul Downward (London and New York, 2003), 170–193, especially, pp. 174–178. To collect and analyze the data I used *kleio*, a free-domain database management program developed by medievalists, that is source oriented. The researcher does not begin with a ready-made template, but instead determines the fields in the database in a continuous process of recording and evaluating the data. The conclusions of this book were not generated by the application of software developed for uniformly produced data suitable for advanced statistical analysis. The analysis here is the result of a commonsense study of patterns revealed by the data.

Fortunately, the data is abundant, at least from a medievalist's viewpoint. The *Memoriali* are a gold mine of information, revealing the actions and aspirations of thousands of individual Bolognese from the rich and famous, the educated and the landed, to artisans and even some of the lowest paid wage earners. The legal parameters surrounding the testament and its preservation through the Office of the *Memoriali* or the mendicant sacristies of Bologna constructed evidence that allows us to lead a detective-like investigation of life during the epidemic. Each will is an excellent window to view a gathering of about a dozen people, brought together for reasons of piety, charity, kinship, and social and legal norms. Each piece of information has value and each is referenced in the hope that others may be able to use this study as a finding guide for their own interests.[19] It is the assumption of this work that to understand how people and communities behaved during this time of unprecedented crisis, we must follow their actions, not any preconceived notions of how we thought they might have behaved.

Chapter One explores the consumer side of notarial culture, setting out the social and gendered profile of late medieval testators. It also explains the intricacies of medieval Bologna's most famous source, the *Libri Memoriali*, as well as the accompanying series of the *Provvisori* and the alternative deposit for testaments, the *Demaniale*. Instituted during Bologna's golden era in the late thirteenth century, the *Memoriali* underwent important institutional changes in the mid fourteenth century. This book is the only major study of the *Memoriali* after the introduction of the *Provvisori*, and the first chapter can serve as guide to those doing research on this time period. The results of a detailed analysis of how the source functioned during the epidemic reveals that, although it entered into crisis, the office continued to work and was not abandoned. Chapter Two uses information from the wills to build a picture of life in Bologna during one of its darkest periods, which has seen little scholarly attention. While prosperous and growing thirteenth-century Bologna continues to be an object of study, there is a need for work on the fourteenth century, because new institutional and political structures, such as the *signoria*, developed at that time. Similarly, although the university was past its peak, the early

---

[19] I agree and comply with Martin Bertram's call for "an ironclad rule of testament research that each individual piece used must be documented so that it can be traced back in the archive": Bertram, "'Renaissance Mentality'?," p. 368.

to mid fourteenth century was the age of the famous legists, such as Giovanni d'Andrea and Jacopo Bottrigari, both of whom show up in the testaments as do their family members. This second chapter finds that many of the political, intellectual, and economic centers of Bologna's thirteenth-century "golden age" endured with continued vitality into the fourteenth century. It also presents a social and economic profile of fourteenth-century Bologna that delineates wealth and economic activity by quarters, parishes, and zones circumscribed by the city walls. In the third chapter we turn to the people and how they experienced the epidemic of plague. The popular image of the Black Death today is that family members abandoned each other, and people streamed out of the city gates in order to escape the disease. Certainly the medieval chroniclers encourage us to think this way, and perhaps it makes sense for many, because that is how we assume people would have behaved when faced with such a disaster. The evidence that remains suggests otherwise. There was no massive flight, no extensive family abandonment. Chapter Four closely examines the behavior of professionals such as doctors, notaries, priests, friars, and the *ministrali* or parish leaders during the epidemic to arrive at similar conclusions of stability and resilience in the face of disaster. Chapter Five studies the community of neighborhood by tracing the activity of witnesses in wills redacted during the months of plague. The bonds of neighborhood are revealed through the actions of individuals. The final layer of community investigated is the family, the subject of Chapter Six. The focus is on inheritance, that is, strategies for the continuation of the family. Much of the scholarly discussion of late medieval inheritance has been based on laws of intestacy that dictated rigid, patrilineal rules for the transfer of property. However, when we examine the actual wills, we find that people were more flexible in their choices and that the patterns set out in intestacy law were not always followed in the actual transmission of property set out by testaments. The narrative of this book, thus, moves from the source and the city to the people who produced them both, populating and preserving these historical forms as monuments to the amazing resilience of medieval society.

CHAPTER ONE

THE NOTARIAL EVIDENCE: TESTAMENTS IN THE *LIBRI MEMORIALI, DEMANIALE*, AND THE *PROVVISORI*

In order to best learn what life was like in late medieval Italy, it is imperative to understand and investigate the notarial culture that permeated and reinforced nearly all human interactions of daily life. During the thirteenth century, Italy underwent what Jean-Claude Maire Vigueur has called a "documentary revolution", an "explosion" of writing and documentary practice, that extended into all fields of administration—legislative, judicial, fiscal, military, and accounting. Vigueur emphasized the political aspect of the thirteenth-century transformation, but notarial records went beyond the political.[1] These sources afford investigation into all aspects of medieval life because of the complete permeation of a contractual culture: the economy depended upon notarial contracts; the social bonds of marriage, guardianship and maintenance of family wealth and kinship strategies were enabled through acts and testaments; products of art were arranged with the aid of notaries; and even the religious used notarial acts to authenticate miracles and record candle offerings.

Bologna offers superb opportunities for examining notarial culture in action, because of its exceptional city registers, the *Libri Memoriali* and *Provvisori*. Of all notarial records, the testament offers perhaps the best window on to late medieval urban life, not only because it records people's views on piety, charity, burial, and inheritance, but also because, like a net, it captures many historical subjects who were engaged in the socially significant behavior of making a will. Medieval people from all walks of life, except the destitute, were testators, and their decisions depended on the assistance of many others who served as notaries, witnesses and executors for their last wishes. The copies of testaments registered in the *Memoriali* and the original parchment wills that are preserved in the *Demaniale*, the archival holdings of the

[1] Jean-Claude Maire Vigueur, "Révolution documentaire et révolution scripturaire: Le cas de l'Italie médiévale," *Bibliothèque de l'École des chartes* 153 (1995), 177–185, esp. p. 184.

suppressed religious houses, retain for investigation the actions and intentions of many men and women.

The testament is a rich and highly descriptive source, which has been intensively studied by historians of the social and religious history of medieval and Renaissance Italy.[2] It is the contention of this work that the testament is one of the best, if not the best, source to study the experience of the Black Death because of the large number of people who wrote, or, more accurately, dictated wills and participated in the process of their production and preservation. Furthermore, during the epidemic, notarial activity was focused almost exclusively on producing testaments, thus it makes sense to aim our sights there. For the historian, the State Archives of Bologna provide perhaps the highest known concentration of wills remaining in northern Italy from the Black Death. While from the "normal" year of 1337 there remain 315 copies of wills in the *Memoriali*, for 1348 there are 1098 wills, 17 codicils for which there is no accompanying testament, 13 codicils for which the matching testament is preserved in 1348, and 19 wills that I have identified as duplicate and entered erroneously into the *Memoriali*.[3] The corpus of extant wills from 1348 is completed by a further 85 parchment testa-

[2] The study of medieval Italian wills has generally fallen into two types of analysis, that of the history of religion or religious mentalities, and that of the history of the family or inheritance practices. Some American historians have used many wills as their primary source, such as Samuel Kline Cohn, Jr. who studied the religious mentalities of Renaissance Tuscans and Steven A. Epstein and Sally McKee who explored family and inheritance in thirteenth-century Genoa and Venetian Crete, respectively. Others have used wills as supplement to other sources, such as Dennis Romano's work on communities in Renaissance Venice, Robert Brentano's studies of religious ideas in Rieti and the social history of thirteenth-century Rome, Roisin Cossar's study on confraternities of Bergamo, and Diane Owen Hughes's work on the social world of artisan families in medieval Genoa. Unlike the Americans, Italian scholars have tended to focus on the religious mentalities. An example of such work for central Italy is the study by Bonanno, Bonanno and Pellegrini of *pro anima* legacies of Florentine testaments and for the Emilia Romagna region the studies of Antonio Samaritani on Ferrara, Cento, and Massafiscaglia. Recent work, however, on testamentary inheritance and the family has been carried out by Linda Guzzetti on Venice, by Elena Brizio and Gianna Lumia on Siena, Maria Luisa Lombardo-Mirella Morelli on Rome (see references in Bibliography). For a comprehensive study of the historiography of studies based on medieval Italian testaments see Martin Bertram, "Mittelalterliche Testamente: Zur entedeckung einer Quellengattung in Italien," *Quellen und Forschungen aus italienischen Archiven und Bibliotheken* 68 (1988), 509–545 and for European wills see Linda Guzzetti, "Testamentsforschung in Europa seit den 1970er Jahren: Bibliographischer Überblick," in *Seelenheil und irdischer Besitz: Testamente als Quellen für den Umgang mit den 'letzten Dingen'*, eds. Markwart Herzog and Cecilie Hollberg (Constance, 2007), 17–33.

[3] Apart from the examination of codicils below, I have not used the 13 codicils corresponding to extant testaments nor the 19 duplicate wills in the analysis of this book.

ments, which can be found in the papers of the suppressed religious houses held today in the *Demaniale* collection.

This chapter will examine the medieval will as historical source by explicating testators and testamentary practices in mid fourteenth-century Bologna. With the focus on gender, social status, and identity, I will demonstrate the breadth of the will-making public. In analyzing testaments and other notarial acts, it is important to recognize that we are not dealing with standardized practices across the notariate. While notaries followed rules from formularies that included how acts ought to be dated, witnessed, and signed, and in particular, for wills, who could be testator and witness, they did not have specific instructions on how the notary ought to identify the testator. Parties to acts were to be recorded by name, which, according to Rolandino Passaggeri's well known and influential Bolognese manual of notarial law, *Summa totius artis notarie*, included at least two of the following: prenomen (first name), cognomen (family surname), and agnomen (named based on place of origin, office, or trade).[4] Almost always notaries went beyond the name to note also the testator's title and parish, and about a third also listed a trade and citizenship. Thus valuable information can be gleaned from the notarial record about civic identity, but researchers must confront, in addition to the familiar problem of lack of standardization in spelling, the problem of lack of uniformity in notarial practice. With this caveat in mind, the present chapter hopes to add to current ideas on how men and women in the medieval Italian town viewed and lived the realities of social status and occupation.

The intent of this chapter's focus on testaments, then, is to go beyond the traditional direction of historical inquiry into notarial culture, that is, the institutional history of the notariate, and instead illuminate its popular, or consumer, side. Nevertheless, a central aspect of notarial culture was the complicated bureaucracy of notaries, and no study is complete without an explanation of this amazing medieval invention. Therefore, this chapter will outline how the office of the *Memoriali* and its two dozen notaries carried out the task of registering and recording the contractual obligations of the townspeople. The abundant testaments

[4] The notary was instructed to include the six *publicationes*: year, indiction, day, place, names of witnesses and name of the notary. See the section on "De publicationibus instrumentorum" in *Tractatus Notarularum* by Pietro de Unzola added to Rolandino Passaggeri, *Summa totius artis notariae* (Venice, 1546; repr. Bologna, 1977), fols. 470v–473v.

of 1348 are an excellent guide, because they employed more than two hundred notaries who worked in the city writing up legal documents for clients. The aim of this chapter is not to produce a guidebook to a complicated medieval bureaucratic procedure—although it can serve as such since no study has been made of the *Memoriali* after the introduction of the *Provvisori*—but instead to bring to light the efforts of medieval notaries, men of *fides publica*, during the worst catastrophe in medieval history. These men continued to register and record notarial contracts even during the height of the epidemic. A detailed investigation of the source demonstrates the strain on the system, but shows too that the notariate did not collapse but continued to function through out the crisis. The analysis of the source is the foundation for our understanding of the experience of the Black Death.

Testators: Gender and Marriage Status

Who was the will-making public? We can characterize this group by gender and social status. Beginning with gender, it would appear from the Bolognese evidence that more women made wills than men, since in the *Memoriali* of 1337, 203, or 64.5 per cent, and in 1348, 585, or 52.5 per cent, of testators were female. These numbers differ from other scholars's estimates of the gender ratio of testation in urban areas of northern and central Italy during the fourteenth and fifteenth centuries. For Tuscany and the Veneto, Samuel Kline Cohn, Jr., Ann Crabb, and James Grubb found that testation rates for women ranged between 34 and 39 per cent.[5] Anna Vallaro found for testaments from San Gimignano during the first half of the fourteenth century that testation was equal between the sexes.[6] The highest participation of

---

[5] See Samuel Kline Cohn, Jr., *Death and Property in Siena, 1205–1800: Strategies for the Afterlife* (Baltimore, 1988), p. 200 and his "Last Wills: Family, Women, and the Black Death in Central Italy," in his *Women in the Streets: Essays on Sex and Power in Renaissance Italy* (Baltimore, 1996), pp. 39–56; Ann Crabb, *The Strozzi of Florence: Widowhood and Family Solidarity in the Renaissance* (Ann Arbor, 2000); James S. Grubb, *Provincial Families of the Renaissance: Private and Public Life in the Veneto* (Baltimore, 1996), p. 81.

[6] Anna Vallaro, "Il significato religioso dei testamenti sangimignanesi in tempo di peste," *Studi Medievali*, ser. 3, 41 (2000), pp. 375–6. For an earlier period, Epstein also found near equality in testation for Genoese wills, with 49 per cent of the 632 testaments in all extant notarial registers belonging to women: Steven Epstein, *Wills and Wealth in Medieval Genoa, 1150–1250* (Cambridge, Mass., 1984), p. 38.

women in will-making appears in Venice where Stanley Chojnacki and Linda Guzzetti discovered that women made wills more often than men. Working with wills of the patriciate they found that women made wills frequently because they faced more life-threatening situations, especially, childbirth.[7] The Bolognese wills, however, cannot be used to confirm the Venetian example because the cause of higher female testation in Bologna appears to be due to the legal option of the "secret will" detailed below that was open only to men after the rise of the *Provvisori* in 1333. Women had to have their wills registered with the office of the *Memoriali* where their wills would be public record, while men could choose to deposit their wills in secret at a mendicant house.[8] The normal level of female testation in the *Memoriali* after the introduction of the *Provvisori* is around 60 per cent: 204 of 315 or 64.7 per cent for 1337, and 61 per cent for the months before plague arrived in Bologna (viz., January through May). However, when the epidemic was in full force, fewer men may have used this option and, instead, had their wills registered immediately in the *Memoriali*. Thus, the percentage of female wills drops from 53 per cent in July to 40 per cent and 35 per cent in August and September, numbers that conform better to other studies. Bertram's calculations from the *Memoriali* for the years before 1333 also demonstrate a female testation rate of 40 per cent, bringing Bologna in line with rates common in late medieval and Renaissance Italian cities.[9]

Was will-making a gendered experience in that men and women responded to different gender-specific requirements or circumstances when they made a will? In other words, could such factors as pregnancy for women and travel for work or study for men influence will-making?

[7] Chojnacki found that, for 1371–1410, 66 per cent of 121 testators were women and, for 1411–1450, 71 per cent of 120 were women: Stanley Chojnacki, "Dowries and Kinsmen," reprinted in his *Women and Men in Renaissance Venice: Twelve Essays on Patrician Society* (Baltimore, 2000), pp. 140–41. See also discussion in Linda Guzzetti, "Le donne a Venezia nel XIV secolo: Uno studio sulla loro presenza nella società e nella famiglia," *Studi Veneziani*, n.s. 35 (1998), 15–87.

[8] See Martin Bertram, "Testamenti medievali bolognesi: Una miniera documentaria tutta da esplorare," *Rassegna degli Archivi di Stato* 52 (1992), 307–323. Despite their disadvantage compared to men's wills, women in Bologna did not need to have a *mundualdus* or have their husband's consent recorded in the will (even though this phrase does appear in a few wills).

[9] Martin Bertram has determined the percentage of women's wills in the *Memoriali* for 1268 and 1300 as 41 per cent and 40 per cent respectively. See Bertram, "Bologneser Testamente: Zweiter Teil: Sondierungen in den *Libri Memoriali*," *Quellen und Forschungen aus italienischen Archiven und Bibliotheken* 71 (1991), pp. 212–215.

In fact, for most testators the impulse to make a will came near the end of life, since most testators were ill: for the non-plague year of 1337, 82.2 per cent declared themselves to be ill, while during the plague-filled year of 1348, 90 per cent were ill.[10] For the minority who did declare they were healthy, men and women differed in their motivations. Healthy male testators sometimes indicated plans to go on pilgrimages to Rome, while business may have offered the occasion for others who came into Bologna from villages in the contado and had their wills drawn up at a notary's workshop (*statione*).[11] Men and women, both, could be forced to make wills in prison, but these were rare.[12] For the most part, women's wills do not declare the circumstances for making a will, so we must examines several factors to estimate their motives.

Since more women than men chose to write their wills when they were healthy, it would appear that gender was key here.[13] A first guess might be that Bolognese women were making their wills when they were pregnant, as Guzzetti and Chojnacki have found was the case for Venetian patrician women. There was, however, only one healthy married woman (out of 100 healthy female testators) who stated that she was pregnant.[14] Instead, husbands mentioned their wives's pregnancy when they nominated their heirs, of which there are five examples.[15] The majority of these healthy female testators were, in fact, either widows or unmarried: for 1337 only 23.6 per cent of the healthy testators were married and for 1348 20.9 per cent were married.[16] There must have

[10] Each will contains a declaration of health along the lines of either "sanus[a] mentis licet languens [or, eger] corpore" or "sanus[a] mentis et corpore".

[11] For example, on 31 March, 1337 one contado resident came to a notary's workshop at the central square to dictate his will "intendens beatorum Petri et Pauli Apostolorum de Roma lumina visitare": Archivio di Stato di Bologna, Memoriali [hereafter as Mem], vol. 191, fol. 383v.

[12] Mem, vol. 191, fol. 180v (woman from the contado) and vol. 192, fol. 427v (male citizen of Bologna).

[13] In 1337, 18.6 per cent of female testators were healthy compared to only 14.2 per cent of males, and in 1348, 10.5 per cent of female testators were healthy compared to 5.2 per cent of males.

[14] Mem, vol. 230, fol. 172r.

[15] Mem, vol. 191, fols. 59v, 535r; vol. 192, fol. 461v; vol. 193, fol. 69r; vol. 229, fol. 95r.

[16] The lack of pregnant testators in Bologna indirectly supports Isabelle Chabot's argument that female testators of the Venetian elite were making wills frequently because they were not satisfied with the intestacy law which granted equal inheritance to sons and daughters. Venetian wives were making wills so often not because of factors that affected all wives, such as the dangers of childbirth, but because they wanted to act against the possibility of intestate succession more often. Venetian testators' behavior was different from testators elsewhere because of the different intestacy law

been some reason other than pregnancy at work for these women to make their wills when they were healthy. Unlike men, healthy women frequently declared their last wishes in a church. Among pre-plague testators the largest group (half) of these women were widows, who made their wills equally as often in a church, in a nunnery, in the mendicant schools (*in scolis Fratrum Predicatorum* or *Fratrum Minorum*). Healthy women who were not married, about a quarter of them, also met in churches or nunneries, but not at the mendicant schools, while the remaining quarter, wives, were present in churches and the mendicant schools, but not in nunneries.[17] The majority of these testators had elite surnames, so it is possible that some were, as widows, retiring to convents. As for the wives, it is not clear why they shared in this unusual practice. We can only definitively state that, while some gendered experiences such as travel for work for men and retirement to a nunnery for women were factors in will-making, the most common experience of testating sick and near the end of one's life was shared by women and men alike.

The largest group of female testators was widows, but wives were also common testators. It is fairly easy to garner reliable statistics for the marriage status of testatrices because, next to being her father's daughter, marriage to a man was the principal form of identification for a woman. She was either *uxor* or *uxor olim* of a man. Men, on the other hand, were identified always in relation to their father—signifying whether or not they were *sui iuris*—and sometimes by their occupation or citizenship, but never by their relation to a woman. Therefore, male marriage status can be discerned only if they named their wife in their testament. Unlike female testators, most males named a wife and thus were married at the end of life, rather than single or widowed. This dearth of widowers in Bolognese society conforms to late medieval

---

in place there. See "A proposito di 'Men and Women in Renaissance Venice' di Stanley Chojnacki" with contributions by Isabelle Chabot, "Ricchezze feminili e parentela nel Rinascimento. Riflessioni intorno ai contesti veneziani e fiorentini" and Anna Bellavitis, "Genere e potere politico tra medioevo e età moderna," *Quaderni Storici* 118 (2005), pp. 203–238.

[17] Four widows were in the nunneries attached to San Lorenzo, San Vitale, San Pietro Martire, and Santa Maria di Castel dei Britti, and two unmarried women were in the nunneries of Santa Cristina and San Francesco. On the nunneries of Bologna see Sherri Frank Johnson, "Women's Monasticism in Late Medieval Bologna, 1200–1500" (PhD diss., University of Arizona, 2004). Women also had their wills drawn up in parish churches. Being healthy and at home was rare: only two healthy widows, one healthy wife and one healthy man did this.

and Renaissance Italian marriage practices of frequent remarriage by men.[18] While more men testated as widowers during the plague year than before, the rates of testation for wives, widows, and unmarried women were the same for the pre-plague and plague years: for both 1337 and 1348, 40 per cent were widows, 35 per cent were wives, and 25 per cent were single women.[19] The numbers of wives and widows do change as a result of plague mortality during the summer months—a fact which will be discussed in greater detail in Chapter Three—but the testation rates overall suggest that for married and widowed women there were general, societal, reasons to provide for the institution of an heir that remained fixed.

For most women, testamentary decisions would have been made within the larger structure of familial relations, but this would not always have been the case for single women, i.e., those female testators who were only identified only as the daughter of a father and who did not name children in their testaments. As other recent studies have found, women who never married are difficult to locate in the sources, and because they are a remarkably frequent testator in Bologna it is worth examining who these women were.[20] Apart from nine women—a small minority of five per cent—who were tertiaries (labeled as *soror*) that had never married, we do not know their vocations. Another ten per cent of the unmarried female testators may have had some connection with the church, for they dictated their wills as healthy testators inside of a church. Most of these women had elite surnames, and some

---

[18] I have identified two widowers (men who name a deceased wife and no living wife) and two likely widowers (men who named children, but no wife) in the pre-plague year. Steven Epstein found only one widower in his *Wills and Wealth*, p. 102. For Renaissance Florentine society see Christiane Klapisch-Zuber and David Herlihy, *Tuscans and Their Families* (New Haven, 1985), pp. 211–215 and Christiane Klapisch-Zuber, "'The Cruel Mother': Maternity, Widowhood, and Dowry in Florence in the Fourteenth and Fifteenth Centuries," in her *Women, Family, and Ritual in Renaissance Italy*, trans., Lydia Cochrane (Chicago and London, 1985), p. 120. However, on the basis of memoirs and tax returns from fifteenth-century Verona and Vicenza, Grubb has questioned the traditional assumption of asymmetry of remarriage in his *Provincial Families*, pp. 31 and 223.

[19] For 1337 there were 54 widows, 47 wives and 37 unmarried female testators and in 1348 there were 242 widows, 198 wives, and 143 unmarried female testators. During the pre-plague months of 1348, for which there are only 29 female testaments there were twice as many widows as wives, and only 11 per cent of females were single.

[20] See Sharon Farmer on the difficulty of finding single women in the Parisian records in her *Surviving Poverty in Medieval Paris: Gender, Ideology, and the Daily Lives of the Poor* (Ithaca, 2002), pp. 140–144.

appear to be fairly young, since their mothers were alive. However, the practice of dictating one's will inside a church was also done by wives and widows, so it is not a certain guess that these were daughters going into convents.

Several single women appear to be from the ranks of the working poor and some were immigrants depending on the help of others. For example, Caterina fq Azolini Gerardelli from the village of Monte Calderaro lived in the home of a parchment worker in San Biagio and named as her executor a female *cartolaria*, so it is likely that Caterina also practiced that trade. A certain Bona, also from the working-class parish of San Biagio, came from a poor family—she is noted as the daughter of Matheus who used to sell wine in the fields—and did not live in her own home. Another Bona may have been the servant in the home of a law professor, since she dictated her will there and asked the professor's wife to be her executor. Benvenuta fq Bigoli was the servant (*familiana*) of a member of the elite Armi family. She made her will in his house and named her master as executor.[21] Three single women lived in the homes of notaries, while a handful of others stayed in homes that were owned by women. Thus it does appear that some single women testators were disadvantaged and came from the ranks of the working poor, but we must not make too much of these numbers. The majority of single women (sixty per cent for both 1337 and 1348), however, dictated their wills in their own homes, at least according to the standard phrase "actum in habitatione testatricis". Of course, without other evidence we do not know who were the actual property owners, and I am not suggesting that all these single women were heads of households.[22] Most likely they were living in households with other relatives, but it should be noted that these single women appear to have come from across the social classes since a little less than half had elite surnames while the rest bore simple patronymics. This initial evidence on the gender of testators suggests that there was wide participation in notarial culture.

---

[21] Mem, vol. 193, fol. 205r; vol. 229, fol. 428r; vol. 230, fol. 392r.

[22] Some notaries did note, in the case of a few single women with elite surnames, that the residences belonged to their brothers or other male relatives. Nevertheless, I would not want to suggest that when this was not the case the testatrix was necessarily the owner of the residence.

Testators: Occupation and Social Status

The fact there were any wills of the working poor among the Bolognese testator class goes against the common assumption that wills were written only by the elite classes of society. The intent of this book is to provide the fullest description of the experience of the Black Death, so it is imperative that any conclusions based on testaments be understood as representative of a large part of society. It is possible to gain some idea of the social levels of testators from information in the wills. A sum of bequests would not be a good estimate of a testator's wealth, because the primary purpose of the medieval will was to transmit an inheritance—which was not itemized—to a named heir. While most wills contain long lists of bequests to individuals and religious institutions, such charitable and pious giving is not a necessary part of the will. According to notarial law, the principal purpose of a will—the *caput et fundamentum testamenti*—was the institution of the heir. The bequests and conditions, as the professors of notarial law emphasized, were not necessary and completely up to the will of the testator.[23] Some wills, in fact, are very short documents that simply record the name of the heir after a few standard bequests of alms to the church and, therefore, there is no way to monetarily estimate the wealth of the testator. Furthermore, for the many wills that do list legacies and charitable bequests, the will is the record of distribution of assets (and debts) at only one time of life. That this time was the most crucial and final time of giving and thus represented a more complete picture of an individual's wealth is probably the case for most testators. But there is no way to know what went on before the will was drawn up.

A better way of determining social status is by examining occupations, but, unfortunately, many testaments do not provide the testator's profession. As noted above it was up to the notary whether or not anything beyond the name would be recorded. The name and parish were sufficient for identity, and, thus, there are many testators who appear without an occupation but surely did work for a living. In fact, notaries only recorded the occupation of the testator for approximately one third

[23] According to Rolandino, "sine heredis institutione non valet testamentum". Furthermore, Pietro Aldobrandini stated in his accompanying gloss that "reliqua tria sunt voluntaria, videlicet legata substitutiones et provisiones, quia potest stare testamentum sine legatis et sine substitutionibus et aliis variis provisionibus". Rolandino, *Summa*, fols. 230v–232v.

of the male testators.[24] Nevertheless, the 233 recorded occupations for testators of 1337 and 1348 represent a significant amount of information, which is presented in Table 1.1. Although testaments cannot provide as much information on occupations as guild matriculation lists do, the wills have the advantage of specifying individual occupations that would not have been distinguished in guild lists, in which several occupations would fall under an umbrella guild. Thus the information of Table 1.1. provides a more nuanced picture of the various types of metal workers and meat processors working in Bologna. Moreover, wills expand our knowledge of workers by including among the testators those who were prohibited from forming guilds in Bologna, viz., taverners, barbers, some food sellers and grain providers, such as fisherman, bakers, millers, and market gardeners, as well as some wool workers, such as dyers.[25] Most of the information on occupations comes from testaments drawn up in July when plague was rampant. Nevertheless, the high numbers of butchers, shoemakers, and notaries is not because plague killed more of them, but because the late medieval economy of Bologna was based on leather-working and the mortality brought many more people than a normal year into the record.

Table 1.1. reveals a wide range of occupations covering much of the social scale. Most testators come from middling professions, such as shoemaker, tailor, and draper, but there appear members of the wealthy, educated elite, namely, university professors, lawyers, merchants, goldsmiths, notaries, and doctors, as well as small artisans and even laborers. The income levels of many professions are difficult to measure and some may have involved greater wealth than generally assumed. For example, butchers were also landowners and this could also extend to millers or, perhaps, even market gardeners (*ortolanus*).[26] Nevertheless, it is not possible to speak of a will-making class of elites

---

[24] For 1337 and 1348 the percentages are equal: 29.5 per cent and 29.8 per cent of male testators, respectively, have a recorded occupation.

[25] According to the statute of 1288 on "De societatibus inhibitis": Ordinamus quod pistores, fornarii, tabernarii, aburatatores, brentatores, molendinarii, victurales, ortolani, barberii, lardaroli vel formaglarii, tessarii pannorum vel battarii, tintores vel lavatores lane, tricoli vel tricole erbarum, fructuum vel pullorum, palee, feni vel lignaminum non possint inire vel facere aut contrahere aliquam societatem…" See Gina Fasoli and Pietro Sella, eds., *Statuti di Bologna dell'anno 1288*, 2 vols. (Vatican City, 1937 and 1939), 2:220.

[26] Butchers often were owners of land beyond the walls, for they dealt in cattle, not simply the preparation of meat. See Antonio Ivan Pini, "Gli estimi cittadini di Bologna dal 1296 al 1329: Un esempio di utilizzazione: il patrimonio fondiario del beccaio Giacomo Casella," *Studi Medievali* 17 (1977), 111–59.

Table 1.1 Occupations of Testators in 1337 and 1348

Occupation	Group Total
Leather/Fur Artisans & Retailers:	45
shoemaker (*calzolarius*), 19	
tanner (*peliparius*), 14	
bootmaker (*calegarius*), 12	
Textile Artisans & Retailers:	36
clothes dealer (*strazarolus, strazarius*), 11	
tailor (*sartor*), 10	
clothier (*draperius*), 4	
cloth finisher (*cimator*), 3	
woolmonger (*lanarolus*), 2	
dyer (*tintor*), 2	
jacketmaker (*zubonerius*), 2	
wool worker (*bixilerius*), 1	
weaver (*tessarius*), 1	
Legal Professionals:	27
notary (*notarius*), 24	
lawyer (*iurisperitus*), 2	
judge (*iudex*), 1	
Butchers:	24
butcher (*becarius macellator*), 18	
pork butcher (*lardarolus*), 6	
Food Preparers and Retailers:	18
cook (*chogus*), 1	
baker (*fornarius*), 9	
market gardener (*ortolanus*), 8	
fishmonger (*piscator*), 1	
Wood or Stone Workers:	16
master carpenter (*mag. legnaminis*), 11	
mason (*murator*), 3	
paver (*planelarius*), 2	
Metal Workers:	13
smith (*faber*), 9	
farrier (*feraterius*), 2	
sword maker (*spadarius*), 1	
armorer (*armarolus*), 1	

Occupation	Group Total
Medical and Health Practitioners:	13
druggist (*spetiarius, spezialis*), 9	
doctor (*medicus*), 3	
barber surgeon (*barberius*), 1	
Miscellaneous Artisans & Retailers:	9
innkeeper (*hospitator, tabernarius*), 4	
comb seller (*petenarius*), 2	
mercer, haberdasher (*mercarius*), 1	
sieve maker (*sedazarius*), 1	
painter (*depintor*), 1	
Agricultural/Manual Laborers:	9
agricultural worker (*laborator*), 2	
winnower/sifter (*mundator et aburatator*), 2	
miller (*munarius, molendinarius*), 2	
porter (*portator*), 3	
Merchants and Goldsmiths:	7
merchant (*mercator*), 5	
goldsmith (*aurifex*), 2	
University: Professors & Book Trade	8
doctor medicine, professor phisicae, 3	
doctor legum, 1	
doctor grammatice, 1	
parchment maker (*cartolarius*), 2	
bookseller (*stazionarius*), 1	
Government Employees:	7
messenger of the commune (*nunptor*), 2	
constable of Pepoli signori (*chonestabilis*), 1	
mercenary (*stipendarius ad stip. comunis*), 1	
familiar of noble Pepoli knight, 1	
trumpeter (*trombator*), 1	
measurer (of land) *mensurator*, 1	
Total number of occupations listed:	233

Source: ASB, Memoriali, vols. 191, 192, 193, 228, 229, 230

when we have testators such as a comb seller, a sieve maker, an agricultural worker, a winnower and sifter, and porters.[27]

One glaring omission, however, in this list of occupations from a town famous for its university is the student population, which has been estimated at around 2,000 during the late thirteenth century. Their numbers may have decreased somewhat during the first half of the fourteenth century, but they and the university body continued to be a powerful presence in the town, as will be discussed in the following chapter.[28] There are no student testators from both the pre-plague and plague years, so their absence is not because the students left town en masse during the epidemic—something that no social group in Bologna seems to have done. As will be noted in Chapters Four and Five, students do appear among the lists of witnesses to testaments during the plague epidemic. Thus, at least some students were in town during the epidemic and would presumably have had the chance and reason to make a will as their fellow townsmen did in such large numbers. Moreover, although the impecunious student has always been a familiar figure, poverty did not prevent all of them from being testators because many students in Bologna were well off financially—their money fueled the town's economy. Their absence from the lists of testators, instead, has to do with their will-making habits. Some students may also have been young men whose fathers were still alive, and therefore they had not entered into succession. Older students pursuing the advanced degrees of law and medicine in Bologna, as unmarried men without children, may have been content with intestacy laws governing succession and thus did not feel the need to designate an heir by testament. We have seen, however, that many unmarried women without children in fact did write a will, so the reason may lie elsewhere. Julius Kirshner has argued that students gained the legal status of pilgrim and, in fact, the civic statutes establishing the *Memoriali* included students with pilgrims and foreigners in the declaration that their wills could be deposited in the mendicant sacristies instead of the city registers.[29] Therefore, it

[27] The kind of economy that this table describes, with its large numbers of butchers and notaries, confirming the epithets of *Bologna la grassa* and *Bologna la dotta*, will be discussed in the following chapter.

[28] Luigi Dal Pane, "Lo 'Studio' e l'economia," in *Atti del convegno internazionale di Studi Accursiani*, ed. G. Rossi (Milan, 1908), 1:43–53, esp. p. 49.

[29] Julius Kirshner, "Made Exiles for the Love of Knowledge: Students in Late Medieval Italy," forthcoming in *Atti del Convegno su Bartolomeo Cipolla: un giurista veronese del Quattrocento tra cattedra, foro e luoghi del potere (Verona, 15–16 ottobre 2004)*. Fasoli and Sella, *Statuti*, 2:83: "...scolarium vel peregrinorum vel viatorum vel forensium".

is likely that some students followed the behavior of pilgrims as well as merchants who wrote their wills in their home town before their departure. Others surely wrote their wills in Bologna and deposited them in the *Demaniale*, but because the notaries did not identify these testators as students their presence has gone undetected.

Members of the clergy and religious communities of Bologna are another under-represented group. Monks, nuns, and canons regular were not allowed to make a will, and therefore do not appear as testators. Among the wills of male clerics that were deposited in the *Memoriali* there appear four rectors and three priests (two from 1337) of parish churches in Bologna, a priest and archpriest of churches in the diocese of Bologna, and a chaplain of the cathedral of Saint Peter in Bologna (who used to be a rector of a parish church in town). All but one of these men made their wills in their parish church or a home belonging to it. The two clerics of rural churches were in parish churches in town when they dictated their wills and the cathedral chaplain had returned to his former parish church, while one priest, not linked to any church in his title, was in the home of his kinsman (*cognatum*) and heir. Having no children, these testators named as their heirs either siblings or other men of the church. Other testators who were members of Bologna's religious communities include a servant (*famulus*) of the nunnery of Santa Maria della Vergine and two novitiates (*novicius*) of the Dominican order (both from 1337), who lived and made their wills in homes attached to the convent and friaries.

It was fairly common for members of the tertiary orders of the convents, particularly the Benedictines, to write wills and name family members or others as their heirs. Thirteen women were identified by notaries as *soror*, which represents a proportionally larger group than male tertiaries. Unfortunately we know little about their religious careers as only two were named as sisters of penitential orders and one of the tertiary "order of Saint Bernard". Most likely all of these testatrices had taken on lesser orders of the Benedictine rule. Only six male testators were members of tertiary orders. They were either labeled as tertiaries by the notary or who were simply called *frater*, such as a shoemaker who identified himself as a *frater ordinis Sancti Francisci*, a clothes dealer (*strazarolus*), and another brother claiming to be of the Carmelite order. No mendicant friar appeared as testator. However, they were frequent witnesses, in which capacity they will be discussed in Chapters Four and Five.

Also missing from the lists of testators are women with a job. Of course women worked for a living in Bologna, but one must dig deep into testaments to find hard evidence of their occupations. There are frequent bequests made to *famulae*, but women legatees also had jobs more often assigned to men, such as baker (*fornaria*), parchment maker (*cartolaria*), and apothecary (*specialis*).[30] David Herlihy commented on the lack of female occupations in a contemporary fiscal document drawn up by the city's notaries, viz. Bologna's salt tax of 1395 (that has been edited by Paolo Montanari).[31] Despite the fact that they do not appear as workers in this source and in the wills, I do not agree with Herlihy that "[w]omen participated minimally in the Bolognese work force" or that the largest profession was prostitution. It simply was not standard notarial practice to record a woman's occupation. Working on data produced in a similar notarial culture, namely, the *Liber Divisionis* of Avignon in 1371, Joelle Rollo-Koster found evidence for a wide array of female employment but at the same time notes that women declared an occupation much less frequently than men (64 versus 20 per cent).[32] This conception of women's identity as devoid of occupation was not limited to the Mediterranean notarial environment. Working on Parisian evidence, Sharon Farmer has shown how scribes failed to record occupations for women. This corresponded to clerical attitudes that men's identity was linked to productive labor while women were associated with reproductive labor.[33]

Mediterranean notaries and northern scribes alike shared the cultural attitudes of clerics who viewed women in regards to their reproductive relation to men: only women were identified by the spouse's name (as *uxor*, *uxor quondam* or *uxor olim*). All men and women carried their father's name (and often a family name). We can use this information to get some sense of what occupational circles many of the female

---

[30] One testator named as executrix *dominam Meldam filiam quondam Ranucini specialem*: Mem, vol. 228, fol. 77v. It is possible, though not certain, that she was an apothecary like her executrix, because the occupation *specialis*, listed after her identification as the wife of Petrus Francisci Ravigni, does not reveal gender.

[31] David Herlihy, *Opera Muliebria: Women and Work in Medieval Europe* (New York, 1990), pp. 155–58.

[32] Joelle Rollo-Koster, "The Women of Papal Avignon: A New Source: The *Liber Divisionis* of 1371," *Journal of Women's History* 8 (1996), 36–59.

[33] Farmer, *Surviving Poverty*, pp. 113–119.

testators may have frequented. The notaries recorded a profession for the fathers or husbands of female testators about twenty per cent of the time. This evidence is shown in Table 1.2 demonstrating that women's relatives cover the same range of professions as their male testator counterparts. Many of these woman would not have practiced the trade of their husband, but would have shared their social status, as would have been the case for the many widows and daughters of law professors, doctors, and notaries. But others may have worked along side their husband and even taken over their trades after death, such as the wives of bakers, mercers, fishmongers, and innkeepers. Again, there are examples of the lowest paid professions, such as the daughter of a man "who used to sell wine in the fields".[34]

Only for women of very low or very high social status is there an indication of social standing linked to the woman alone. As noted above, one female testator was the *familiana*, or servant, of a man of the prominent Armi family. She is unique, but her presence in the documents demonstrates, as Giovanna Benadusi has found for Italian wills of the sixteenth century, that it was not common but certainly possible for servants and members of subaltern classes to write wills.[35] The very elite women stand apart from most women by virtue of their titles. The title *domina* was not reserved for elite women, but instead was generally used for a woman who had married: virtually all married or widowed women in Bologna were identified as *domina*, while most unmarried women were not. In order to go beyond the simple "Mrs." to indicate social prestige, the notaries repeated *domina* and added other terms of social status. The most common such terms were *discreta* or *provida*, borne by the daughter of a physician and widows of a spice dealer and of a *civis*, as well as other women noted only by family surnames. These were also common titles for men (held by a merchant, a professor, three notaries, and several men identified only as *civis*). Women were also called *honesta*, which sometimes was a first name, while for men only clerics held that title. Three widows—of a member of Bologna's knightly order of the *frati gaudenti*, a *civis*, and a notary—were granted the unusual title *sapiens*. This was also rare among men, as there were only two male testators noted as *sapiens*, viz.,

---

[34] Mem, vol. 229, fol. 428r (will of Bona fq Mathei "qui consueverat vendere vinum ad campos").

[35] Giovanna Benadusi, "Investing the Riches of the Poor: Servant Women and Their Last Wills," *American Historical Review* 109 (2004), 805–826.

Table 1.2 Occupations of Husbands and Fathers of Female Testators (1337, 1348)

Occupation	Daughter of	Wife of	Widow of	Total
Notary (*notarius*)	6	6	8	20
Shoemaker (*calzarius/calegarius*)	5	6	3	14
Butcher (*beccarius*)	4	2	5	11
Tailor (*sartor*)	1	4	5	10
Professor (*doctor/professor*)	3	0	6	9
Tanner (*peliparius*)	3	3	3	9
Medical (*barberius/medicus*)	6	0	2	8
Apothecary (*speziarius*)	2	3	3	8
Smith (*faber*)	2	3	2	7
Textiler (*lanarolus/strazarolus*)	2	3	1	6
Dyer (*tintor*)	1	0	4	5
Baker (*fornarius*)	1	2	1	4
Mason (*murator*)	1	2	0	3
Carpenter (*magister lignaminis*)	0	1	2	3
Goldsmith (*aurifex*)	1	0	2	3
Mercer (*merzarius*)	2	0	1	3
Clothier (*draperius*)	0	1	1	2
Jacketmaker (*zubonerius*)	1	1	0	2
Innkeeper (*tabernerarius*)	1	1	0	2
Salt seller (*salarolus*)	1	1	0	2
Saddler (*selarius*)	1	0	1	2
Judge/Lawyer (*iudex/iurisperitus*)	0	0	2	2
Weaver (*tessarius*)	1	0	0	1
Napperer (*napparius*)	0	1	0	1
Wine seller (*qui vendit vinum*)	1	0	0	1
Fish seller (*piscator*)	0	0	1	1
Parchment maker (*cartolarius*)	0	0	1	1
Merchant (*mercator*)	0	1	0	1
Miller (*mollendarius*)	0	1	0	1
Total	46	42	54	142

Source: ASB, Memoriali, vols. 191, 192, 193, 228, 229, 230

a tertiary and a *civis*.[36] The only titles that women did not share with men, apart from the occupational designation of *magister* or *ser*, were "honorable" (*honorabilis*, of one *civis*, or *spectabilis*, of one butcher) and the knightly title of *generosus et magnificus* (held by the knight, Eganus Lambertini de Lambertinis).

[36] Two other men who appear in testaments as relatives and legatees of testators, viz., a lawyer and a professor, also bore this rare title.

A few women and men stand out among the elites as members of the nobility, with the word *nobilis* added usually to *discreta* or *provida*. With noble status came power and prestige in the medieval Italian town. Thus, families of commoner status, i.e., *popolani* or members of the popular societies of the *Armi* and *Arti*, tried to garner nobility for their members in order to gain political power. Contemporary examples include the ruler, Taddeo Pepoli, who came from a commoner banking family and was proud to have his sons knighted in 1345 by a visiting dignitary from Austria, while his nephew, Giovanni di Zerra Pepoli went to work as retainer at the court of Robert of Anjou in Naples and gained knighthood there. When he took over his father's reign in 1348, Taddeo's son, Giovanni, knighted the orphaned sons of a key ally of his father, the law professor and frequent ambassador, Maccagnano Azzoguidi.[37] Nobility, however, could represent an obstacle to success since in the statutes of 1288 nobles were equated with magnates who were dealt harsh penalties for harming members of popular families and whose business activities and political participation were severely limited.[38] The law, it turns out, did not always reflect practice. Sarah Blanshei has determined that the boundaries between magnate and *popolano* were porous and there were many ambiguities over status in definition and practice. For example, magnates who should have been excluded from political life were present on communal councils and as officials in civil courts, while *popolani* were named among lists of *milites*. Furthermore, magnate status was mutable, since whole groups of families had their status changed from *popolano* to magnate (or vice versa) and back again depending on the political regime. Blanshei concludes that in late medieval Bologna, status was ambiguous and social identity blurred.[39]

The testamentary evidence at mid fourteenth century supports this view. Nobility does appear as a hereditary trait for some among the privileged and powerful, since all testators who bore the title *nobilis* specified the nobility of their father in their name, such as a brother from

[37] Guido Antonioli, *Conservator pacis et iustitie: La signoria di Taddeo Pepoli a Bologna (1337–1347)* (Bologna, 2004), pp. 18, 178,

[38] See Sella and Fasoli, *Statuti*, 1:357, on the law "De penis impositis contra magnates..." identifying "magnatem, nobilem vel potentem vel militem" and "magnati vel nobili" in "De contractibus factis seu faciendis cum magnatibus et de non faciendo" on 1:69.

[39] Sarah Blanshei, "Politics and Justice in Medieval Bologna" (book manuscript), chapter IV.

the magnate Garisendi family, *nobilis et prudens vir dominus Nicholas olim nobilis militis domini Lanze de Garisendis*, and the daughter of a law professor, *nobilis et discreta domina domina Laxia filia quondam nobilis militis domini Egidii de Malavoltis legum doctoris* who married into the branch of the ruling Pepoli family and had a daughter, *nobilis et discreta domina domina Johanna filia quondam nobilis viri domini Philippi olim domini Zohannis de Peppolis*. Nevertheless, not all children of noble knights, nor wives for that matter, were granted the title *nobilis* by notaries.[40] Some children of nobility did not even bear a title, at least in the records. Many testators bore the names of families that had been given magnate status, but they were not considered *nobilis* by notaries.[41] Furthermore, it seems that nobility was a rare commodity in mid fourteenth-century Bologna, since only six female testators and five male testators in the *Memoriali* were labeled as noble, while a further ten who were children or spouses of nobility were not so labeled. Keeping in mind Blanshei's argument that status was mutable, I use the term "noble" only for those few individuals who bore a noble title in the documents and instead use the term "elite" for those who were of the landed, wealthy, and privileged social levels.

The most common single identifying term among testators was *civis* or citizen, but again this term was subject to the non-standardized practices of notaries. Only 31.6 per cent of male testators were named as *civis*. It is more difficult to determine if *civis* applied to a female testator or to her father or husband, but only 42 or seven per cent of female testators record the possibility, while only one of these women has the term *civis* recorded not after the name of her husband or father, but after her parish and thus it appears to apply to her.[42] The notaries who

[40] For example, Bertolomea fq Ramberti de Ghixilleriis, widow of the noble knight Petrus fq Henrigitii de Galuciis (Mem, vol. 193, fol. 292r) and Bertolomea fq domini Francisci de Galucis, widow of the noble knight Philippus de Asinellis (ASB, Demaniale [hereafter as Dem], F.P, Miscellanea, busta 168) do not bear the title *nobilis*. Padoanus fq nobilis militis domini Liazarii de Liazariis (Mem, vol. 191, fol. 187v) is not titled.

[41] Borniollus fq domini Blanchi de Galucis is not titled *nobilis*. Non-noble male testators from magnate families include men of the Galluzzi (Mem, vol. 230, fol. 249r), de Simopizolis (Mem, vol. 229, fols. 192r, 350r), Malavolti (Dem, F.P., 193, 7527, no pages numbers and Mem, vol. 229, fol. 186v), Torelli (Mem, vol. 228, fol. 143r; vol. 229, fol. 255r), de Manzolino (Mem, vol. 230, fols. 144v, 320v), de Savignano (Mem, vol. 230, fol. 448r), Prendipartis (Mem, vol. 229, fol. 355r), Ramponi (Mem, vol. 230, fol. 12v), Buvalelli (Mem, vol. 229, fol. 169v and vol. 230, fol. 39v), Basacomari (Mem, vol. 193, fol. 55r, vol. 229, fol. 322v and vol. 230, fol. 251v).

[42] Mem, vol. 230, fol. 47r: Benvenuta dicitur Guidolla fq Johannis olim Maxini capelle sancte Marie Mascarelle civis. For most women, *civis* came after their father's and husband's names and before their parish.

did take the time to write this term were fairly consistent among themselves: none of their female clients was a citizen and the few male clients who also lacked that designation were originally from other towns or villages. The difficult conclusion from the practice of such notaries is that women were not considered citizens. Yet these women were from Bolognese families and were the wives and daughters of citizens, so by law they were citizens. The notaries were most likely recording the view that women, because they were ineligible for office, were not full, participating, citizens.[43] Moreover, it is unlikely that all of the clients of these notaries who came from other towns and declared a residence in a parish were new immigrants without citizenship. Furthermore, among the clients of those notaries who did record citizenship there are some exceptional cases of men who clearly were citizens, i.e. men of prominent Bolognese families.[44] The ambiguous notarial record provides indirect support for the situation that Julius Kirshner has argued existed in medieval Italian towns, viz., "the dynamic amalgamation of different forms of citizenship".[45]

Citizenship, as listed in the wills, was wide ranging, as it was adjoined to a whole range of occupations that, although in reduced numbers, roughly followed the frequency among the general list of occupations: among the testators of 1348, fourteen notaries, six shoemakers, six drapers, five master carpenters, and five butchers were noted as citizens. The other citizens claimed occupations ranging from the public figures of judge or town crier to the middling trades of baker and tailor to the lower ranked occupations of barber or winnower and sifter (*aburatator*). For those citizens who did not list a trade, a significant number

[43] As Anna Bellavitis has shown for Renaissance Venice, women garnered a secondary sense of citizenship for the purposes of work that excluded them from election and office. They were granted citizenship *de intus* instead of the full rights of citizenship. Anna Bellavitis, "Donne, cittadinanza e corporazione tra Medioevo ed età moderna: ricerche in corso," in *Corpi e storia: Donne e uomini dal mondo antico all'età contemporanea*, eds. N. M. Filippini, T. Plebani, and A. Scattigno (Rome, 2002), pp. 87–104.

[44] For example, the careful notary Bertolomeo Petri de Codagnellis did not record citizenship for Bonbolognus Cavalleri de Cavalleris (Mem, vol. 229, fol. 21r).

[45] Kirshner based on his argument on the views of the jurists of the mid fourteenth century, Bartolus of Sassoferato and the Bolognese Jacopo Bottrigari. Speaking about naturalized citizens, Julius Kirshner states, "[t]he rights of these citizens, although normally granted *in perpetuum*, often proved to be ephemeral. Their rights were challenged, abridged, and even melted away in times of rampant nativism and social conflict, as happened in fourteenth-century Florence." See his "*Civitas sibi faciat civem*: Bartolus of Sassoferato's Doctrine on the Making of a Citizen," *Speculum* 48 (1973), pp. 695–6 and 710.

were among the well off. About one third of the men identified as *cives* in 1348 were members of prominent families such as the Azzoni, Basacomari, Buvallelli, Cavaleri, Garisendi, Lambertini, Lazari, Pepoli, Prendiparti, Torelli among many others. Among these appear five men who bore titles indicating magnate status, such as *nobilis vir* or *generosus et magnificus miles*. The few magnates all bore citizen status with the sole exception of one nobleman who may not yet have gained it. He was described as *habitator* or resident of the parish of Santa Maria dei Galluzzi, a parish dominated by the elite families of the Galluzzi and their allies, and was originally from Lodi. Forty-one other male citizens had titles that indicated some elevated social or occupational status. Eleven of these bore the distinguishing titles of *discretus*, *providus*, or *honestus vir*, while twenty other male citizens bore the simple title of *dominus*.[46] That leaves ten citizens with titles for whom a profession was recorded: two tertiaries (including the shoemaker and draper noted above); three *magister* or masters, one of whom was a physician and another a smith; and five artisans titled *ser* (not notaries since that was not Bolognese custom), all partaking in the social classes of citizens listed above.[47] Citizenship therefore as one would expect encompassed a broad range of the working population of the late medieval town, of which women were not seen as participants.

For most testators, the notary followed the formularies and did the minimum, i.e., he wrote their names. For this majority it is possible to assign a general social status of elite or non-elite by means of a combination of factors. Historians have generally used surnames as an indication of high, even noble, status, but this alone is not sufficient since individuals without surnames may have considerable wealth or may be married to another with a surname and thus have garnered status through marriage. For example, Francesca fq Benvenuti Petri was the daughter of a deceased smith, but as wife of Albertinellus de Bentivoglis (the family that would rise to power as *signori* at the beginning of

[46] *Dominus/a* appears to have marked higher social status among men than it did among women, for whom its use was so frequent it must simply have meant "Mrs.".

[47] This last label illustrates just how localized usage of titles was in medieval Italian towns. The Tuscan model of *ser* as notary does not apply to Bologna where *ser* was more commonly used by men whose occupations were listed in the testamentary evidence as very different from notaries. They include: shoemaker, draper, market gardener, comb maker, and paver (as testators); innkeeper, butcher, miller, goldsmith, and wine porter (as legatees or witnesses). Although notarial culture was widespread through out medieval Italy, local customs could be quite pronounced.

the fifteenth century) she would have shared in her husband's higher status.[48] To go beyond reliance on names, researchers can add dowries to the equation for a more accurate indication of social status. As Anthony Molho and others have made clear, dowry amounts reflected social status.[49] Each married male testator was supposed to use the will to return his wife's dowry and specify amounts for his daughters. With this information we can assign status more accurately as for example, the butcher, Matheus fq Phylippini Crestenci who did not have a dignifying surname, was clearly part of the Bolognese elite because he returned a large dowry of 525 *lire* to his wife.[50] Jacobus fq Tholomei de Tholomeis, on the other hand, appears to have an aristocratic name, but he was an innkeeper whose wife's dowry of 60 *lire* puts him into the class of non-elites.[51] Dowry amounts confirm the expected low economic status of a porter and a shoemaker who returned dowries of 36 *lire* and 60 *lire* respectively.[52] Putting all of the various factors together, I have determined that about one third of all testators were elite members of society.[53]

Testaments as Sources

Thus, wills have their problems in representation—they include no poor, few religious, and no identifiable students—but they do record the wishes of a large part of the general population. Are they, however, accurate representations of those wishes? What exactly do they tell us? Some have argued that testaments reveal very little of what actually happened. Thomas Kuehn, in particular, has argued that much historical work on testaments has neglected to realize that inheritance was a dynamic process. The testament was only one stage in "a whole complex

[48] Mem, vol. 230, fol. 56v.
[49] Anthony Molho, *Marriage in Late Medieval Florence* (Cambridge, Mass., 1994).
[50] Mem, vol. 229, fol. 77v.
[51] Mem, vol. 192, fol. 443r.
[52] Mem, vol. 229, fol. 12v and vol. 192, fol. 340r.
[53] The numbers are for 1337: elites make up 29.7 per cent of all testators of whom male elites comprise 23 per cent of all males and elite women are 33 per cent of all female testators. For 1348: elite testators comprise 33.0 per cent of all testators, of whom elite men are 26.4 per cent of all males and elite women are 39.1 per cent of all women.

of operations that came into play (or could) after an individual died".[54] Furthermore, instead of offering certain information about testator's wishes for the future, "the testament could generate untold forms of uncertainty, notably in relation to legal mechanisms to interpret and validate a testator's intent".[55] He emphasizes that since wills could be repudiated by the heir, they reveal only the intentions of the testator, not the actual transmission of inheritance. The heir was not legally constrained to accept the inheritance and could, in fact, arrange a contract of *repudiatio hereditatis* in order to reject it. Repudiation, Kuehn shows, was a tool for heirs to protect themselves from financial ruin in the case of an estate burdened with debt. What we need to know, however, is how active repudiation was in comparison with the use of testaments, that is, we need to know the actual incidence of rejection of the testament, rather than simply the presence of the institution of repudiation, before we can reject the testament as a source representing actual transmission.

The data from Bologna provide evidence of how often wills were repudiated. Although I will not attempt to track each will that was repudiated, an estimate of frequency of repudiation can be made by simply counting the number of wills and comparing that with the number of repudiations during one year. The *Provvisori* are the best source for counting acts, since not all acts made it through the final steps of registration to be copied into the *Memoriali*. In the *Provvisori* of 1337 there are 274 testaments, 11 codicils, but only five repudiations, i.e., only about two per cent of wills were repudiated.[56] Two of these repudiations only reject a part of the inheritance, i.e., a choice of guardian and, for the other, a legacy of 50 pounds, while the other three reject the entire inheritance.[57] The *Provvisori* of 1348 are useful only for the

[54] Thomas Kuehn, "Law, Death, and Heirs in the Renaissance: Repudiation of Inheritance in Florence," *Renaissance Quarterly* 15 (1992), p. 486 and now his *Heirs, Kin, and Creditors in Renaissance Florence* (Cambridge, 2008). See also his review of Steven Epstein, *Wills and Wealth in Medieval Genoa, 1150–1250* in *Speculum* 61 (1986), p. 145 and his "Introduction" to *Law, Family, and Women: Toward a Legal Anthropology of Renaissance Italy* (Chicago, 1991), p. 15.

[55] Kuehn, *Heirs, Kin, and Creditors*, p. 92.

[56] This information comes from the remaining five out of six possible parchment registers for the *Provvisori* of 1337. The parchment register at the *Cambium* from the first semester is missing.

[57] This proportion of partial to full repudiations is double that found by Kuehn for Florence where 20 per cent were partial repudiations, except in the 1450s when they rose to over 40 per cent. Kuehn, *Heirs, Kin, and Creditors*, pp. 131–132.

first semester (that should, in any case, come closer to representing normal testamentary behavior), during which time no repudiations of inheritance were drawn up. For the second half of the year the *Memoriali* contain nine repudiations (three of which are included with guardianship contracts), as compared to 919 testaments from that time. Two wills were repudiated in July and August, but the rest were from September to December. Most likely these were in response to wills made in July, when 579 testaments were copied out, the largest single month of notarial output. It is possible that wills from that month were repudiated during the following year, but Kuehn has found that most were repudiated within a few months. The repudiations that remain represent only 1.5 per cent of the number of testaments from July.

The *Provvisori* of 1362, when plague returned for a second time to Bologna, are preserved in all of their parchment registers (and are discussed further in Chapter Three with the accompanying Figure 3.3). As was the case with the Black Death, a very large number of wills were produced during that year, and we can assume that each posed the sorts of problems for heirs that Kuehn emphasizes. There were 1,453 testaments, but only 50 repudiation acts registered during 1362. Repudiations had increased, but they still remained a tiny fraction of testamentary activity, i.e., representing only 3.4 per cent of possible testaments. Again, most repudiations were made in reaction to the large number of testaments made during the months affected by plague, since 16 repudiations were registered in the first half of the year and 34 in the second half, mostly during the last three months. It is possible that between 1365 (after two onslaughts of plague) and 1534—the dates for evidence in the Florentine records utilized by Kuehn—repudiation of inheritance grew to become the significant phenomenon that he believes it is.[58] What is clear from the late medieval evidence, however, is that the vast majority of wills were not repudiated and that the testament stands firm as a source of viable historical study of both intentions and actions.

Instead of repudiations, the activity concerning the revision of testaments includes, in descending order of frequency, codicils, entries into or acceptances of inheritances (*aditio hereditatis*), nomination of heirs

[58] There needs to be more work comparing the Florentine evidence with other Italian towns. Studies of the notarial evidence that examine several types of records as they act in conjunction with each other in practice—and not in theory—would be very beneficial. At the moment, not only was Florence the worst place to be born a woman, as Cohn has said, it appears to have been the worst place to be a testator.

(*nominatio heredis*), which was used to name the receiving poor when a testator nominated the "Poor of Christ" as universal heir, and division of inheritance (*divisio hereditatis*).[59] Codicils, then, more closely represent the fulfillment of the dynamic process of inheritance that Kuehn emphasizes. For the "normal" year of 1337, the *Provvisori* contain 15 codicils, as compared to 275 testaments (there are no codicils in the *Memoriali* of 1337). There remain 30 codicils in the *Memoriali* of 1348. Of these, 13 correspond to extant testaments, which were all drawn up during the second half of the year (70 per cent of them from the summer plague months). All but two of these codicils were made within the same day or four days after the original will. Some record a change in choice of heir (generally because of the death of the original choice), but it was not necessary to use a codicil for this purpose, since testators provided for substitutions to the heir in their original will. The numbers demonstrate that even the more frequent codicil was not a common practice resorted to by most testators: they appear for 5.4 per cent of the wills in 1337 and 2.7 per cent of the wills in 1348. In addition to their infrequency we should remember that codicils and the other testamentary contracts providing for changes to a will, apart from the even less frequent repudiation, contain the instructions of the testator and should be understood as an accurate reflection of the fulfillment of the testator's wishes.

Another criticism of wills is that they are formulaic, that they represent the notary's views more than the testator's. Indeed notaries had to follow legal language and rules; they were supposed to assist their client so that legal problems would not arise in future as a result of the declaration. Instead of assuming that notaries would automatically shape their clients's words, however, we should examine what the notaries themselves thought about this issue. Rolandino was emphatic that notaries should be sure they were recording testators's wishes. In a section on witnesses, he stressed that testators should not be coerced—according to the notary, it was the witness, not the notary who could shape the testator's declarations. When Rolandino did instruct notaries on what might have been expected of testators's last wishes, it was to caution that the testament should be favorable to widows and orphans, and he

[59] In the *Provvisori* of 1348 there were 23 entries or acceptance of inheritance and 12 divisions of inheritance with 18 nominations of heirs. For a description of these types of contracts see Rolandino Passaggeri, *Contractus*, ed. Roberto Ferrara (Rome, 1983).

stated that the notary must carefully write what the testator says when there were any instructions concerning the wife. Rolandino was also concerned that notaries make certain that the testator was mentally capable to make a will. He stressed that it was enough that the testator was properly identified and of sound mind and encouraged notaries not to worry if she or he were sick and spoke in a difficult fashion as a result, as long as the testator was expressing his or her own wishes.[60] Such instructions would have been particularly resonant during the Black Death. Guided by Rolandino's practical advice, the notaries enabled the town's populace—men and women of the elite and nonelite classes—to undertake the important task of making known and preserving their last wishes for the future of their souls and their families.

Notarial Bureaucracy: the Memoriali *and* Provvisori

The notaries of Bologna were the product and producers of a large and complicated bureaucracy that since the early fourteenth century revolved around the offices of *Memoriali* and *Provvisori*. It is due to the notaries's efforts to produce their registers and staff these offices that the history of one of the worst human catastrophes can be accurately told. But even beyond the year of the Black Death, the amount of material recording the transactions of late medieval urban life extant in the *Memoriali* is nothing short of phenomenal.[61] An investigation of its contents is clearly essential for a thorough understanding of the contract-based culture characteristic of late medieval Italian towns, but it is also important to know how the notarial bureaucracy that produced this material functioned—during non-plague years as well as during the epidemic. While the origin and evolution of this source has been described by Giorgio Tamba and Luisa Continelli, there has been no detailed analysis of how it functioned during the fourteenth century, when it had undergone important transformations.[62]

---

[60] Rolandino, *Summa*, fol. 294r–v.

[61] The *Memoriali* span over 200 years and comprise 322 large parchment volumes, each containing the *liber memorialium* or *memoriale* of several notaries. See Luisa Continelli, ed., *L'Archivio dell' Ufficio dei Memoriali: Inventario: Vol. I Memoriali 1265–1436, Tomo I 1265–1333* (Bologna, 1988), pp. xiv and xvi.

[62] The inventory for the *Memoriali* after the rise of the *Provvisori* has now been produced: Luisa Continelli, *L'Archivio dell'Ufficio dei Memoriali: Inventario, Vol. 1 Memoriali, 1265–1436; Tomo II, 1334–1436* (Bologna: Bononia University Press, 2008).

The *Memoriali* were established in 1265 during a time of crisis in the popular government, when two friars from the order of the Santa Maria Gloriosa, the *frati gaudenti*, were given exceptional powers with which they passed a series of ordinances intended to rein in factional hostilities. Chapter XLI of these statutes required the public recording of certain types of contracts dealing with articles of a value higher than 20 *lire*.[63] Contracts were recorded at the office of the *Memoriali* in registers that were deposited and preserved at the Camera degli Atti, the communal archives of Bologna.[64] Bologna did not follow the trend of cities such as Genoa and Venice which set up public archives to preserve the cartularies of deceased notaries (or of notaries temporarily away from the city).[65] Instead, the commune was concerned with registering the documentation of active notaries. According to Giorgio Tamba, the creation of the *Memoriali* represented an effort, on the part of the commune, to control the activities of the many notaries in the city. The private citizens for whom the contracts had been drawn up paid the taxes due for this registration and, as a concession by the commune to the notaries, only the parties of the transaction or their *procurators* were responsible for making sure registration was carried out within the time limit. The contract had to be registered on the day that it was drawn up or on the following day (with a third day allowed for holidays), otherwise the contract would be invalid: *illud instrumentum sit cassum et nullius valoris, nec ex eo aliquid possit peti vel exigi*. True to the institution's stated purpose of protecting citizens against fraud, it was further declared that anyone trying to use an unregistered contract for legal purposes was subject to a fine of 100 *lire*. For its part, the city guaranteed these contracts eternal protection against falsification or loss.[66]

The *Memoriali* contain a large variety of contracts illuminating late medieval urban life, but not all contracts drawn up by the notaries of

---

[63] At the time of the *Memoriali*'s institution, 20 *lire* was equal to the price of two work cattle or one *tornatura* (equal to about half an acre) of land.

[64] Giorgio Tamba, "I Memoriali del comune di Bologna nel secolo XIII: Note di diplomatica," *Rassegna degli Archivi di Stato* 47 (1987), pp. 235–236.

[65] Giorgio Tamba, "Un archivio notarile? No, tuttavia...," *Archivi per la Storia* 3 (1990), pp. 41 and 72–95.

[66] Fasoli and Sella, *Statuti*, 2:80–81: "Dicimus etiam quod in armario populi Bononiae semper sint et esse debeant et remanere omnes libri contractuum memorialium et ultimarum voluntatum facta ab eo tempore...et in predicto armario perpetuo conserventur".

Bologna were subject to registration. Apprenticeship and work contracts were excluded because of the difficulty of establishing a value for the object of the contract. Juridical contracts also were excluded since they would have been recorded and preserved in administrative offices and would not require guarantee through the office of the *Memoriali*. Thus the bulk of contracts in the *Memoriali* are financial contracts (i.e., sales, loans, and other financial settlements). There also appear contracts of a less financial nature such as pacts and agreements between parties, dowry and emancipation contracts, and testaments, which were most likely to be of values higher than the 20 *lire* minimum and, thus, their numbers better reflect the number of actual contracts redacted in the city. Petty business transactions, however, were much more likely to escape registration in the *Memoriali*.[67] The many small loans and rentals of work animals of artisans, shopkeepers, and peasants would often have been left out of this source. In fact, individuals requiring such contracts purposely avoided registration by subdividing these transactions into smaller deals which each involved transactions below the 20 *lire* limit.[68]

The procedure of registration was complex in 1265 and became even more complicated and difficult as the source continued over time. In 1285 the law required that the notaries themselves report to the office of the *Memoriali* or request that the contracting parties report and deposit, for each contract requiring registration, the *nota* (i.e., the initial *rogatio* or *scheda* which the notary wrote down in his cartulary during the transaction, and not the *imbreviatura* or final copy which remained with the clients). The *Memoriali* notary would then copy out the following information in his *quaternus* or *liber memorialium*: the name and parish of the contracting parties, the object and value of the contract, the principal witness, and the notary who wrote up the contract. As the *nota* had to be deposited within two days, the *Memoriali* notary also noted this date with such formulas as "nota data fuit", "notam dederunt dicta die", or "dictus notarius notam dedit".[69] Thus, only the essential information, and not the entire contract was copied out into

[67] Giorgio Tamba estimated that, during the late thirteenth century, the *Memoriali* contained between one third and one fourth of the actual number of contracts produced in the city. See Tamba, "Un archivio notarile?," pp. 43–45.

[68] Tamba discovered this by examining the *imbreviature* of a cartulary of 1305, the only cartulary remaining from the beginning of the fourteenth century. See Tamba, "I Memoriali," pp. 280–281.

[69] Continelli, *L'Archivio, Tomo I*, p. xx.

the *Memoriali*. The founding principles of the *Memoriali* were careful not to institute a substitution for the actual notarial documentation. This was in deference to the notaries of Bologna who wished to keep intact the patrimonial value of the unique and unduplicated *instrumenta* in their personal archives.[70] Because of these rules we can learn very little in the early period from complex contracts such as wills, since none of the testamentary bequests was recorded.

Laws of 1290 stipulated that for wills the name of the heir and substitutions, in addition to bequests of more than 10 *lire* be copied out. According to Martin Bertram, between 1290 and 1335 the registrations are very irregular, since different notaries chose to include different amounts of information. From about 1290 there developed a tendency to copy out more and more of all types of contracts, not simply wills. Finally in 1335, new laws ordered that all registered contracts were to be copied out in full.[71] This was an enormous task, and the *Memoriali* notaries were probably chronically behind in the copying of the full contracts. In the case that a contract was copied out at a later date by a notary of the office of the *Memoriali*, that notary sometimes wrote an additional note stating his name and the date.

During the late thirteenth century, contracts were entered by type and in chronological order. The number of registrations preserved in the *Memoriali* for these early years is, on average, about 8,000 to 10,000 a year.[72] During the second decade of the fourteenth century, the contracts no longer appear in chronological order. It seems that notaries of the office of the *Memoriali* were no longer able to keep up with the burden of copying out the contracts entirely on each day. According to the inventory compiled by Luisa Continelli, during the early 1300s notaries began to add sections at the back of their registers which contained contracts copied "out of order" and omitted "by mistake".[73] These *quaterni extraordinarii* became the norm as time went on since there was no attempt at maintaining a chronological order by the 1330s. The problem of random order among contracts was remedied by the introduction in 1333 of a parallel series, the *Libri provvisorum* or *Provvisori*, which were kept in strict chronological order. New laws of 1335

[70] Tamba, "I Memoriali," p. 262.
[71] Bertram, "Testamenti medievali bolognesi," pp. 313–314.
[72] This estimate is based on calculations in Tamba, "Un archivio notarile?," pp. 44–45: c. 20,000 for late 1265–1268, c. 12,000 for 1288, and c. 8,000 for 1305.
[73] Continelli, *L'Archivio, Tomo I*, pp. xxv–xxvi.

recognized and authorized the existence of the *Provvisori* while setting out new and reaffirming old guidelines for the *Memoriali*.

The primary purpose of the *Provvisori* was to collect the taxes due for registration, not to avoid fraud as was the purpose of the *Memoriali*. The notaries of the office of *Provvisori* were the first to receive the *nota* and payments for registration. The city notaries were now required by the new laws of 1335 to deposit the *nota* at the office of the *Provvisori* within three days for contracts made in the city and within 15 days for those in the contado. Notaries were posted at three areas of business and commercial activity in the city: the *Cambium*, *Gabella*, and *Scarania*. The *Cambium* was located near the central commercial zone of Bologna, viz., the Piazza di Porta Ravegnana (the site of Bologna's iconic two towers), where bankers and moneychangers worked. The *Gabella* was the Customs House located near the central piazza, while the *Scarania* was located on the central piazza (the Piazza del Comune) at the *palatium vetus*, which together with the *palatium novum* held the offices of government across from the palace of the guild of notaries. At each location the notary of the *Provvisori* had to copy out on that same day into his register (or *provvisore*) the essential data for each contract (i.e., date and place where the contract was drawn up, the subject matter, and names of parties involved and principal witness). This task rotated through the week to the seven notaries at each site. After the registration, each notary had 15 days to copy out in full—as now required by the 1335 law—the information of the contract, taken from the *nota*, in his *liber memorialium*. All of the notations in the *Provvisori* registers are in a strict chronological order, but contracts recorded in the *Memoriali* from then on are without order. The notaries of the *Provvisori* were required to keep two copies: an original in parchment and a copy in paper.[74]

The task of copying out in full thousands of contracts each year may have become too burdensome for the officials and perhaps not very useful for the citizenry of Bologna. Once the tax had been collected by a notary of the *Provvisori* and the contract's information registered in brief, there was less incentive to copy out the entire contract in the *Memoriali*. Citizens of Bologna may have made more use of the private

[74] The parchment *provvisori* consist of 421 registers, spanning the years 1333–1434, while the paper *provvisori* consist of 834 registers and lasted until 1452. There are more paper registers in this series, because contracts from the city and contado were kept in separate paper registers.

archives of notaries for authorized copies of contracts than resorting to the *Memoriali*. In fact, the numbers of contracts in the *Memoriali* declines severely after 1335, the date of the establishment of the *Provvisori*.[75] Tamba estimated that during the last decade of the fourteenth century there appear about 3,000 notations in the *Provvisori* each year, while the registrations in the *Memoriali* do not reach ten per cent of those in the *Provvisori*.[76] Indeed, the *Memoriali* from 1385 to 1436, the year that the series ended, make up only seven volumes (unlike 1348 which encompasses three volumes of approximately 500 folios each).[77] The office of the *Memoriali* and its functions were taken over in 1452 by a new institution, the *Registro*, which continued the financial function of the *Provvisori* with the exclusion of more types of contracts and an increased limit on the value of transaction for registration. Thus, in terms of quantity and quality of extant material, the period shortly after the beginning of the *Provvisori* and before the onset of severe decline at the end of the fourteenth century offers the best window of opportunity for the research in the *Memoriali*.

Secret Wills of the Demaniale

Ever since the introduction of the *Memoriali*, there had been the option of depositing one's will to be kept "secret" in the Franciscan and Dominican sacristies. The laws of 1333 that instituted the *Provvisori* limited this option to men only. My search through the collections of the suppressed religious houses, known as the *Demaniale*, has resulted

[75] There are 4836 contracts in the *Memoriali* of 1348 (including 3567 from the city and 1269 from the contado). Nevertheless, despite the decline in number of contracts in the *Memoriali*, the introduction of the *Provvisori* brought distinct advantages to the researcher. The requirements of the *Provvisori* produced a source of internal consistency in documentation and no further changes in the nature of the content or registration were ordered. The contracts and testaments in the *Memoriali* are complete copies, and the reproduction of contents is no longer subject to the inclination of the individual notaries in the Office of the *Memoriali*.

[76] Tamba, "Un archivio notarile?," p. 17.

[77] The *Provvisori* fared somewhat better than the *Memoriali* since the paper series lasted until 1452. The parchment *Provvisori*, however, ended in 1434. One must take this into account when using the series to make comparisons of the contents of the *Memoriali* over time. Samuel Kline Cohn, Jr. has used this series to compare mortalities in plague years between 1362 and 1423. The decline in numbers of testaments is primarily because of a decline in the quality of this source. See Cohn, *The Black Death Transformed*, pp. 160, 166.

in 12 wills of female testators and 73 wills of male testators for the year of the Black Death. The women's wills are not secret wills at all, but rather copies of wills, some of which are extant in the *Memoriali*. Most of the men's are secret wills—the testator declared that this was his intention—but a few are wills from the *Memoriali* for which the mendicants wanted their own copies. Nearly half of these secret wills were dictated in the sacristy of the Franciscan or, more rarely, the Dominican convent, with a smaller number in a home belonging to the convent or in a chapel in the mendicant church. The rest, about a third, were written up in the home of the testator, with the specific instructions that the will was to be deposited in the sacristy, not the *Memoriali*, and to remain secret.

With an elaborate bureaucracy dedicated to preserving the populace's documents and protecting them against fraud, why would testators want to bypass the system to make a secret will? It certainly was not necessary to use the friars for secrecy, since male and female testators who had their wills registered with the city could and did give secret instructions. Several wills in the *Memoriali* instructed executors, relatives, or clerics with "secret commissions" involving the distribution of sums. These could be prodigious amounts of money, such as the bequest by Bella of the noble Prendiparti family who left 500 *lire* to her brother asking him to distribute it for her soul *in secreto commissionis*.[78] These secret bequests were not usually *pro anima*, however. A certain Martinus made his uncle executor with separate bequests to him of seven *lire* "to the poor and other pious places" and ten *lire* "to distribute according to secret commission".[79] Other men turned to their wives: a member of the elite Conforti family entrusted to his wife 35 *lire* instructing her "to give it to people and places in secret" and a blacksmith named his wife with three other men as executors to arrange for the transfer of half of his house and its furnishings "which money and goods are to be given as he has instructed them in good faith and in secret" (*prout eis commisit in fide et secreto*). The blacksmith relied on more (presumably not secret) written acts, since he had separate arrangements with another guildsman (*socius*) to whom he bequeathed in his testament his share in the capital and profits of the workshop: *prout eis continet*

[78] Mem, vol. 229, fol. 113r (Bella olim nobilis viri domini Tani de Prendipartibus).
[79] Mem, vol. 229, fol. 75r (Martinus fq Jacobi olim Martini Alexii).

in scripturis factis inter ipsos.[80] Others turned to friars or confessors to distribute secret funds.[81] Thus the testament did not preclude separate confidential instructions.

It does appear, however, that a couple of testators of the secret wills in the *Demaniale* either may have had more complicated reasons for secrecy that could not be handled by means of a single bequest or indeed last wishes that they preferred to declare only in the confines of the sacristy. A noble knight originally from Trapani in Sicily went to the Franciscan church to make his will. He was married and had an illegitimate son by a servant from Malta. After returning to his wife her dowry, this knight left money to the son and dowries for the son's daughters (one received clothes and the other the knight's arms).[82] The other example is a widowed doctor of medicine who made a will at home, but declared that it should remain secret. While making large bequests to his legitimate children that were consistent with his station, he also was concerned with his illegitimate family: he provided a dowry of 100 *lire* to the daughter of the woman who lived with him, named only Emanuela, 150 *lire* to each of her sons by him, as well as a dowry of 50 *lire* for Emanuela.[83] These two testators, however, are exceptional. There were no other examples of testators who used secret wills to provide for illegitimate families.

In terms of profession, a greater percentage of the *Demaniale* testators had connections to the church: three were tertiaries, one was identified as brother of the order of Saint Bernard, and one was a rector of a church in the contado. There are also strong examples of religious forms of charity since five testators made the Poor of Christ their heirs—seven per cent of testators is a greater proportion than such

[80] Mem, vol. 228, fols. 112r (Nicolaus fq domini Bitini de Confortis), 181v (Johannes fq Gerardi de Feraciis).

[81] Zanobia, originally from the Florentine contado, left four gold florins to her parish priest "for a certain person" (Mem, vol. 229, fol. 5v); Soane fq ser Dominici asked his parish priest to give away 30 *lire* "to those persons" (Mem, vol. 229, fol. 82r); Margarita, daughter of a saddler (*selarius*), left 5 *lire* to a Franciscan (Mem, vol. 228, fol. 217v); and Bertolomea fq nobilis militis Thomaxini de Sasuollo, widow of a law professor, left 25 *lire* to a Dominican friar for such purposes (Mem, vol. 228, fol. 411r).

[82] Dem, F.M., Camp. Rossi, 340, fol. 43 (nobilis et egregius miles dominus Laurentius fq Rugerii de Mamellis de Trappani regni Sicilie). The servant was named Johana Santori.

[83] Dem, F.P., 193, 7527, unnumbered pages (magister Jacobus olim magistri Merchadantis Venanci Azzis *medicine doctor eximius civis*). See Chapter Two for a discussion of his will in the context of other professors's wills.

bequests in the sample of wills from the *Memoriali*—and six named as heirs *familiares*, or servants of the Franciscans, which was a very unusual choice. However, as in the public wills of the *Memoriali*, sons were the favorite choice of universal heir. Furthermore, most of the testators of secret wills were not clerics, but elite citizens. Unlike testators from the *Memoriali*, very few were from the middling artisanal classes. The few artisan wills that are found in the *Demaniale*, viz., those of two shoemakers, a clothes dealer, and a *laborator* (agricultural worker), are actually not secret wills, but copies made by the religious house. Thus it appears that dictating one's will in the sacristies and having it deposited it in secret was a sign of prestige, rather like being buried in the mendicant churches. Elite women as noted above also dictated their wills in the church. They relied on the same friars as witnesses and executors, the only difference was that their wills did not remain in the sacristies.

A secret will had the usual legal form of a testament, that is, it was dictated to a notary before seven witnesses. Instead of being copied into the public registers, however, the document would be sealed with the seal of the Franciscan or Dominican convent and would remain there unopened and secret until sometime after the testator's death, at which point it would be opened and read.[84] This added another layer of notarial authentication to an already complicated system. The fact that the will was delivered into the hands (*in manibus*) of the sacristan and sealed and deposited in a religious house (and not a public office) was treated as a separate legal act from the declaration of the will, and therefore required a separate declaration by a notary with two additional witnesses (by means of a new *actum* clause written at the end of the testament). It is important to keep in mind these multiple layers of legal requirements—fulfilled by notaries—that encompassed so many aspects of civic life. The notaries underwrote and sustained people's interactions and intentions, and thus it is imperative to understand their activity and the functioning of their bureaucracy during the Black Death.

[84] Testators of secret wills stated that they wanted their will to be secret, deposited, and sealed by the mendicant order of their choice, and opened after their death. The typical phrase was "voluit secretum et ut secretum deponi debere in sacristia [F.P. or F.M.] et sigillari debere sigilo conventus [F.P. or F.M.] secundum formam statuti Bononiensis et post mortem dicti testatori publicari et aperiri debere".

The Notarial Bureaucracy During the Black Death

The system of registration in the *Provvisori* and reproduction in the *Memoriali* was supposed to follow an organized procedure, but, in fact, the reality was more complicated and erratic. In theory, the *Provvisori* registers should work as a finding key for acts in the *Memoriali* registers, since one could quickly identify material in a given *Provvisori* register, note the notary who copied down the *nota* and then locate his *memoriale* and, ideally, sort through the randomly ordered contents and find a specific contract. In reality, the contracts registered by one notary could end up copied out into the *memoriale* of another, who might even have been working at a different location in the city.[85] That this departure from the ideal was in fact the norm can be demonstrated by tracking testaments in the *Provvisori* and the *Memoriali* for the year 1348.[86]

For the first semester of 1348 there remain the parchment registers of the *Provvisori* for contracts registered "a latere gabelle" and "a latere scaranie", while those registered "a latere cambii" are missing, but can be retrieved by means of the paper register copy.[87] The wills registered in these *provvisori* registers were then copied into various *memoriali* which today compose a single volume of the *Memoriali*.[88] The *Provvisori* registers of the *Cambium* are missing in both the parchment and paper copies for the second semester, so it is not feasible to carry out a comparison of the contents of the *Memoriali* and *Provvisori* for the second half of the year. Because the *Memoriali* contracts were entered without chronological order, the only way to systematically analyze their contents is through a database of names that can be compared with a corresponding database for the *Provvisori*. This comparison demonstrates

[85] Another departure from the rule was that the number of notaries working under the *provvisore* were not always seven. When this happened the notaries would rotate more quickly through the week.

[86] A comparison of the testaments registered in the first semester of the *Provvisori* with those copied into the *Memoriali* is the best way to determine the actual functioning of this remarkable source, since, because of their formulaic nature, they are generally the easiest kinds of sources to identify in the *Memoriali*. All the contracts registered in the *Provvisori* are identified by an abbreviated rubric, but rubrics are erratic and unreliable in the *Memoriali*. A comparison of the more numerous and varied business contracts would be much more difficult and open to errors.

[87] ASB, Provvisori pergamenacei [hereafter as Provv. perg.], reg. 16 and ASB, Provvisori cartacei [hereafter as Provv. cart.], reg. 152.

[88] Mem, vol. 228 (1348). For a list of the names of the *Provvisori* notaries see Bertram, "Zweiter Teil," p. 217.

the error of the traditional assumption that contracts in *provvisori* and *memoriali* registers corresponding to the same notary went through the registration and reproduction process completely. Furthermore, one should not assume that when there is no corresponding *memoriale* for a register in the *Provvisori*, then those contracts never went beyond the registration phase. On paper, the *Memoriali* appear to be missing many *quaterni*, when, in fact, some contracts from those missing *quaterni* were copied out into the *memoriale* of a different notary. This was the case even for contracts written in the months before plague struck, that is, in the normal functioning of the source. For example, Bitinus fq Jacobi de Castro Sancti Petri registered contracts at the *Gabella* for the *Provvisori*. Since there remains no *memoriale* for Bitinus Jacobi in the *Memoriali*, it could be assumed that the contracts he registered were never copied out and do not appear in volume 228 of the *Memoriali*. Nevertheless, some do appear, because they were copied out into the *memoriale* of Jacobus de Policino, who also worked at the *Gabella*.[89] Similarly, Francolus Mundini Francoli worked at the *Gabella*, but his *memoriale* is not extant in the *Memoriali*. Yet wills that he registered appear in the *memoriale* of Johannes Jacobi Perini, who was working at the *Scarania*.[90] Johannes seems to have substituted for Francolus only occasionally, for his *memoriale* contains testaments for which he registered the *nota* in the *Provvisori*, as well as testaments that were registered at the *Gabella*. Most of the extant wills registered at the *Cambium* in the *provvisore* of notary Bitinus Jacobi Bitini Azolini were from June and were later copied out, according to the correct procedure, by Bitinus, into his *memoriale* (volume 228, fols. 257–316), but other testaments that he registered during that month, were, in fact, copied out by Antonius Dominici de Pizanis, who worked at the *Scarania*, in his *memoriale* (volume 228, fols. 319–366).[91] The examples can be multiplied, but what is clear is that the notaries substituted among

[89] See, for example, the testament of Jacobus fq Gerardi de Foratiis redacted on 12 April, registered "a latere cambii" by Bitinus Jacobi Bitini in Provv. cart, vol. 152, no page number, but copied into the *memoriale* of Jacobus de Policino, working at the *Gabella*, in Mem, vol. 228, fol. 181v.

[90] See, for example, the testament of Magdalena fq ser Santi, redacted on 19 April, registered "a latere gabelle" by Francolus Mundini Francoli in Provv, perg. reg. 16, no page number, but copied into the *memoriale* of Johannes Jacobi Perini, who was working at the *Scarania*, in Mem, vol. 228, fol. 70r.

[91] Proper procedure was followed for the wills redacted on 18 June of Margarita fq ser Pizoli (Mem, vol. 228, fol. 274r) and of Diana Johannis de Beccadellis (Mem, vol. 228, fol. 307r) which are both in the *memoriale* of Bitinus Azolini. The will of Costancia

themselves, and furthermore, that this was part of the standard *modus operandi* even before plague arrived.

When plague entered the city it put great strain on the bureaucracy of the *Memoriali*.[92] Notaries managed to continue to enter information into the *provvisori* registers, but it became increasingly harder to carry out the second task of copying contracts into their *memoriali*. This is demonstrated in the first graph (Figure 1.1), which records the total number of testaments in the *Provvisori* and *Memoriali*. Even in the beginning of the year, before plague entered the city, the *Provvisori* contain the registrations of wills that were never copied into the *Memoriali*, however, the tendency to neglect this second step is more pronounced once plague entered the city. Change is apparent in the second half of May, when the gap between the number of testaments in the *Provvisori* and *Memoriali* widens. During the month of June, the *Memoriali* is in a state of crisis. The preserved material represents about one third of the actual number of wills redacted and registered in Bologna.

It was not, however, an across-the-board crisis, since the notaries acting at each of the three designated areas of the city managed to carry out their work with different levels of success. The next three graphs display the extent to which the notaries succeeded in copying out the full contracts, i.e., they demonstrate the numbers of wills registered in the *Provvisori* from each of the three areas as well as the number of those wills that appear anywhere in the *Memoriali* (as we know, not necessarily in the *memoriali* of notaries working in a given area). The *Scarania* (Figure 1.2), under the direction of Paulus Jacobi de Raffanellis, did very well for the early months, especially March, when more contracts were successfully copied than not, but there is less success for May. Plague has clearly had an effect by the second half of June when the number of testaments registered at the *Scarania* that never made it

---

Garietis also registered by Bitinus on 18 June was instead copied into the *memoriale* of Antonius Dominici de Pizanis (Mem, vol. 228, fol. 365r).

[92] Another sign of stress and irregularity in the *Memoriali* is the presence of 19 duplicate wills in the *Memoriali*, 12 of which were originally redacted during the summer months of plague. Three of these duplicates are the fault of the notary to whom the contracts were given to copy out—they duplicated their own work since they appear in the same *memoriale*. However, the remaining 16 duplicates are wills that were copied out by different notaries and appear in different *memoriali*. This is another indicator that notaries were used to copying into their *memoriali* contracts for which they were not assigned the *nota* according to regular procedure.

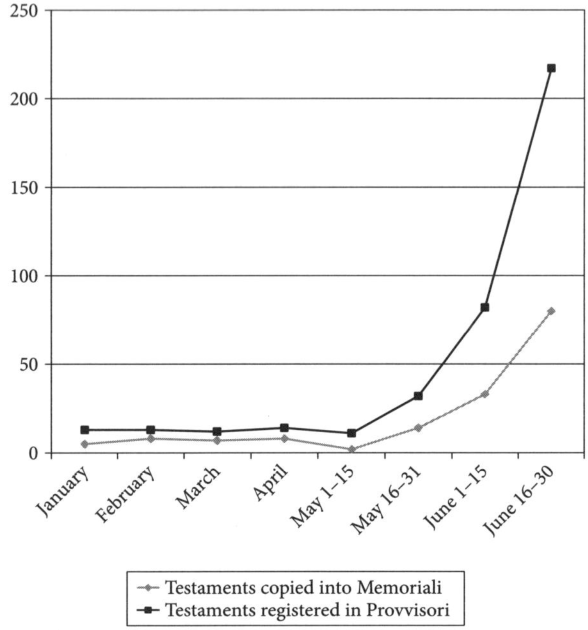

Figure 1.1 Testaments in the *Memoriali* and *Provvisori* in 1348

into a *memoriale* is nearly twice that of those completed. The *Gabella* (Figure 1.3) under the notary-in-charge *provvisor* Nicolaus Petri de Castagnolo, registered roughly the same numbers with a similar pattern of success. The *Cambium* (Figure 1.4), on the other hand, under Michael Jacobi de Nugareto, managed to deal with the strain of copying out testaments much better. During the second half of May, when plague had already caused problems for notaries working at the other two locations, those at the *Cambium* copied out all testaments redacted during the last two weeks of May. It was only the exceptionally high number in June that resulted in a significant amount of testaments not reproduced in the *Memoriali*. There were fewer wills registered at the *Cambium* than the other locations, and this may have been a reason for the better rate of completion. However, according to the proper procedure of registration, it should have been the case that very few testaments from the *Cambium* would have ever made it into the *Memoriali*, because there are only two extant *memoriali* of the notaries to whom the *nota* were designated at the *Cambium*. Yet they did make it in, as the graph demonstrates, because Bonbolognus Panigalis, who was working at the *Gabella*, copied most of them into his *memoriale*.

Thus, the notaries were arranging things among themselves, and the bureaucracy functioned during the epidemic, just not according to the original plan.

The *Memoriali* certainly do not contain all the wills that were registered in the *Provvisori*: for the first semester there are 176 testaments in the *Memoriali* (not including codicils or duplicate wills) versus 402 registered testaments, while for the second semester there are 1095 testaments compared to 1235 in the remaining (incomplete) *Provvisori* registers.[93] Yet, the fact that so many were copied out during an epidemic is astonishing. The notaries were making the effort to carry out the second and final step in the procedure of registration, and most wills that survive as complete appear to have been copied into the individual *memoriali* during the year of plague. The epidemic did, nevertheless, cause considerable difficulties for the source and its compilers. Some of the *Memoriali* notaries spent the next 14 years finishing the tasks of 1348. Many testaments in the *Memoriali* of 1348 contain addenda stating that the act was copied into the *memoriale* at a later date. However, once again, the difficulty and gaps in the source were not across-the-board. Of the *memoriali* from the first semester, eight appeared to have been completed during the year of plague (at least there is no notation to the contrary in any testament written therein), while three were finished in later years. There were more problems for the second half of the year when six registers had to be completed later, but, it should be noted that ten *memoriali* appear to have been fully finished during the year of the epidemic. It is interesting that among the wills added later in years after 1348, in "extraordinary" sections of the *memoriali*, there appear four wills that were never originally registered in the *Provvisori*—they appear to have completely bypassed the first step of registration.[94] They were redacted in the second half of June when the notaries were having problems keeping up with copying their contracts. Again, we see that plague caused disruption and forced some changes in procedure, but the demanding system was not abandoned.

[93] I have used Bertram's count for the number of testaments in the second semester. Our numbers differ slightly for the first semester, perhaps, because I have not included codicils in my count. Bertram, "Zweiter Teil," p. 219.

[94] These are the testaments of Mina Cavalieri de Cavalieris redacted on 16 June, Landa fq Fratris Doxii on 20 June, Egidius fq Auliverii olim Egidii de Scudellis on 25 June, and Franciscus fq domini Oselitii de Oselittis on 28 June: Mem, vol. 228, fols. 109r, 250v, 251r, 318r.

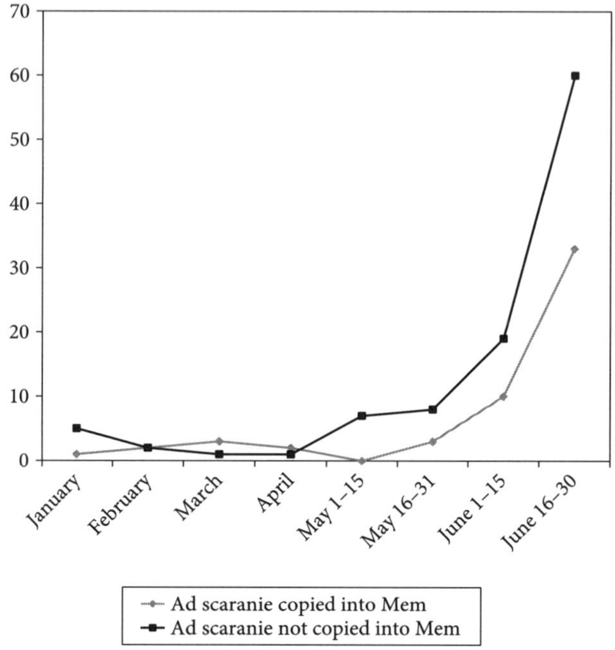

Figure 1.2 Testaments Registered *Ad Scaranie* and Those Copied in the *Memoriali*

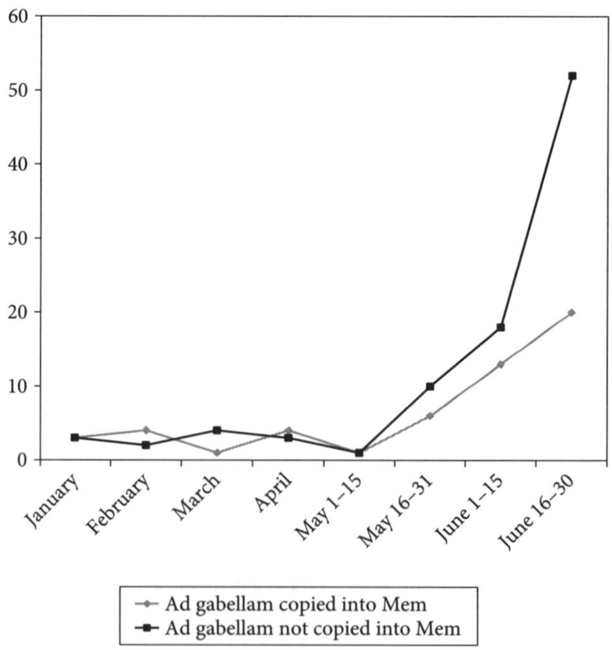

Figure 1.3 Testaments Registered *ad Gabellam* and Those Copied in the *Memoriali*

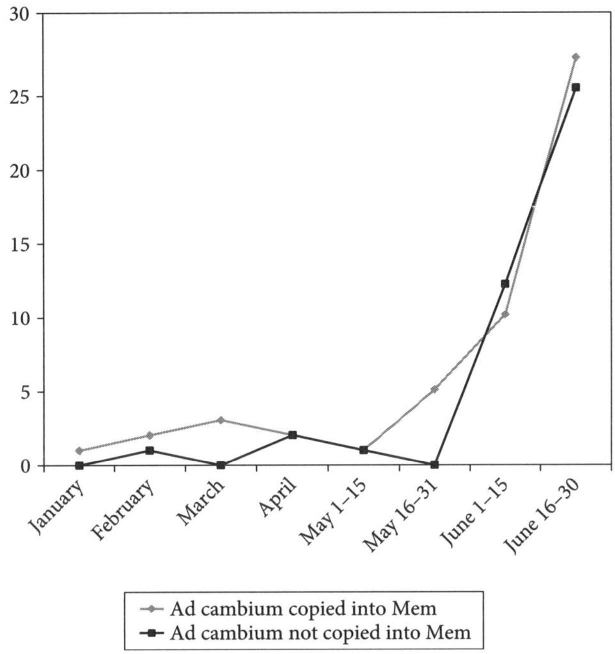

Figure 1.4 Testaments Registered *Ad Cambium* and Those Copied in the *Memoriali*

The last year that testaments registered in 1348 were still being copied into a *memoriale* was 1362 when Jacobus Johannis de Albertuciis finally completed his *memoriale* by copying out two testaments on 22 March and 28 August. Jacobus had survived the Black Death and was still serving as notary in 1362, although no longer for the Office of the *Memoriali*.[95] Interestingly, this was during the second onslaught of plague in Bologna. Thus, while plague was raging for a second time, this notary was still laboring to copy out contracts from the first epidemic. The cruel coincidence of the situation must have been painfully clear to this notary, but the message to us should be that in both episodes of plague these men of the *Memoriali* continued to carry out their work. The conclusion is that the *Memoriali* suffered during the Black Death, but this complicated bureaucratic institution did not collapse. The *Provvisori* were completed during the epidemic and much of the

[95] In the note following these two wills he identifies himself as "notary and at one time notary for the Office of Memoriali for the second six months of 1348". The wills were redacted on 21 August and 10 October of 1348: Mem, vol. 229, fols. 98r and 99v. See Chapter Four and Appendix for a discussion of *Provvisori* notaries who survived the first epidemic and appear in official capacities at the office of the *Memoriali* in later years (some until 1363).

immensely difficult work of copying out the contracts into the *Memoriali* was also carried out. Nevertheless, this was a time of crisis and thus there were problems, for as we have seen many of the contracts were not copied immediately. They were not completely neglected by the notaries, but were laid aside to be dealt with at a later date.

Will-Making During the Black Death

Testaments were the act that probably required the most effort on the part of notaries.[96] Notarial law laid out specific parameters for the drawing up of a valid will. There were also special rules for the redaction of wills dictated in the *Statuti* establishing the *Memoriali*. The first and foremost concern of notarial and communal law was that the testament be authentic, i.e., an accurate and un-coerced statement of the wishes of the testator, and that it be recognized as such by witnesses beyond the testator's immediate family or legatees. The widely used notarial manuals of Bologna, the *Ars notarie* of Salatiele and the *Summa totius artis notarie* of Rolandino Passaggeri, gave specific instructions about witnesses. There had to be seven male witnesses, who were not hermaphrodites, slaves, insane, mute or deaf, nor subject to the legal

[96] Some wills, especially of the wealthy, are very long documents covering three to four large parchment folios, but most are short. As noted above, the length and number of bequests does not, however, always correspond to the wealth of the testator. Testaments could be a good source of income for notaries, since the more complicated demanded higher fees than other types of contracts. Payment varied according to the value of pious bequests (*pro anima*). According to the communal statutes of 1288, the fees started at three *solidi* for the redaction a will containing less than six *lire* of pious bequest and went up to six *lire* for a will containing between 500–1000 *lire* of pious bequests. The only types of contracts demanding anything near these high fees were "big" inventories, which garnered 10 *solidi*, or sales of property worth over 500 *lire*, which cost 12 *solidi*. The notaries of the *Memoriali* who registered the testaments, received for their labor, the fixed sum of 12 *denari*, equal to that of many other types of contracts. Fees are listed in Fasoli and Sella, *Statuti*, 2:77–79. The testament also required a high level of technical skill and more legal knowledge than any other contract. In the comments on the testament, the "Flos testamentorum" of his *Summa*, Rolandino was emphatic that a notary must know the law before attempting to redact a testament, since the material and spiritual well-being of the testator and many others depended on it. Imprudence and incompetence on the part of notaries were "unpardonable offenses". See Giovanni Chiodi, "Rolandino e il testamento," in *Rolandino e l'ars notaria da Bologna all'Europa*, ed. Giorgio Tamba (Milano, 2002), pp 465–472.

authority (*in potestate*) of the testator.[97] In the case of ill or female testators, the *Memoriali* also required the presence of a priest, preferably from the testator's parish, who could also vouch for the testator's identification.[98] In fact, almost all of the wills of 1348 had at least one priest, or sometimes two friars, officiating, even for those testators who were healthy men. This meant that each will required the gathering of at least ten people: the testator, notary, priest and seven witnesses. Most likely female family members were at the making of the will, but their presence is not recorded.

These requirements demanded a lot of effort from the notaries and townspeople who were living and dying in the midst of a frightening epidemic. Nevertheless, once again, the notaries, assisted by neighbors and clerics in this case, fulfilled their obligations to the law and their clients. The twenty-seven complete testaments extant in the *Memoriali* from the first four months of the year—before plague had disrupted town life—all have at least the required number of witnesses. Twenty-five of these had eight, nine, or ten witnesses, while two had 11 and 12 men listed. After plague arrived there is some slippage, but it is just enough to remind us that plague had brought on a difficult situation, but did not cause a complete breakdown. Out of a sample of 255 wills redacted in June, July, and August—the months in which plague was at its height—only 14 (or five per cent) fall short of the required eight witnesses (with six or seven men listed, including the priest).[99] 186 wills

[97] Rolandinus, *Summa*, fols. 235r–235v: "In testamentis exiguntur regulariter septem testes qui presentes sint". Eight witnesses were required for wills drawn up "in scriptis," i.e., written by the testator (or a scribe), or for testators who were blind. The "in scriptis" testament was rare in late medieval Bologna. The common practice was the nuncupative or "sine scriptis" testament, which was also written down, but, most importantly was the result of an open declaration before witnesses and the notary by the testator of his or her intentions. In villages or places where no more could be found, only five witnesses were required. The same requirements for witnesses are expressed in the earlier formulary by Salatiele, which was eventually supplanted by Rolandino's *Summa*. See Salatiele, *Ars Notarie*, ed. Gianfranco Orlandelli, 2 vols. (Milan: Giuffrè, 1961), 2:176–177.

[98] Fasoli and Sella, *Statuti*, 2:82: "in qua ultima voluntate mulierum et infermorum sit presens unus sacerdos, qui publice habeatur sacerdos in contrata ubi habitat, qui cognoscat condentem ultimam voluntatem, vel aliquis alius sacerdotes de aliquo loco religioso civitatis Bononie vel prope ad unum miliare".

[99] This sample is not statistically random or at least it was not generated with a plan to achieve statistical randomness, but instead is the result of disjointed efforts at entering data from testaments over several years. There are more wills in the sample from volumes 228 (which includes contracts from January to June) and 229 (from July to December) than from volume 230 (also from July to December), and the data

have eight or nine witnesses, while 55 (over twenty per cent) involved groups of 10, 11, and even 12 men. In July, at the height of the epidemic, there were seven large gatherings of 11 and 12 witnesses meeting either within a home or in the more public space of the *Gabella*, a church or a house belonging to a hospital.[100]

Clearly, the law was followed in most cases and even the customary behavior of large social gatherings of nine and more witnesses continued despite plague. Moreover, the fact that the notaries recorded such large groups of witnesses indicates that these men were actually present at the dictation of the will. If notaries had suspended normal practice and were simply recording names without their real presence, one would expect the numbers of witnesses to remain at the legal minimum without fluctuation. There is no legal loophole in the notarial manuals for fewer than seven witnesses at the dictation of a will, other than it being carried out in the countryside. Furthermore, there are no notarial notations in the wills that either state explicitly or suggest that legal norms were suspended. The townspeople came together to ensure the validity of the wills and honor the last wishes of the dying.

The bureaucracy of the *Memoriali* demanded other additional steps beyond the requirements of notarial law in order for the will to be valid in Bologna. Testators had to come with the notary and priest to register the will at one of the three *Memoriali* locations. If the testator was ill or female, a *procurator* was assigned to take his or her place. The notaries were less diligent about assigning proctors than they were about ensuring the proper number of witnesses, since 83 per cent of ill testators in July and 72 per cent in August instituted a *procurator* in their will. It may have been a harder task to find a witness willing to accompany the notary to the *Memoriali* office within the required time limit of one day. Although each proctor was selected from the witnesses present at the will, the person enlisted for such a duty was usually someone with whom the testator had a closer bond and thus would be more likely

came from more wills in the first registers of each volume, i.e. from the first 200 to 250 folios and less from folios 250–500.

[100] A healthy elite widow had her will made in the church of San Giacomo with 12 witnesses including two Augustinian friars, a notary, tanner, barber, butcher and others, all hailing from four parishes (Mem, vol. 229, fol. 210v); two wills of healthy men in July, one made in a house of a hospital and the other at the *Gabella*, each had 11 men assisting (Mem, vol. 229, fols. 194v, 266r). The other four gatherings of 11 witnesses during the epidemic were in the homes of sick testators—the usual redaction site.

to carry out this added task. Among the proctors appeared a husband, a brother, a brother-in-law, a guardian, executors, notaries, and parish priests. Nevertheless, the wills of July and August do not show a greater failure to follow the strict communal requirements than do those of the last four months of the year, after the epidemic had waned, when only 78 per cent of the wills had the required procurators.

The final step demanded by the *Statuti* in assuring the validity of a testament was the *crida*. When a testator sent a *procurator* before the office of the *Memoriali*, that notary would send a *nuncius* or town crier to the testator's house and, at the testator's or proctor's expense, he would loudly announce to two neighbors of the parish that so and so had made a will.[101] The *crida* was carried out infrequently during the pre-plague period (less than one fourth of the time it should have been), and much less so during the epidemic. Nevertheless, it is surprising that there were any announcements of wills made at all during the epidemic, given towns's decisions to do away with excessive lamentation at funerals and the tolling of bells in order to provide relief from the constant messages of grief among the populace.[102] The message, again, should not be that the system had broken down during the Black Death, but rather that it resisted and remained functioning.

In summary, testaments and the bureaucracy and notaries who produced them remain an exceptionally rich source for understanding late medieval urban life. Like a net, the notarial record captured the actions and decisions of a broad section of the populace. As they served their clients, notaries appear to have responded to the fluid nature of status and identity in urban life, at least in terms of the attribution of noble titles and citizenship. They worked in a complex bureaucracy

[101] Fasoli and Sella, *Statuti*, 2:82–83: "Et etiam teneatur ipse tabellio quoram [sic] quo iverit, mittere aliquem nuntium comunis ad domum condentis qui non venerit personaliter sed per procuratorem, in qua habitat, expensis conditoris vel procuratoris qui ibidem alta voce coram duobus vicinis dicte contrate quo scriptum est coram tabellione, scilicet quod talis condidit suam ultimam voluntatem in presentia talis sacerdotis, scriptam manu talis notarii, quam cridam ipse tabellio tenatur postea scribere, scilicet proclamationem factam in presentia dictorum vicinorum."

[102] A. Chiappelli, "Gli ordinamenti sanitari del comune di Pistoia contro la pestilenza del 1348," *Archivio Storico Italiano* ser. 4, 20 (1887), p. 11: "Item providerunt et ordinaverunt, ad hoc ut sonus campanarum non invadat infirmis, nec contra eos timor insurgat, quod campanarij seu custodes stantes super campanile maioris ecclesie cathedralis civitatis Pistorij non permictant pulsari aliquam campanam occasione funeris mortuorum existentem super dicto campanile".

following strict norms of notarial law. Yet the institution and law were not so rigid that they did not allow flexibility and practicality. In the face of severe crisis, the notaries and their bureaucracy struggled, but did not abandon their goals to ensure and preserve the legal force of their clients's interactions and intentions. The next chapter will use the information resulting from their efforts to examine the social and economic environment of Bologna during the fourteenth century.

CHAPTER TWO

ILLUMINATING THE DARK CENTURY: NOTARIAL EVIDENCE ON BOLOGNA'S CIVIC LIFE

The history of late medieval Bologna begins during the city's "golden century" (*secolo d'oro*), the Duecento.[1] The physical form of the city was transformed by the massive building and canalization projects of this era. The population increased, requiring the erection of two sets of city walls, and the economy and university flourished. The popular commune ruled with the support and administration of notaries, who had so much power in thirteenth-century Bologna that it has been called a "Republic of notaries".[2] Traditionally, the last two decades of the thirteenth century are seen as the beginning of a strong decline in Bologna. This was manifested politically in Bologna's submission to papal authority after 1278 and the destructive factional politics within the city that pitted the Guelf Geremei against the Ghibelline Lambertazzi parties in violent struggles. The repeated expulsions of the Lambertazzi, beginning in 1274 and ending in 1306, did not stabilize the situation and real political power passed increasingly into the hands of a *signore*, or lord. The process began with the "crypto-signoria" of banker Romeo Pepoli who was expelled in 1321, continued with the authoritarian rule of papal legate Cardinal Bertrand du Pouget from 1327 to 1334, and culminated in the naming of Taddeo Pepoli in 1337 as "general and perpetual preserver and governor of the Commune, the Popolo, and the

[1] Antonio I. Pini, "Bologna nel suo secolo d'oro: Da 'comune aristocratico' a 'repubblica di notai'," in *Rolandino e l'ars notaria da Bologna all'Europa: Atti del convegno internazionale di studi storici sulla figura e l'opera di Rolandino*, ed. Giorgio Tamba (Milano, 2002), pp. 3–20.

[2] For the powerful and ubiquitous nature of the notarial guild see Pini, "Bologna nel secolo d'oro" and Gina Fasoli "Il notaio nella vita cittadina bolognese," in *Notariato medievale bolognese*, 2 vols. (Roma, 1977), 2:134–141. From the first half of the thirteenth century onwards, the commune increased its control over notarial activity by means of registration and admission exams imposed on notaries. See Brigide Schwarz, "Das Notariat in Bologna im 13. Jahrhundert," *Quellen und Forschungen aus italienischen Archiven und Bibliotheken* 53 (1973), 49–92; Giorgio Tamba, *Teorie e pratica della "commissione notarile" a Bologna nell'età comunale* (Bologna, 1991). Tamba sees the institution of the *Memoriali* as part of the commune's long-term efforts at control over the notaries.

territory of Bologna".[3] The nadir of this political decline came in 1350 when the sons of Taddeo, Giovanni and Giacomo Pepoli, sold the city to Giovanni Visconti, archbishop of Milan. For historians of Bologna's politics, the bleak picture continued with return of Church rule over Bologna until the revolt against the papal legate in 1376 and the establishment of the "second commune".[4] Magnate families, however, again gained the upper hand and at the start of the fifteenth century Bologna succumbed to the *signorie* of Renaissance rulers such as the Bentivoglio and the Visconti followed later by submission to the Church.

In a similar, though perhaps protracted, fashion, the material urbanistic forms, i.e., the construction projects of walls, canals, towers and palaces, and the socio-economic characteristics of the city, i.e., its well-known guilds and popular associations, continued to develop in the late thirteenth century. But, the traditional historiography emphasizes, towards the beginning of the fourteenth century the civic and urbanistic sectors suffered a decline that would last until the communal renewal at the end of the fourteenth century, when building projects begun at the end of the previous century, such as the third set of walls, finally reached completion. The historians of the urban fabric match their evidence to the political decline. Thus in the 1330s when Taddeo Pepoli constructed his massive *palazzo* on Via Castiglione, south of the city's center, its great size and location are interpreted as symbolic of the rise of signorial power in Bologna, distinct from the older political and commercial arena, the Piazza del Comune. According to this view, the population came to be concentrated along the principle access roads, abandoning the commercial and political zones that had developed in the previous century.[5] The implication is that the thirteenth-century nucleus of Bologna had become enervated with the rise of signorial power, and that the commercial life of the city had radically changed, because the massive building projects of the Duecento had stopped. The history of Bologna's most famous institution, the *Studium*, also fits the

---

[3] On Romeo Pepoli, see Massimo Giansante, *Patrimonio familiare e potere nel periodo tardo-comunale: Il progetto signorile di Romeo Pepoli banchiere bolognese (1250 c.–1322)*, Università degli Studi di Bologna, Dipartimento di Paleografia e Medievistica, Fonti e saggi di storia regionale, 1 (Bologna, 1991); Niccolò Rodolico, *Dal comune alla signoria: Saggio sul governo di Taddeo Pepoli in Bologna* (Bologna, 1898), pp. 65–72.

[4] See Antonio Ivan Pini, "Origine e testimonianze del sentimento civico bolognese," in *La coscienza cittadina nei comuni italiani del Duecento* (Todi, 1972), pp. 184–185.

[5] Maurizio Armaroli, "La costruzione della Mercanzia," in *La Mercanzia di Bologna*, eds. Dondarini et al. (Bologna, 1995), p. 32.

picture of political and economic decline.[6] The traditional bleak picture becomes darker as the decline was further deepened by the Black Death, with its profoundly negative social, demographic, and economic effects. Economic renewal came with the return of the popular commune in 1378 that initiated new projects for the economy such as the first gold "bolognino", coined in 1380 with the inscription *Bononia docet*, and a new silver "grosso" with the inscription *mater studiorum* and a picture of San Petronio on the reverse. Antonio Pini considered these inscriptions symbolic of the revival the university was experiencing at that time. The cultural revival of this period was also embodied in the construction of the civic cathedral of San Petronio in 1390.

The people revealed in the *Memoriali* and *Demaniale*, the subjects of this book, were living during the worst period of what Italian historians call Bologna's "black century" (*secolo nero*). While I will not argue that this was a time of expansion, it appears to this student of Bologna that the darkest aspect of their existence is that they have been left in the shadows of historical scholarship. This chapter seeks to illuminate life during the mid fourteenth century by demonstrating continuity from the thirteenth century and arguing against severe economic decline in the first half of the fourteenth century.[7] The subjects of this study were clearly a product of the thirteenth-century city. They maneuvered its waterways and built their homes along the remains of walls constructed in the thirteenth century. They lived in quarters delineated by the commune in the early thirteenth century, when most of their parish churches were built and their neighborhoods took shape along the canals supervised by that commune.

---

[6] Albano Sorbelli links the decline of the university to the political history of the commune. As the commune intervened in the life of the university, according to Sorbelli, it deprived the *Studium* of its liberty. With the factional fighting at the end of the century, the commune's efforts to ensure the appointments of only trusted Guelf professors resulted in the dismissal of professors, the emigrations of students, and the formation of a caste of teachers, united not by their love of knowledge but by political ties. See Albano Sorbelli, *Storia della Università di Bologna* (Bologna, 1944), vol. I: Il Medioevo (secc. XI–XV), pp. 91–94.

[7] I follow Douglas Dowd's conclusion that the decline began in the second half of fourteenth century. See Douglas F. Dowd, "Power and Economic Development: The Rise and Decline of Medieval Bologna," *Journal of European Economic History* 3 (1974), 424–452. Giuliano Milani has presented evidence against the traditional view of political decline setting in during the last quarter of the thirteenth century, because he argues that exiling the Lambertazzi was neither the symptom nor cause of a moribund commune, but the means by which it actively redefined itself politically. Giuliano Milani, *L'esclusione dal comune: Conflitti e bandi politici a Bologna e in altre città italiane tra XII e XIV secolo* (Roma, 2003).

This chapter will present both a diachronic and synchronic analysis of life in late medieval Bologna. By means of studies carried out by historians of Bologna, such as Antonio Ivan Pini, Rolando Dondarini, and Francesca Bocchi, it will briefly examine the urban development of Bologna during the thirteenth century. The bits of information from the many remaining wills, especially the occupations and residences of the individuals who appear in the capacity of testator, relative of testator, or as witness to a testament, will then serve as raw material to build a picture of life during the mid fourteenth century. The many extant wills of ordinary Bolognese allow an examination of the city's economic vitality, while individual testaments shed new light on the extraordinary individuals and families of Bologna's intellectual and political powerhouses. The 1330s marked the golden age of medieval jurists as it was distinguished by the careers of the celebrated canonist of Bologna, Giovanni d'Andrea, and the great jurist of civil law, Bartolo da Sassoferato, who received his degree at Bologna in 1334 and taught there briefly. Both of these men were connected to testators of the 1348 *Memoriali* and *Demaniale*. Giovanni d'Andrea died during the Black Death, and although his testament is not extant, that of one son, Federicus, remains and another son, Bonincontrus, was named in another testament. Bartolo's teacher was Jacopo Bottrigari, whose son Jacopo, also a jurist, was a testator during the Black Death. Jacopo junior and his brother were on the examining committee that granted Bartolo's degree. The wills of these jurists and their family members as well as other professors and their families provide a unique glimpse into the life of the *Studium* during this largely unexamined period. Other extraordinary people revealed in the testaments are the ruling Pepoli, the family that gave Bologna its first *signoria*, marking Bologna's transition from the Middle Ages to the Renaissance.

Thirteenth-Century Developments

The study of Bologna's waterways has been an invaluable contribution to the understanding of this city. As Pini emphasized, "the city lived on water".[8] Until the construction of canals in the last quarter of the thirteenth century, Bologna had to rely on the Aposa stream, which

[8] Antonio Ivan Pini, "Energia e industria tra Sàvena e Reno: I mulini idraulici bolognesi tra XI e XV secolo," in *Tecnica e società nell'Italia dei secoli XII–XVI* (Pistoia,

flowed along the western edge of the early medieval city, providing water for the moats of the first set of walls, the "Selenite circle" begun perhaps at the end of the fourth century. As the population and economy revived and expanded in the twelfth century and the need for water increased, construction projects were undertaken. The canals provided water for transportation, irrigation, and production in many industries working with leather, iron, bricks or glass, as well as for hydraulic energy at mills. The first major canals of Bologna, drawn from the Savena and Reno rivers, were constructed in the last quarter of the twelfth century when the commune, strengthened and emboldened by the defeat of Emperor Barbarossa at the Peace of Constance, was able to turn its attention away from consolidation of its control over the contado toward the management of resources within the city.[9] The Savena canal and its accompanying mills were built in 1176 at the expense of the commune. According to Pini, the waters may have been used for the moats of the new circle of walls being constructed around that time, the "Torresotti Circle", that were needed for the expanding city.[10] The expenses seem to have burdened the commune greatly, since the second great waterway, the Reno canal constructed in 1183, was the project of a consortium of private individuals known as the *Ramasani*. The commune, recognizing the vital importance of this second canal to the stability of the economic and political life of the city—disorder could result if complete control of grain supplies were left in private hands—bought the water rights to it in 1208, although they allowed the *Ramasani* to remain owners

1987), pp. 1–25, reprinted in Pini, *Campagne bolognesi: Le radici agrarie di una metropoli medievale* (Firenze, 1993), p. 15.

[9] The twelfth-century commune is known by historians as the "consular aristocracy" since it was made up of a group of powerful aristocratic families. For the rise and expansion of the commune see Alfred Hessel, *Storia della città di Bologna dal 1116 al 1280*, trans. and ed. Gina Fasoli (Bologna, 1975). For the commune's early canal projects see Pini, "Energia," and Francesca Bocchi, *Bologna, II: Il Duecento*, Atlante Storico delle Città Italiane (Bologna, 1995), p. 21.

[10] Bocchi argues instead that that there are no archeological remains confirming the use of the Savena canal for the moat of the *cerchia dei Torresotti*. According to Bocchi, use of this water in moats would not have left water for the mills in the northern area. See Francesca Bocchi, "Dalla Grande Crisi all'Età Comunale (secoli IV–XII)," in *Da Felsina a Bologna dalle origini al XII secolo*, eds. Giuseppe Sassatelli, Cristiana Morigi Govi, Jacopo Ortalli, Francesca Bocchi (Bologna, 1996), pp. 50–114. The exact dates of construction for the first two sets of walls—the Selenite circle of the fourth century and the Torresotti of the twelfth—remain unknown, since the documents only refer to them once they are completed. Construction began on the third and last set of walls during the late thirteenth century, but they were not completed until 1374. Nevertheless these walls are mentioned in the testaments of the mid fourteenth century as *circla* and are clearly an important physical and social boundary.

of the mills they had constructed along its banks. The commune was then able to undertake the massive technical and financial enterprise of building the Navile canal that would eventually connect commercial traffic from Bologna to the Po valley in the north.

Complete control over the canals came about with the rise of the *Popolo* in the next decades. Its members were the increasingly wealthy artisans and businessmen with economic and demographic clout in the parishes of Bologna who had been shut out of political power. They had organized themselves into the *arti*, or guilds, and the *armi*, or voluntary defensive corporations organized by parish or neighborhood. The leaders of the *arti* and *armi* entered the government in 1217, but were thrown out by an aristocratic reaction in 1219, while the merchants and bankers, who had previously allied with the aristocratic commune, were allowed to remain. Only after a popular revolt in 1228 was the *Popolo*, with the support of the merchants and bankers, able to establish a popular government with its own council members, the *anziani*.[11] The new popular commune expropriated all the private mills along the Reno canal and bought those along the Navile. These investments were very costly, but proved to be a good source of revenue for the commune in the future.[12]

The Quarters

At the same time that it established governmental control over the water arteries of the city, the commune instituted a powerful new administrative tool that was to become a permanent aspect of city life. In 1219, the commune divided the city into new administrative divisions—quarters—which were called *porte*, or gates, distinguishing them from the early medieval division based on the Germanic *guaita*, or

[11] Gina Fasoli, "Bologna nell'età medievale (1115–1506)," in *Storia di Bologna*, eds. A. Ferri and G. Roversi (Bologna, 1984), pp. 151–154; Hessel, *Storia*, pp. 173–176. The *anziani* united with the *consules* of the bankers, the *ministrales artium et armorum*, or leaders of the guilds and armed societies, and the *ministrales contratarum*, or leaders of the parishes, to form the new senate that ruled the city with the *podestà*.

[12] Revenues and expenditures are calculated by Pini in "Energia," pp. 35–36. The rental and control of mills were matched by the prohibition of millers, bakers, and transportation workers to associate themselves as guilds. The commune did not want the basic food to be out of its control when times of famine, and possible revolt, may threaten.

military watch.[13] The new terminology expressed the reality of expansion and growth for the city, nourished by Bologna's "nodal" position for commercial traffic along the via Emilia.[14] Money and people flowed into Bologna through its gates. There was a strong political aspect to this new administrative tool, since the members of the *compagnie d'armi e d'arte*, the political arms of the *popolo* government, were divided by quarter. The *anziani*, the political leaders of the *popolo*, chose the quarter as the principal division over the ancient territories of parishes, in which aristocratic circles continued to exert considerable influence.[15] Taxes were imposed and public works were assigned by quarter. A further example of how the quarters served the political needs of the *popolo* is the extension of the quarter system into the surrounding contado in 1223. The boundaries of the city's quarters were simply extended outwards dividing the contado into "quarters". This was another step in the city's ongoing conquest of the contado.

The city's quarters were created to represent population distribution equally and therefore were not of equal size. For example, the quarter of Porta Procola sprawled across the entire southern section of the city. The oversized northwest quarter of Porta Stiera contained the area known as *bononia antiqua rupta*, which had been abandoned in the early medieval period and still had not gained in population levels with the rest of the city during the thirteenth century. Porta Ravennate in the southeast contained by far the most dense population, since it was about half the size of each of the other three quarters. Strada Maggiore, the continuation of Via Emilia, ran through the crowded quarter of Porta Ravennate and served as witness to the continued importance of Romagna (and not Emilia to the west) in the economic life of Bologna. The boundaries of all quarters met in the central square or Piazza del Comune, today's Piazza Maggiore. The boundaries of

---

[13] The *guaita* was established in the early Middle Ages when Bologna was not much more than a small, irrelevant fortified *oppidum*, subsumed under the political domination and military needs of the patriarchate of Ravenna. I am following Pini on the date for the establishment of the quarter system as 1219. This has been challenged by Bocchi who noted that the quarters are mentioned in a document of 1131. See Bocchi, "Dalla Grande Crisi," p. 90. However, in her "Duecento," p. 21, she presents the traditional date for the quarter system.

[14] The expression is Antonio Pini's.

[15] Antonio Ivan Pini, "Le ripartizioni territoriali urbane di Bologna medievale: Quartiere, contrada, borgo, morello e quartirolo," *Quaderni Culturali Bolognesi* 1 (1977), p. 39.

the quarters were maintained in the fourteenth century, despite the inevitable demographic change.

Evidence from the mid fourteenth-century wills provides an estimate of change in population growth from the time of the quarters's institution to the mid 1300s. It appears that the population density had not changed a great deal from the early thirteenth century because the 1225 testators who declared residence in a parish in Bologna were roughly equally divided across parishes: 17.2 per cent in the largest quarter of Porta Procola, 17.4 per cent in Porta Stiera, the area of *bononia antiqua rupta*, 19.5 per cent in the small and densely packed Porta Ravennate, and 22.1 per cent in Porta Piera. According to these numbers, the only area of the city which may have experienced greater population growth would appear to have been Porta Piera in the northwest. However, these figures do not capture all parishes (and, thus, the percentages do not total 100 per cent) because the boundaries of the quarters overlapped and some parishes were thus located in two quarters. If we look at the quarters according to the cardinal directions, there are more apparent differences in population density. The area with the highest density of population (51.3 per cent of all Bolognese) lay in the eastern quarters of Porta Piera and Porta Ravennate, whilst the least dense area was in the west in Porta Stiera and Porta Procola, which held only 37.0 per cent of the population at mid century. From the evidence of the wills it appears that the western area of the city, with its abandoned Roman area, was still lagging behind in growth in the fourteenth century. The eastern commercial focus of thirteenth-century Bologna thus continued well into the fourteenth century.

Since the thirteenth century, the quarters were also used for military purposes, as the commune assessed and mobilized recruits, from the city and contado, based on the quarter in which they lived. Soldiers were deployed by quarters, with two quarters sent out into the field and two remaining at home.[16] All men able to bear arms (i.e., those between 18 and 70 years of age, excluding clergy, students, and professors) were organized into groups of 25 called the *venticinquine*, who served as infantry, or groups of 10, called *decine*, who served in the cavalry.[17] These were drawn up according to the smallest subdivision, the parish

[16] Ibid., p. 18.

[17] Antonio Ivan Pini and Roberto Greci, "Una fonte per la demografia storica medievale: Le 'venticinquine' bolognesi (1247–1404)," *Rassegna degli Archivi di Stato* 26 (1976), 337–417 and Fasoli, "Bologna," pp. 144–145.

or *cappella*, as it was called in Bologna, by the administrative heads of the parish, the *ministrales cappellarum*.[18] All these groups were organized by quarter under the leadership of two *gonfalonieri*, or standard-bearers, per quarter—one for the infantry and one for the cavalry. The *gonfalonieri* and *ministrales* represented the popular elements of the government and populace. These men were members of the *arti* and *armi*. They had important roles for the life of the populace beyond fiscal and military recruitment, such as responsibility for safety and morality at the parish level.[19] These were the men who controlled the Duecento government and oversaw the urban construction projects that shaped medieval Bologna. Although they lost political power with the rise of the *signoria* of the Pepoli in the fourteenth century, their institutional forms remained and their positions still carried social relevance on the level of the parish. Indeed, as we will see in the following chapters, the *ministrales cappellarum* were active citizens coming to the aid of their neighbors during the Black Death. Many of the testators examined in this book were these men of the *popolo* and their families, and the areas of their social activity—the parish, neighborhood, and quarter—are the focus of analysis.

Commercial Activity and Occupations

The thirteenth century was a time of great effort and investment by the *popolo* as it worked to gain control over the economy and public spaces of Bologna. Through the early Middle Ages the center of commercial activity had been the area where the three principal roads leading east met at the city gate, i.e., the Piazza di Porta Ravegnana, where today stand the famous two towers (see Map of Bologna). Since the beginning of the thirteenth century there had been fish- and meat-markets here, which the commune regulated in the late thirteenth-century Statutes, although it did not yet have direct rights over this area. A

[18] Most testators declared a parish, but the quarters do not appear in the testaments, apart from the few parishes which incorporate a quarter into their name in order to distinguish churches with the same name. For example, the parish of San Bartolo in Porta Ravennate is distinguished from that of San Bartolo in Palazzo, and San Lorenzo di Porta Stiera from San Lorenzo de' Guarini.

[19] The *ministrales* had the duties of denouncing thieves, prostitutes, gamblers, and sodomites and maintaining wells and sewers and preventing and fighting fires. See Fasoli, "Storia," p. 152.

great variety of commercial activity went on in this piazza and along the street that led from here to the Piazza del Comune. According the Statutes of 1250 and 1288 this area contained stalls for vegetables, cheese, poultry, grain, wine, livestock, and shops with cloth of linen or wool, wood, hay and straw.[20] The testamentary evidence of the mid fourteenth century suggests that this area continued to be the site of the meat- and fish-markets (*beccaria et pescaria Porte Ravennate*), but was also a center of expanded economic activity.[21] Testators that lived in this area came from retail and artisanal professions. For example, here were the homes of two apothecaries or spice dealers (*spetiarius*), two pork butchers (*lardarolus*), a draper, a baker, a master carpenter, a merchant, a mercer, a dyer, a doctor, and a notary, as well as the relatives of several others from such mixed professions, among whom those of notaries prevail.

The workers for which Piazza di Porta Ravegnana was most well-known, viz., butchers and fishmongers, did not live in this area during the Duecento nor, as the wills suggest, in the Trecento (except for the two pork butchers noted above). The fishmongers worked in the central fish-market of Porta Ravegnana and, after mid thirteenth century, at a second market near the communal *curia*.[22] Using the *Libri matricolarum* or guild membership lists of the fishmongers of 1294, Pini found that most lived outside the early medieval center, mainly in the northwest area of Porta Piera, near the roads and waterways leading to the marshes and rivers of Romagna. Since the fishmongers were bound by law to unload at their homes that served as workshops (*domus vel stationes*) wares which would later be sold in the communally-regulated market areas, fishmongers's residences were the site for exchange with fishermen of the contado. No testators were identified as fishmongers in the wills of the mid fourteenth century. Of the five female relatives of fishmongers that appear as testators, however, two lived in the area of concentration identified by Pini, while the other three are spread out in the three other quarters. Three of the four witnesses identified as fishmongers lived in the area noted by Pini. Thus we see both continuity

[20] See, for example, Fasoli and Sella, *Statuti*, vol. 2: book 10, rubrics 1 and 3; book 12, rubric 5.

[21] For example, in the wills the Hospital of the Battuti is noted as being *iuxta becarias et pescarias*, or *prope plateam sive piscariam*, or *prope plateam comunis*.

[22] Antonio Ivan Pini, "Pesce, pescivendoli e mercanti di pesce in Bologna medievale," *Carrobbio* 1 (1975), 329–349.

and change in the dispersion of some of the residences of fishmongers beyond their traditional areas of concentration.

The second prominent trade of the central markets, the butchers, are much better represented in the wills. Indeed, they are the most numerous among those professions named in the testaments, perhaps because they enjoyed high political status in Bologna.[23] According to the *Statuti* of 1288, butchers were allowed to sell their meat only in the city's two meat-markets, located in the Piazza di Porta Ravegnana and near the Piazza del Comune. They were permitted to slaughter only in the area near the third walls where the Aposa stream entered the city. Mario Fanti identified a concentration of butchers's residences, a real *contrata beccariorum*, in this area of slaughter, although they too lived in all four quarters. The picture was substantially altered by the mid fourteenth century when the 20 butcher testators (as *beccharius* or *macellator*) resided in all four quarters and in 13 parishes, near or outside the second set of walls, but not near the central markets of Porta Ravegnana. It appears that the particular zone of the *contrata beccariorum* had changed by mid fourteenth century and moved away from the Aposa canal. Eight were clustered in three parishes that stretched along the Savena canal in the southwest area of town—perhaps too large an area to be a real *contrata*—while two other groups of three were near the Reno canal in the west and near the market in the north.[24] If we add the parishes of the 12 relatives (alive or deceased), viz., fathers and husbands who were butchers, and wives and widows of butchers who were not testators, the results are similar. There are no relatives of butchers who lived within or close to the Selenite walls. There are several witnesses who are named as butchers and their residential pattern fits the butcher testator: most are grouped near the southern part of the Savena canal between the second and third walls.[25]

The butchers did not live near their place of business, since this was fixed by communal statute. Other workers, free from the restrictions imposed on the workplace of the butchers, fishmongers, and bankers, probably worked closer to their homes, as has generally been found

[23] Mario Fanti, *I macellai bolognesi: Mestiere, politica e vita civile nella storia di una categoria attraverso i secoli* (Bologna, 1980).

[24] Eight are from San Leonardo, San Biagio, San Tommaso della Braina; three from San Felice, San Nicolò del Felice, San Lorenzo; three from Santa Maria Maggiore and San Tommaso del Mercato.

[25] Of 23 witnesses whom notaries noted as butchers and gave a parish, 18 are in this area.

for medieval towns.[26] However, we cannot assume that all workers lived close to their business, as is clear from the will of one smith who lived in the parish of Santa Maria Maggiore, northwest of the Piazza di Porta Ravegnana. He left to his wife his equipment (*furnimentum*) from his workshop, where "he worked continuously", that was located at the boundaries of the *foro medio*, i.e., the central market of Piazza di Porta Ravegnana.[27] Not as far from his workplace lived a certain Bertonus, who is identified only as living in the parish of San Vitale, but who left his nephew his *stationem*, or workshop "with all its things and equipment" that was located on Strada Maggiore in the house of another owner.[28] Nevertheless, members of professions other than butchers and fishmongers, which were not regulated in the same manner, did tend to live in defined areas or neighborhoods based on one or more trades, as will be further demonstrated in Chapter Four. Residential zoning by occupation was present to a certain degree in mid fourteenth-century Bologna.

The third occupational group that was forced by law to work in the central commercial area of Porta Ravegnana were bankers and moneychangers. Indeed, since the thirteenth century, the area around Porta Ravegnana had been the financial center for the town.[29] The guild of *campsores* ruled that no one could carry out this activity beyond the area known as the *Cambium*, which was centered on the parish and church of Santa Maria di Porta Ravennate. This area also held the old customs house or *Gabella* which was replaced in 1380 by the *Mercanzia*—still one of Bologna's most evocative and beautiful reminders of its late medieval past.[30] This occupation had had its heyday in the Duecento, but with the entry of Tuscan bankers into Bologna the fortunes of the local men declined. In fact, there is only one testator identified as *campsor* in the wills, and five merchant testators. However, of these individuals, three lived in the area around the *Cambium* and one in the area of the

[26] Pini, "Ripartizione topografica," pp. 161–162.

[27] Mem, vol. 229, fol. 205v (Bernardus Petri Dominici).

[28] Mem, vol. 229, fol. 73v (Bertonus fq Gerardi).

[29] Antonio Ivan Pini, "L'arte del Cambio a Bologna nel XIII secolo," *L'Archiginnasio* 57 (1962), 20–81; Antonio Ivan Pini, "Le piazze medievali di Bologna," *Annali di architettura* 4–5 (1992–1993), 122–133.

[30] The guild did not have its own seat, but met in the church of Santa Maria di Porta Ravennate throughout the thirteenth and fourteenth centuries. See Pini, "L'arte del Cambio," pp. 53–54. For the construction and role of the *Mercanzia* in late fourteenth-century Bologna see the essays by Rolando Dondarini, Pier Luigi Cervellati, and Maurizio Armaroli in *La Mercanzia*, pp. 8–37.

general market to the north. Numbers are also small for goldsmiths, of whom two testators lived in San Simone e Giuda, a parish just north of Piazza di Porta Ravegnana, and Santa Lucia, further out towards the south near the second walls. The parishes of goldsmiths who appeared as witnesses and testators who were relatives of goldsmiths were similarly spread around the city with some representation in the central area of the *Cambium*.

A new element is apparent in the *Cambium* area in the period under examination here. According to the will of Zunta fq Lotti of the parish of Santa Maria di Porta Ravennate, next to the Mercanzia, his workshop was located "at the market of apothecaries above the *Cambium*".[31] There are eight apothecaries represented among testators in mid fourteenth century. These men were wealthy and many lived near this new market or commercial area. Of these testators, half lived in the area of the *Cambium*: two were at the market area in the parish Santa Maria di Porta Ravennate and two along roads leading to the market in San Biagio and San Vitale. Of the others, one lived next to the Piazza del Comune, two lived in San Gervasio and San Barbaziano at the western edge of the second walls, and one was a resident of Venice, who originally came from San Biagio.[32] The eight testators who had apothecaries as relatives also mostly lived along the streets that fed into the *Cambium* or in parishes on the *Cambium*. Some historians have noted an early coincidence of the workplace of spice traders and moneychangers, perhaps, as Pini hypothesized, because pepper and others spices were used as a valid form of exchange.[33] According to the wills, this matching of workplaces appears to have continued in the later medieval period.

While the markets at the Piazza di Porta Ravegnana grew naturally in the early Middle Ages as a result of its location at the confluence of the major roads to Romagna and flourished under communal control through the Duecento, the Piazza del Comune was the result of planned, energetic urbanistic programming on the part of the consular aristocracy and later the *popolo* in the mid Duecento. A second fish-market was instituted here, and from the mid to later decades of the Duecento this open square or *platea* was the construction site of several new *palazzi*

---

[31] Mem, vol. 229, fol. 199v (Zunta fq Locti).

[32] Also living in the central area of the *Mercanzia* were the wife of one living and daughter of another deceased spice dealer.

[33] Pini, "L'arte del Cambio," pp. 34–35.

relating to the government: the *palatium novum* supplementing the earlier Palazzo del Comune or *palatium vetus*, as it is referred to in the fourteenth-century testaments, the Palazzo del Capitano, and the *palatium bladi* or public deposit of grain.[34] Numerous artisans had their shops in the Piazza del Comune, and, according to Pini, in the Duecento a wide variety of merchandise was sold in this area. According to the wills, the testators with a named profession living in this area included three master carpenters, a tanner, a merchant, and an apothecary. But the principal kind of work-related activity for this area that is noted in the wills is that of the notaries, many of whom had their *stationes* at the *palatium vetus*. Since the last decades of the thirteenth century, when the notaries were at their peak of political power and had set up their Palazzo dei Notai in the Piazza del Commune, this area had been a special zone of notarial activity.[35] Although Bologna was under the lordship of the Pepoli and the notaries no longer had much political power in the mid fourteenth century, the wills reveal that the *platea* remained a focus of their attention and work. Several wills were redacted at the *stationes* of notaries next to the *palatium vetus* and the Palazzo dei Notai. Testators came here to dictate their wishes from all over town, from beyond the third walls and from villages in the contado.[36] Presumably they had come to the *platea communis* for other business as well, since usually the notary traveled to the testator's home to redact a will.[37] The only workplaces of notaries that are named as such are located in the Piazza del Comune next to the *palatium vetus* and

[34] The great basilica of San Petronio, it should be remembered, was not yet built. Its construction in 1390 drastically changed this area, since many houses and several churches were destroyed to make room for the monumental square and church. See Pini, "Le piazze di Bologna".

[35] On the notaries who rented stations from the commune in this location at the end of the thirteenth century, see Brian Carniello, "The Notaries of Bologna: Family, Profession and Popular Politics in a Medieval Italian City-State" (PhD diss., University of California at Santa Barbara, 2005), pp. 181–196.

[36] There are eight wills from 1337 and 1348 redacted at these locations. As will be further demonstrated in the next chapter these testators were traveling *into* the town, not exiting, from destinations outside the third set of walls, such as a testator from Sant'Egidio, and the contado during the height of the epidemic: Mem, vol. 230, fols. 45r (on 8 August 1348) and 371v (on 13 August 1348).

[37] Gina Fasoli describes the Piazza del Comune as the center of civic life, not only based on the market and government offices, but also a place to come to for an exchange of news, political and commercial information, to listen to storytellers and watch acrobats, to gamble—much as it is today. During times of civil strife, factions would amass their supporters here and riots would spread out into the city. See Fasoli, "Storia di Bologna," p. 169.

Palazzo dei Notai. Other sorts of shops existed here, but the wills give no information of their type of trade. Still, it was clearly a lucrative area for shopkeepers as evidenced in the will of an elite woman who lived in the parish of Santa Maria delle Muratelle near the second set of walls in the southwest and owned a workshop at the corner of the central square (*super angulo platea comunis*). She bequeathed the significant proceeds from this property for the saying of masses for three years by the mendicant orders of Bologna.[38] This kind of aristocratic ownership of shops to rent in the center must have been fairly common. Another example is an aristocrat in the parish of San Bartolo, which abutted the Piazza di Porta Ravegnana, who owned several homes "and shops within those said homes" in that parish.[39] He bequeathed the ownership of the homes and shops to his cousin, but let his wife enjoy the usufruct of the property as long as she remained a widow.

The strong economic decline that prompted the abandonment of the traditional thirteenth-century commercial and political zones does not appear to have materialized, according to the testamentary evidence.[40] The wills of mid fourteenth-century Bologna do not speak of building projects, but they do provide evidence of people's activities and residences that suggests the nerve center of the city continued to be the area of Piazza di Porta Ravegnana, Piazza del Comune, the Mercato di Mezzo, and the *Gabella* or customs house. Changes had certainly taken place, but a thirteenth-century inhabitant would still have recognized the vitality and importance of these areas to the economic life of the city.

Social Composition of the City

The social composition of the town also inevitably changed, but its underlying thirteenth-century structure remained similar in the fourteenth. Most studies in this area have made use of tax records with

---

[38] During the first year after her death the funds went to the Dominicans, the second year benefited the Franciscans, and the third year was shared by the Augustinian Hermits and Servites. The fourth year's profits went to an unrelated woman. See Mem, vol. 229, fol. 98r (Jacoba Raynerii de Dalfinis).

[39] Mem, vol. 229, fol. 328r (Franciscus fq Oseliti de Oselictis).

[40] Maurizio Armaroli, "La costruzione della Mercanzia," in *La Mercanzia*, p. 32.

fruitful results, but unfortunately there are no extant, complete tax records for the fourteenth century until the salt tax of 1395.[41] However, the testaments survive in large enough numbers to provide an estimate of the social composition of the town at the middle of the fourteenth century. If we follow the medieval administrative division of quarters, we find that there is little difference in wealth among them. No one quarter was the preferred residential area of elite or non-elites, since 19.9 per cent of elites and 19.3 per cent of non-elites made their homes in Porta Ravennate; 16.4 per cent of non-elites vs. 18.9 per cent of elites lived in Porta Procola; 16.1 per cent of elites and 18.1 per cent of non-elites lived in Porta Stiera; and 22.1 per cent of both elites and non-elites lived in Porta Piera.[42] As noted above in the discussion of quarters and parishes, several parishes were considered as belonging to two quarters. To generate these percentages of elites vs. non-elites in each quarter these parishes of ambivalent location were not counted. In order to count all parishes we have to examine quarters by the four cardinal directions with the result, again, that there is no significant difference between the percentage of elite and non-elites found in parishes lying to the north, south, east, or west.

There do, however, appear to be class divisions if we divide the city up into zones defined by its circles of walls (see Map of Bologna). Studies of the tax records of 1296/1297 found the highest concentration of wealth and of magnate families within the Selenite walls. A second zone between the first and second walls housed merchants and magnates, while a third semi-rural zone between the second and third walls was the site for "popular" and immigrant settlements.[43] The second wall of

---

[41] See the study of this source by Paolo Montanari, ed., *Documenti su la popolazione di Bologna alla fine del Trecento*, Fonti per la storia di Bologna, 1 (Bologna, 1966).

[42] These numbers are the composite of the years 1337 and 1348. Examined individually, there is a difference in wealth by quarter. The figures for the elites of 1337 differ the greatest from those of 1348, while non-elites across both years produce roughly equal results. For example, the percentage of elites of 1337 living in Porta Piera is 15.7 per cent, while for those of 1348 it is 23.6 per cent, but the percentage of non-elites from 1337 living there is 21.4 per cent and from 1348 it is 22.2 per cent. The differences between the years most likely arise, not from any residential pattern shift, but because the number of elites from 1337 is so much smaller (76) than any other group of testators.

[43] Massimo Giansante, "Il quartiere bolognese di Porta Procola alla fine del Duecento: Aspetti economici e sociali nell'estimo del 1296–97," *Il Carrobbio* 11 (1985), p. 126. A similar pattern has been found in Florence during the fifteenth century. Samuel Cohn stated that the *popolo minuto* of the fifteenth century formed "working class ghettoes" focused around parish churches on the city's periphery. However, this marked a change from fourteenth-century Florence when he found that the *popolo minuto*

Torresotti, called in the tax records *seralium*, was no longer needed for military purposes, but appears to have had meaning as a social boundary in thirteenth-century Bologna. The area within the Selenite walls, called here zone 1, was the smallest area, containing 34 tightly packed, densely built, parishes. The second zone contained 40 parishes and formed a donut shape between the Selenite walls and the *cerchia dei Torresotti* built towards the end of the twelfth century. The Selenite walls no longer existed after the new walls were built, but the moat would have continued to be used and may have acted as a kind of social barrier. The third zone, lying between the third and final circle of walls, was the largest area containing 20 large parishes. This was the least densely occupied area as it was the site of many vineyards and fields. Outside the walls lay five remaining parishes. These formed part of the *guardia civitatis*, a three kilometer wide zone that surrounded the city, having rights as being part of the city, but not considered part of the contado or district in the countryside.[44] At mid fourteenth century the third walls were still being built but, of all Bologna's walls at the time, they represented the clearest barrier.

The center was home to the fewest number of families in Bologna because of its small area, but there are clear differences between the social makeup of this area. Using the parishes identified for 404 elite and 911 non-elite testators from 1337 and 1348 we can examine the rings of wealth that characterized late medieval Bologna.[45] Most elites can be found in the second zone, i.e., 53.7 per cent of the 404 elite testators lived there. Yet about a third of these wealthy households can be found in the parishes outside, but adjacent to, the remains of the Selenite walls. These are the parishes mentioned above that surround the key market areas, such as San Bartolo, San Marco, and Santa Maria di Porta Ravegnana, and the political and commercial center of the Piazza del Commune, such as Santa Margarita, San Martino dei Santi,

were distributed throughout the city in roughly the same proportion as the general population. See Samuel Kline Cohn, Jr., *The Laboring Classes in Renaissance Florence* (New York, 1980), pp. 119–121. Bologna appears to have developed a "class geography" much earlier than Florence.

[44] On the *guardia civitatis* see Francesca Bocchi, "Suburbi e fasce suburbane," *Storia della città* 5 (1977), 15–33; Giancarlo Benevolo, "Espansione urbana e suburbi di Bologna nel medioevo: La 'Guardia Civitatis'," *Ricerche storiche* 22 (1992), 455–81.

[45] There were 327 elite and 713 less wealthy testators from 1348, and 77 elite and 198 less wealthy from 1337. The percentages of elites and non-elites living in the various zones did not change significantly between 1337 and 1348. Thus we can combine the numbers for a mid fourteenth-century snapshot.

or San Giacomo Carbonesi (see Map of Parishes of Bologna). Thus a fair number are clustered towards the central part of town. As we move outward towards the third zone, the percentage of elite homes diminishes to 27.9 per cent. Beyond the third set of walls, in the area known as the *guardia civitatis*, there are very few wealthy homes. Only 16 per cent of the elites of Bologna lived in zone 1, simply because this was the smallest area with the fewest homes. Out of all the mid fourteenth-century testators with an identified parish (1,315) only 130 individuals make this area their home. But elite testators are more likely to do so than non-elites, since only 7.0 per cent of the less wealthy populace was living in the urban nucleus. Thus, although as many elite as non-elite testators (66 and 64 respectively) can be found in this area, those wealthy testators were behaving more like their peers than the less wealthy who lived in that part of town. In fact, the wealth of the town declined as one moved away from the center. The raw numbers of non-elite testators rises as we move outwards: from 64 in zone 1 to 386 in zone 2 and 393 in zone 3. Thus the less wealthy were equally inclined to live in the second and third zones (42.3 per cent and 43.1 per cent respectively), which is much different behavior from the wealthy whose numbers in the third zone had dropped by about half. While only 8, or 1.9 per cent, of wealthy testators made their homes beyond the last set of walls, 68, or 7.4 per cent, of the non-elites lived there.

Historians have long recognized the outer areas of late medieval cities as homes to the lower classes. In Bologna the second important city market (other than the Piazza Ravegnana) lay in the third zone, in the northern part of the city between the second and third walls. This had been set up by the commune in 1219 as a weekly market, but it was also the site of bi-annual fairs. Known as the *campus fori* it was surrounded by the industrial areas of the northern canals and their mills, and, according to Pini, was the home of very humble citizens.[46] The occupations of mid fourteenth-century testators living in the two parishes closest to the market, viz., in San Benedetto di Borgo Galliera and San Giuseppe di Borgo Galliera, tell little about the activities that must have gone on in this area. The occupations of these testators include an innkeeper, a baker, a smith, a shoemaker, a miller, and a

[46] Pini, "Le piazze," pp. 131–133. Paolini also found this area to be preferred by heretics, especially Cathars in the late thirteenth century. See Lorenzo Paolini, "Domus e zona degli eretici: L'esempio di Bologna nel XIII secolo," *Rivista di storia della chiesa in Italia* 35 (1981), 371–387.

notary. One would expect to find notaries and innkeepers near this area of constant traffic. But most notaries preferred to live in the parishes near the market that were within the more upscale second zone. The nearby parish of San Tommaso del Mercato (the name refers to this weekly market) was the home of three notaries. If we move beyond the few occupations to examine social status, we find only four elites close to the market—and only then in the parish of San Giuseppe di Borgo Galliera nearer to the center—while 19 non-elites lived here, appearing also in the more remote San Benedetto di Borgo Galliera. Certainly, this zone appears in the mid fourteenth century to have maintained its less prestigious character.

Immigrants

Traditionally, historians have viewed the peripheral areas of late medieval towns as more likely to house immigrant and poorer populations. We have in fact found that zones 3 and 4 are the preferred addresses of more non-elites than elites. It is possible to also examine immigrant settlement by means of the wills, since some notaries recorded that the testators had originally lived in a different location. Ninety-nine wills make such a declaration.[47] The largest number of immigrants (49) came from the contado of Bologna. From the regions beyond Bologna's contado, Tuscany provided the most foreigners, since 39 came from either Lucca (15), Florence (13), Pistoia (4), Piacenza (1), Barga (1) or a village in the contado of Florence or the contado of Lucca (5). There were four immigrants from Lombardy (from Lodi, Cremona, and Brescia) and only one from the Veneto (from Padua).[48] Surprisingly, there are not more immigrants from the Emilia region, since only six people came from Modena or its contado, Reggio, and Bobbio. The majority of these immigrants to Bologna are not, in fact, residing in

[47] It is interesting to note that a fair degree of mobility existed also within the town, since 69 testators declared that they had moved to a new parish.

[48] I have not included as an immigrant, the apothecary, Antonius fq domini Ugolini Bellondi who is identified as having lived in San Biagio but as being currently from the contrata of Santi Apostoli of Venice. He left a bequest of "38 or 39 ducats which he has in the form of linen cloth". He nominated as executor and principal heir a Bolognese notary, in whose house the will was redacted. He appears to have been an emigrant returning to Bologna temporarily, but remaining there because of the outbreak of plague. See Mem, vol. 228, fol. 153v, redacted on 10 June 1348.

the outskirts of the city, but within the first and second walls, the area we are calling zone 2.

Immigrants, however, were not all alike, since their patterns of residence changed according to their provenance. This is clear if we compare the residence patterns of the two larger groups of immigrants, viz., those coming from Tuscany and those coming from the Bolognese contado. Three Tuscans lived in the aristocratic nuclear area, while most of them (75 per cent) lived in zone 2 and not a single Tuscan immigrant settled in the area between the third and fourth walls, in zone 3. Thus it appears, according to what we have learned about the economic and social characteristics of the zones of Bologna, that the Tuscans as a group were of high status.[49] Unfortunately, the number of occupations stated by immigrant testators is very low, but the few recorded confirm this picture of Tuscan wealth, since there are three merchants (*mercator*) from Florence and Lucca, and an apothecary (*spetiarius*) from Pistoia. The apothecary, Zunta fq Lotti, was a very wealthy man who dealt largely with foreign money—gold ducats and Venetian grossi—and credit, judging from the bequests in his will.[50] He left huge bequests, such as 700 golden ducats to his wife, *provida domina* Nicholeta fq ser Zanis, originally from Podium Bonici (Poggi Bonsi in Tuscany), who distributed this money in her will redacted on 8 August for several large charitable bequests.[51] She left 100 ducats divided into smaller bequests to poor people in Venetian prisons, to religious men in Venice and Bologna, to several hospitals in Bologna and to "poor and miserable persons in pious places according to the wishes of her executors". Bequests to individuals including her mother, brother, servants, two orphans, and her executor were also specified in ducats. The Tuscan wills are unusual when compared with those of the Bolognese or any other immigrant because they deal mainly in foreign monies: ducats, florins, or grossi. These immigrants appear both well integrated into Bolognese cultural and commercial life—several leave

[49] One Florentine stands out among the other Tuscans as a temporary or new immigrant to Bologna. Jacobus Philippi Placiti lived in the central parish of San Marco but is identified as Florentine. Unlike other immigrants, he is identified as a citizen of Florence belonging to the district of San Giacomo oltre Arno (*popolli Sancti Jacobi ultra Arnum*). The date on this will is described as being written "according to the custom of Bolognese notaries" (*die secundum cursum et consuetudinem notariorum civitatis Bononiensis*).

[50] Mem, vol. 229, fol. 199v.

[51] Mem, vol. 229, fol. 79r.

instructions for burial at the principal mendicant churches—but they also maintained contact with their Tuscan origins as some bequeathed money for churches in Florence.

The wealthy merchants from Tuscany may well have dominated high commerce in Bologna in the late Middle Ages, since, of the five merchant testators who appeared in the wills, three are from Tuscany. It is likely that they dealt in silk cloth, but that distinction is not noted in the statement of occupation in their wills. It is well known that silk workers emigrated from Lucca in 1314, as a result of political upheaval there, and settled in various northern Italian towns, thereby encouraging the silk industry in their new home towns.[52] For Bologna, the silk industry, i.e., the production of cloth for exportation worked from imported raw silk, became a dominant force in the late medieval and Renaissance economy as a major employer and source of the city's wealth and fame.[53] The first extant statutes of the Silk guild, which included merchants and workers in the craft, date from 1372, but historians have argued that the silk industry developed much earlier in Bologna with water-driven silk spinning machines set up in the city in the 1340s.[54] The evidence from the wills suggests that at mid-century the silk industry did not yet play as important a role in Bologna's economy, since there appear few workers or merchants identifiably occupied with this industry. One might counter that testaments are a poor source to identify the presence of textile workers in a city, since it could be argued that such workers would not have customarily written a will, but there are, in fact, two such individuals among the testators: a cloth shearer or *cimator* of

[52] G. Livi, "I mercanti di seta lucchesi in Bologna nei secoli XIII e XIV: Notizie e documenti," *Archivio Storico Italiano*, ser. 4, 7 (1881), 29–55. See also Francesca Bocchi, "Trasferimenti di lavoratori e studenti a Bologna nel basso Medioevo," in *Forestieri e stranieri nelle città basso-medievali*, Atti del Seminario Internazionale di Studio Bagno a Ripoli (Firenze), 4–8 giugno 1984 (Florence, 1988), 249–261, esp. pp. 256–258.

[53] Jacopo Volpi, "Mercanti e setaioli a Bologna intorno a 1400," *Archivio Storico Italiano* 570 (1996), 583–614. For the first wave of textile workers from Verona and Florence, who came for the enticements and tax relief offered by the commune of Bologna in 1231, see Maureen Fennell Mazzaoui, "The Emigration of Veronese Textile Artisans to Bologna in the Thirteenth Century," *Atti e memorie dell'Accademia di Agricoltura, Scienze e Lettere di Verona*, ser. 6, 18–19 (1967–68), 275–322. See also Antonio Ivan Pini, "Produzione artigianato e commercio a Bologna e in Romagna nel Medio Evo," in *Storia della Emilia Romagna*, ed. Aldo Burselli (Bologna, 1975), 1:519–547.

[54] Gina Fasoli, "Le Compagnie delle Arti in Bologna fino al principio del sec. XV," *L'Archiginnasio* 30 (1935), 237–280 and 31 (1936), 46–79; Giancarlo Roversi, "Le arti per l'arte: Le sedi e il patrimonio artistico delle antiche corporazioni di mestiere bolognesi" in *La Mercanzia*, pp. 149–154.

Florence and a dyer or *tintor* from Lucca. These men may well have worked in the growing silk industry of Bologna, but that cannot be discerned from information in the testament. A few more men working in this industry appear among the lists of witnesses discussed in Chapter Five. Nevertheless, textile workers, such as weavers, dyers, and cloth shearers, form a minority of other less-paid occupations listed in the occupations of testators and witnesses. Thus it appears that, in the fourteenth century, textile production continued to take a backseat in Bologna's economy to commerce in textiles, which had flourished from the thirteenth century.[55]

The wills do, in fact, indicate the presence of wealthy silk merchants in mid fourteenth-century Bologna, because there is evidence of two families originally from Lucca, who were active in the silk trade. The Di Poggio and Ubaldi families had been exiled from Lucca in 1314 and during the last quarter of the fourteenth century, according to Jacopo Volpi who has studied the commercial correspondence of the leading Lucchese silk companies, participated in a network of companies of exiled Lucchese based in Bologna, Florence, Genoa, and Venice with commercial dealings beyond the Alps.[56] Francisca de Pozio was a wealthy widow who lived in San Biagio, but was originally from Lucca.[57] Her many large bequests are specified in Bolognese *lire* and florins and demonstrate continued contacts in Bologna, Lucca, and Florence. She owned "land, homes, and goods" in Lucca, which she left, along with a good-sized dowry of 300 *lire* and 50 florins worth of "cloths and ornaments", to her niece or granddaughter living there. She distributed candles worth 25 *solidi* to her parish church and the Servites in Bologna as well as to the church of Santa Maria Novella in Florence. One of the witnesses at her will was a resident of Bologna who was originally from Lucca. The other testator connected to a silk merchant family was Turellus de Ubaldis of the parish of Santa Cecilia, but originally from Lucca—although, again, there is no specific designation in his testament as working in the silk industry.[58] Wealth and connections to Bologna and Lucca also appear in the will of ser Datus de Ugolinellis of San

[55] Massimo Giansante, "L'età comunale a Bologna: Strutture sociali, vita economica e temi urbanistico-demografici: Orientamenti e problemi," *Bullettino dell'Istituto Storico Italiano per il Medio Evo e Archivio Muratoriano* 92 (1985/1986), pp. 161–165.

[56] Volpi, "Mercanti e setaioli".

[57] Mem, vol. 229, fol. 30v.

[58] Mem, vol. 230, fol. 161r.

Procolo who owned land in Pietrasanta (in the district of Lucca), left large bequests in the currencies of Florence, Lucca, and Bologna, and whose executor and several witnesses were originally from Lucca and its district.[59] The evidence from these wills suggests that the commercial trading of cloth, which had a long tradition in Bologna involving Tuscan merchants, continued to flourish in the mid fourteenth century, with a decidedly Lucchese tint.[60]

As further evidence of their wealth and solid social connections, other Tuscans appear to have had important connections with the ruling Pepoli family. Johannes fq Lapi of the parish of San Biagio, but originally from Florence, was noted as a *stipendarius ad stipendum de civitate Bononiense*, a mercenary soldier. His sister, who lived in the centrally located parish of Santa Maria di Porta Ravennate, was married to Ugolinus fq Zengali de Pepollis.[61] Ghirardinus Pelossi, known as Toschetius, from the Valdelsa in Tuscany, was a mercenary soldier working for the lords of Bologna, Giovanni and Giacomo Pepoli. He is noted as a constable working at the pay of a foot soldier (*chonestabilis ad stipendum pedestrem*).[62] Thus the Tuscans played an important role in late medieval Bologna, spurring their textile economy and assisting the ruling family in its first *signoria*.

Immigrants from the contado displayed a different pattern from the Tuscans. They were the only immigrants who lived near the third walls or in the *guardia civitatis* (10 per cent did so). Twenty, or 40 per cent of them, lived in the second zone, but an equal number lived in the third zone, while five lived in the elite center. The occupations of the immigrants from the contado are even less well represented than the Tuscans, but the few occupations listed are not wealthy: a servant in a convent from Borgo Panigale, a tailor from Cento, and a porter from Ugiano. In general, the wills of these contado immigrants are simple, with few bequests of moderate size, and only one testator bore what appears to be an elite name.[63] A typical example is the will of Jacobus

---

[59] Mem, vol. 229, fol. 9v.

[60] The Florentine merchants had organized themselves into a *societas* in 1278–1289 and were active in the importation of Flemish and English cloth, which was distributed around northern Italy. See A. Gaudenzi, "Statuti dei mercanti fiorentini dimoranti in Bologna negli anni 1279–1289," *Archivio Storico Italiano*, ser. 5, 1 (1881), pp. 1–19.

[61] Mem, vol. 229, fol. 201r; vol. 230, fols. 137r, 144v.

[62] Mem, vol. 230, fol. 9v.

[63] Mem, vol. 230, fol. 175r (will of Jacobus fq Petri de Fabris of San Biagio, originally from Varignana, redacted on 18 October 1348).

ser Amodei from Castel dei Britti who lived in the *guardia civitatis*. He had no distinguishing wealth or land and had retained connections to people in the contado, both in offering and receiving support. He left four small bequests of 20s to men of his village, plus a larger bequest of 5 *lire* to a woman of a different village for her dowry. He named two men from the nearby village of Iola as his executors, and as guardians and substitute heirs for his son. Three of the witnesses to his will were brothers from the parish of Santa Maria Allemani, located outside of the third set of walls, while the other three came from villages in the contado.[64] Immigrants from the villages of the contado, then, like this Jacobus, were generally poorer than their counterparts from the towns and villages of more distant regions and maintained links to their contado origins.

The Studium

The immigrants we have examined came to Bologna for a trade, but many were attracted, especially during the thirteenth century, by the university, which was the powerhouse behind Bologna's golden-age economy. At that time it was a large, well-organized institution. The students had organized themselves into one large association, the *universitas scholarium*, which had its own statutes and officials called rectors. It was divided into two sections: the *ultramontani* consisting of foreigners from beyond the Alps and the *citramontani* consisting of Italians. These two groups were subdivided into "nations" consisting of Lombards, Tuscans, and Romans for the Italians and French, English, Spanish, German, Polish, and Hungarians for the foreigners. Excluded from these groups were students who were citizens of Bologna and professors or *doctores*. It has been estimated that there were about 2,000 students in Bologna at this time.[65] Early on, the commune recognized the economic advantage of the university and its students, many of whom came from wealthy families. The students, who were often accompanied by their servants, provided an enormous stimulus to the

[64] Mem, vol. 229, fol. 10r.

[65] Hessel, *Storia*, pp. 217–219; Fasoli, "Storia di Bologna," p. 142. On the university see the bibliography in Carlo Dolcini and Girolamo Arnaldi, *Università e studenti a Bologna nei secoli XIII e XIV* (Torino, 1988).

economy in their need for food, lodging, books, and cash.[66] Thus, in the early decades of the century, the commune sought to prevent the loss of this important revenue by ordering the professors to swear they would not leave the town. It was this action that brought about the organization of the university, as the students viewed these government requirements as an attack on their freedom. The government's demands set the commune and university on a rocky road of confrontation involving the departure of students every time a new university was set up in another town, as for example in Padua in 1222 and Naples in 1224. This contentious relationship lasted until the middle of the century when the commune changed tactics and tried to encourage the students to stay by granting them the same rights as citizens and by protecting their economic interests, such as controlling the price of books.[67] Not only did the individual merchants who served the needs of the students become wealthy—such as the merchants and bankers who formed an early, powerful guild and the booksellers or *stationarii* who were important figures often serving as bankers for the university—but the students played a large role in shaping the economy of Bologna into one based on commerce and the sales of goods and services, not on industry.[68]

As noted above, the traditional view of the *Studium* in the fourteenth century, as of the town, is one of decline. The university certainly went through some tough years: in 1304 the city was placed under an interdict by Cardinal Orsini, the papal legate of Pope Clement, that shut down the *Studium*, and in 1321 most of the student body transferred to Siena. Nevertheless, there is evidence pointing to its continued importance in the city life in the mid fourteenth century. In fact, the exodus of students is proof of the vitality of the university, for within 16 years of the interdict it had reopened, returned to fame, and had become the object of desire for competing towns. When the students and professors left Bologna for Imola in 1321, ostensibly because one of their own had been executed for committing rape, but also because of factional fighting within the town, the Sienese sent ambassadors to Imola to entice the university to their town. The government of Siena paid out large sums to transport the Bolognese students and their books, set up schools and

[66] Dal Pane, "Lo Studio," pp. 48–53.
[67] Hessel, *Storia*, pp. 219–223.
[68] Dal Pane, "Lo Studio," pp. 51–53.

free lodging for them, and pay the masters's salaries.[69] Padua, and even Florence with its declaration of a new university, also tried in 1321 to lure the Bolognese professors, but Siena, for the moment, won the race.[70] However, the commune of Bologna made concessions to the students and most returned to Bologna in 1322.[71]

Antonio Favoro uncovered a fascinating attempt by the rulers of Padua to again lure away students around the middle of the fourteenth century. Padua financed a certain Gardino Fini del Vedovaccio of Bologna who organized a conspiracy to get all the foreign students to move to the university of Padua. Two students, a Hungarian and a German, did go to Padua, but the attempt appears to have failed, and Gardino was prosecuted in Bologna (although we do not know the judgment and sentence).[72] The commune of Bologna recognized such attempts as detrimental to its economic health and prosecuted the conspirators involved.[73] It fought back with renewed laws. Just as it had done in the thirteenth century, the commune passed a law in 1357 making it a capital crime for masters to leave the city to teach elsewhere.[74] It appears, then, in terms of prestige and importance—it is useless to argue for decline on the basis of numbers of students, since there were no definite numbers for the thirteenth century to work with—the *Studium* did not

---

[69] Luciano Banchi, "Alcuni documenti che concernono la venuta in Siena nell'anno 1321 dei lettori e degli scolari dello studio bolognese," *Giornale storico degli archivi toscani* 5 (1861), pp. 237–247.

[70] F. Filippini, "L'Esodo degli Studenti da Bologna nel 1321 e il 'Polifemo' dantesco," *Studi e memorie per la storia dell'Università di Bologna* 5 (1921), pp. 124–129; Antonio Favoro, "Nuovi documenti intorno all'emigrazione dei professori e degli scolari dallo Studio di Bologna, avvenuta nel 1321," *Atti e memorie della Deputazione di storia patria per le provincie di Romagna* ser. 3, 10 (1893), pp. 315–321.

[71] Filippini, "L'Esodo," p. 147. The students won the right to be judged by the *capitano del popolo* and not the *podestà*, who had ordered the student accused of rape executed.

[72] Antonio Favaro, "Di un tentativo per procurare una nuova emigrazione di scolari dallo studio di Bologna a quello di Padova intorno alla metà del secolo XIV," *Nuovo Archivio Veneto* 31 (1916), pp. 254–259 and his "Ancora del tentativo di procurare una nuova emigrazione di scolari dallo studio di Bologna a quello di Padova intorno all metà del secolo XIV," *Atti e memorie della Deputazione di storia patria per le provincie di Romagna* ser. 4, 7 (1917), pp. 195–202.

[73] Favaro, "Di un tentativo," p. 258, reproduces the act from the criminal investigation of one such attempt carried out c. 1357 by a Bolognese acting in consort with other unnamed Bolognese, who was probably supported by his brother, a lawyer living in Padua, and that commune.

[74] For the text of a law making the attempt to lead students to another city a capital crime, with the rubric "De tractantibus seu settam facientibus vel conspirationem pro Studio transferendo extram civitatem Bononie" see Favaro, "Di un tentativo," p. 257.

suffer a marked decline in the fourteenth century. What is clear is that the population of students continued to diversify: the Statutes of the law students of 1317–1347 show that the *ultramontani* were then divided into 14 nations, while the Italians remained the original three groups. Furthermore, the *Studium* continued to draw the attention of both the commune of Bologna and communes with competing universities.[75]

We have noted that the presence of students in town is not matched in the testamentary evidence, although their existence can be documented since they appear in the record as witnesses. This is also the case for another important group for the university, the *stationarii* who sold and rented books using the *pecia* system.[76] They had been important to the Bolognese economy since the twelfth century and played a crucial role in the university as the only official providers of the texts set by university statute, a function which they acknowledged annually in an oath before the rectors.[77] Historians of the *Studium* have determined there were five *stazionari* in Bologna at the end of the thirteenth century, but there are no published figures for the fourteenth century.[78] The mid fourteenth-century testaments, however, do document their presence: three booksellers appeared as witnesses and executors.[79] Most visible is Andriucius Raynaldi de Libris, a *stationarius librorum* living in the parish of Sant'Andrea degli Ansaldi. He is a good example of endurance over time within the overlapping communities of work, family, and neighborhood in late medieval society, because he belonged to a family that had been booksellers in that parish since the thirteenth

[75] Bocchi, "Trasferimenti di lavoratori e studenti," pp. 252–253.

[76] See Sorbelli, *Università*, pp. 192–199; Hastings Rashdall, *The Universities of Europe in the Middle Ages*, 3 vols. (Oxford, 1936), 1:191–192, and Sven Stelling-Michaud, *L'Université de Bologne et la Pénétration des Droits Romain et Canonique en Suisse aux XIIIe et XIVe siècles* (Geneva, 1955), pp. 102–109 on *stazionari* and the *pecia* system at Bologna.

[77] Only *stazionari* could sell books as a business in Bologna. According to Ludovico Frati, merchants and even professors could have a *statio librorum*, loaning out books as well as money to students. Students were allowed to sell books to each other. Ludovico Frati, "Gli stazionari bolognesi nel Medio Evo," *Archivio Storico Italiano* ser. 5, 15 (1910), p. 381.

[78] Dal Pane, "Lo Studio," pp. 51–53 and Stelling-Machaud, *L'Université*, p. 104.

[79] Two booksellers, magister Masinus of Cremona and Guidonus fq magistri Johannis, are named executors in the will of a widow of San Procolo: Mem, vol. 229, fol. 94r. Connected to the *stazionari* were copiers or *scriptores*. There are five *scriptores* listed as witnesses in the database of wills from 1348.

century.[80] The notarial evidence shows that a contract of the sale of a book (*venditio libri*) was drawn up at Andriucius's shop, or *statione*, in May of 1337 in which a copy of the *Digest* sold for the price of 57 *lire*. Andriucius was active during the plague year since we find him as executor for a neighbor, Bazomeus Toti de Tossignano from Lucca, who was wealthy in cattle and may have been a student or connected to book production (perhaps providing skins for parchment). Bazomeus certainly had strong links to the university, since he named as universal heir a son of jurist Giovanni d'Andrea, he had books in pawn (*Decretals* and *Novella*), he left a bequest of bedding to a student from Pescia, and made Andriucius, to whom he owed money, a witness and his executor.[81] The social status of booksellers may be indicated by the testament of Andriucius's sister who was the widow of a judge. According to the *actum* clause of this will, Andriucius's home also served as the school where the law professor Mino Azzoguidi taught.[82]

This evidence of classes in a bookseller's shop can be added to the information known from earlier studies of university life by historians such as Francesco Cavazza and Albano Sorbelli who explained that early on classes were either in private homes—the homes of professors or rooms that they rented for their classes—or, especially for Theology, Philosophy, and Canon Law, in churches.[83] The Law faculty held their meetings to elect rectors and other important business in the church of San Domenico, while the school of Medicine and the Arts met in San Francesco. The notarial evidence from the mid fourteenth century indicates that the Dominicans's property still served as meeting halls for the university, since six wills were made in houses belonging to the

[80] Frati reports that the Libri family had their houses in the area of the parish of Sant'Andrea degli Ansaldi in the thirteenth century and records the sale of the house and shop of Alberti dei Libri in 1247. Alberto's son Matteo apparently did not continue the profession, since he became a notary. Other lines of the family carried on in that trade even beyond the fourteenth century, since Gaspare dei Libri had his shop in the parish of Sant'Andrea degli Ansaldi c. 1420. Ibid., pp. 384–385.

[81] Mem, vol. 229, fol. 8v. An additional hint to some connection with the university is the fact that one witness to this will, Paulus de Ravignani de Baldoinis, was the brother of a certain Philippus who bought a copy of the *Decretum* on 11 June, 1328 as evidenced in Gianfranco Orlandelli, *Il libro a Bologna dal 1300 al 1330: Documenti con uno studio su il contratto di scrittura nella dottrina notarile bolognese* (Bologna, 1959), p. 119. None of these men is identified as *scolaris* however.

[82] For other examples of contracts redacted in the *stationes* of booksellers during the thirteenth century see Orlandelli, *Il libro a Bologna*, p. 381.

[83] Francesco Cavazza, *Le scuole dell'antico Studio bolognese* (Milan, 1896), part 2, chapters 1 and 2; Sorbelli, *Università*, pp. 189–190.

Dominicans "in the schools in which the students of the university of Bologna meet", while only the mendicant schools, and not the *Studium*, are documented as being connected to the Franciscans (three wills were made in "in scolis inferioribus Fratrum Minorum").[84] Sorbelli states that before the commune established a fixed area for the university in the fifteenth century and the first university building was erected in the sixteenth, the medieval university tended to be separated by two rival zones: the jurists taught in a zone south of the center around the church of San Domenico, which included the parishes of San Procolo, Sant'Andrea degli Ansaldi, and San Giacomo dei Carbonesi, while the Arts were taught in an area closer and slightly west of the center in a zone comprising the smaller parishes of Santa Margherita, Sant'Arcangelo, San Tecla di Porta Nova and others near the church of San Francesco.[85] Andriucius's shop which held classes on law was in the parish of Sant'Andrea degli Ansaldi—in the jurists's area.

We can further decipher the topography of the fourteenth-century university and its members by examining the best-represented university group, viz., the professors and their families. The five wills of professors and 13 wills of their relatives (widows, wives, and children), as well as other notices of professors's children in the testaments, provide some indications of the social geography of this elite intellectual class.[86] Two of the medical professors lived in the central parishes San Martino dei Santi and Sant'Arcangelo, the area where classes for the school of Medicine and the Arts were held, so it is possible they held classes in their homes.[87] The third medical professor, however, lived

[84] Mem, vol. 191, fols. 328v, 389r; vol. 192, fol. 192v; vol. 193, fol. 368r; vol. 228, fol. 367v: testaments redacted "in domo Fratrum Predicatorum in scolis in quibus congregantur scolares universitatis studii Bononensis" or as "in domibus ecclesiae Domenici conventus Fratrum Predicatorum in scolis ubi congregatur universitas scolarium studii Bononensis". For the testaments redacted "in scolis inferioribus Fratrum Minorum": Mem, vol. 228, fols. 106v, 409r, 426r.

[85] Sorbelli, *Università*, pp. 191–192.

[86] There appear in the *Memoriali* of 1337 and 1348: four widows of law professors, one widow of a professor of notarial law, one widow of a professor of logic and philosophy, four daughters of law professors, two sons of the law professor, Giovanni d'Andrea, one son of a professor of grammar, and one brother of a professor of medicine.

[87] These Arts professors would have been close neighbors with three professors of logic and philosophy, medicine, and grammar who lived in San Salvatore and one professor of medicine in San Martino di Porta Nova. These are the four Arts professors living during the first half of the fourteenth century for whom a parish is noted in Andrea Tabarroni, "Notizie biografiche su alcuni maestri di arti e medicina attivi nello *Studium* bolognese nel XIV secolo," in *L'insegnamento della logica a Bologna nel*

outside the walls in Sant'Omobono, and the grammar professor lived in San Michele dei Leprosetti near the bustling commercial center. Both of these parishes were connected by Strada Maggiore and were away from the traditional university zones. No parish is given for Jacopo Bottrigari—presumably this was public knowledge and the notary did not need to include it for identification—but he seems to have closer connections to the Franciscan church than the Dominican, since the witnesses for his will were all Franciscan friars. We know that a law professor, Giovanni di Paolo Guiberti, was living in Bologna in San Barbaziano near San Francesco (in the Arts zone!), when his daughter Phylippa, of the parish of San Michele dei Leprosetti, made her will on 12 July 1348. Federicus, the son of the famous jurist, Giovanni d'Andrea, who died in the Black Death, lived in the area of the law schools around San Domenico, that is, in the parish of San Giacomo dei Carbonesi. His father, who had died only eight days before his son dictated his will, also lived there.

The wills of other faculty family members show a similar mix. Two widows and two daughters of law professors lived in the traditional jurist parishes of San Procolo and Sant'Andrea degli Ansaldi, while two other law faculty widows and three daughters lived along Strada Maggiore in parishes near the market center of Porta Ravegnana.[88] As for the families of the Arts faculty, widows of a doctor of notarial arts and a doctor of logic and philosophy had remained in the traditional Arts zone, while the son of a grammar professor was in the more commercial parish of San Tommaso della Braina along Strada Maggiore. Thus the social geography of faculty in mid fourteenth-century Bologna shows that for the most part the faculty remained in their traditional areas (except for the jurists Paolo Guiberti and perhaps Jacopo Bottrigari who lived near San Francesco), or they were neighbors in parishes stretching along Strada Maggiore from outside of the walls (Sant'Ombono) to the central markets (Santa Maria di Porta Ravennate). They did not live in the northern and less prosperous quarters of Porta Stiera and Porta Piera.

XIV secolo, eds. Dino Buzzetti, Maurizio Ferriani, and Andrea Tabarroni (Bologna, 1992), pp. 607–616.

[88] The law faculty widows and daughters living near Piazza di Porta Ravegnana were in the parishes of Santa Maria di Porta Ravennate, San Michele dei Leprosetti, San Donato, and San Tommaso della Braina.

In addition to being classrooms, professors's homes were significant locations in civic life. Even after the professors had passed away, their homes and the relatives who lived there continued to be marked by their earlier owners. Bologna's later fourteenth-century statutes specified that the town heralds, the *bannitores*, issue their proclamations, or *cride*, at specific sites such as crossroads, wells, crosses, and the homes of leading families or individuals (e.g., *ante domum illorum de Ramponibus* or *ante domum domini Iacobi de Tenchararriis*). Several homes of professors are noted, including those of the famous dead, who were distinguished with the epithet *bone memorie*.[89] Testators sometimes chose to have their wills made in the homes of professors. We noted, in Chapter One, the will of a woman living in the home of Paolo Liazari who may have been a servant, but there are other examples of less servile connections, such as a tailor who had his testament written in the parish of Sant'Isaia (near San Francesco and school of the Arts) in the home of the daughter of Marsilio Mantighelli, a famous professor of canon law who died in 1300.[90] Of course, the daughter may not have been living in her father's house, but it is interesting to note that nearly 50 years after her father's death, the notary chose to identify her with her father's profession. In fact, almost all of the relatives of deceased professors in the testaments bore the patronymic introduced by the title "olim bone memorie".

With this fame came wealth and power. The fact that the university professors moved in the privileged circles of Bologna is clear from their elite surnames, their noble wives, and the large bequests they left in their wills. The most famous of the famous were the law professors. They received the highest pay for their classes, to which the government contributed usually 50 *lire*, but sometimes 100 *lire*, for a year's worth of lectures.[91] But what most distinguished the law professors were their

---

[89] Thus we learn that Giovanni d'Andrea lived near San Domenico ("in burgo Sancti Mamme, ante crucem ipsius burghi, in bocha vie que itur ad Sanctum Dominicum, prope domos bone memorie domini Iohannis Andree"). Either Jacopo Bottrigari senior or junior may have lived near the main square since after leaving there the heralds were to stop *ante domum bone memorie domini Iacobi de Butrigariis legum doctoris*. See Valeria Braidi, *Gli Statuti del Comune di Bologna degli anni 1352, 1357, 1376, 1389: Libri I–III*, 2 vols. (Bologna, 2002): 2:174, 946 and 950.

[90] Mem, vol. 228, fol. 62v. The home of Paolo Liazari is considered so well known that the notary did not record a parish: Mem, vol. 192, fol. 266r. On Marsilio Mantighelli, see Sorbelli, *Università*, p. 81.

[91] Comune Governo, Riformagioni et Provvigioni, ser. cartacea, II, 38 record that during 1348 the government paid for 12 professors of which eight taught law (usually

connections through marriage to Bologna's political elite. Perhaps the best examples of political ties noted by historians for the mid fourteenth century are the Azzoguidi brothers Maccagnano and Nicola, law professors active in the 1330s and grandsons of another famous jurist, Maccagnano Azzoguidi of the thirteenth century. Their sister, Ghixia, was married to Giovanni Pepoli, son of the *signore* Taddeo and lord from 1348–1350; Maccagnano was married to Zanna Pepoli, the daughter of Taddeo.[92] The testamentary evidence allows further reconstruction of similar ties. Laxia, daughter of the knighted *doctor legum* Egidius de Malavoltis and testator in 1337, married Philippus Zohannis Pepoli.[93] While not marrying into the Pepoli, Chastelina fq Nicholai de Musollinis, the widow of the law professor Matheus de Gandonibus, came from an important aristocratic family. Her daughter, Phylippa, married another law professor bearing an elite name, Saldonus Bertholomei de Rustighanis.[94] Bertolomea fq Thomassini de Sasuollo was the daughter of a noble knight and widow of the famous doctor of law, the "noble and magnificent" Bonifacio Galluzzi, who had been ambassador to the pope and to princes before he died in 1346. Their daughter, Johanna, married into the Basacomari family, which could boast the famous jurist Basacomater Basacomatri among its ancestors.[95] A final example of these jurist dynasties revealed in the testaments is Laxia, daughter of Albertus de Malavoltis, from a family that produced many jurists. She can be found in the wills as widow of the *sapiens et discretus* professor of law, Paulus, son of the famous jurist Martino Sillimani, the teacher of Giovanni d'Andrea.[96]

The testaments of Bologna's finest reveal the immense wealth created by these elite connections. The most famous professor testator was the

civil, but in two cases canon law). Salaries were 50 *lire* for lectures in civil or canon law, except for the exceptional case of Thomas de la Fossa who received 100 *lire* for lectures on the *Digestum Novus* (*pro lectura digesti novi voluminis*), in contrast to Mino Azzoguidi who was paid 50 *lire* (*pro lectura digesti veteris*). Professors's salaries rose, as the later fourteenth-century statutes dictate them to be usually 100 *lire*, or, for a morning course on the *Decretals*, 150 *lire*. See Braidi, *Statuti*, 2:278–279. The morning lecture, summoned by San Pietro's bell announcing mass, was the longest and most important one of the day. See Rashdall, *Universities*, 1:218.

92 See Antonioli, *Conservator pacis et iustitie*. Taddeo Pepoli who became *signore* in 1337, it should be remembered, was a doctor of law himself. The commune had celebrated with his father, Romeo de Pepoli, the granting of his doctorate in 1320.

93 Mem, vol. 191, fol. 437v.

94 Mem, vol. 229, fol. 83r.

95 Mem, vol. 230, fol. 113r.

96 Mem, vol. 230, fol. 140r.

"esteemed" professor of civil law, Jacopo Bottrigari.[97] Jacopo's father, as noted above, was teacher of Bartolo da Sassoferato and frequent ambassador for the commune before his death in 1347.[98] His brother, Lorenzo, was on the important commission that wrote the laws of 1355—the first time the law professors had redacted the city's statutes. According to Jacopo's testament he was married to the granddaughter of Giovanni d'Andrea, Bertolomea, called Muncia, who was the daughter of the wise (*sapientis viri*) Bonincontrus. Jacopo nominated Bertolomea as the guardian for their infant daughter and his universal heir, Margarita. His will offers a glimpse at the wealth of a famous jurist: he returned his wife's enormous dowry of 1000 *lire* along with clothes, pearls, silver, and gold found in his house; he paid off debts to a cloth merchant and returned many law books to various creditors (he pawned his wife's crown for one), while also distributing various charitable bequests to his beadle (*bidellus*), servants, friends, and clerics; he also chose burial in an ancestral tomb in a chapel in San Francesco.[99]

The Faculty of Medicine and Arts was separate from the Faculty of Law. The medical professors were granted the same pay by civic statute and displayed similar wealth, but do not appear to have had the same sorts of political and hereditary connections.[100] They are, however, better represented in the wills.[101] An examination of these three wills shows some difference in their social status. The simplest will is of magister Stephanus fq Jacobi de Tempestis, a *doctor medicine*, who lived in the parish of San Omobono. He was unmarried and named as heirs the sons of a cousin. His residence outside of the city walls and

[97] Mem, vol. 229, fol. 7v (egregius doctor dominus Jacobus fq recollende memorie Jacobi de Butrigariis).

[98] Jacopo Bottrigari also worked as ambassador to win back the students who left Bologna for Imola in 1321. See Filippini, "L'esodo degli studenti da Bologna," p. 117, drawn from the biographical information in Maurus Sarti and Maurus Fattorini, *De claris archigymnasii bononiensis professoribus a saeculo XI usque ad saeculum XIV*, 2 vols. (Bologna, 1888–1896), 1:299–303.

[99] Sarti and Fattorini relate that Jacopo's father was buried in San Francesco before an altar that he had constructed. See Sarti and Fattorini, *De claris professoribus*, 1:302. According to Rashdall, each doctor had his own special beadle "who looked after his school, opened and shut the door, swept it out twice a day, strewed the floor with straw in winter and carried his Doctor's books to school". See Rashdall, *Universities*, 1:194. Jacopo Bottrigari is the only professor testator to leave a bequest to his beadle.

[100] A doctor of medicine could receive 100 *lire* per course.

[101] None of these three professors appears in the list of professors of the Arts of the fourteenth century in Sorbelli, *Università*, pp. 121–124 or in Sarti and Fattorini, *De claris professoribus*.

small bequests place him as a middling-class Bolognese: he left 15 *lire* for the mendicant churches, ten *solidi* to his parish priest for masses, and requested burial at his parish church. His parish priest was a witness to his will, and all of the other nine witnesses also resided in his parish—again, typical of the not-so-wealthy.[102]

The will of his colleague, the *doctor medicine* and *eximius civis*, magister Jacobus olim magistri Merchadantis fq Venancii Azzis, is a much more complicated document demonstrating his status as "excellent citizen". Magister Jacobus was a widower who lived with a concubine, a woman named only as Emmanuela. As noted in Chapter One, he may have chosen to deposit a secret will with the Dominicans because he wanted to provide for his legitimate and illegitimate children as well as a concubine. His legitimate daughters from his marriage were given large dowries of 600 *lire* with 200 *lire* for sumptuous apparel, which would allow them marriages suitable to maintain the social status of their father, and his minor son was made his universal heir under the guardianship of a notary who was also his executor. His illegitimate daughter, instead, received only 100 *lire*, and any other children of his that Emmanuela bore were to get 150 *lire* if male or 100 *lire* if female, assigning them to the artisanal classes. Emmanuela, who is not named as concubine, but only as the woman "who lives with him", got the least security for her future with a bequest of 50 *lire* for a dowry. His concern for the security of his soul elicited more money: magister Jacobus left 40 *lire* for a chapel and altar in the principal church of San Pietro, made generous bequests of ten *lire* to the Franciscans and Dominicans, and had his executors distribute a further 80 *lire*. The remaining bequests were salaries with added gifts of 20 *solidi* to a servant (*famulus*), who was a barber, and retainers (*familiaris*, *domicellus*).[103]

Unencumbered by complicated familial legacies but demonstrating the same elite attentions to mendicant charity and pious monuments, is the will of the third medical professor, the "prudent and discrete man" magister Saraconus fq magistri Doni, a professor of natural philosophy (*professor physice*). Magister Saraconus was a bachelor who, unlike other men of his class (as will be demonstrated in Chapter Six), was generous to and relied on his female relatives by naming as his heirs his two sisters and his mother. He provided dowries to nieces of his

[102] Mem, vol. 230, fol. 176v.

[103] Dem, F.P., 193, 7527, unnumbered page.

mother and to his unmarried sister, already named as universal heir, along with an additional gift, and for his married sister he added money to the dowry she had received from their deceased father.[104] He was also charitable to the poor, as he left the sizeable amount of 100 *lire* for poor orphans. But the greatest expenditures went to benefit both his soul and memory. His parish church was to receive 400 *lire* for an altar, and however much the executors chose to give for a new tomb to be placed on the external wall of that church (which he wanted to look like the tomb of the noble Garisendi family in the church of San Marco). Although the sisters of magister Saraconus would not be able to marry into the elite circles with the dowries he left them—perhaps he was expecting other relatives to assist—he certainly believed that the memory of him as an elite would be honored.

The last professorial will from 1348 is that of a faculty member of the lowest rung of university teachers, a professor of grammar (*doctor grammatice*), magister Tarducius fq Bonavogli de Piro.[105] He was unmarried and the only relatives to benefit from his will were two sisters who gained land in usufruct. Without family he turned to the officers of the hospital of the cathedral of San Pietro, where he lay ill when he dictated his last wishes, for assistance in executing his will. San Pietro would also have had professional significance for this university professor, because it was the site where exams were administered.[106] Like the medical professors, he did not list any books in his will. He stands out as a creditor, perhaps to students, since he forgave many debts made in various currencies, including 250 florins. His charitable bequests to the standard choices of the mendicant houses were quite small—20 *solidi* each—but he left the significant amount of 200 *lire* to provide a chalice, missal, and other liturgical objects for an altar in San Pietro, his burial choice. Although he does not display the enormous wealth, social connections, and prestigious addresses of the jurists, this grammar

[104] Mem, vol. 229, fol. 319r. The dowries of 150 *lire* were supplemented by gifts of 100 *lire* "pro ornamentis", which would not have been sufficient for these women to have his social status, so they may have been supplements to dowry amounts provided by other relatives.

[105] As Rashdall noted, the title of *doctor* spread from the Law faculties to all other faculties. While the titles of doctor, professor, and master were synonymous, the law professors never used the title *magister*. Of all the professors in the Faculty of Medicine and the Arts, the doctors of medicine garnered the highest salaries and grammarians the least. See Rashdall, *Universities*, 1:20–21, 207, and 240.

[106] Sorbelli, *Università*, p. 192.

professor was a well-off resident of the commercial zone inside the second walls near Porta Ravegnana.

It is clear that the professors were doing well in mid fourteenth-century Bologna. The law professors, in particular, were recognized as important citizens and assets to Bologna's political life since this was the period in which they wrote the city statutes, frequently served as arbitrators, and acted on the highest committees for the Pepoli lords.[107] The examples of wills here show they were connected with ruling families in wealth and marriage. Massimo Vallerani cited this kind of evidence in his study of the famous generation of *moderni*, the jurists who became doctors in 1260s and 1270s and were at heart of political decisions for the popular commune. They arbitrated, they served on emergency committees that deliberated on war, and they met with the pope as ambassadors representing Bologna. According to Vallerani, in late thirteenth-century Bologna there was an "indissoluble link between juridical culture and political power".[108] The evidence of this study of the mid fourteenth century shows that the link was not broken. Although historians have judged the *Studium* as an institution in decline during the fourteenth century, the reality for the people who lived and worked in that institution appears to be different.

The Pepoli

We turn lastly to information about the political landscape revealed in the mid-fourteenth century wills. This "darkest period" for Bologna began with the political crisis of the exile of the Lambertazzi in 1274. This first expulsion is believed to have forced 12–14,000 people to leave the city. However, most of them returned in the following months, to be subsequently expelled, again allowed to return in 1299, and finally sent out for good in 1306. The numbers of individuals that permanently left town as a result has been estimated at 4,500–5,000, but the overall demographic impact is uncertain due to the probable entry of many

[107] See Shona Kelly Wray, "Instruments of Concord: Making Peace and Settling Disputes Through a Notary in the City and Contado of Late Medieval Bologna," *Journal of Social History* (forthcoming 2009).

[108] Massimo Vallerani, "The Generation of the 'Moderni' at Work: Jurists Between School and Politics in Medieval Bologna (1270–1305)," in *Europa und seine Regionen: 2000 Jahre Rechtsgeschichte*, eds. Andreas Bauer and Karl H. L. Welker (Cologne, 2007): 139–156.

Guelf supporters.[109] The final expulsion appears to have had a long-term impact since among the thousands of names of testators, their relatives, witnesses or legatees in the database there appears only one member of the Lambertazzi family, a widow of a noble knight of the Galluzzi family.[110] However, the family that guided the politics and wealth of the first half of the fourteenth century in order to rise to signorial power, namely, the Pepoli family, does make a strong showing in the wills.

The Pepoli were a commoner family, of banking stock, who climbed the ladder of power and wealth. The epitome was Taddeo, a doctor of law, son of the richest man in Italy, and father of knighted sons. The Pepoli made marital matches suitable for political power: several members were married to leading Bolognese families of jurists who had attained noble titles, such as the Basacomari and Malavolti, as well as outside wealth, especially Florentine.[111] They lived near the banking area of the *Cambium* in the parish of Santa Maria di Porta Ravennate, along one side of which runs Via Castiglione, the street of Taddeo Pepoli's *palazzo*. That they were closely linked with their neighbors in this parish is suggested by the will of a neighbor who left three small bequests of about ten *solidi* to two Pepoli, and by the fact that their homes were the sites of the redaction of wills by testators not related to them.[112] Next to this parish was that of Sant'Agata where the Pepoli also owned much property, ever since Romeo Pepoli had bought up several homes there in the 1280s and 1290s. Johannes, a bastard son of Tarlatus, son of Romeo Pepoli, lived in this parish with his wife from the Bonazzi family.[113]

The only Pepoli testator who did not live in the traditional family stronghold was Juliana, the daughter of Romeo and sister of Taddeo,

---

[109] Rolando Dondarini, *Bologna medievale nella storia delle città* (Bologna, 2000), pp. 167–168.

[110] Mem, vol. 191, fol. 42v (Beatrisia Nicholay de Lambertucis).

[111] Mem, vol. 229, fol. 201r and vol. 230, fol. 144v (Ghita fq domini Lapi de Schandici of Florence and her husband Ugolinus fq domini Zengali de Peppollis); vol. 191, fol. 437v (nobilis et discreta domina Lassia fq nobilis militis domini Egidii de Malavoltis legum doctoris); vol. 230, fol. 113r (nobilis et discreta domina Johanna fq nobilis viri domini Philippi olim domini Zohannis de Peppolis, widow of dominus Albertus Petri domini Bolognini de Baxacomatribus). Johanna had moved back into the house of her deceased father in the parish of Santa Maria di Porta Ravennate. The notary was careful to record that the house belonged to the deceased patriarch.

[112] Mem, vol. 228, fol. 88r (Michaelis fq Johannis left bequests to Pepoli on 19 July 1348).

[113] Mem, vol. 191, fol. 590r.

who had married into the Baldoini family and lived in the parish of San Damiano outside the second walls between San Vitale and Strada Maggiore. A widow in 1348, her extensive will demonstrates the broad pious obligations that a ruling family had towards the religious houses in their city—she lists dozens of bequests to the mendicant houses, churches, monasteries, and nunneries of Bologna. The gifts range from small donations of 20 *solidi* to six or ten *lire*, but probably the most valuable gift was a house that went to the nunnery of Sant'Agnese where her niece, Jacoba, the daughter of her brother Andreas, was a nun.[114] Juliana's executor was her widowed sister-in-law, Bertolomea di Bonifacio Samaritani, who had married Taddeo and then retired to Sant'Agnese after his death. Assisting Bertolomea as executor was the prior of San Domenico. This choice was very characteristic of the Pepoli family, which had long ties to the Dominicans of Bologna. Taddeo's brother Tarlato and his sister Giacoma as well as his young son Romeo were all buried in S. Domenico before Taddeo built and left his body to the monumental tomb there as a reminder of this family's power and wealth. Taddeo's sons Giovanni and Giacomo chose San Domenico as the site for their knighthood ceremony.[115] That the prior of San Domenico should act in tandem with the Pepoli was also known by an elite testator of the Tencarari family (a family which, as far as I can tell did not have marriage ties with the Pepoli), who named a woman from a lesser branch of the Pepoli family to act as her executor along with the prior of the church of San Domenico.[116]

In many ways mid fourteenth-century Bologna shared the light of her brighter past. The economy was geared towards serving the university, which still had a powerful presence in its home town and was attractive to competing towns. As Table 1.1 of Chapter One shows, the economy was heavily based upon the production and use of animal products, especially leather goods, and retail exchange dominated the textile trade.[117] The interests of commerce and wealth remained focused on the

---

[114] Of all the Pepoli offspring named in the charts in Antonioli, *Conservator pacis et iustitie*, Giacoma di Andrea Pepoli seems be the only female who did not marry and instead entered a convent.

[115] Antonioli, *Conservator pacis et iustitie*, pp. 185–186.

[116] Bertolomea fq Thome de Tenchararriis was unmarried and named Margarita fq domini Bonbologni de Pepolis as her heir and executor: Mem, vol. 228, fol. 267r.

[117] See Roberto Greci, "La tariffa daziaria bolognese del 1351," *Il Carrobbio* 4 (1978), 265–289, esp. pp. 274–277, on the presence of shoemakers and the production in leather, furs, and metals in the Bolognese economy of the mid fourteenth century.

center of town linking the Piazza del Comune and the Piazza di Porta Ravegnana. Wealth radiated out from this area, as it had done in the early and high Middle Ages, in consecutive rings of diminishing prosperity. In the fourteenth century, there appears to have been, however, a greater amount of intermingling between the social levels than in the earlier periods, with more elites and non-elites living together between the second and third walls. Immigrants, especially from Tuscany, were integrated well in the economy and prosperity of the town.

We can identify examples of renewal and of prestige in Bologna's civic culture during the 1330s. The Office of *Memoriali*, as we saw in the last chapter, went through an attempt at renewal in the 1330s with the institution of the *Provvisori*. The *Memoriali* continued to decline and was finally replaced in 1436 by the *Registro*, but the *Provvisori* did well. The university was not expanding, but maintained power and prestige, and its most famous professors, the jurists, entered a golden age. While Tuscan merchant-bankers pushed out the natives, the economy received a boost from Lucchese immigrants in terms of silk production. Thus the cultural and economic picture is mixed.

This was the society that faced the onslaught of plague. Forty per cent of the populace, Pini has estimated, died in the cruel summer months of 1348.[118] Pini and others have argued that plague hit a population already weakened from at least 50 years of demographic and economic decay.[119] The height of Bologna's medieval population has been established by Pini at approximately 49,500 persons in 1294. He calculated that in 1324 the population had declined to around 43,500.[120] Decline may not yet have been so steep, however, since this figure does not take into account clergy, students, invalids, and foreigners.[121] Although Bologna

---

[118] Antonio Ivan Pini, "La società italiana prima e dopo la 'peste nera'," *Incontri Pistoiesi di Storia Arte Cultura* 8 (1981), p. 9; Antonio Ivan Pini, "Problemi di demografia bolognese del Duecento," *Atti e Memorie della Deputazione di Storia Patria per le Provincie di Romagna*, n.s. 16–17, (1969), 180–222; and Pini and Greci, "Una fonte per la demografia".

[119] For Pini and others, the political decline began with the expulsion of the Lambertazzi in 1274.

[120] For a critique emphasizing the problems, especially the household coefficient, inherent in generating these estimates of Bologna's population during the thirteenth and fourteenth centuries see Rolando Dondarini, "La popolazione del territorio bolognese fra XIII e XIV secolo: Stato e prospettive delle ricerche," in *Demografia e società nell'Italia medievale*, Società per gli Studi e Storici della Provincia di Cuneo (Cuneo, 1994), 203–230, esp. pp. 206–208.

[121] Pini's population figure for 1324 is based on 12,435 men able to bear arms multiplied by a coefficient of 3.5 to arrive at c. 43,500 for the general population. However, as Pini notes, one must add to this number those who do not appear in the

and Italy suffered famines during the early decades of the fourteenth century, the precise impact is not known and we cannot assume that it was equal to the better studied famines north of the Alps.[122] It is usually estimated, based on Pini's calculations of a declining population, that Bologna's population was reduced to 20–25,000 after the epidemic. The next firm population estimate for Bologna is from the *Descriptio civitatis Bononie* carried out in 1371 under the direction of the papal vicar, Cardinal Anglic Grimoard de Grisac of Avignon, that Pini used to estimate a population of 32,000. Thus, according to this scenario, within 20 years the population had regained much of its losses. At the same time it was undergoing a political and cultural rebirth that began after the revolt against the government of the Vicars of the Church in 1376 and the institution of a new commune. The material signs of this late fourteenth-century renewal are the building of the Mercanzia in 1380 and the "civic temple" of San Petronio in 1390, the minting of a new gold coin in 1380 as well as the completion of the third set of walls in 1374. Important growth also occurred in the university after mid-century: the Theological Faculty began granting degrees in 1352, the College of Spain was founded in 1364, and the Collegium Gregorianum in 1371. It is difficult to see how such rapid and strong re-growth could occur within 25 years of a devastating epidemic in a population and economy that had been suffering from a steep, long-term deterioration. Perhaps David Herlihy's proposal of a population at saturation point and remaining on a plateau until the onslaught of plague is a better scenario for the pre-plague decades.[123] The trajectory of economic decay also is not clear, but the notion of stagnation may fit better here as well. Pini's own evidence does not support an economic downturn beginning before the second decade of the fourteenth century. According to the

venticinquine, viz., clergy, students, invalids, and foreigners. The clergy may have added another 1,500 (according to Pini's previous estimates), but the student population may have declined from the estimated 2,000 in the thirteenth century. Yet, the number of foreigners could have been significant. It would not be unreasonable to add a further 2,500 to the total, which would mean a decline of 3,500 from the figure of 49,500 in 1294. Other demographic evidence provided by Pini also does not support steep demographic decline in the early fourteenth century. His examination of the membership lists for the *società delle armi* of 1274 and 1314 reveals that out of 24 *società* only three had decreased its numbers (with four groups suppressed before 1314). See Pini, "Problemi di demografia," p. 189.

[122] See William Chester Jordan, *The Great Famine* (Princeton, 1997).

[123] David Herlihy, *The Black Death and the Transformation of the West* (Cambridge, 1997).

guild matriculation lists nearly all occupations had expanded, sometimes doubled, their membership between 1274 and 1294.[124]

After 1300 there is little to go on, but the evidence from the wills does not point to a radically different economy or social composition at the mid-century point: economic life was vital and both were still focused on the thirteenth-century centers of growth and wealth. Thus for the first half of the fourteenth century the picture may not have been as black as is commonly depicted. In other words, Bologna may have entered the Black Death in a less weakened state than generally assumed. It was a city no longer at its thirteenth-century economic, demographic, and political peak, but in 1348 plague entered a society that was stagnant or had only recently entered decline, not one wasted by 50 to 75 years of deep decline. We now turn to the social experience of that devastating epidemic.

---

[124] Pini, "Problemi di demografia," pp. 195–197.

CHAPTER THREE

SOCIAL REACTIONS OF THE POPULACE DURING THE BLACK DEATH

On 8 July 1348 Mengonus fq Fratris Ugolini a *strazarius* or second-hand clothes dealer of the parish of San Biagio drew up his will. He returned to his wife, Ysabeta, her modest dowry of 100 *lire* and left her a small gift to help her buy a widow's gown as well as the use of his household goods. The twelve witnesses to his will included two parchment makers, two smiths, and a cloth dealer. Also present were Ysabeta's three brothers, Tomas, Bernardus, and Johannes. Serving as principal witnesses to guarantee that Mengonus was of sound mind were two Augustinian friars Nicola and Zacharias and dopnus [dominus] Gerardus, the parish priest of San Biagio.[1] This rather large gathering was documented by Johannes Laurentii Stephani, a notary also living in the parish of San Biagio. On the same day, Ysabeta and her brothers were joined again by dopnus Gerardus and Johannes Stephani at the house of their father, Figliocharius, known as Charinus, a parchment maker who lived in the same parish, to hear him dictate his will. Charinus returned to his wife, Ursollina, her dowry of 130 *lire*, gave her use of his household goods as long as she remained a widow, and named his three sons as heirs. Ysabeta, his daughter, received only a token blessing of 20 *solidi*. The wishes of Charinus were noted by four other men of his trade living in the same parish who served as witness to his will. Within a couple of weeks Ysabeta's husband and father were both dead, when once again she joined her brothers and the notary, Johannes Stephani, at the side of their mother, Ursollina, on 23 July. Again, her three brothers were named as heirs, while she, the married daughter, received a gift, this time a more sizeable one of 20 *lire*. Also at the side of her mother acting as witness, was Petrobellus, the brother of Ysabeta's deceased husband, who shared his brother's trade and parish. Two days later on 25 July, Petrobellus himself lay ill, dictating his last wishes to Johannes Stephani, as dopnus Gerardus and most likely Ysabeta looked on. Petrobellus did

[1] The standard title for priests in Bologna was *dopnus*.

not have any children but left his young nephew Nicola, Ysabeta's son, his property, half of which she would receive if Nicola died while still a child. Petrobellus named her as his executor and rewarded her with a bed and bedding. Her brother Bernardus was witness to this arrangement along with eight other residents of San Biagio and their parish priest, dopnus Gerardus. Bernardus was still alive five days later, for he was named heir by his brother Johannes, whom we first saw on 8 July at Mengonus's side, in his testament of 30 July.[2]

These five artisans's wills reveal the strong network of social bonds that existed between artisan families living within a neighborhood circumscribed by the religious boundary of the parish. The notary who lived in the parish helped his neighbors who were his clients. The parish priest came to administer last rites, hear confession, and witness their wills. Neighbors, related by work and marriage, assisted each other to prepare for death and pass on their property. We also see at work within these artisan families, the typical social institutions of late medieval urban Italian life: namely, the use of inheritance divided among a testator's sons who practiced his trade, and the exclusion from inheritance of daughters due to the use of dowry. What *is* unusual about this scene of familial and neighborly cohesion among artisans is the epidemic that struck down these individuals forcing them to prepare for death by writing their wills in quick succession.

Similar scenes were taking place during the summer of 1348 in other neighborhoods. The elite citizens of Bologna were faced with the same horrific and unprecedented spectacle of plague. Their wills offer the following set of testamentary scenes of family members of the Dessideri, Caselle, Basacomari, and Bonacatti families linked by marriage that played out in a similar fashion. On 26 June, Andriucia Philipi Dessiderii, a widow of the parish of San Michele dei Leprosetti, stood before the altar of Saint Catherine of the Augustinian Friars's church of San Giacomo, and dictated her will. She was healthy as she told the notary and nine friars before her that she would leave 50 *lire* in charitable bequests for the benefit of her soul to their church, her parish church, and the other mendicant churches of Bologna. She requested burial at the Church of San Giacomo. Thinking of her family she provided an

[2] Mem, vol. 229, fols. 9r (Ursollina fq domini Thomacis Ursii), 77r (Petrobellus fq Fratris Ugollini), 77v (Johannes fq Carini); vol. 230, fols. 97v (Mengonus fq Fratris Ugolini), 98r (Figliocharius fq Fratris Donisdei).

annual payment of eight *lire* to her daughter, a nun, and named her two sons as universal heirs. She asked that all of her clothes be distributed for the benefit of her soul to the poor by her executors, namely, the prior of the Augustinian church and her brother Romaninus.

On 15 July, Andriucia's brother, Romaninus Philippi Dessiderii, a wealthy citizen of the parish of Santa Maria di Torleone lay ill in his home and prepared his will. After two large *pro anima* bequests for masses and for charity distributed to the poor, he returned his wife's large dowry of 700 *lire* as well as 200 *lire* he owed her for the sale of pearls and jewels that she had brought to the marriage. He further granted her a bed, with linens and clothing and all their gold and silver appurtenances. He provided his daughter with a dowry of 600 *lire* and his servant, Margarita, with a bequest of eight *lire* that he claimed she had lent him. His son, still a minor, was named heir under the guardianship of his wife, whom Romaninus also named as executor. She was to be aided in this task by her brother-in-law, Albertus Thomacis de Basacomatribus, the husband of her sister. Albertus had come to witness the will from the adjacent parish of San Tommaso della Braina for he is listed among the witnesses. Also at the side of Romaninus were five men of his parish as well as a notary, Johannes de Venario, who lived in a different parish.

Within three weeks, Romaninus was dead since on 6 August his widow, Misina Jacobi Chaxelle, dictated her will to Johannes de Venario, the notary who had assisted her husband. Like her husband, Misina made charitable donations for her soul to the poor, but, in addition, she left several small bequests to the daughters of men and women living in Bologna and in rural villages to aid in their dowries. Three female servants, including Margarita, Romaninus's servant whom Misina called her nurse (*baiula*), got small *pro anima* bequests of 20 and 40 *solidi*. She added to her daughter's dowry and, following her husband, she named her small son as heir, but arranged that he should be substituted by her sister, Bertolomea, the wife of Albertus de Basacomatribus. If Bertolomea died, half of Misina's wealth would then go to her grandchildren, Bertolomea's children, and half would go to the Franciscan church of Bologna. Bertolomea was to serve as Misina's executor aided by a Franciscan friar. On the same day that Bertolomea was attending to her sister's needs, her husband Albertus was helping a neighbor in his parish, for he appears among the list of witnesses. He too quickly fell ill and on 8 August we find him dictating his last wishes in his home.

The following month we find another relative, Fixia de Boncaptis of the parish of Tommaso del Mercato who had married Bertolomea's and Misina's brother, Johannes. She was a widow and was healthy when she made her will on 1 September in the Carmelite church of Santa Maria de Monte Carmello. When Fixia's brother-in-law Guilielmus fq Nicholai Jacobini Mathei, a notary living in Santa Maria Mascarella, made his will on 10 October, we see further connections to the Carmelites, since he named the prior of the Carmelite church as his executor along with his wife, Fixia's sister, Montina. Fixia was still alive on 17 November after the epidemic had died down, when Montina, now widowed, lay ill and dictated her will in her home. After Montina's will no others from these elite families connected through marriage appear in 1348.

These seven elite wills paint another remarkable picture of families remaining in town throughout the entire epidemic from June through November.[3] For these privileged Bolognese, family members were spread around town but came together to help each other as witnesses and executors, who assisted them by arranging for the distribution of their goods after they were dead. In the home they were assisted by their servants. As we saw for the artisan families, the traditional patterns of property devolution were followed in which the bulk of these families's great wealth went to their children in the form of dowries and inheritance. But unlike the artisan class they left considerable sums to the poor, sometimes in the form of dowry aid, and to the mendicant orders of Bologna whose friars aided them by witnessing their will, providing for their burials, and managing their estates as executors.

This picture of stability and cohesion among urban communities of piety, kinship, and neighborhood is not what we would expect of the period in which epidemic plague struck the city, but it is demonstrated by the notarial record. This chapter will examine the immediate experience of the Black Death as evidenced in the actions of the townspeople recorded in the notarial contracts and wills of the *Memoriali* and *Demaniale*. Their decisions in terms of inheritance, piety, and charity will be examined in Chapter Six, while the actions of notaries, priests, friars, and neighbors who enabled the populace to make contracts and wills (and ultimately enabled us to know them) will be examined in

[3] Mem, vol. 228, fol. 432v (Andriucia fq domini Phylippi Desiderii); vol. 229, fols. 76v (Mixina fq Jacobi Chaxelle), 99v (Guiliellmus fq Nicholai Jacobini Mathei), 322v (Albertus fq domini Thomacis de Basacomatribus); vol. 230, fols. 126r (Romaninus fq domini Philippi Dessiderii), 239v (sapiens domina domina Montina fq domini Pauli olim domini Jacobi de Bonacaptis), 502r (Fixia fq domini Pauli de Bonacatis).

Chapters Four and Five. This chapter will track the activity of families and individuals through acts demonstrating the commercial life of the city, acts of family concerns such as dowry, guardianship, and emancipation, and lastly through the wills. As normal life collapsed and people became ill, they turned away from their usual daily activities to make their wills, which survive for study in enormous numbers. In effect, testaments constitute an exceptional window into the past, since they document the whereabouts of thousands of people during the epidemic. The notarial record allows us to investigate the issue of flight, which is assumed to have been the typical reaction to plague in cities, and track the progress of the disease in town in May, June, and July. In addition, by means of names of testators in databases of wills from the *Memoriali* and *Demaniale*, we will trace spouses, siblings, and parents and their children to propose a reconstruction of life during the epidemic.

The vignettes of the artisan families of Mengonus and his kin and the elite families of the Dessideri, Caselle, Basacomari, and Bonacatti are strikingly different from the portrayal of reactions to plague found in medieval literature. We will begin this chapter by reviewing and critiquing the common literary evidence for the history of the Black Death and then question its primacy in historical analysis by offering a new and different picture based on notarial evidence.

Literary Evidence

The most famous literary account is the Introduction to Giovanni Boccaccio's *Decameron* in which life during the epidemic in Florence is characterized by fear, panic, and flight. The situation was so bad that even society's core, the family, dissolved. The height of pathos is reached in the passage:

> It was not merely a question of one citizen avoiding another, and of people almost invariably neglecting their neighbours or rarely or never visiting their relatives, addressing them only from a distance; this scourge had implanted so great a terror in the hearts of men and women that brothers abandoned brothers, uncles their nephews, sisters their brothers, and in many cases wives deserted their husbands. But even worse, and almost incredible, was the fact that fathers and mothers refused to nurse and assist their own children, as though they did not belong to them.[4]

[4] Giovanni Boccaccio, *Decameron*, trans. G. H. McWilliam (London, 1972, repr.

Gabriele Zanella has demonstrated that in this passage Boccaccio was making use of a common literary theme of Italian chronicle accounts of 1348.[5] The same phrase expressing abandonment can be found repeated in Latin or Italian in several texts. Marco Battagli of Rimini wrote "father shunned his sick son, brother his brother, wife her husband, and so all healthy persons avoided the sick".[6] The *Storie Pistoresi* announced that in Tuscany, and especially in Pisa, "father abandoned son, children abandoned their mother and father, and one brother abandoned the other".[7] Guglielmo Cortusi wrote in his city chronicle of Padua that during the epidemic "wife fled the embrace of a dear husband, the father that of a son, and the brother that of a brother".[8] Modern readers may be more familiar with the work of Agnolo di Tura del Grasso, an eyewitness of the Black Death in Siena, who stated that "[f]ather abandoned child, wife husband, one brother another".[9] The word-for-word repetition in these accounts makes plain we are dealing with literary convention.

1995), pp. 8–9. "[L']un fratello l'altro abbandonava e il zio il nepote e la sorella il fratello e spesse volte la donna il suo marito; e, che maggior cosa è e quasi non credibile, li padri e le madri i figliuoli, quasi loro non fossero, di visitare e di servire schifavano" in Giovanni Boccaccio, *Decameron*, ed. Vittore Branca (Torino, 1980, repr. 1987), pp. 21–22.

[5] Zanella countered Vittore Branca's argument that this passage was an example of literary *imitatio* of a passage in Paul the Deacon's *History of the Lombards*. See Gabrielle Zanella, "Italia, Francia e Germania: Una storiografia a confronto," in *La peste nera*, pp. 49–135. I have argued that, in addition to drawing from chroniclers, Boccaccio was making direct use of plague tractates written during 1348 in order to criticize the advice set forth by doctors during the epidemic. See Shona Kelly Wray, "Boccaccio and the Doctors: Medicine and Compassion in the Face of Plague," *Journal of Medieval History* 30 (2004), 301–322.

[6] "Marcha di Marco Battagli da Rimini," ed. A. F. Massèra in *Rerum Italicarum Scriptores* [hereafter as *RIS*], n.s. vol. 16, pt. 3 (Città di Castello, 1912), 54: "pater postea infirmum filium evitabat, frater fratrem, uxor virum, et sic de singulis sani infirmos penitus evitabant".

[7] "Storie Pistoresi," ed. S. A. Barbi in *RIS*, n.s. vol. 11, pt. 5 (Città di Castello, 1906), 235: lo padre abbandonava li figliuoli, e' figliuoli lo padre e la madre, e l'uno fratello l'altro".

[8] "Chronica de Novitatibus Padue et Lombardie Guilielmi de Cortusis," ed. B. Pagnin in *RIS*, n.s. vol. 12, pt. 5 (Città di Castello, 1941), 120–121: "Uxor fugiebat amplexum cari viri, pater filii, frater fratris". English translation in Horrox, *The Black Death*, p. 34.

[9] The translation is by William Bowsky from his *The Black Death: A Turning Point in History?* (New York, 1971), p. 13. The original is "El padre abbandonava el figluolo, la moglie el marito, e l'uno fratello l'altro" in "Cronica senese di Agnolo di Tura del Grasso," ed. A. Lisini and F. Iacometti in *RIS*, n.s. vol. 15, pt. 6 (Bologna, 1935), p. 555.

Although he does not repeat the same phrase, Gabriele de' Mussis, writing between 1348 and his death in 1354, described the epidemic in his home town in Piacenza with the same emphasis on the dissolution of families. In one instance it is death that causes the unwanted separation of family members: "Oh hard death, impious death, bitter death, cruel death, who divides parents, divorces spouses, parts children, separates brothers and sisters". But elsewhere he exhorts the reader to "[l]isten to the tearful voices of the sick" and then records the cries of sick people abandoned by friends, of children crying out for their father or mother, and of parents asking why their children have run away. De' Mussis's account is often treated as a good report of the epidemic, but it was meant to be, as Rosemary Horrox has pointed out, "an extended meditation on the plague as an expression of divine anger".[10] The beginning of the tract is not as often repeated as his description of the epidemic, but here we can see the moral framework of this piece. It begins with a conversation between God and earth in which God states his anger at the hateful and loathsome behavior of humans and his intention to seek "savage vengeance" upon them. Boccaccio also had a moral purpose in writing his account of the Black Death and repeating the theme of abandonment. His rendition of the epidemic had great success and resonance among readers. It was repeated by authors writing well after 1348, some of whom, such as Marchionne di Coppo Stefani working in the 1370s, were certainly borrowing from Boccaccio.[11] Pietro Azario found plague a useful literary tool to introduce and close his entire chronicle. Although the body of the chronicle does not mention the Black Death of 1348, the *Proemium* and *Finalis Conclusio* contain descriptions of the outbreak of plague in 1361 with the same repetition of the abandonment theme. For Pietro Azario, plague served to remind how "fragile and fleeting" human life was and to emphasize the necessity and importance of his work as a chronicler.[12] The description of life

[10] Horrox, *Black Death*, p. 19.

[11] "Cronaca Fiorentina di Marchionne di Coppo Stefani," ed. N. Rodolico in *RIS*, n.s. vol. 30, pt. 1 (Città di Castello, 1903), 230: "Lo figliuolo abbandonava il padre, lo marito la moglie, la moglie il marito, l'uno fratello l'altro, l'una sirocchia l'altra".

[12] In the proem, Pietro Azari followed Boccaccio's description with the inclusion of friends and neighbors: "propter infestionem si quidem morbi vidi patrem de filio et filium e contra de patre, fratrem de fratre, amicum de amico, vicinumque de vicino penitus non curare". In the conclusion, like Agnolo, he related the deaths of his children. The body of the chronicle, does not mention the Black Death or the second outbreak, but only relates the political events of those years. See "Liber Gestorum in Lombardia Petri Azarii" in *RIS*, n.s. vol. 16, pt. 4 (Bologna, 1925–1939), pp. 7 and 177.

during plague, then, was an allegory, a tool that many authors used to emphasize or frame their own literary purpose which may have been to comment on society, the role of the author, or some such aim. The purpose of these texts was not exclusively to report on the epidemic.

Other authors's descriptions of the Black Death are much less dramatic than Boccaccio et al., since their focus was on events outside the epidemic. For most Italian city chroniclers the focus of attention was politics and war and, thus, many provided only short descriptions of the year's events.[13] Bologna's principal chronicler, Matteo Griffoni, simply stated that plague entered in May, lasted for the rest of the year, and killed two thirds of the population, among whom were two "world famous" professors of law (presumably Giovanni d'Andrea and Jacopo Bottrigari junior).[14] Occasionally a chronicler preferred to pass over the local details and instead gave a description of the disease's origins in the East. For example, the author of the *Annals* of Forlì stated "there was a great mortality throughout the entire world" and then described the events of Louis of Hungary's military campaigns in the south, and followed with a telling of the spread of plague in the eastern Mediterranean by the Genoese.[15] There are, in fact, chronicles which do not depart

[13] Short descriptions of the epidemic (which is generally referred to as *mortalitas*) are: for Rimini "Cronaca Malatestiana del secolo XIV," ed. A. F. Massèra, *RIS*, n.s. vol. 15, pt. 2 (Città di Castello, 1922–1924), 17 ("Cominzoe in Arimino una grandissima mortalità, e durò infina adì primo de decembre. E morì de tre persone le doe."); for Subiaco, "Chronicon Sublacense," ed. R. Morghen, *RIS*, n.s. 24, pt. 6 (Città di Castello, 1927), 44 ("Fuit autem tempore maxime mortalitatis que extitit anno ab incarnacione domini MCCCXLVII."); for Venice, "Chronica Raphayni de Caresinis Cancellarii Venetiarum," ed. E. Pastorello, *RIS*, n.s. vol. 12, pt 2 (Città di Castello, 1922), 4–5 ("Anno Domini 1348, inguinaria pestis, incipiens in partibus Tartarorum, et se, peccatis exigentibus, ad universum orbem contagiose extendens, adeo terribiliter desaevivit, quod penitus nulli loco pepercit"); for Apulia, "Chronicon de Rebus in Apulia Gestis," ed. A. Sorbelli in *RIS*, n.s. vol. 12, pt. 3 (Città di Castello, 1903), 49. The anonymous fourteenth-century "Cronaca Senese" simply states that in "1348 fu una grande moria in Siena, e per tutto el mondo e bastò tre mesi, giugno, luglio e agosto, e moriro de' quattro e tre" eds. A. Lisini and F. Iacometti in *RIS*, n.s. vol. 15, pt. 6 (Bologna, 1935). For Orvieto, we learn that the epidemic lasted from May to September, that shops closed and 500 people died, with death coming sometimes over night. See "Ephemerides Urbevetanae" or "Discorso Historico con Molti Accidenti Occorsi in Orvieto," ed. L. Fumi in *RIS*, n.s. vol. 15, pt. 5 (Città di Castello, 1920), 25–26.

[14] "Memoriale historicum de rebus Bononiensium," eds. L. Frati and A. Sorbelli in *RIS*, n.s. vol. 18, pt. 2 (Città di Castello, 1902), 56.

[15] "Annales Forolivienses," ed. G. Mazzatinti, in *RIS*, n.s., vol. 22, pt. 2 (Città di Castello, 1903), p. 66, which account continues with the military activities of King Louis of Hungary and the spread of plague by Genoese ships from "parts of Persia" to Constantinople, Sicily, and Genoa.

from the usual subjects of political intrigue and battles to make any mention at all of plague in 1348.[16] Thus, despite the fact that chronicle and literary accounts are the starting point for much of our modern understanding of the epidemic, they are not ideal sources. The military and ruling elite were the subject material for most medieval chroniclers. Many of these writers were not interested in reporting the actions of townspeople in their chronicles except when those actions directly affected the lives of the elite, such as riots. And for the accounts that do give us a detailed description of the actions of individuals during the epidemic there is clearly a moralizing purpose at work.

Historians have turned to other sources produced within medieval towns during the epidemic and their work has tempered the picture of panic presented by Boccaccio and chroniclers. Utilizing municipal records and legislation, Italian historians of the later nineteenth century stressed the active and aggressive efforts to manage disease during the crisis on the part of the governments of Florence, Pistoia, and Venice.[17] More recently, William Bowsky and Élisabeth Carpentier have argued that governing councils in Siena and Orvieto, respectively, were less active during the Black Death. Nevertheless, according to their investigations, the social fabric in these towns did not collapse during the crisis. Gene Brucker reviewed wills, diaries, and letters of Florentines during the epidemic and also concluded that society remained stable.[18] Aliberto Benigni Falsini examined a sample of notarial records written in Florence during 1348 to find notaries and witnesses to acts remaining in town during the epidemic.[19] Investigations of notarial records of France, that remain in much smaller numbers than Bologna's, have

[16] Instead of the Black Death, the Carrara lords in the Veneto are the subject of Galeazzo and Bartolomeo Gatari's "Cronaca Carrarese," ed. by R. Cessi in *RIS*, n.s. vol. 17, pt. 1 (Bologna, 1931). The subalpine region is discussed without mention of plague in the "Chronicon Parvum Ripaltae," ed. F. Gabotto in *RIS*, n.s. vol. 17, pt. 3 (Città di Castello, 1911–1912). For Lombardy, Pietro Azari's chronicle also does not discuss the Black Death (see footnote 12 above).

[17] Mario Brunetti, "Venezia durante la peste del 1348," *Ateneo Veneto* 22, n. 1 (1909), pp. 290–311 and 22, n. 2 (1909), pp. 5–42; A. Chiappelli, "Gli ordinamenti sanitari," pp. 3–21; Francesco Carabellese, *La peste del 1348 e le condizioni della sanità pubblica in Toscana* (Rocca San Casciano, 1897). These will be discussed in Chapter Four.

[18] Gene Brucker, "Florence and the Black Death," in *Boccaccio: Secoli di vita: Atti del Congresso internazionale Boccaccio 1975*, eds. Marga Cottino-Jones and Edward Tuttle (Ravenna, 1977), pp. 21–30.

[19] Aliberto Benigni Falsini, "Firenze dopo il 1348: Le conseguenze della peste nera," *Archivio Storico Italiano* 129 (1971), 425–503.

produced similar pictures of stability and resilience in society.[20] The notarial records of Bologna provide the best evidence for this growing picture of stability during the Black Death and are an excellent foil to the chronicle accounts.

Business Activity and Testaments

We begin our investigation with the most common forms of notarial records: commercial acts, most of which are loans, and testaments. Figure 3.1 shows the extant wills plus codicils and miscellaneous business contracts registered in abstract form in the *Provvisori* for the first half year, when several quaderni are missing from the *Memoriali*, and for the second half of the year, those copied into the *Memoriali*.[21] Also included in the graph are the wills from the *Demaniale* holdings for 1348 comprising the "secret" wills of men who chose to have their wills deposited in the sacristies of San Francesco and San Domenico and

---

[20] Based on a study of three surviving notarial casebooks and other judicial sources, Daniel Lord Smail found social stability in his "Accommodating Plague in Medieval Marseille," *Continuity and Change* 11 (1996), 11–41. Richard Emery also used notarial evidence in his study of "The Black Death in 1348 in Perpignan," *Speculum* 42 (1967), 611–23. His study of 63 wills during the three months in which plague was active determined that the social organization in Perpignan remained "cohesive, intact, and functioning" (pp. 620–21). For a discussion of the change in modern historical interpretations of the Black Death from a "gothic" epidemiology emerging in 1832 with Justin Hecker's *Der schwarze Tod im viersehnten Jahrhundert* and continuing to the early twentieth century, in which plague had immediate, dramatic, transformative effects on society, to a de-emphasis on the impact of plague, see Faye Marie Getz, "Black Death and the Silver Lining: Meaning, Continuity, and Revolutionary Change in Histories of Medieval Plague," *Journal of the History of Biology* 24 (1991), 265–89.

[21] The data for the following graphs are taken from Provv. cart. 152, 153, 154, 155 and Provv. perg. 16 (for the first semester), Mem, vols. 229 and 230 (for the second semester) with wills from Dem: Instrumenti, Campioni Rossi, and Miscellanea. As explained in Chapter One, the *Provvisori* contain only the essential information from each contract—name, type of contract, and value—which was later to be copied out in full into the *Memoriali*. Twelve out of the 25 *quaderni* or registers are missing from the first six months of the *Memoriali*. I have counted 1360 contracts in the first semester of the *Memoriali*. All of the registers for the *Provvisori* from the first semester are extant. There remain 2708 notations of acts (twice the number of contracts in the *Memoriali*). In terms of wills, in the *Memoriali* there remain 137 wills from June, but there are 309 in the *Provvisori*. On the other hand, for the second half of the year, there are more wills in the *Memoriali*, e.g., 585 in July, versus 463 in the *Provvisori*. There are 2207 acts remaining in the *Memoriali* from the second half of the year. It must be noted that also these registers are not complete—9 out of 25 or 34 per cent of the *quaterni* may be missing.

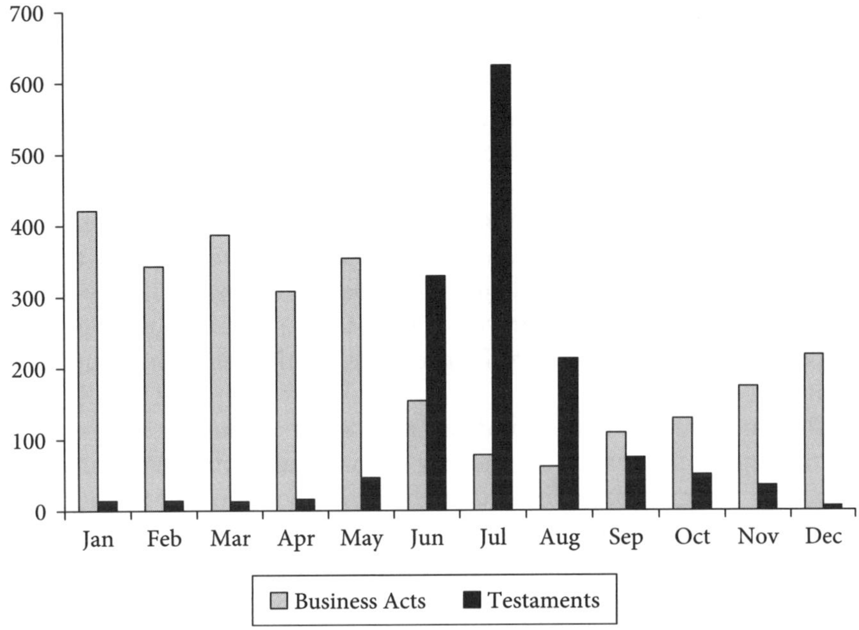

Source: ASB, Provvisori, reg. cartacei 152–155 and Memoriali vol. 229, 230

Figure 3.1 Business Contracts and Testaments of 1348

not the *Memoriali* as well as copies of wills of men and women that for some reason the religious houses chose to preserve and which are not extant today in the *Memoriali* registers. This inventory of the total corpus of 1,434 wills and codicils from the city during 1348 (that does not include 19 wills that were duplicated by accident in the *Memoriali* nor four wills which appear in both the *Memoriali* and *Demaniale*) can be paired with the 2,736 business contracts, consisting mainly of loans, sales, and settlement of debts, to provide the fullest understanding of the people's experience of the Black Death.

The impact of plague is clear. We see regular commercial activity for the months of January through May. The number of business contracts stayed high for the first five months of the year, ranging from about 420 in January to 310 in April. The reaction to plague in the business acts shows up in June when for the first time there is a significant drop followed by a continued decline. The reaction in testaments begins in May and appears most clearly in June. In fact, on a day-by-day level life looks very normal until the last two weeks of May and first week of June when there is a small increase of wills followed by a huge jump in activity on 8 June, when more Bolognese decided to make their wills than on any other previous day that year. The wills appear to confirm May as the date of plague's entry reported by the chronicler Matteo Griffoni and argue against the entry date of March proposed in the *Historia Miscellanea* (and accepted by general works on the epidemic in Italy and Europe, such as those of Lorenzo Del Panta and Jean-Noël Biraben).[22] Ole Benedictow's recent study of the Black Death in Europe, which repeats the March date, proposes a tempo-spatial formula according to which plague deaths occur in general 39 days after the entry of infected rats into an area. It is possible, then, that plague entered Bologna during April, spreading north after it had infected Florence in March.[23]

Plague rapidly took hold and was at its most vicious in the summer. According to the graph, the months of June, July, and August display the most aberrant behavior with wills taking over most of the notarial activity. Business contracts decrease to unprecedented numbers during July and August. July appears truly horrific as plague overcame the city. The 624 testaments redacted in July and preserved in the *Memoriali* and *Demaniale* represent a much larger number of acts and effort on the part of notaries and families than any other month that year, whether pre- or post-plague. Deaths and will-making still outstrip business in August, but, finally, in September wills diminish and no longer surpass other more typical activities as the number of business contracts steadily increase. For the year of the Black Death, then, there were three distinct periods of 1) normalcy, i.e., January through April, 2) the epidemic, comprising the transitional month of May followed by three months of severe mortality, and 3) gradual recovery at diminished capacity comprising the last four months.

It is important to note that Figure 3.1 includes all extant urban wills from 1348, generated from sources found in collections produced under

---

[22] Matthaeus de Griffonibus, "Memoriale Historicum de rebus bononiensium," ed. L. Frati and A. Sorbelli, *RIS* n.s. vol. 18, pt. 2 (Città del Castello, 1902), p. 56; Jean-Noël Biraben, *Les hommes et la peste en France et dans les pays européens et méditerranéens*, Civilisations et Sociétés, 35, 2 vols. (Mouton, 1975), 1:74; Lorenzo Del Panta, *Le epidemie nella storia demografica italiana* (Turin, 1980), pp. 111–113.

[23] Benedictow, *The Black Death 1346–1353*, pp. 58–59, 79, 92. While his spatio-temporal formula is useful, Benedictow's view that notarial evidence and chronicles reflect the actions and interests of the upper classes only is less applicable here. It is the contention of this study that Italian wills and notarial records encompass also the less-well-off, though not the poor, and are a good indicator of general civic life.

different conditions: the *Provvisori* and *Memoriali* were instituted by the commune through statutes requiring public deposit of testaments of men and women in the *Memoriali* after first being registered with the *Provvisori*, while the *Demaniale* contain testaments deposited either by the choice of individual men who wished to have their wills kept secret or by the choice of the mendicant houses who wished to have copies retained for their own purposes. Therefore, it is prudent to examine the trends during 1348 of testaments in each archive to avoid distortion in the data. The secret wills in the *Demaniale*, in fact, follow the same pattern of the *Memoriali* with a blow-up of wills during the summer plague months, although in much smaller numbers: there are four wills extant from January through April, then another four in May, by June that number had quadrupled to sixteen extant wills, with a high of 28 in July, and back down to 14 in August, 6 in September and then three remaining for the rest of the year.

How does this pattern compare to non-plague years? Could the summer spike in will-making during 1348 actually reflect normal behavior? Figure 3.2 shows wills redacted in the *Memoriali* from the year 1337, which, apart from some factional violence between the Scacchesi and

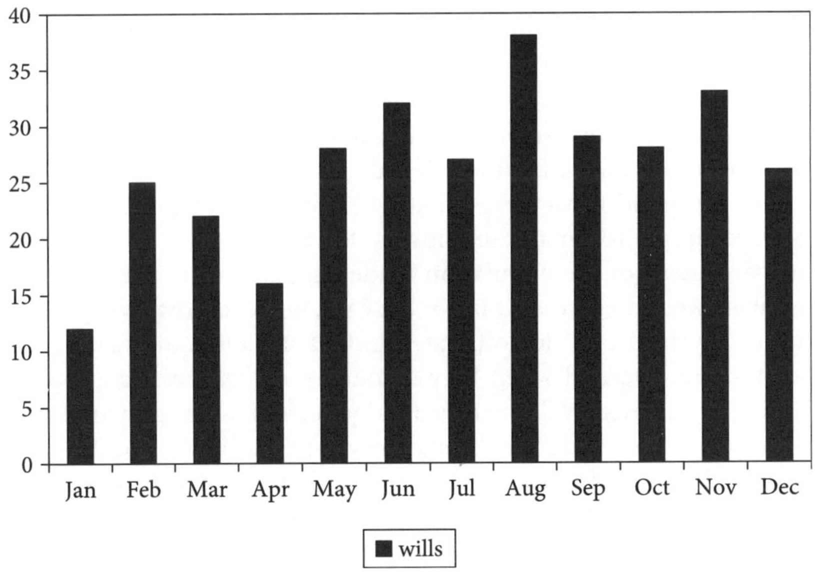

Source: ASB, Memoriali, vols. 191, 192, 193

Figure 3.2 Testaments in the *Memoriali* of 1337

Maltraversi as a result of the rise of the Pepoli *signoria*, was a relatively tranquil year for Bologna, without famine, major disease or war. The number of wills fluctuates month by month with no specific trend. Although more wills were redacted in August than any other month, the differences are never as great as the year of plague. A further comparison can be made with the numbers of wills charted by Martin Bertram for the years 1268 and 1300. There are similar patterns in the 577 registered wills of 1268 only in that August had the highest (80) and December had the fewest (28), but the range of numbers of registered wills each month for the remaining months (i.e. between 41 and 54) is narrow and does not conform to the changes of 1348. There were 1,264 wills registered in the *Memoriali* during 1300. Unlike the year of the Black Death, for this year the months of the highest numbers of registered wills were April (172), May (183), and September (219), while the summer showed a decline (with 99 in June, 140 in July, and 104 in August). Again, the number of wills fluctuate month by month with no clear trend. Thus evidence from non-plague years demonstrates that the numbers from 1348 are the result of abnormal and exceptionally high mortality.[24]

The unprecedented mortality must have brought on shock and fear in the populace. How much was will-making a result of this fear? The graph's spike for July would seem to indicate a massive reaction, but should we understand their presence, as Benedictow argues, as the "result of mass psychosis in face of terrifying mortality" and thus consider wills to be an over-reaction and misleading representation of the experience of the Black Death?[25] Benedictow is correct in arguing that wills are not good tools for estimating population or mortality rates. There are simply too many unknowns: for example, we do not know what percentage of the population made wills nor what percentage of those wills were preserved. It is not the case, however, that wills are the result of psychosis. As demonstrated in Chapter One, the vast majority of testators were ill when they dictated their testaments and were behaving as late medieval testators usually did when they prepared their last wishes. Wills produced through psychotic behavior would—presumably—be made in large numbers by healthy individuals reacting abnormally in fear expecting, but not yet experiencing, the worst. The

---

[24] Bertram, "Zweiter Teil," pp. 212–215.
[25] Benedictow, *Black Death*, pp. 268–269.

reactions of wills to the epidemic in Bologna can be compared with Florentine numbers of deaths during plagues derived from evidence that some may see as less psychologically motivated. David Herlihy and Christiane Klapisch studied two necrologies of Santa Maria Novella and references from 21 family memoirs to count deaths by month during plague and non-plague years between 1251 and 1500. In Florence deaths in May comprised 11.40 per cent of all deaths over the plague years, but in Bologna the *Provvisori* wills of May represent only 3.36 per cent of the total for 1348. The plague entered Florence in March, earlier than in Bologna, and this pattern may have characterized the other plague-year data compiled by Herlihy and Klapisch, so May was not as deadly a time in Bologna as Florence. Nevertheless, if wills were an over-reaction to an epidemic, even only at its beginning stage, one might expect a greater reaction in Bologna in the wills of May. In Florence deaths in June during plague years were 20.98 per cent of the total, and this number is roughly matched in Bologna where the wills of June are 25.3 per cent of the year. No psychosis here. But the situation in July is different. Deaths in Florentine plague years during July form twenty-six percent—the most lethal month of plague years—while in Bologna the wills of July take up 38 per cent of the yearly output. Nevertheless, this difference may not be due so much to over-reaction by testators, but simply because the summer of 1348 was deadlier than any other plague year.[26]

The Black Death, then, had a powerful impact on daily life in Bologna. Daily business was abandoned as the ill turned to preparing for their imminent death. The records demonstrate—just as emphatically as the pitiful words of chroniclers or authors like Boccaccio and de' Mussis—that the summer of 1348 was a profound shock to society. Sam Cohn, however, has repeatedly argued to the contrary that the second onslaught of plague, not 1348, had the greatest psychological impact. Cohn is interested in change in mentality. He finds in 1363 a new sense of piety among Tuscan testators who were interested in promoting their own and their family's memory and a new sense of medical progress among doctors—both mentalities being part of a new Renaissance psychology.[27] While Cohn's aims of tracing long-term mentalities are

[26] Herlihy and Klapisch-Zuber, *Tuscans and Their Families*, pp. 78–80.

[27] Cohn, *Black Death Transformed*, chapter 9; Cohn, *Death and Property*, p. 45. I see no great difference between the views and actions of doctors during the Black Death and the second onslaught. See Wray, "Boccaccio and the Doctors".

very different from this book's close investigation of the immediate experience of an epidemic, it may be useful to examine briefly this issue of psychological impact of the second outbreak through the notarial records. The *Provvisori* of 1362, when plague returned to Bologna for a second time, demonstrate that, at least in the short-term, the social response was very different than during the Black Death.[28]

Figure 3.3 shows the impact of the second outbreak on business acts and testaments. As was the case for 1348, a reaction sets in during June. Again, the number of wills increases greatly in July, however not to nearly as high numbers (351 wills and codicils compared to 588 for 1348). Unlike 1348, August is the month in which the highest number of wills were written (402 as compared with 195 for 1348). The decrease in wills is not as steep as that of 1348, which may indicate that mortality or at least apprehension of death on the part of the townspeople

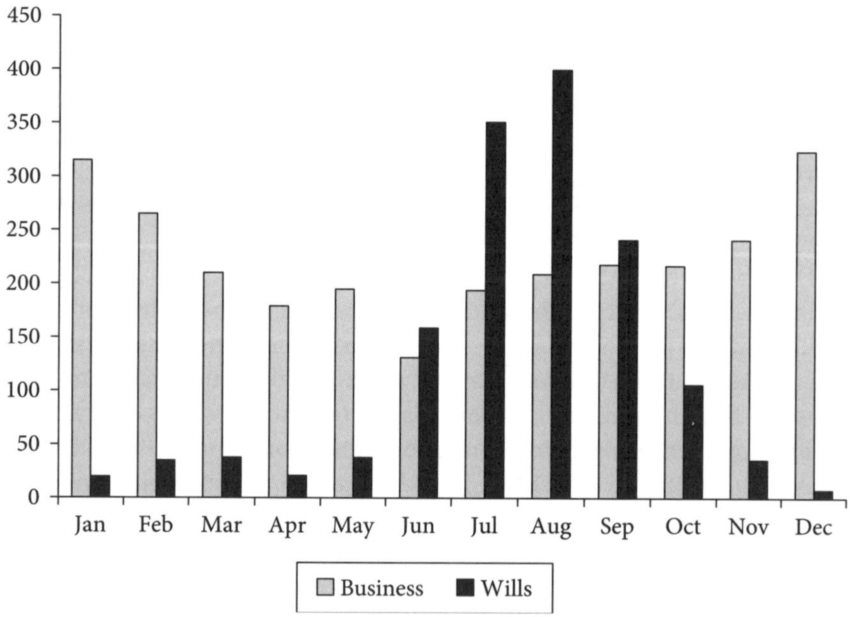

Source: ASB, Commune, Provvisori pergamenacei, 30

Figure 3.3 Business Contracts and Testaments of 1362

[28] The *Memoriali* of 1362 are missing several volumes, since the first semester contains *quaterni* of only eight notaries (out of a possible 20 to 24), while an even fewer six remain for the second semester. For this reason I have used the *Provvisori* of 1362.

remained high for a longer period in 1362. Clearly by November (one month later than in 1348) the effects of plague were over. Again, there is a marked decrease in business activity in June, though not as great as that of 1348. Very different from 1348 is the fact that business activity always remained fairly strong, even in July and August. After summer, it reached pre-plague levels with the first and last two months of the year almost mirroring each other. From this evidence, it appears as if people may have been able to adjust to the renewal of the second epidemic slightly better. That is, they do not appear to have abandoned all other activity to make their wills, although clearly they did make their wills in large numbers. There is not, however, the same appearance of shock.

The testaments and commercial notarial acts are eloquent witnesses to the severity of the impact of plague in 1348. While the chaos emphasized in literary accounts is mirrored in the disruption of daily business activity, their insistence on the breakdown of social relations and the abandonment of the family is not. Due to legal requirements for witnesses and testamentary purposes of providing for the testator's soul and family, wills are eminently social documents, incapable of being produced during mass social breakdown.

Family Matters

In addition to wills and business contracts the notarial registers demonstrate other kinds of social activity that took place during the Black Death. Figure 3.4 displays contracts concerned with family life, namely, the arrangement of dowry, the assignment of guardians, and procedures for inheritance.[29] Various kinds of dowry contracts make up a large part of this social activity registered in the *Memoriali* and *Provvisori*.

[29] I have not included here emancipation acts by which a father removed a son from his *patria potestas* allowing him to become *sui iuris*, because, as Thomas Kuehn has shown for fourteenth- and fifteenth-century Florence, the act was generally used by fathers for financial purposes, that is, to release their sons from financial liability and protect property from creditors by passing it to emancipated sons. See Thomas Kuehn, *Emancipation in Late Medieval Florence* (New Brunswick, N.J., 1982). There were 30 emancipation acts drawn up during 1348, but most of them (ten) were redacted in January, while every other month except June and September had one, two, or three such acts. These numbers do not reveal any patterns of behavior by fathers towards their sons during the epidemic, but instead present information on presiding officials which will be analyzed in Chapter Four.

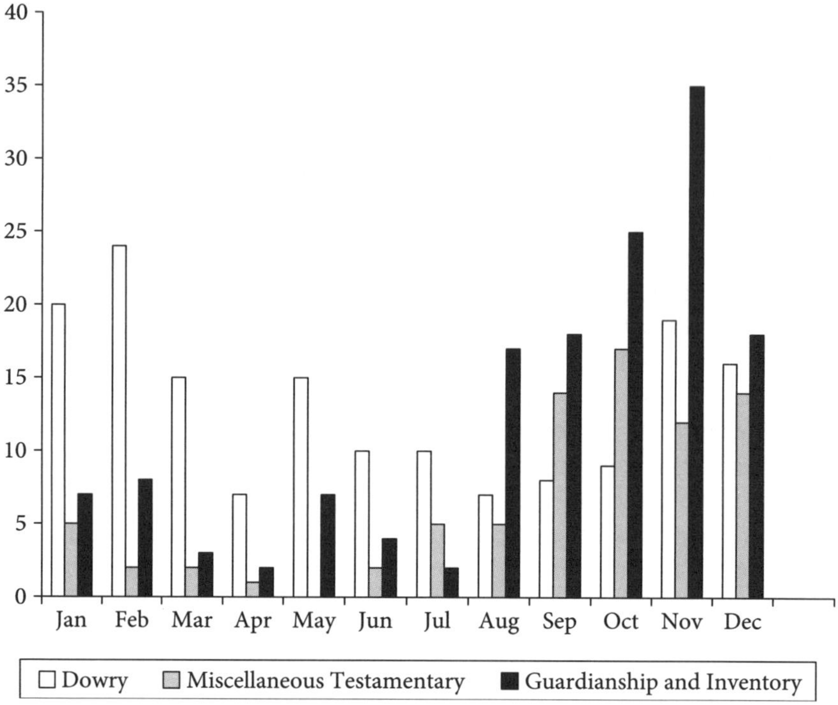

Figure 3.4 Dowry, Testamentary, and Guardianship Contracts in the *Provvisori* and *Memoriali* of 1348

Among the graphed dowry contracts appear not only the standard declaration of reception of dowry from a marriage about to take place (*instrumentum receptionis dotis*), but also acts concerning increases in an already established dowry (*instrumentum augmenti dotis*), restitution of a dowry (*instrumentum restitutionis dotis*), and other acts concerning dowries of marriages already carried out.[30] It is not possible from this graph to determine the number of marriages that took place during the epidemic. However, I have included dowry contracts as a general category in the figures as these types of contracts do involve activities that primarily centered upon the family and were distinct from the business activity represented in the graphs.

The numbers demonstrate the impact of plague on such family-centered concerns such as dowry, since of the 160 total dowry acts, 66

[30] Examples of the many varying types of dowry contracts can be found in Salatiele, *Ars Notarie*, 2:267–272, and Rolandino, *Contractus*, pp. 125–134.

(or 41.25 per cent) were written during the stable periods of first four months of the year, while a much lower number of acts, viz. 42 or 26.25 per cent, remains after the entrance of plague in May and through the summer. In each of the three months of the plague's most virulent time (June, July, and August) the numbers of act generated were half those during each of the first three months of the year. Nevertheless, activity had hardly ceased and, if we were to take into account the potential third of contracts missing from the second semester, the decrease would appear much less significant. In any case it appears that people in Bologna were arranging marriages, and possibly marrying, during the epidemic. In the winter months the number of such contracts rose to almost normal levels 52 (32.5 per cent) during the final months of recovery. Again, with the potential missing contracts, what may be reflected here is a strong upsurge in marriages that may well have surpassed pre-plague activity.

Guardianship contracts, in which a *tutor* is established for a child and an inventory is generated, demonstrate another side of parental concern. They appeared less frequently in the notarial registers than dowry acts (on average there were five acts in each of the first four months) and this pattern continued well into the epidemic (with an average of four such acts during May, June, and July). But in August the number of guardianship and inventories grows much larger than before (17) and continues high throughout the remainder of the year (reaching a high of 35 acts in November). This is also the case for miscellaneous testamentary contracts, i.e., contracts recording entry into inheritance entitled *aditio hereditatis* and the repudiation of inheritance, or *repudiatio hereditatis*. Normally these acts represent only a tiny proportion of notarial output, but they rise in number once the disease had died down. After the epidemic, as chroniclers reported, there were many problems over inheritance that had to be addressed. Thus, although some family arrangements such as dowry were curtailed during the summer months of plague, parents and guardians did address the needs of their children, especially when faced with problems of inheritance and wardship as a result of the summer's mortality.

A contract that represents both family concern and business activity is the *curatele* or *cure* contract. These involve the appointment of a *curator* or advisor for a minor carrying out a financial transaction.[31] Usually they

[31] For an example of *instrumentum curatoris* see Salatiele, *Ars Notarie*, p. 302. For a discussion of this form of contract in the notarial manuals, see Maria Gigliola di Renzo

include one or two adult brothers who request permission from a judge of the *podestà*, the leading judicial official of the city, to serve as *curator* for a younger brother in some kind of business transaction. They are always followed in the registers by the relevant financial contract and, therefore, can also be used as indicators of business activity. It is best to treat them separately from the first graph as their inclusion would inflate business activity. Figure 3.5 charts *curatele* contracts remaining in the *Provvisori* and *Memoriali* from the same months as Figure 3.1.

The picture is similar: plague brings on a small reaction in May that grows in June to show the disruption caused by disease and death in July and August. As we saw with dowry contracts, there remains some activity of families making arrangements for each other during the height of the epidemic. The city starts to recover in September with increased *curatele* and business contracts appearing in October and November.

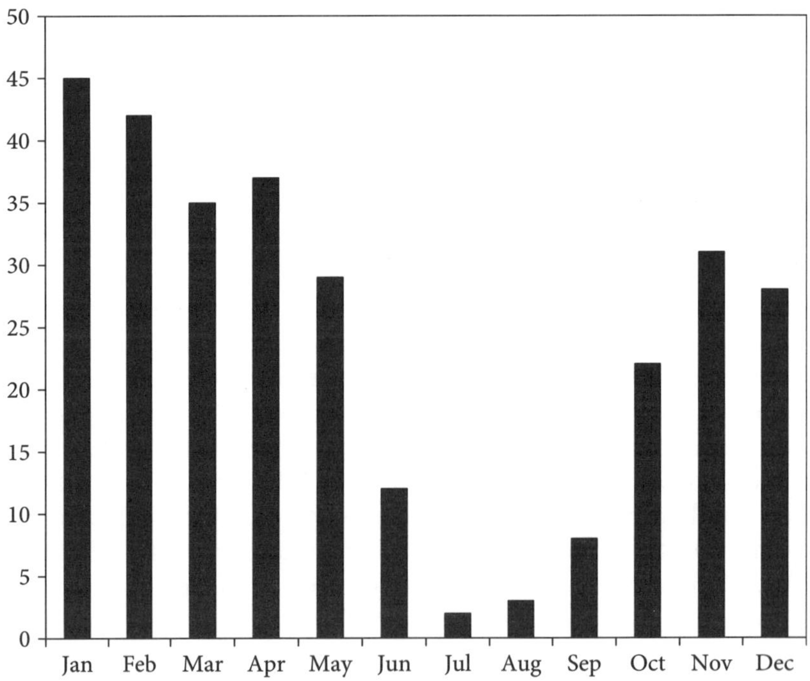

Figure 3.5 *Curatele* Contracts in the *Provvisori* and *Memoriali* of 1348

Villata, "Il volta della famiglia medievale tra practica e teoria nella *Summa totius artis notariae*," in Tamba, *Rolandino e l'ars notaria*, pp. 439–441.

The reduced number of contracts at the end of the year may be due to mortality from plague, but is also the result of gaps in the *Memoriali* registers. Once again, the notarial evidence demonstrates, in contrast to the chronicles, that families continued to engage in commercial and social transactions that directly benefited their members despite the difficulties of the epidemic.

Crime

According to chronicles, there was a rise of violence and crime during the Black Death. There is one type of notarial contract in the *Memoriali* that provides a glimpse into the world of crime. This is the fascinating *instrumentum pacis et concordiae* or pact of peace. These are pacts made between two or more parties after a violent crime has been perpetrated against one party. They involve a description of the violent act, an agreement that the aggressor be removed from any ban placed upon him or her and freed from the possibility of suit by the offended, and lastly a statement of the fine that the victim or his or her party agrees to pay if they break their promise not to pursue the case in the future.[32] There are 32 registrations of such peace contracts in the *Provvisori* for the first semester and 23 such contracts in the *Memoriali* for the second semester. The majority of crimes involved in these contracts are personal injuries (usually involving one aggressor and one victim), while murder is the second most common crime.[33] The date of the crime is usually not specified in the contract, but since the name of the *podestà* who ruled at the time is generally given, it is possible to determine a range of time in which the crime took place.[34]

---

[32] For more information on these pacts in Bologna see Wray, "Instruments of Concord" and Sarah Rubin Blanshei, "Criminal Law and Politics in Medieval Bologna," *Criminal Justice History* 2 (1981), 1–30. For elsewhere in Italy see Glenn Kumhera, "Making Peace in Medieval Siena: Instruments of Peace, 1280–1400" (PhD diss., University of Chicago, 2005) and Katherine L. Jansen, "Peacemaking in the Oltrarno, 1287–1297," in *Pope, Church, and Society: Essays in Honour of Brenda M. Bolton*, eds. Frances Andrews, Christoph Egger and Constance M. Rousseau (Leiden, 2004), 327–344 with accompanying bibliographies.

[33] Most of the peace contracts involved crimes between individuals and settlements drawn up between those individuals. Only a small number of contracts were concerned with feuds or vendetta. This fact is contrary to the traditional view that the peace contract's primary purpose was to settle vendetta.

[34] The *podestà* ruled for six months and usually did not repeat his term for many years.

Twenty datable peace contracts reveal that many involved crimes committed over a year before the contract was written: the intervals between the crime and pact range from one year to thirteen years. And for the nine contracts concerning violent acts carried out in 1348, all are from the first semester of the year. It is possible that crimes carried out during the height of the epidemic were settled in the later months of 1348, but we should not conclude that since there are no such acts, there was no such crimes. Instead it would be better to examine peace contracts of 1349 and the criminal court records to determine levels of violence during the epidemic. Nevertheless, it is useful to examine the numbers for 1348.

Figure 3.6 shows that the number of pacts drops during the plague-ridden months with the biggest decline in August. At the outset of the epidemic the need for this kind of social activity—the private settlement of injury and reintegration into society of a banned criminal, which was the purpose of the most of these peace contracts—continued to be important. However, with the resulting two months of high mortality the Bolognese populace had to turn to address other social needs, such as guardianship and testamentary activity. These reconciliations return to importance and begin to rise at about the same time that regular business activity picks up.

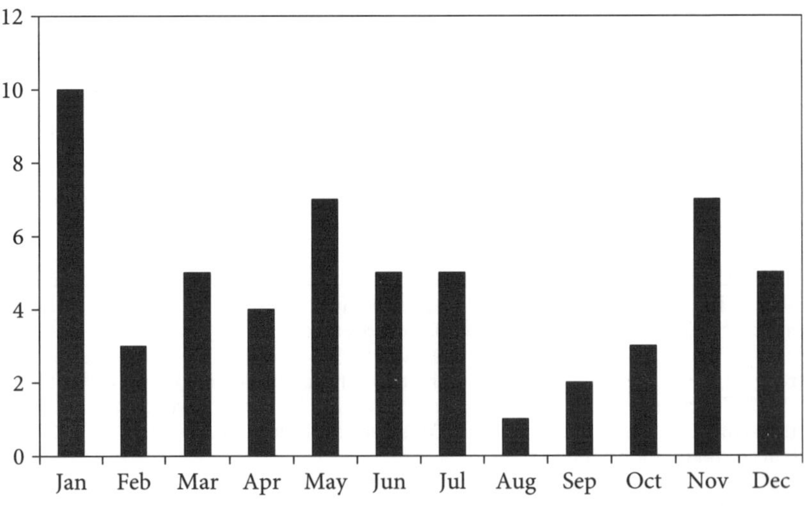

Figure 3.6 Peace Contracts in the *Provvisori* and *Memoriali* of 1348

Tracking Disease and Flight

The notarial contracts and wills demonstrate a reaction to plague beginning in May and manifest in June. The wills allow us to track the progress of the disease in the city. Each testator is usually identified by a parish, or *cappella*, for which we know the location of the church—the borders of each parish are completely unknown. He or she makes a brief formulaic statement about his or her health, usually "sound in mind, but sick in body". Given the certain presence of epidemic disease, it is likely that the ill testators are suffering from plague.[35] With this information we can track the progress of the disease. One should not assume that the disease started in a particular area of town, say, the poorer periphery as Benedictow believes. This may have been the case and, if so, might not show up in the wills, but as we have learned from Cohn's study, we should not assume that it was a disease of the poor.[36] In fact, we should assume nothing and proceed only with the medieval evidence.

The first map shows that location of the 15 testators who specify a parish for the month of May. During this first month of plague, there is no clear clustering of ill testators by parish, quarter, or zone. The testators are roughly divided between the northern and southern quarters. Over half were located in the third zone, while only one fifth were in the central zone within the first walls. Unfortunately the number of remaining wills is very small for May, but June offers more information since 126 testators provided a parish.

The second map shows the location of 35 ill and healthy testators during the first two weeks of June. Again the ill are scattered throughout the city, but a larger number appear in the north. The greatest number of ill lived between the second and third sets of walls. There appears to be little clustering, but several adjacent parishes had ill testators: San Felice and San Niccolò del Borgo di San Felice along the western stretch of the continuation of the Via Emilia; Santa Maria Maddalena and San Sigismondo along Strada San Donato; and San Martino dell'Aposa, San

[35] As discussed in Chapter One, most medieval testators dictated their wills from their deathbeds. Those arranging a will in advance generally did so for reasons of travel. The few healthy testators in June may, however, have been anticipating plague.

[36] Cohn argues that we cannot assume that plague must have started in poorer neighborhoods of town. These would have been in the periphery, but there homes were not so crowded since the population had shrunk since its height in the thirteenth century when walls were begun. Cohn, *Black Death Transformed*, p. 129.

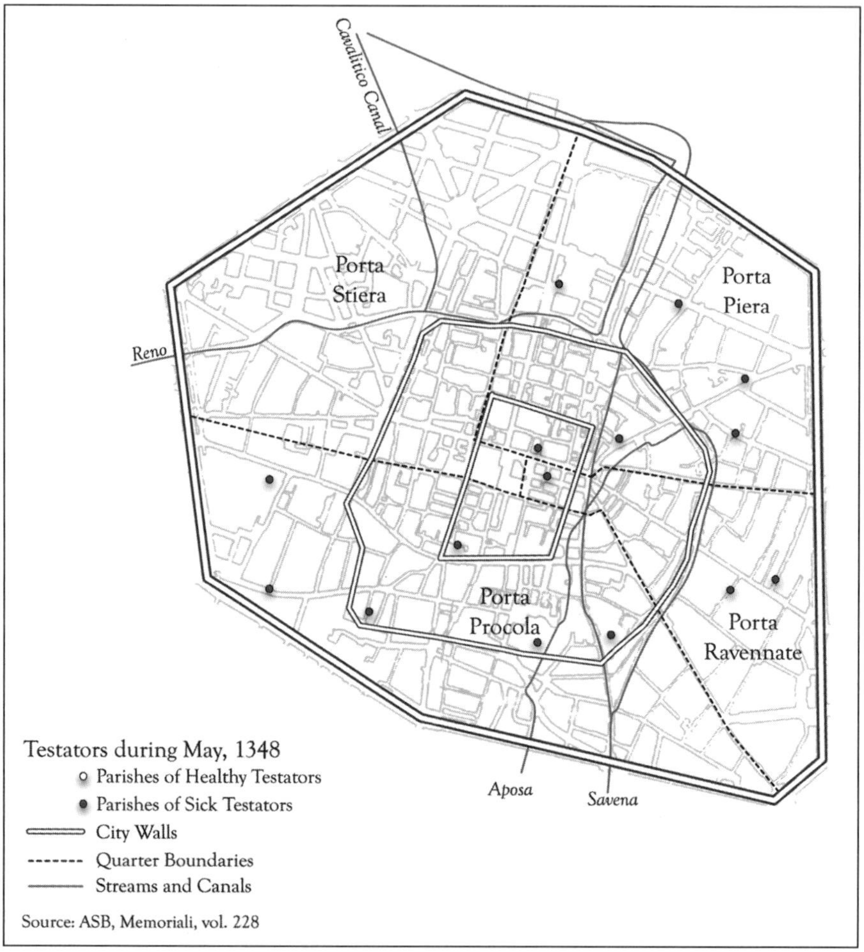

Testators During May, 1348

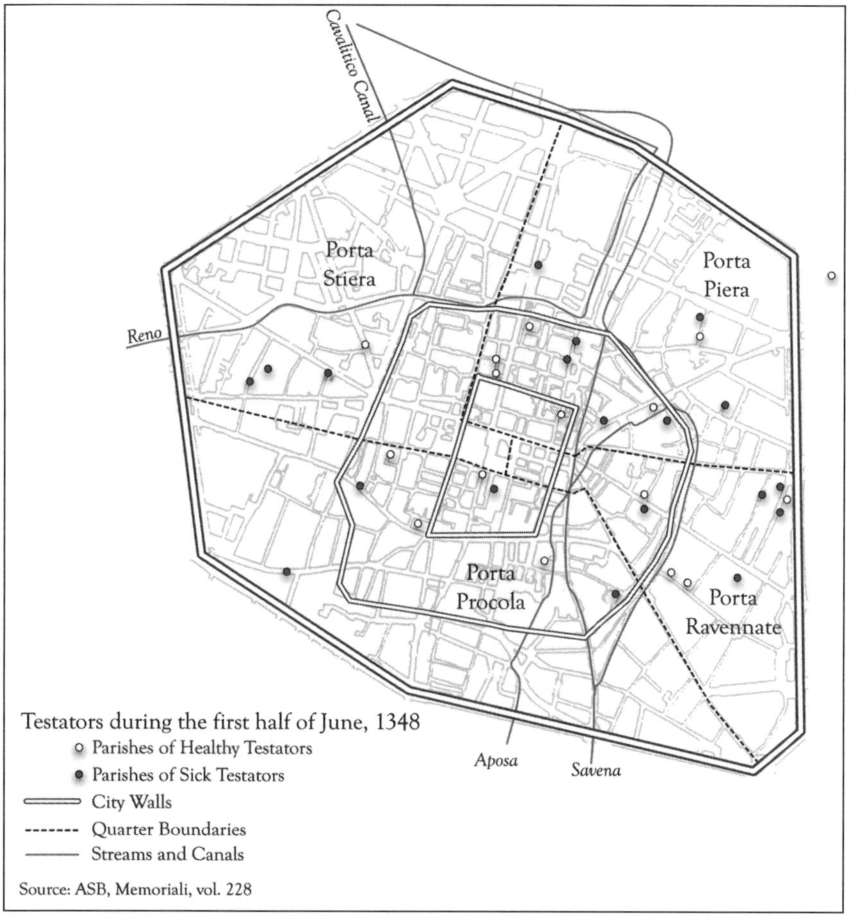

Testators During the First Half of June, 1348

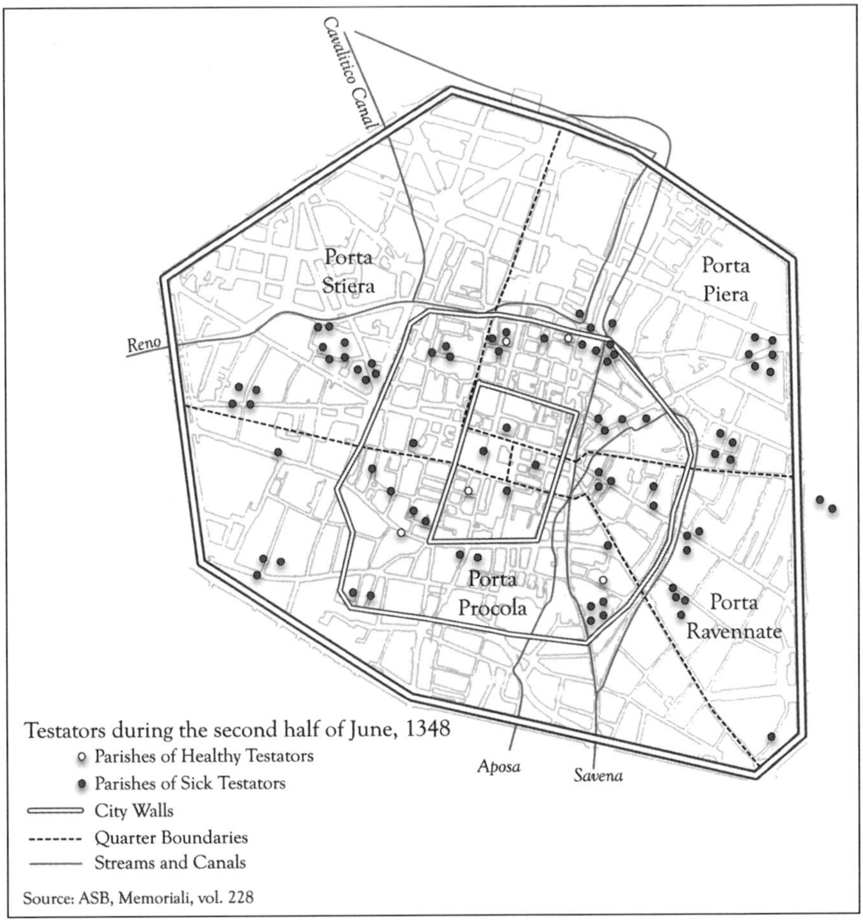

Testators During the Second Half of June, 1348

Tommaso del Mercato, and Santa Maria Maggiore, which were located near the main market. During the second half of June (the third map) there is more clustering in areas, such as the parishes around San Martino dell'Aposa, along the Savena canal along the second walls (San Biagio, San Tommaso della Braina) and the neighborhood of San Felice and San Nicolo di Porta Felice. Without a precise knowledge of the borders of the parishes it is difficult to know how close these households were.

During June more of the ill were located in the northern parishes, with Porta Piera holding the highest number. This is significant since the weekly market was located here and may have been a source of influx of the disease. The disease is divided equally between the two outer zones, that is, beyond the first set of walls. Again, the central city represents the minority (6 per cent) of all cases in June. For the first time three testators appear in the *guardia civitatis*, the broad suburban zone outside the city walls. By July the disease has spread all over the city: the 553 identified parishes of testators were evenly divided between north and south; 45 per cent are in the second zone, 40 per cent in the third zone, 9 per cent in the center, and 5 per cent in the *guardia civitatis*. These 553 testators lived in 79 per cent of all parishes, a remarkable increase from June when 52 per cent and May when 15 per cent of all parishes in the city were represented. From August there remain the wills of 183 testators with a parish. The representation of total parishes in the city drops back to 54 per cent, but there is a similar distribution of plague cases around the city by zone and quarter.[37]

As more people became ill, areas of Bologna not often represented in the testaments become visible. For example, there were six testators among the July wills who lived in the *guardia civitatis*, the broad suburban zone outside the third set of walls.[38] This was not part of an exodus of people from the city center, because, although one testator originally came from a village in the contado and two others had

[37] The percentage of cases in the early medieval nucleus rises to 12 per cent (22 cases), while the representation in the second zone (80 or 44 per cent) grows with respect to the third (65 or 36 per cent). There also appear 12 testators from beyond the third walls and four from towns in the contado.

[38] Also from this part of the city are one testator in August, two in September, and one in November.

earlier addresses within the city walls, all testators in the *guardia* were in their own homes.

The number of testators who came from locations outside of Bologna does increase throughout the summer. At first sight it appears that this may indicate flight from the contado into the city during plague (i.e., people fled their homes to come to town and dictate their last wills). However, a closer examination reveals that these were not newcomers from the contado, but Bolognese residents returning to town. The single example of movement into the town in June was a wealthy apothecary, originally from Bologna, but living in Venice, who made his will in the home of a notary whom he made his executor and heir.[39] Two of the three outsiders among the testators in July came from villages in the contado but were originally from Bologna. Both were healthy and had their wills made in a church.[40] The third, an unmarried woman from Varignana in the contado, had been living in the home of a widow in Bologna. Her ties to this household appear more than temporary since she made the widow her heir, left money for burial and masses in the local parish church, and drew witnesses from that parish and an adjacent one.[41] It is noteworthy that the widow remained in her home throughout the crisis, because one month later she had a codicil drawn up in her home.[42]

The situation does appear to be different in August when there is a much greater proportion of people from the contado who had come, apparently temporarily, into the city during the epidemic. These cases included a married couple from the nearby village of Borgo Panigale, with no apparent ties to Bologna, who made their wills together in a church while they were both sick, and another ill man from the contado who was guest in a home outside the city walls of Bologna. The fourth man who was from the contado but made his will in town was originally from Bologna, and his will was drawn up while he was healthy in a public location, viz., a notary's *statione*. Thus only three examples in August look like they may have been newcomers from the

---

[39] Mem, vol. 228, fol. 153v (will of Antonius fq Ugolini Bellondi on 10 June 1348).

[40] Mem, vol. 230, fol. 506r (Bertolomeus fq Turelli olim Alberti Zacarie, a citizen of Bologna originally from the parish of Santa Cristina della Fondazza, on 30 July) and vol. 229, fol. 112r (Johanna fq Federici de Sala, originally from the parish of Santa Maria delle Muratelle, on 15 July).

[41] Mem, vol. 229, fol. 75v (Gasdia fq Guidonis on 30 July 1348).

[42] Mem, vol. 230, fol. 120v (Mina fq Anthonini de Tabulis, codicil redacted on 29 August 1348).

contado with few demonstrable ties to the city (the kind of testators who could be indicative of flight, in this case into the town in order to escape plague that had abated in the city, but not in the countryside).

It is possible to check for flight out of town during the height of plague by examining the residence of testators whose wills were redacted in the contado. In the two *Provvisori* registers remaining from July appear the registrations of 132 wills that were redacted in 66 communities in the contado.[43] The *Provvisori* notaries did not always record a testator's parish, but the site of the redaction is given and this is usually noted as the testator's home. In fact, there are only three testators who had their wills drawn up by a notary in the contado who are identified as residents of Bologna.[44] Apart from a nobleman who came from Mantova, all other testators who had their wills made in the contado during the height of the epidemic were residents of the contado. Thus the evidence from wills drawn up in the contado also goes against notions of massive flight out of the town.

The wills drawn up in the town during the Black Death remain in much larger numbers than the contado and they strongly counter the notions of widespread flight and family abandonment. There were 976 wills registered in the *Provvisori* in the town during the plague months of June, July, and August.[45] Not all of these wills were eventually copied out into the *Memoriali*, since for that source there remain 913 testaments from the three months of plague. Instead of movement, these testaments demonstrate stability during the epidemic, because the vast majority were written up in the testators's own homes. Ninety-two of 134 *Memoriali* testaments of June had been drawn up at home. In July, 429 of 586 testators were in their homes. In August, 136 of 193 testators were in their homes or homes of their close family. The other places of

---

[43] The largest single group of testators in the contado were ten men and women from San Giovanni in Persiceto, followed by seven from San Lorenzo in Collina and five from Borgo Panigale. Most communities, however, produced only one or two testators during July.

[44] Provv. cart., registers 152, 153, no page numbers: Tommaso Petri Bernabe was from the parish of Santa Caterina di Saragozza, but dictated his will on 12 July in the house of ser Albertus, his heir, in Casalecchio di Reno; Bertolomeus Petri was a butcher from San Tomaso del Mercato who dictated his will in an acquaintance's house on 26 July in the village of Santa Maria in Duno; and, lastly, Nicolaus Ugutonis de Oxellis, declared that he came from the parish of San Michele, but he was in his own home in a village when he dictated his will at the end of July.

[45] The numbers are 324 for June, 463 for July, and 189 for August. See Bertram "Zweiter Teil," pp. 219–220.

redaction (in declining order) include inside mendicant convents, in parish churches, in homes attached to convents, at notaries's workshops (four in July and three in August), and in hospitals or homes belonging to a hospital (of which there are only one case in June and four in July). The thirty-five testators who deposited their wills with the Franciscans and Dominicans (the *Demaniale* wills) during the summer behaved differently. For these wills, only a minority each month were made at home: 4 of 16 in June, 6 of 29 in July, and 7 of 15 in August.[46] Instead, the testators writing secret wills were inside the mendicant houses, most commonly in the sacristy of the Franciscans, but occasionally in the sacristy and schools of the Dominicans, the chapel and choir of the Franciscans, even in the rooms of friars. It must be remembered that each of these 948 testators, whether they were in their homes or the mendicant houses, were surrounded by a small crowd of at least nine people: the notary, the presiding cleric, and seven witnesses who were usually laymen but in the case of the secret wills were normally friars. Because of the legal requirements of the testament, it appears extremely unlikely that so many could have been completed during a climate of general social breakdown. Thousands of individuals were needed in order to produce, register, and preserve these wills. Moreover, this group of testators was not a particularly unusual group, but were representative of a large section of the population, as the following analysis of the gender and social status of these testators reveals.

Gender and Plague

We have seen that the social activity of dictating a will—with the purpose of safeguarding the future of one's soul and one's loved ones—and the social activity of listening to those wishes was widespread geographically throughout the city. The high mortality from plague brought in people from all stages of life, except minors under the age of 25 who had not been emancipated from the *potestas* of their fathers.[47] Before the Black Death men were seldom widowers when they made their wills; only 1.3 per cent of the male testators in 1337 mentioned a deceased

[46] These numbers do not include the few wills of females (i.e. not secret wills) which were kept as copies by the mendicant houses.

[47] The percentage of testators who were emancipated children remained the same between 1337 and the plague months, viz., c. 0.5 per cent.

wife (although there could, of course, have been more of them who did not have reason to mention her). After plague entered, the percentage of men who were widowers rose to seven percent. The biggest change in testators, however, is the increased percentage of male to female wills. As explained in Chapter One, the number of women's wills in the *Memoriali* before the epidemic was very high, because men took advantage of the option of a secret will that was barred to women, whose wills had to be public record in the *Memoriali*. During the height of the epidemic, fewer men used this option and, instead, had their wills registered immediately in the *Memoriali*. The plague months of July, August, and September are closer to more familiar levels of female testation found in other Italian towns: women's wills are 42 per cent of the total for those three months. However, the percentage of women's wills in June (75 per cent) is higher than the pre-plague months or the later plague months, when more men were entering the record. It is possible, then, that women were the early victims of plague.[48] Exactly why this would be this case is not clear. Contrary to chronicles which generally state that plague affected all, young and old, men and women, Ole Benedictow proposes that women and children suffered "supermortality" because they remained inside more often (closer to rats).[49] The fact that women were the first victims in Bologna does not contradict Benedictow's argument based on a rat-borne disease, but since such supermortality did not continue beyond June, it does not corroborate it either.

[48] Reinhold Mueller surveyed chronicle literature to argue that more women than men died during the Black Death in Venice. See Reinhold Mueller, "Aspetti sociali ed economici della peste a Venezia nel Medioevo," in *Venezia e la peste 1348/1797* (Venice, 1979), pp. 71–76. The percentage of women's wills in June is as high in the better represented *Provvisori* examined by Bertram: 77 per cent of the 324 wills are women's. See Bertram, "Zweiter Teil," p. 219. The physician and professor of medicine at Naples, Giovanni della Penna, stated in his plague tract of 1348 that children and women died more than others. He added, however, that the elderly and the weak also suffered more, thus covering much of the population. Karl Sudhoff, "Pestschriften aus den ersten 150 Jahren nach der Epidemie des 'schwarzen Todes' 1348," *Archiv fur Geschichte der Medizin* 5 (1912), pp. 341–348. In fact, evidence from chronicles and plague tractates can be found for particularly heavy mortality among all classifications: rich and poor, young and old, men and women. When plague was in full force in 1348, it appears to have impacted all social groups. As post-Black Death art emphasized, death was an equal opportunity killer.

[49] Benedictow, *Black Death*, ch. 27, esp. pp. 266–268. His statistics on women's mortality are drawn from modern plague episodes.

Since women are almost always identified by their marriage status, as wife or widow, a more detailed picture of this gender emerges (see Figure 3.7). During the height of the epidemic in July, the testaments describe a broad cross-section of women: 35 per cent of female testators are wives, 37 per cent are widows, and 28 per cent are unmarried. Whereas unmarried women appear much less frequently as testators before the plague spread—they make up 11 per cent of female testators in the first five months—the widespread mortality brings them into the historical record more prominently. However, we see the results of the advance of plague in August and September when the percentage of widowed testators grows to 44 per cent and 67 per cent respectively. For the remainder of the year, the majority of female testators are widows, a telling reminder of the mortality at work.

Occupations and Plague

As illustrated in Table 1.1, the occupations of these testators are representative of people working in trades from all areas of the economy. For many shopkeepers and artisans leaving their workshops unattended

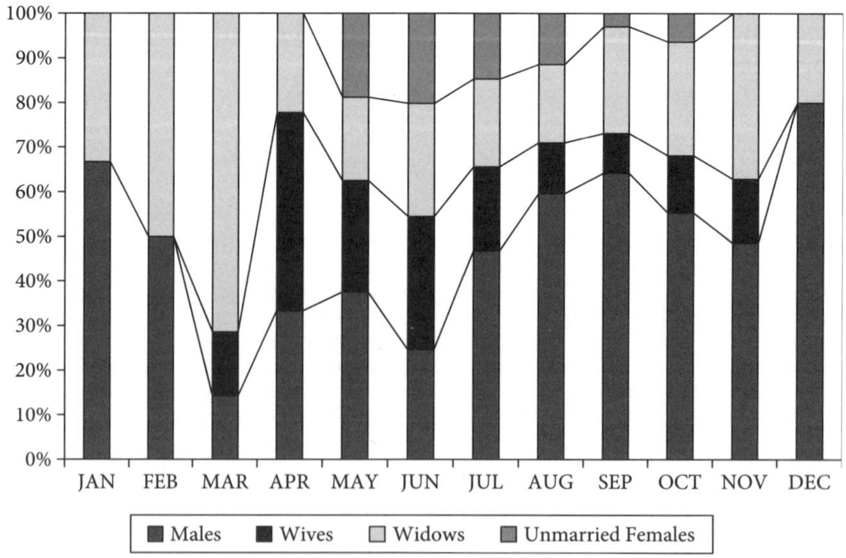

Figure 3.7 Percentiles of Male and Female Testators in the *Memoriali* of 1348

in order to flee the city may not have been an option. But for professionals, such as notaries and professors, flight may have been easier. Nevertheless, as we will see in the next chapter, the Bolognese were well served by notaries who stayed with their families during the Black Death. Some of Bologna's most famous citizens, the professors of the *Studium*, also stayed put. The law professor, Giovanni d'Andrea, died during the epidemic and was buried in the church of San Domenico, as noted in Bologna's chronicle. Despite the fact that his will does not appear in the *Memoriali* or the *Demaniale*, it is likely that he remained in the town. His son, Federicus, was also in town, since he made his will on 13 July.[50] Another son, Bonincontrus, survived the epidemic, and it is possible that he also stayed in Bologna, since he was nominated heir by Bazomeus fq Totti de Tossignano and offered his house for the redaction of this testament on 13 October.[51] His daughter, Bertolomea was married to Jacopo Bottrigari junior, who remained in town during the epidemic with his wife and baby daughter. He dictated his will on 18 July before ten men, including eight friars and a student (*scolaris in iure civilli*).[52]

The professor of law, Bonromeus de Suricis, whom the government had paid 50 *lire* on 17 March for lectures on civil law beginning in October, was also victim of plague.[53] He was dead by 10 July when his daughter made her will "in the home of the heirs of Bonromeus". The government may not have lost its money on another professor, Filinus de Barberiis who was paid 50 *lire* on 20 April for "extraordinary" (afternoon) lectures on the *Decretals* to begin in October.[54] He may have carried out his contract since he was still alive on 17 July, described as a *sapientissimus et eloquentissimus vir* though not as *doctor legum*, when his daughter made her will. The widow and daughter of another famous professor may have been early victims of plague, but members of this famous family also stayed in town. Bertolomea, daughter of the

[50] The will of Federichus olim bone memorie d. Johannis Andree decretorum doctoris is transcribed and published in Bertram, "Zweiter Teil," pp. 233–35.

[51] Mem, vol. 229, fol. 338r. Bonincontrus was beheaded in 1350 for conspiring to kill the lords of Bologna. For this and information about Giovanni d'Andrea see Bursellis, "Cronica gestorum ac factorum memorabilium civitatis Bononie edita a fratre Hyeronimo de Bursellis ab urbe condita ad a. 1497," A. Sorbelli, ed., *RIS*, vol. 23, pt. 2 (Città di Castello, 1911–1929), p. 43.

[52] See Chapter Two, pp. [] and footnote 97.

[53] Comune Governo, Riformagioni et Provvigioni, s. cartacea, II, 38, fols. 24r–25r.

[54] Ibid.

noble knight Tomas de Sassuolo and widow of the famous and knighted law professor Bonifacio Galluzzi who died in 1346, dictated her will at her home on 14 June. Ill, she designated her three daughters as heirs. Three days later one of those daughters, Bernardina, prepared her last will, leaving her inheritance to the brother and sisters of her husband, Guidotinus fq Francisci de Plantavignis, who is named as witness to a will on 24 July.[55] A final example is Paulus, son of the law professor Giovanni Guiberti, who appeared as witness on 25 April and again during the height of the epidemic on 27 June, while his sister Philippa made her will on 12 July.[56] Although she was married and living in a parish in the eastern quarter of Porta Ravennate, Philippa had returned to her father's house in San Barbaziano in the university zone to dictate her will. These examples show not only the strong familial connections of law and power in Bologna, but also that the faculty families themselves remained strong despite tragedy in the face of plague.

The land-owning elites would have been in a better position than most to flee to country homes, yet some of their most prominent members appear among the testators of June, July and August: men and women bearing the names Armi, Cavaleri, Garisendi, Lambertini, Magnani, Odofredi, Pepoli, Torelli and other aristocratic lineages. With them stayed their large households, including retainers, servants, and family members, who served as witness for their wills.[57] The nobility, as evidenced in the discussion of the Garisendi family below, aided their peers and clients since they appear in the wills as executors and witnesses in June, July, August, and September. One would expect non-noble people with occupations that supported landholding, such as butchers, to have been able to flee the city for the contado if they had wanted.[58] Again, we find them remaining in town as testators, witnesses, legatees, and executors.

---

[55] Mem, vol. 229, fols. 102v, 206v, 411r. The will of Bonifacio Galluzzi's widow reflects her social status by her provision for a tomb in San Domenico—a popular choice among Bologna's elite—and her selection of a Pepoli widow as executor. Her special ties to the Dominicans are revealed by the fact that she left them 25 *lire* and a bed for the infirmary of San Domenico, named two as executors, and was surrounded by four on her death bed. A copy of her will is preserved in the *Demaniale*.

[56] Mem, vol. 228, fols. 140r, 176r; vol. 230, fol. 326v.

[57] For example, the *familiar* of the noble knight, Nicolaus de Pepoli, appears as testator on 8 August (Mem, vol. 229, fol. 84v). Another of this knight's servants (*famulus*) is listed among the witnesses at the will of the wife of Ugolino Zengali de Pepolis on 29 July (Mem, vol. 229, fol. 201r). See also discussion of the Garisendi family below.

[58] Butchers often were owners of land beyond the walls, for they dealt in cattle, not simply the preparation of meat. See Pini, "Giacomo Casella". For example, see the testa-

Many of the town's inhabitants, nevertheless, remain invisible: the very poor, clergy, and students do not appear as testators. At least we know that many clergy—parish priests and friars—remained in town acting as principal witnesses at the bedsides of the ill. Testators left bequests to these men for "their necessities" and for the singing and or saying of masses *pro anima*. The students of the university may be a different case, as they were a more transient population. As discussed in Chapter One, they most likely made wills before coming to town to begin their studies—their lack of appearance among the testators is not due to poverty—and flight may have been a less vexing question for them.[59] Indeed, Pearl Kibre found that most students of the German nation left the town during the Black Death and Francis Aiden Gasquet cites a chronicle of Prague noting students who left Bologna to return home to Bohemia (only one made it).[60] As for the poor with no wealth to leave in a will, there seems no reason to assume that they would have left their friends, family, and neighbors in greater numbers than the portion of the populace revealed in the wills. Their exact identity and actions remain a mystery. Like the poor without wills who remain lost to us, we can only speculate that many potential testators died intestate due to the difficult circumstances of plague. Nevertheless, the many wills that remain reveal the actions of a significant part of the populace. While we can never hope to have every will that was made, the testators in the *Memoriali* are representative of much of Bolognese society.

Families During the Black Death

It could be argued that these testators had been abandoned by their families, even though they were served by notaries, priests, and neighbors

ment of the *macellator*, Jacobus fq Lamberti, who was ill during the epidemic and left bequests of land in the contado to charity (Mem, vol. 229, fol. 15r on 28 July 1348).

[59] Many of the students of Bologna were well-off and, thus, were a powerful stimulus to the economy. Other students, however, had taken orders and would not have left wills in the *Memoriali*. Alfonso D'Amato claims that a large part of the student population were Dominicans. See Alfonso D'Amato, *I Domenicani e l'Università di Bologna* (Bologna, 1988), pp. 125–134.

[60] According to Pearl Kibre, most of the students of the German nation had fled or died by mid-June of 1348. The rest met to elect a custodian to guard their possessions, while others left the city for the summer. See her *The Nations in the Medieval Universities* (Cambridge, Mass., 1948), p. 38. See also Francis Aiden Gasquet, *The Black Death of 1348 and 1349* (London, 1908), pp. 37–38. The few students who appear as witnesses will be discussed in the next chapter.

who acted as witnesses for the legal redaction of their wills. With such a large number of wills it is possible to identify connections of kinship among testators. The following tables represent this further magnification of our lens on the epidemic. Table 3.1 displays information on 56 testators whom I have been able to identify as spouses. They include nobles as well as artisans: a master carpenter, tailor, shoemaker, innkeeper, spice trader, two butchers, and a baker. Throughout the entire epidemic these couples stayed in town and at home even after the death of a spouse. The only woman who left her husband's home was an elite widow, Xina fq Jacobi de Foghariis who had moved to her sister's home in August.

No death records remain from Italian towns during this period, but by means of these wills it is possible to identify an antequam date of death for a few testators. The intervals between the appearance of an ill spouse and the certain death and possible infection of another range from as little as four days to three weeks to three months. There are two examples of testators who were healthy when they make their wills in Bologna at the end of July: the butcher, Mathiolus, and the noblewoman Ghita fq Lapi Schandici, wife of a member of the Pepoli family. When their respective spouses appear towards the end of the epidemic in August and November, these two testators were still alive. In fact, a testament made in the church of San Domenico on June 8 of 1362 for Ghita fq ser Lapi Schandici was registered in the *Provvisori* of that second year of plague.[61] Ghita and Mathiolus probably fled Bologna, after first ensuring that their wills be properly redacted by notaries in town. Both of these testators were members of a class that had access to land beyond the city walls. But these examples are the exception to the many other cases of noble, landowning families whose members became ill and died in the town. There are also two testators who were sick at the redaction of their wills but still appear alive at the time their spouses made their wills: Dolce lasted at least five days, and Caterina's husband was optimistic enough to name her as his heir three days later.

Table 3.2 contains the names of 12 parents and their 13 children that I have been able to identify among the testators. Sons and daughters who were *sui iuris*, i.e., no longer under their father's authority, had to be older than 12 years if female, 14 years if male.[62] If their father were alive,

[61] Provv. perg., reg. 30 (1362).
[62] Chiodi, "Rolandino e il testamento," p. 477.

Table 3.1 Testator Spouses During the Black Death

Date	Name	Site	Information
11 March	Ymelda fq ser Johannis Rubei	Home	Still alive on 27 August
27 August	ser Baldus fq Bonacurxii	Sacristy	Secret Will
1 May	Philippa fq Francisci de Blanchucis	Home	
26 June	Tomas Petri de Garisendis	Home	Brother is witness for other wills
30 May	Margarita fq Fratris Michaelis	Home	Dead by 29 June
29 June	Taurelus fq Gerardi de Taurellis	Home	
8 June	Figliocarius fq Fratris Donisdei, *cartolarius*	Home	Dead by 23 June
23 June	Ursolina fq Thomacis Ursii	Home	
13 June	Dolce fq Azolerii	Home	Alive on 18 June
18 June	Conteus fq Albertini, *magister lignaminis*	Home	
20 June	Pax fq ser Johannis, *salarolus*	Home	Dead by 15 July
15 July	Madalena fq Palmerii de Canzolis	Home	
21 June	Manina fq Bertolotti Morandi	Home	
21 June	Antonius fq Ugolini de Mataratiis	Home	
21 June	Francisca fq Jacobi	Home	Dead by 29 June
29 June	Johannes fq Azolini Strazavache, *calzolarius*	Home	
25 June	Benvenuta fq Christianii	Home	
25 June	Mantoanus fq Stephanii, *sartor*	Home	
2 July	Ursollina fq Lanfranchi de Muzollis	Home	Dead by 18 August
18 August	Johannes fq Johannis magistri Amadoris	Home	
3 July	Benvenuta fq Rolandi	Home	
3 July	Johannes fq Jacobi Capestrarii	Home	
6 July	Checha fq Loti	Home	Dead by 10 July
10 July	Petrutius fq Alberti, *hospitator*	Home	
6 July	Petrus fq Ser Ugolini de Condatis	Home	Dead by 2 August
2 August	Xina fq Jacobi de Foghariis	Sister	
9 July	Mixina fq domini Francisci Orandi	Neighbor	Dead within 4 days
13 July	Petrus fq Zanzi Martelli, *notarius*	Home	
9 July	Bona fq Leonardi Bertholli	Home	Dead by 8 September
8 September	Paulus fq Jacobi Spighei	Home	

Table 3.1 (*cont.*)

Date	Name	Site	Information
14 July	Pax olim Bonacose de Suricis	Home	Dead by 6 August
6 August	Ghixia fq domini Jacobini de Ripolli	Home	
15 July	Romaninus fq Philippi Dessiderii	Home	Dead by 6 August
6 August	Mixina fq Jacobi Chaxelle	Home	
17 July	Pagnolas fq Laurentii de Passarellis	Home	Dead by 26 July
26 July	Gixia fq Jacobi de Magnanis	Home	
17 July	Francesca fq Fellini de Barberiis	Home	Dead by 31 October
31 October	Bonbolognus fq Panichalis de Gato	Home	
20 July	Johannes fq Nicholai de Manellis	Home	Dead by 25 July
25 July	Egidia fq Jacobini de Guidizagnis	Home	
20 July	Zunta Lotti Sparini, *speciarius*	Home	Dead by 6 August
6 August	Nicoleta fq ser Zanii	Home	
29 July	Mathiolus fq Johannis Bonaguide, *becarius*	Home	Alive on 4 November
4 November	Jacoba fq Donellis	Home	
29 July	Caterina fq ser Beliotti	Home	Alive on 1 August
1 August	Guilielmus fq Benventi, *fornarius*	Home	
29 July	Ghita fq domini Lapi Schandici	Home	Alive on 29 August
29 August	Ugolinus fq domini Zengali de Pepolis	Home	Healthy
29 July	Phylippa fq Arardi	Home	Dead by 9 August
9 August	Philippinus fq Laurentii, *becarius*	Home	
3 August	Michaele fq Pirolli	Church	Both sick even though
3 August	Bertolomea fq Ture Padullis	Church	they are in a church
14 September	Orellus fq Bitini de Orellis	Home	Dead by 17 September
17 September	Agnesia fq Thomacis fq dmi Jacobi iudicis	Home	Brother is testator on same day
10 October	Guilielmus fq Nicholai Jacobini, *notarius*	Home	Dead by 17 November
17 November	Montina fq Pauli de Bonacaptis	Home	

(Mem, vols. 228, 229, 230 and Dem: San Francesco, Instr. and Camp. Rossi; San Domenico, Instr. and Misc.)

Table 3.2 Parents and Children Who Were Testators During the Black Death

Date	Relation	Status	Name	Parish	Site	Information
13 June	Daughter	Married	Caterina fq Johannis de Villanova	No parish recorded	Home	
20 Dec.	Mother	Widow	Adella fq Nicholai de Galutiis	S. Maria dei Galluzzi	Church	Sick, but in a church
14 June	Mother	Widow	Bertolomea fq Thomasini de Sasuollo	S. Andrea degli Ansaldi	Home	Widow of law professor
17 June	Daughter	Married	Bernardina fq Bonifacii de Galuciis	S. Donato		Daughter of law professor
30 June	Mother	Widow	Valente fq Nicholay de V[anis?]	S. Maria Maddalena	Domenican schools	Healthy
30 June	Daughter	Married	Clara fq Phylippi de Montanariis	S. Dalmazio	Domenican schools	Healthy
3 July	Daughter	Married	Malgarita fillia Ser Facioli fq Paganini	S. Felice	Father's home	
20 July	Father	Married	Faciolus fq Paganini	S. Felice	Home	
6 July	Mother	Married	Bexia fq Magistri Francisci	S. Bartolo	Home	Wife of napperer
11 July	Son	emancipated	Johannes filius Santi Lamberti	S. Bartolo	Home	Father alive
25 July	Son	emancipated	Bertholanus filius Santi Lamberti	S. Bartolo	Home of father	Father alive
7 July	Mother	Widow	Castelina fq Nicholai de Musollis	S. Tommaso del Braina	Home	Widow of law professor
17 Oct.	Daughter	Widow	Phylippa fq Mathei de Gandonibus	S. Tommaso del Braina	Home of brother	Widow of law professor
11 July	Mother	Widow	Bitixia fq Felloni de Bassacomatribus	S. Donato	Church next to altar	Healthy
11 July	Daughter	Widow	Beleza fq Bertolucii de Manticis	S. Donato	Church next to altar	Healthy
11 July	Mother	Widow	Roxa fq Juliani, widow of *selarius*	S. Martino dell'Aposa	Home	Dead by 8 September
8 Sept.	Daughter	Widow	Agnes fq Ugollini	S. Martino dell'Aposa	Home	*Pro anima* bequest for mother
19 July	Mother	Widow	Gexia fq Alberti de Picigotis	S. Maria del Turleone	Home	
22 July	Son	Unknown	Salamon fq Johannis de Cavaleriis	S. Maria del Tureone	Home	Dead by 4 August
26 July	Mother	Widow	Francesca fq Alberti de Santo Alberto	S. Cecilia	Home	Not in son's will
17 Sept.	Son	Single	Francescus fq Coradini de Santo Georgio	S. Donato	Home	
27 Oct.	Son	Unknown	Buvalinus fillius Alidoxii B. de Buvalellis	S. Cristoforo dei Geremei	Home of testator & father	Dead by 29 November
29 Nov.	Father	Widower	Alidoxius fq Buvalelli de Buvalellis	S. Cristoforo dei Geremei	Home	
17 Nov.	Daughter	Widow	Soldana fq Mathei de Malavoltis	S. Luca di Castello	Home	Alive on 27 November
27 Nov.	Mother	Widow	Lipa fq Francischi Guidocheri de Galuciis	S. Luca di Castello	Home	

(Source: Mem, vols. 228, 229, 230)

they must either no longer be a minor or emancipated. The fathers of all but three of the children listed here were dead. The daughter whose father was still alive was married, but she had returned to her father's home to dictate her last wishes (she did not need her husband's consent to make her will). The two sons of a living father were emancipated (and, thus, under age 25) and may have still been living with their father. It is hard to tell if all of these parents and children were living in the same household, nevertheless they remained closely connected as most children continued to live in the same parish as their parents. For example, Castelina Nicholai de Musollis, the widow of a professor of law, made her will in her home in the parish of San Tommaso della Braina. Her daughter, also a widow of a law professor, is found in the house of her brother in the same parish. Although Castelina, the mother, is noted as being in her own home, this may in fact be the same household as her son's, but in any case it is surely nearby.

The best example of a coherent household in the same spot is the family of Santus Lamberti, a napperer, whose wife and sons were testators in July. Here we have the touching example of Santus who remained alive and at home with his family as they all became ill and died through the month of July. His will does not appear in the *Memoriali* of 1348.[63] Another family is that of the communal *nuncius*, Cosolle Blaxii of the parish of Sant'Alberto. He appeared as witness to a will on 9 July, and his son, Blaxius fq Cosolle nuntii, appeared on 3 August for neighbors in San Leonardo. With *quondam* before his father's name, we learn from Blaxius that Cosolle had sickened and died not long after we first found him. His son may have taken over his duties during the epidemic since one will on 1 August notes that the *crida* was carried out by *nuncius* Blaxius. In any case this family remained in town, together through illness and death, as we learn from the will of Cosolle's widow, Catillia fq Lipi, on 18 August. She made as universal heirs their children, Blaxius and Malgarita. Another daughter, Bertolomea, who was still a child (*pupilla etate*), was granted a house, which she presumably would have used for her dowry.

Lastly, I have identified 33 groups of sibling testators (Table 3.3) from the months of plague, as well as three other groups of siblings

[63] Mem, vol. 229, fol. 87r (Bertholanus filius Santi on 25 July 1348); vol. 230, fols. 328r (Johannes filius Santi on 11 July 1348), 449r (Bexia fq magistri Francisci on 6 July 1348).

Table 3.3 Sibling Testators During the Black Death

Date	Name	Parish	Site	Information
15 June	Philippa fq Marchi de Albergatis	S. Lorenzo P.S.	Home	Alive on 16 June, heir of sister
16 June	Bitina fq Marchi de Albergatis	S. Lorenzo P.S.	Home	
16 June	Mina fq Cavalleri de Cavalleriis	S. Bartolo	In son's home	Not in brother's will
4 Aug.	Bonbollogus fq Cavalleri de Cavalleriis	S. Maria del T.	In home of uncle's heirs	
18 June	Bertolacia fq Johannis de Sancto Alberto	S. Martino A.	In Carmelite sacristy	Alive and healthy on 26 June
26 June	Francescus fq Johannis de Sancto Alberto	S. Martino A.	In home of unrelated man	
3 Aug.	Petrus fq Johannis de Sancto Alberto	S. Martino A.	Home	Healthy; does not mention siblings
18 June	Bertolomea fq Johannis Castellani	S. Martino A.	Home	Not in brother's will
13 Aug.	Jacobus fq Johannis Castellani	S. Martino A.	Home	
19 June	Chatellina fq Francisci de Artunixiis	S. Stefano	In San Francesco	Healthy; cousin also testator in 1348
19 June	Zanna fq Francisci de Artunixiis		In San Francesco	Healthy
20 June	Margarita Facioli		Home	Named her sister as universal heir
10 July	Chatellina fq Ture Facioli	S. Leonardo	Home	
22 June	Francescus fq Jacobini Caprarie	S. Tommaso B.	Home	Not in brother's will
8 July	Ugolinus fq Jacobuci Caprarie	S. Tommaso B.	Home	
25 June	Egidius fq Auliverii Egidii de Scudellis	S. M. Maggiore	Home	Not in sister's will
13 July	Margarita fq Auliverii Egidii de Scudellis	S. M. Maggiore	Home	
26 June	Caterina fq Nicholai Johannis Pellachanis	S. Martino A.	In friend's home in S. Cec.	
14 July	Margharita fq Nicholai de Pellachanis	S. Biagio	In friend's home in S. Cec.	
1 July	Bitixia fq Thome de Tencharariis		Home	Dead by 16 July
16 July	Bertolomea fq Thome de Tencharariis		In home of female friend	
2 July	Dominicus fq Rodulfi Rolandi	S. Vitale	In home of brother-in-law	Not in sister's will
25 July	Chatellina fq Rodulfi Rolandi	S. Michele L.	Home	

Table 3.3 (*cont.*)

Date	Name	Parish	Site	Information
3 July	Petrus fq Bertoluci de Minarolis	S. Siro	In sacristy, San Francesco	Secret will; alive on 11 July
11 July	Zacharias fq Bertholuci de Munarolis	S. Siro	In chapel, San Francesco	Secret will
5 July	Vivianus fq magistri Amodei	S. Nicolo Albari	Witness for testament	
13 July	Johannes fq magistri Amodei	S. Nicolo Albari	Home	
7 July	Jacoba fq Johannis olim Dominici	S. Michele L.	Home	Daughter of farrier
7 July	Belda fq Johannis olim Dominici	S. Michele L.	Home	Daughter of farrier
8 July	Mengonus fq Fratris Ugolini, *strazarius*	S. Biagio	Home	Dead by 25 July
25 July	Petrobellus fq Fratris Ugolini, *strazarius*	S. Biagio	Home	
9 July	Bertus fq magistri Guarneni [Guarneri?]	S. Alberto	Home	Not in brother's will
10 July	Maxolinus fq magistri Guarnini [Guarneri?]	S. Alberto	Home	
9 July	Mina fq Stephani	S. Egidio	Home	Not in brother's will
1 Aug.	Dominicus fq Stephani	S. Egidio	Home	
9 July	Johannes fq Mathyolli Martelli, *spezarius*		Home	Not in brother's will
26 July	Bertolomea fq Mathyoli Martelli	S. Lorenzo P.S.	Home	Not in brother's will
7 Aug.	Franciscus fq Mathioli Martelli	S. Martino C.	Home	
11 July	Johannes fq Jacobini Aioli, *beccharius*	S. Tommaso M.	Home	Not in sister's will
20 July	Mandina fq Jacobini Aioli	S. Tommaso M.	Home	
11 July	Betixia fq d. Felloni de Baxacomatribus	S. Donato	In church of San Giacomo	Not in sister's will
31 July	Ghisutia fq d. Feloni de Baxacomatribus	No parish	In home of female friend	
12 July	Johanna fq ser Partis de Stupa	S. Domenico	Home	Dead by 15 July
15 July	Daxia fq ser Petris de Stupa	S. Domenico	Home	

Table 3.3 (*cont.*)

Date	Name	Parish	Site	Information
13 July	dopnus Thomas fq Jacobi Bonandi, *rector*	S. Tommaso B.	In a home of parish church	Not in sister's will. She is his heir.
18 July	Agnexia fq Jacobi Bonandi	S. Tommaso B.	In a home of parish church	Her daughter is her heir
14 July	Francisca fq Zanini Ugutionis	S. Lucia	Home	Widow of tailor; brother of notary
17 July	Margarita fq Zanini Ugutionis	S. Bartolo	Home	Sister of notary active in epidemic
3 Aug.	Tomas fq Zanini Ugutionis	S. Tommaso B.	Home	Brother of notary active in epidemic
15 July	Jacobus fq Ducii	S. Leonardo	Home	
15 July	Dominicus fq Ducii	S. Leonardo	Home	
15 July	Petrus fq Francisci Sanuti	S. GiuseppeB.G.	In home of unrelated man	He is *ministrale*; alive on 22 July
22 July	Jacobus fq Francisci Sanuti	S. GiuseppeB.G.	In sacristy, San Francesco	He is notary and *civis*
15 July	Johanna fq Federici de Sala	In the contado	In church of S. Lorenzo	Healthy; not in sister's will
5 Sept.	Fiona Federici de Salla	S. Antonino	Home	
16 July	Dana fq Mei de Sabadinis	S. Michele L.	Home	Not in sister's will
23 July	Anthonia fq Mei de Sabadinis	S. Michele L.	Home	
18 July	Symolinus fq Zonis	S. Leonardo	Home	Same notary redacted both wills
18 July	Johannes fq Zonis	S. Leonardo	Home	
18 July	Marina fq Fratris Jacobi de Ronpollis	S. Mamolo	Home	Not in brother's will
20 July	Cristoforus fq Fratris Jacobi de Rompollis	S. Mamolo	In home of father's heirs	
22 July	Flora fq Belli Bernardini	S. Stefano	In home of brother	Not in brother's will; niece is testator
7 Aug.	Bernardinus fq Belli Bernardini	S. Stefano	In home of unrelated man	
28 July	magstr. Thomaxinus fq magistri Lanzallocti	S. Donato	Home	Not in brother's will
13 Sept.	Zacharias fq Lanzalocti	S. Tommaso B.	In home of female friend	

Table 3.3 (*cont.*)

Date	Name	Parish	Site	Information
29 July	Bonvixinus fq Johannis Bonvixini, *notar.*	S. Tommaso M.	At *palatium vetus*	Dead by 25 August
25 Aug.	Giullius fq Johannis Bonvixini, *notarius*	S. Tommaso M.	Home	
29 July	Ghita fq Lapi Schandici	S. Maria di P.R.	Home	Not in brother's will; Pepoli wife
19 Sept.	Johannes fq Lapi	S. Biagio	In home of unrelated man	Employed by the Pepoli family
31 July	Bexia fq Zacharie de Conselminis	S. Damiano	In San Domenico	Healthy; but not in sister's will
6 Aug.	Gesia fq Zacharie de Conselminis	S. Andrea A.	Home	
9 Aug.	Nicholas Lanze de Garisendis	S. Donato	Home	Not in brother's will
15 Aug.	Johannes Lanze de Garisendis	S. Donato	Home	
9 Aug.	Bexia fq Azonis fq Petri de Lambertinis	S. Tecla	Home	Not in brother's will
5 Sept.	Giulius fq Azonis qd Petri de Lambertinis	S. Cataldo dei L.	In home of uncle	
15 Aug.	Malgarita fq ser Johannis	S. Andrea A.	In home of husband's heirs	Not in sister's will
23 Sept.	Luchisia fq ser Johannis	S. Colombano	Home	Widow of notary
1 Sept.	Fixia fq Pauli de Bonacatis	S. Tommaso M.	In Carmelite church	Healthy; alive on 17 Nov.
17 Nov.	Montina fq Pauli Jacobi de Boncaptis	S. M. Masc.	Home	Husband, sister-in-law also testators
17 Sept.	Jacobus fq Thomacis fq Jacobi, *iudex*	S. Cristoforo S.	Home	
17 Sept.	Agnesia fq Thomacis fq Jacobi	S. Cristoforo S.	Home	
1 Oct.	Johanna fq Albertini de Libris	S. Martino A.	Home	Notary's wife; not in brother's will
22 Nov.	Francholus fq Alberti de Libris	S. Martino A.	Home	

(Mem, vols. 228, 229, 230; Dem: San Francesco, Instr, Camp. Rossi; San Domenico, Instr, Misc.)

who made their wills in September, October, or November when the epidemic had died down. The conclusions that may be drawn from this list are similar to what was highlighted for the spouses and parents and children. These family members were from the elite, such as brothers of the leading Garisendi and Lambertini families, and from non-elite families, such as two sisters of a farrier and the children of a mercer. Most siblings, whether single, married, or widows, lived in the same households or locations in the same parish. They remained with their family and kinship groups in their homes in town during all three months of plague. Here, again, is evidence of intact households with sick siblings making their wills together on the same day or within a few days of each other.[64] There is also evidence of households enduring and remaining cohesive over time, since we find siblings who made their wills in the same location, but over a space of time. Nearly all the testators who were not in their homes when they made a will were healthy and had gone to a church to dictate their will. These few examples do not indicate broad dispersal of family members during the Black Death.

It is harder to assess whether or not a testator was alive from information in his or her sibling's will, since siblings were less likely to name each other in their wills and one's identity did not include the name of one's siblings. Nevertheless, four male and female testators can be determined to have died within a month of the redaction of their testament, and, despite the death of that close family member, the other sibling had remained at home, to later fall ill and dictate his or her own will (as seen in the initial example of the clothes dealers of San Biagio, Mengonus and Petrobellus). The examples of these connected individuals can be linked to further larger networks of relatives, of which I have been able to identify only a few: extant in the *Memoriali* are the testaments of a cousin, of two brothers-in-law, of a sister-in-law, of a niece, and of two husbands of testators who appear on this list of siblings.

Further connections of family members staying united throughout the epidemic can be traced from two brothers of the noble Garisendi

[64] For example, Jacoba and Belda, daughters of the late Johannes Dominici, a farrier, were at home on 7 July. Jacobus, a judge, living in San Cristoforo di Saragozza made his will on the same day, and perhaps in the same household, as his married sister, Agnesia. One notary came to the house of two brothers living in San Leonardo to write their wills during the middle of the epidemic on 18 July.

family in Table 3.3, whose members make several appearances in the wills. An early victim was Philippa de Blanchuciis, wife of Thomas Petri de Garisendis. She made her will at her home in May, while her husband made his in June, providing land for their two daughters, naming his brothers as heirs, and leaving a small bequest to a physician's assistant for medication (*pro medicinis et alliis receptis*).[65] Later during the epidemic appear two brothers of the knightly branch of this family, the noblemen Nicolaus and Johannes, sons of the deceased knight Lanza de Garisendis, and residents of the parish of San Donato. Nicolaus was first to succumb to plague, making his will on 9 August. He named Johannes and another brother Tanus as universal heirs. Johannes soon fell ill and on 15 August made his will to nominate Tanus.[66] Five men from other branches of the Garisendi family were at the side of Johannes, joining men of the aristocrat Plantavigni and Cavaleri families. Their brother, Paulus fq Lanze de Garisendis, was probably with them through the epidemic, since he was named as executor by a noble widow on 8 July.[67] This was the same day of the redaction of the will of Romeus de Garisendis's widow, who resided in the same parish as Johannes and Nicolaus.[68] From a different branch, Garisendus fq Johannis de Garisendis was made an executor and guardian for the children of another nobleman at the end of July.[69] Several members of the branch of Petrus de Garisendis appear as testators during May and June or as witnesses to wills of their neighbors or relatives in August and September.[70] The last Garisendi member to appear in 1348 was the widow of Ugollinus Ugoletti de Garisendis who made her will in October.

Of the leading family of Bologna, the Pepoli, there is also evidence of some stability during the crisis of plague. Although we have seen that

[65] Mem, vol. 228, fols. 291v, 309v.

[66] Mem, vol. 229, fol. 24v (Nicholaus fq Lanze de Garisendis on 9 August 1348 and Johannes fq Lanze de Garisendis on 15 August 1348).

[67] Mem, vol. 229, fol. 204v (Pelegrina fq Albucii de Sancto Petro on 8 July 1348).

[68] Mem, vol. 230, fol. 105r (Francisca fq Benedicti on 8 July 1348).

[69] Mem, vol. 229, fol. 89v (Allvixius fq Petri de Boitis named Garisendus fq Johannis de Garisendis as executor and guardian on 30 July 1348).

[70] Mem, vol. 229, fol. 88v (Brandelixius fq Petri de Garisendis was witness for his neighbor on 17 September and for his cousin, Johannes fq Lanze de Garisendis on 15 August); vol. 229, fol. 309v and vol. 228, fol. 291v (Tomas fq Petri de Garisendis was testator on 26 June and his wife, Philippa fq Francisci de Blanchuciis was testator on 1 May); vol. 228, fol. 143r (the wife of Montus fq Petri de Garisendis, redacted on 13 June 1348).

Ghita Lapi Schandici, wife of Ugolinus fq Zengali Pepoli, may have left town, other members of minor branches can be identified as present in the city during the summer months of plague. Ghita's husband made his will on 29 August and Nicolaus fq Andreae de Pepollis opened his home as the site for the redaction of two wills in July and August. He was also the legatee of another testator from his parish in July.[71] Other Pepoli from branches different from the governing line of Romeo and Tadeo Pepoli were testators during the summer months of plague. The only member of the ruling line to appear in the testamentary record was Juliana, daughter of the "celebrated" Romeo Pepoli, who dictated her will in November after the epidemic had subsided.[72] The *signori*, Giovanni and Giacomo, do not figure in the testaments and, as will be noted in Chapter Four, their presence during the Black Death is hard to determine, even though their government continued to function.

Plenty of other not so famous Bolognese had certainly stuck it through, and their webs of connections can be pieced together to fill out the picture of stability during the Black Death. If one looks beyond the testators to their relatives and witnesses, one can tease out many more examples of couples and siblings remaining during the epidemic. For example, as noted above, the town crier, Cossole fq Blaxii of the parish of Sant'Alberto stood as witness for an unmarried woman, Mina fq Stephani, who lay ill on 9 July in the neighboring parish of Sant'Egidio. Cossole was dead by the time his widow made her will on 18 August.[73] Mina, his neighbor, probably died within a few weeks of making her will, because we have her brother's last wishes dictated on 1 August in the same parish as his sister.[74] Beyond the immediate family, more distant kin can be found supporting each other during the worst of the summer. For example, Flore fq Belli Bernardini of the parish of Santo Stefano lay ill on 21 July. The next day her brother, Bernardinus, also of Santo Stefano was witness to the will of their niece, who was married and living in the same parish. Bernardinus remained in town, despite the death of his sister, fell ill, and made his will on 7 August.[75] These

[71] See references for Pepoli in Chapter Two, footnotes 111–113.

[72] Mem, vol. 230, fol. 386r (Juliana olim bone memorie domini Romei de Peppolis on 14 November 1348).

[73] Mem, vol. 229, fol. 109r (Catilia fq Lipi on 18 August 1348).

[74] Mem, vol. 229, fol. 326r (Dominicus fq Stephani on 1 August 1348).

[75] Mem, vol. 229, fol. 2v (Lippa filia Petri olim ser Belli Bernardini on 22 July 1348); vol. 230, fols. 117v and 169v (Bernardinus fq Belli Bernardini on 7 August 1348 and Flore fq Belli Bernardini on 21 July).

families were together and died at the height of plague, but others managed to survive, despite the danger. For example, Nicolaus Johannis Trufarari, a butcher in the parish of Santa Maria del Torleone, made his will on 13 July. His brother, Leonardus, lived in the same parish and worked in the same trade. Though Nicholaus testated ill during the height of the epidemic, Nardus was active in aiding his neighbors on 10 August as a witness for the daughter of a doctor in his parish and after the worst had passed, on 17 October, as witness for the daughter of a law professor, a resident of the adjacent parish.[76] The examples can be multiplied.

This chapter has described the social experience of the Black Death, moving from the aggregate display of the behavior of the populace to tracking the whereabouts of individual family members and their relatives, to argue that, despite the unquestionable horror and severity of the epidemic, medieval society remained intact. This detailed description was made possible by the efforts of notaries, priests, and friars who enabled the production and preservation of testaments during the Black Death. There was a great social effort made to ensure the dictation and perpetuation of last wishes. We will now turn our attention to these men of public faith.

[76] Mem, vol. 229, fols. 29r (Johanna fq magistri Jacobi Bonbaroni on 10 August 1348), 83r (Phylippa filia olim bone memorie domini Mathei de Gandonibus legum doctoris on 17 October 1348); vol. 230, fol. 503v (Nicolaus fq Johannis Trufarari on 13 July 1348).

CHAPTER FOUR

PUBLIC PERSONS DURING THE BLACK DEATH

The previous chapter demonstrated that in Bologna the family remained intact and resilient in the face of plague. The investigation of notarial acts made by individuals for private purposes allowed us to enter into the homes of Bolognese and follow family members throughout the epidemic. Because notarial acts permeated all aspects of daily life and required the cooperation of individuals in addition to the transacting parties of the act, these records can also provide evidence on public life during the epidemic. This chapter examines the activities of public men whose professions involved serving the populace and maintaining public order: men of the law and state, such as government officials, judges, and notaries; practitioners of medicine; the clergy; and parish officials or *ministrales cappellarum*. This investigation of the public response to the epidemic will begin by analyzing the more commonly used records, viz. governmental deliberations, but the principal means of analysis will be to use notarial records to find evidence of what public men did during the Black Death.

As in the previous chapter, the information from notarial acts stands in contrast to that of literary accounts of the actions of public officials during the epidemic. Contemporary Italian authors bitterly lamented the behavior of men of the church and law during the Black Death. In the Introduction to the *Decameron*, Boccaccio initially explained that the Florentine government took steps to remove garbage and prevent infection, but then claimed chaos and anarchy prevailed, stating that no law, either of man or God, held during the epidemic. Michele da Piazza's account of the Black Death in Sicily states that "many Messinese looked to make confession of their sins and to make their wills, but priests, judges, and notaries refused to visit them, and if anyone did visit their houses, whether to hear confession or draw up a will, they were soon sure to die themselves".[1] The *Storie Pistoresi* declared that

[1] *Cronaca* of Michele da Piazza translated in Horrox, *The Black Death*, p. 36.

friars and priests could not be found to serve the sick or bury the dead.[2] Doctors come under severe criticism in these accounts. Agnolo di Tura del Grasso of Siena presented a typical account: "no medicine nor any other remedy worked, and the more remedies were administered, the sooner the victims died".[3] Matteo Villani claimed that the physicians of Florence "had neither explanation nor cure through natural philosophy, or through medicine, or through astrology. Some, in order to make a profit, paid visits and gave their explanations. These showed by their deaths that their art was feigned and not real".[4] Boccaccio's Introduction is emphatic on the inadequacy of medical advice during the Black Death.[5]

As argued in the last chapter, the history of the Black Death should not rest on these accounts, since there is evidence within them that contradicts their claims of abandonment of duty and because the biases and moral intentions of these authors are clear. For example, Michele da Piazza, a Franciscan, wished to draw attention in his report to the exceptional behavior of the mendicants who did visit the sick and died in large numbers as a result. It is possible to go beyond the problematic chronicle sources with information drawn from wills. There are abundant references to the whereabouts and activities of notaries and clergy during the epidemic in the testaments of the *Memoriali* and *Demaniale* of 1348 simply because the presence of these men was necessary in

---

[2] "[N]on si trovava chi volesse servire nullo malato né portare morto a sepoltura né frate né prete che andare vi volesse" in "Storie Pistoresi," p. 235.

[3] "Cronaca Senese di Agnolo di Tura del Grasso," p. 555 translated by Benjamin Kohl in *Major Problems in the History of the Italian Renaissance* (Lexington, Mass., 1995), p. 50.

[4] *Cronica di Matteo Villani a miglior lezione ridotta coll'aiuto de' testi a penna*, ed. Ignazio Moutier (Florence, 1825), 1:8–9.

[5] "A cura delle quali infermità né consiglio di medico né virtú di medicina alcuna pareva che valesse o facesse profitto." Marchionne di Coppo Stefani, writing after Boccaccio, stated that physicians charged exorbitant prices and kept their distance from the patient: "Medici non si trovavano, perocchè moriano come gli altri; quelli che si trovavano, voleano smisurato prezzo in mano innanzi che intrassero nella casa, ed entratovi, tocavono il polso col viso volto adrieto, e' da lungi volevano vedere l'urina con cose odorifere al naso" in Marchionne, "Cronica," p. 230. Petrarch famously attacked doctors in his *Invectiva contra medicum* completed in 1353. This is a forceful invective attacking medicine for its pretensions to rhetorical and philosophical learning, but it is not directed at doctors's activities during the Black Death. Rather it is the result of an affront from an individual doctor called to cure the pope. See Conrad H. Rawski, "Notes on the Rhetoric in Petrarch's *Invectiva contra medicum*," in *Francis Petrarch, Six Centuries Later: A Symposium*, ed. Aldo Scaglione (Chapel Hill and The Newberry Library, Chicago, 1975), 249–277, especially, pp. 249–252.

order to create a valid will. Other important men of public service, namely, physicians and the parish leaders or *ministrales cappellarum*, also appear in the wills when they came to aid the townspeople. Notarial acts allow an investigation of the actions of a few officials during the epidemic and are used here to supplement the legislative records that remain. This chapter begins by examining the response of the government to plague, which has always been a principal subject of scholarly investigation, and then adds new material to the historiography of the Black Death with a reconstruction of the activities of notaries, doctors, clergy, and lastly neighborhood officials during the epidemic.

Government Response

Most examinations of the Black Death in Europe have focused on the response of rulers to the epidemic. Early Italian studies based on legislation revealed cities that responded aggressively to disaster. The best documented example is the Ordinances of Pistoia edited by Alberto Chiappelli in 1895. Early in the year Pistoia set up a committee of men to oversee public health and repress plague (section I of the ordinances). They prohibited the entrance into Pistoia of persons or goods from infected areas, requiring that cloth from these areas or from the infected had to be burnt in the piazza (section II). For disposal of the dead wooden coffins were to be used and placed in deep graves without groups of mourners or the accompaniment of bells or public announcements (sections III–XII). The last and lengthiest part of the ordinances dealt with butchers who were closely regulated and tanners who were banned from inside the city walls to prevent the spread of miasma from rotten meat (*ut fetor et putredo hominibus obesse non possit*) (sections XIII–XXII).[6] As the epidemic grew in intensity, the rulers of Pistoia added more specifics to the regulations on meat, animals, and burials—never abandoning their main principles—in May and June. Beyond Pistoia in Tuscany, Francesco Carabellese related that already in January Pisa prohibited people from Genoa or Catalonia from entering town and issued banns proclaiming similar sanitary measures concerning animals, butchers, and tanners. In Lucca in March the government ordered a new hospital to be built and doctors be provided with stipends to administer

[6] Chiappelli, "Gli ordinamenti sanitari," pp. 7–19.

to its citizens. The legislative records are missing from mid March to mid June, but begin again later in June and July to demonstrate the Lucchese government's concern with replacing officials, overseeing the principal hospital, and garnering funds. The Florentine situation was very similar: banns were proclaimed in January that sanitary laws were to be strictly followed and enforced. Pisans and Genoese were prohibited entrance, cloth of the infected was to be burned or thrown in the Arno, the sale of fish and meat was regulated, and prostitutes had to leave the city (here the Florentine government was apparently following the general belief held by doctors and laymen alike that whatever the physical cause of the epidemic the ultimate cause was divine anger over human sin). These banns were reissued several times into May. After examining the fragmentary records of the councils's meetings during the epidemic, Carabellese concluded that the Florentine rulers were far from apathetic and that, despite Boccaccio's assertion to the contrary, there was no anarchy during the Black Death.[7] Studying governmental records in 1909 Mario Brunetti reached similar conclusions for the experience of the epidemic in Venice where the Great Council of Venice passed legislation in April, May, and June that regulated burials, restricted entry, and promoted sanitation.[8]

More recent studies, based on the remaining records of communal council meetings, produced different conclusions arguing for an apathetic attitude or, at best, inactivity of officials. William Bowsky found that after plague entered Siena in the spring the city council recessed courts and halted its regular sessions from June till mid August.[9] It appears they did not pass any legislation that attempted to counteract or prevent plague. Apart from a council meeting on 13 June to allocate funds for the sick poor, governmental reaction came only later in the year, after the epidemic had died down, when the Nine were concerned with recouping revenues and personnel. Similarly, Élisabeth Carpentier found frustratingly little evidence for the government in Orvieto, which held brief sessions during the months of plague that did nothing other

[7] Carabellese, *La peste del 1348.* For information on the Lucchese situation, pp. 38–39, Carabellese draws on the work of Salvatore Bongi, *I bandi lucchesi del secolo decimoquarto* (Bologna, 1863).

[8] Brunetti, "Venezia durante la peste," pp. 291–294.

[9] William Bowsky, "The Impact of the Black Death upon Sienese Government and Society," *Speculum* 39 (1964), p. 14.

than confirm the appointment of replacement officials. As in Siena, action happened only at the end, when financial concerns took hold and motivated new efforts by the state.[10]

For Bologna, there remains for 1348 no legislation promulgated to counteract the effects of the epidemic on their city. We should not take this as evidence of apathy however. Carabellese stressed for Tuscany that we should not expect new legislation during the epidemic, because communes had laws on the books since the late thirteenth century that dealt with sanitation. As he demonstrated for Tuscany, during the epidemic governments merely turned to laws on public hygiene that had been affirmed and reaffirmed in multiple statutory redactions since the thirteenth century.[11] Bologna was well equipped—for the times—with major legislation on sanitation promulgated since the 1250s.[12] The most likely scenario is that the government of Bologna under the leadership of the Pepoli brothers ordered that banns be proclaimed reasserting the commune's standard sanitary legislation. Instead of legislation we must examine the actions of governmental officials. We begin with the Pepoli lords and their chancery or *curia dominorum*, then move to the judges of the offices of the *podestà*, and lastly to the public criers of banns or *nuncii*.

When Taddeo Pepoli came to power as *signore* in 1337 he disbanded the Consiglio del Popolo of the commune and passed its legislative, executive, and administrative functions directly to his lordship. Instead of communal *riformagioni*, the principal tools of government for Taddeo and his sons were the citizen petitions, or *suppliche*, and the signorial decrees, or *provvigioni*, issued in response. There remain today from 1348 three registers of the lords's *provvigioni* and a few registers of the *suppliche*, organized as approved or rejected, as well as many of the original petitions collected unbound on separate *carte*. The number of petitions dropped drastically, but did not disappear, during the

[10] Élisabeth Carpentier, *Une ville devant la peste: Orvieto et la peste noire de 1348* (Paris, 1962), pp. 124–132.

[11] Carabellese, *La peste del 1348*, pp. iv–v.

[12] Book Ten of the statutes of 1288 is dedicated to public sanitation including the regulation of butchers and fishmongers: Fasoli and Sella, *Statuti*, 2:129–173. On thirteenth-century measures on sewage and water control, refuse collection, etc. see Bocchi, *Il Duecento*, pp. 57–69.

epidemic.[13] These records demonstrate that government continued to function throughout the entire year, since *provvigioni* were issued each month of the year even during the height of the epidemic.

After plague arrived the lords issued decrees (*providerunt, statuerunt et decretaverunt*) on at least eight different days throughout May, on five days in June, on five days in July and on eight days in August, followed by fewer occasions from September through November. Most of the decrees do not directly deal with the crisis at hand, i.e. they do not address the prevention of epidemic disease. Many instead were issued for the cancellation of criminal banns on individuals, including an exceptional decree of 29 August that cancelled the banishments of 95 men. The other principal concerns were the sale of property, especially dotal, and the administration of guardianship (again, usually concerning sale of property).

The epidemic is mentioned only four times, in decrees that either remit tax collection or allow guilds to assemble despite low enrollment. These decrees do not begin with the usual formula "having heard a petition the tenor of which is... the lords decree", but instead provide a rare eloquent statement about the gravity of the situation (thus furnishing the opening quotation of this book). The words of the decree on 24 August that "considering the divine judgement of mortality in this year throughout the world and especially in Bologna, never before seen on earth" were repeated on 4 September and 31 October for remission of tax collection because, the decrees state, it had been impossible for the tax collectors (*conductores*) to carry out their duties. On 2 November, because of "the immense mortality in the city, contado, and district of Bologna" the lords allowed all guilds, but especially those of the notaries, to meet (*coadunari et congregari*) despite low numbers.

Although the records state that the lords made the decrees, there is very little indication of their presence. Nearly every decree includes a marginal notation indicating the party who presented the petition (*ad instantiam*) and the chancery notary who authorized it (*auct. per*). Most decrees were authorized by Egidius de Tebaldis and Richardus de Fantuciis, who were clearly the principal actors in the *curia* and carried out their duties throughout the year. Egidius and Richardus

[13] The numbers in one register of petitions go from a high of 54 in March, 20 in April and May, 10 in June and 6 in July. After that, the numbers pick up again starting at 19 in August. ASB, Provigioni cartacee, Signoria Pepoli, reg. 36.

with their colleagues of the *curia* formed the nerve center of the signorial government. The chancery came under extreme strain, but never totally abandoned its functions. According to one of the registers of *provvigioni*, two notaries of the *curia* died during 1348, but they were replaced almost immediately.[14]

The register containing lists of salaries paid to city officials demonstrates that all the offices were functioning throughout the year. Marginal notations reveal that either Egidius or Richardus authorized every single payment. From the salaries of the lower officials, including the bell ringer, those "who closed and opened the city gates", those "who supervised the watch", and those "to whom foreigners were presented" (all key concerns of governments for the prevention of plague) to the salaries of principal magistrates such as the vicar and *podestà*, the register presents a picture of order and stability.[15] There appears regularity even in those areas of governing where we might expect the Pepoli lords to have acted differently in response to the epidemic. For example, the *curia* issued money for alms to various ecclesiastical houses throughout the year of the epidemic as customary. The payments in June and August to the Augustinian Hermits and the Dominicans were not—apparently—for special expiatory rituals in response to plague, but instead the normal payments donated at the religious festivals associated with those houses.[16]

There may have been particular concern for the epidemic, however, when the Pepoli lords arranged the salaries for professors of medicine. From January through May, the *curia* arranged for payments to five professors for lectures on law and one professor for lectures on astrology, but in August a magister Johannes de Senis *doctor scientie medicine* was hired to teach *practica* in the science of *physica*. In October the government returned to funding lectures on law, but its final payment

[14] Ugolinus de Bonacaptis died on 24 August and was replaced by Jacobinus Petri Angellelli on 28 August; Johannes de Garfagninis died on 4 November and was replaced that day by Minocius Benvenuti de Garfagninis: Commune Governo, Riformagioni e provvigioni, s. cartacea, 245, reg. 36, fol. 1r.

[15] Comune Governo, Riformagioni e provvigioni, s. cartacea, II, 38, fols. 2r–27r.

[16] The *signoria* made donations of 50 *lire* in June to the Humiliati hermits of San Giacomo for the feast of the Apostles; 200 *lire* in August to the Dominicans for the Virgin Mary and the feast day of San Domenico; and 25 *lire* to the Augustinian Hermits for Corpus Christi. It gave 12 *lire* in January and again in October to the hermits at Sasso Grossina for alms as well as for maintaining the road to Sasso. Comune Governo, Riformagioni e provvigioni, s. cartacea, II, 38, fols. 30r–v.

for the year, in December, went again for lectures in medicine.[17] It is pure conjecture that the government hired this professor of medical practice as part of an activist agenda on fighting plague. All we know is that the government functioned throughout the epidemic. It was, however, a very difficult struggle: the expenses of the chancery dropped from an average of roughly 775 *lire* from January to June to only 250 *lire* during July, August, and September. Income appears to have been regenerated after the tax remissions, since the expenses rose in November to meet and then in December to surpass pre-plague figures.[18] The men at the heart of the Pepoli government kept working during the Black Death.

It is possible to follow the actions of officials of the government outside of the *curia domini* by means of private notarial acts. Emancipation contracts took place in the public forum of the *palatium novum* before a judge who worked as *assessor* for the *podestà*. When this act was carried out a father and his sons had to stand and take an oath before a judge (*iuraverunt corporaliter ad sancta dei evangellia*) swearing that they were making the emancipation in good faith and not through fraud. The notary recorded that they were all present before the judge (*existentes... et quilibet eorum personaliter in presentia sapientis et discreti viri...*) and that two witnesses testified to the identity of the parties involved and three others witnessed the act. Also taking place before a judge in the government offices were the *curatele* acts which named an adult financial guardian, or *curator*, for another individual or individuals.[19] In these acts the notary stated that the *curator* approached the judge and in his presence asked for (*petit*) such financial supervision concerning a particular financial transaction, usually a loan or sale, which was drawn up at the same time. Sometimes an oath was requested of the *curator*. According to the locations described in the *actum* clauses, the *curatele* acts took place in either the *palatium vetus* at the court of the *podestà* or the Aquila court, above the steps of the

[17] Comune Governo, Riformagioni e provvigioni, s. cartacea, II, 38, fols. 24r–25r. All professors were paid the same amount of 50 *lire* for a year's course, except for one law professor who received 100 *lire*.

[18] Comune Governo, Riformagioni e provvigioni, s. cartacea, II, 38, fols. 33r–34r. The expenses of the *curia* were: in January 840L 13s 4d; in February 716L 10s 9d; in March 912L 3s 9d; in April 735L 18s 6d; in May 777L 2s 9d; in June 659L 12s 9d; in July 261L 6s 6d; in August 231L 18s 2d; in September 250L 14s 7d; in October 430L 2s 3d; in November 757L 3s; in December 1087L 11s 2d.

[19] See footnote 31 in Chapter Three above.

palatium novum near the chambers of the *podestà*, above the corridor that ran from the *palatium novum* to the *palatium vetus*, or, infrequently, in the house of one of the parties. There was a small group of judges who heard these petitions and oaths, and we can track their presence through the year to see if they had carried out their official duties during the epidemic.

The judge who heard the largest number of emancipations during 1348 (half of the 18 copied into the *Memoriali*) was Johannes de Broilo de Feltro who worked at the Aquila court.[20] After nine such acts in the pre-plague months, he disappeared from the record. He may have fled or died, but his colleagues Marcus da Pistoia doctor of law, Johannes da Pistoia, Morutius de Santo Iusto, and Giullius de Regio all managed to remain at their posts, working hard at authorizing both emancipations and the more frequent *curatele*. After working in March and April, Marcus da Pistoia endured the onslaught of plague to preside over an emancipation act in July at the *palatium novum* and two *curatele* in August. He survived the ordeal since he appears in such acts redacted in October.[21] Morutius de Santo Iusto accepted an emancipation in January, but we last find him during the epidemic at the end of July dealing with two *curatele* and emancipation acts made at the *palatium vetus*.[22] The most frequently cited judge for the common *curatele* acts was Giullius de Regio, but he may have left town during the height of plague since he was back at work from October through December.[23] Perhaps his colleague in the office of the *podestà*, Robertus de Sancto Geminiano, took over his duties during the summer since Robertus supervised *curatele* acts only during the plague months.[24]

The judges who presided over and the notaries who recorded these acts were assisted by yet another public figure who had the responsibility of informing the populace of the decisions made at court. Each emancipation act required a *crida* (a public announcement or bann)

---

[20] Ten emancipations, redacted during the first four months of the year, were copied into the *Memoriali*, while the more complete *Provvisori* (used for Figure 3.5) record the registrations of 19 for that same time. Three registrations took place in May, but none of those were copied into the *Memoriali*. The shock of plague in June may have prevented emancipations, since there are none for that month in either the *Memoriali* or *Provvisori*. In July and August there were three recorded, which is not an inconsiderable amount since only five remain from the following months of the year.

[21] Mem, vol. 229, fols. 115v, 119v, 181r; vol. 230, fols. 164v, 380r.

[22] Mem, vol. 230, fol. 44v.

[23] Mem, vol. 229, fols. 117r, 128r, 140v, 141r, 150r, 159r, 175r.

[24] Mem, vol. 229, fols. 155r, 161v; 230, fols. 37v, 130r.

that the *publicus bannitor* made on the same day, which event the notary duly recorded. The town criers revealed in the emancipation acts were Nicholaus Doxii who worked during the epidemic on 27 July and also served as witness for a testament in August, and Damianus Bertholomei who made *cride* throughout the entire year from January to December, including during the plague months of July and August. These men publicized the facts of the contract loudly by voice and trumpet in the *palatium vetus* and at the top of the stairs of the palace, in the neighborhood, and in front of the home.[25] They were members of a team of seven *trombatores* and *bannitores* who were paid 30 *lire* each for six-month terms (a very good salary). The government registers record their payments in April and December, noting that two men died, but not specifying any replacements for them.[26] *Bannitores* were essential to the proper functioning of civic life in medieval Italian cities, since, in addition to the announcements of private acts such as emancipations and testaments, they publicly "published" the decisions of the governing bodies in terms of laws and banishments. They were the right hand of justice and government in Italian communes and would have been crucial for governmental actions during times of crisis such as the Black Death. Although we do not have the banns remaining for Bologna, as the Pistoese and Lucchese archives are fortunate to preserve, we do know that the men who proclaimed those banns remained at their posts and would have been available to follow the same sorts of orders promulgated by their Tuscan counterparts.[27]

Notaries

Testaments, not legislation or private contracts, were the most abundant records produced during the Black Death. They demonstrate that their producers, the notaries, did not flee the town, but a very large number of them stayed throughout the summer months of plague. As

---

[25] The emancipations acts redacted during the epidemic can be found in Mem, vol. 229, fols. 17v, 221v and vol. 230, fol. 333v. The notarial phrase recording the cry was of the form "publicasse et cridasse alta et preconia voce magnoque sono tube in pallatio veteris et super ambabus schalis pallatii veteris in contrata et ante domum predictorum..."

[26] Comune e Governo, Riformagioni e Provvigioni, s. cartacea, II, 38, fol. 48r.

[27] Bongi, *Bandi lucchesi*, pp. 190–204 reproduces 23 banns of 1348, some dealing with restriction of mobility of goods and people.

demonstrated in the previous chapter, will-making, which was during non-plague times a small part of total notarial activity, pushed aside most other activity during the Black Death and demanded greater efforts from notaries as disease produced more ill testators than ever before. The *Memoriali* registers show that 15 in May, 85 in June, and 185 notaries in July drew up wills. The epidemic resulted in the reduced number of 89 notaries redacting wills in August.

During the epidemic the notaries were working much harder than ever before. Whereas the city's notaries might have written up about 500 acts in a typical working month (that is, acts that would be registered and copied into the *Memoriali*—the real number would be higher), during the height of the Black Death they had to produce about a third more documents than their normal workload. In August their workload dropped to under 300 contracts total, half of what they had to redact in July, but testaments still represented over 72 per cent of their activity. The number of wills rapidly decreased in the fall months, returning to about two per cent of notarial activity, while business and other contracts increased. However, when things had fallen back into the normal pattern, notaries were only producing about half the number of contracts they were producing at the start of the year (at least according the extant registers in the *Memoriali*, for which there are gaps). Most of the 185 notaries working at the worst time—July—redacted only one or two wills (125 notaries did so), which was, in fact, the pattern during the first four months of 1348 before plague had arrived.[28] This is also the way that notaries worked in 1337, the comparative year. During that year, 156 notaries redacted 315 testaments. Seventy-eight per cent of the notaries wrote up only one or two wills. The larger workloads of seven, eight, nine, or thirteen wills were borne by only five notaries. Thus, during the Black Death, although a few notaries did work harder than others, a very large number of the Bolognese notaries continued to carry out their professional duties and did not leave the burden to a small group of loyal public servants. As we will see next, several of these notaries were redacting more testaments than they might have done in a year without plague, when the top number of redactions by

[28] The numbers and pattern of work is similar to what Giorgio Tamba found in his investigations of the *Memoriali* shortly after its inception. In 1270 there were 600 notaries active in the city and suburbs of Bologna. Among these only 66 redacted more than an average of six contracts a month and 295 not more than once a month. See Giorgio Tamba, "I memoriali," p. 261.

notaries was only a third of that produced by the most active notary during the epidemic.

Some of the notaries who wrote up a larger number of wills in July had in fact been working on wills in the earlier months. For example, ser Franciscus de Castagnolo was present in February, April, May, June, July (when he wrote up 22 wills), August, October, and November.[29] Bertolomeus fq Petri de Codagnellis, who was second to ser Franciscus in the number of wills he drew up during the year (39), was also around in March, June, July (when he wrote up 22 wills), August, September, and November. Similarly, Petrus Francisci Ugonis worked on wills in February, June, July (12 wills), August, September, and October.[30] However, the other notaries who redacted many wills during plague-filled July, did not write up wills earlier, and presumably usually concentrated on other sorts of contracts. These men are: Bencevenis de Casola who redacted 15 wills in July only; Bertolomeus fq Vinciguere who redacted 24 wills in July and three in August; and his brother Jacobus fq Vinciguere who redacted one will in May, two in June, 28 in July (he was the busiest notary during this month), one in August, and one in September.

If we track the locations of wills redacted by the most active notaries during the epidemic, we find that notaries tended to focus their attention on testators from one or two neighboring parishes, and occasionally worked for testators from other parishes in the area.[31] It is most likely the case that these areas were their own neighborhoods. This can be verified for a few notaries, i.e., those who appear as testators, who will

[29] Ser Franciscus may have compelled his sons to help him out during the worst stages of the epidemic. Paulus filius ser Francisci de Chastagnolo redacted nine wills in July and two in August, while Johannes filius ser Francisci redacted one each in July and August. The sons do not appear again until December when they each wrote up one will, the month that their father no longer worked on wills. Ser Franciscus is one of only two notaries who used the title *ser*. The other was a testator, but his profession as notary is not certain since the abbreviation "not" follows his father's name could be the genitive "notarii".

[30] These examples demonstrate that some notaries survived the epidemic, at least through 1348. They do not appear to have taken special precautions such as meeting in the open air, since the redaction sites (discussed in the previous chapter) are overwhelmingly inside the ill testators's homes.

[31] Brian Carniello has demonstrated that in order to draw up most types of acts notaries rented stations in the center of town, near the *palatium vetus*, but also circulated throughout the town. The neighborhood-based pattern of the redaction of testaments is exceptional to the notaries's widespread circulation throughout the urban community. See Carniello, "The Notaries of Bologna," pp. 181–196.

be discussed below, and those for whom a close relative is a testator. The most active notary from our evidence of 1348 was ser Franciscus Johannis de Castagnolo whose movements were principally within the quarter of Porta Piera. His workstation was located at the *palatium vetus* in the central square. Out-of-towners would come to dictate their wills to him at his station, as did a healthy man from the village of Tizzano on 13 August.[32] But for much of his business ser Franciscus went to visit clients in their homes, and these clients were his neighbors. We can deduce this from the extant testament of 24 July of his daughter, Margarita, wife of a farrier.[33] Ser Franciscus's work pattern supports the assumption that father and daughter lived in the same parish of San Martino dell'Aposa. He redacted 16 wills in the parish of San Martino dell'Aposa, seven in the neighboring parish of Santa Maria Mascarella, and another ten in three parishes clustered around these two areas of higher activity. He worked in parishes along Strada San Donato (modern Via Zamboni) and along via Mascarella, which form a pie-shaped wedge in the quarter of Porta Piera. However, ser Franciscus was unusual in that he also traveled to the southern quarter of Porta Procola where he redacted nine wills in a number of parishes that formed a band along the second set of walls. The other three notaries who redacted the most wills mainly kept to one area of neighboring parishes (sometimes bordering two quarters) and only occasionally moved to a different area of town to write up one will. Like ser Franciscus, they worked in groups of parishes that formed a wedge from the center of town out to the third set of walls or along a principal street. Each focused most of their activity on one or two parishes.[34] Yet, they were not at all limited to these parishes for three of these notaries worked on an average of 18 parishes each.[35]

This pattern of neighborhood activity supplemented by work outside one's home area is borne out in evidence supplied by notaries who

[32] Mem, vol. 230, fol. 371v (Baldonus fq Alessandri domini Mathioli de Tizano).

[33] Mem, vol. 229, fol. 227v.

[34] Twenty-one of the 33 wills written by Johannes Laurentii Stephani were of testators from San Biagio. Bertolomeus Petri de Codagnellis wrote ten wills in Santa Maria del Tempio and seven in neighboring Santa Maria del Torleone, which comprised less than half of his 39 wills. Jacobus fq Vinciguere de Merlinis, who wrote 33 wills, served six testators from San Michele dei Leprosetti and four from San Leonardo, the next parish to the east along Strada San Vitale.

[35] Johannes Laurentii Stephani was the unusual notary of these four, as he worked in only seven parishes.

appear only infrequently. For example, the notary Franciscus Bedoris Bresche redacted five wills between 23 July and 23 September, three of which were in the adjacent central northern parishes of San Martino dell'Aposa, San Tommaso del Mercato, and Santa Maria Maggiore and two in the parish of Santa Maria Maddalena near the third walls. His mother made her will on 16 June in her home in the parish of San Martino dell'Aposa.[36] We see that his work area comprised her parish and that despite his mother's (presumed) death in June he continued to stay and work in her (and mostly like his) neighborhood through the crisis.

The actions of ser Franciscus de Castagnolo and Franciscus Bresche demonstrate that while the children, wives, mothers, and siblings of notaries were dying of plague, the notaries continued to stay in town and work. I have identified 42 plague testators who were close relatives of notaries actively redacting wills during the Black Death: these include nine widows, eight wives, seven sisters, four brothers (not including brothers who were both notaries), eight daughters of notaries, and six mothers.[37] With this information we can extend the time that we know certain notaries to have been working during the epidemic. Petrus Zanzi Martelli appears in the records only once, i.e., as redactor of a widow's will in the parish of Santa Maria Maddalena on 25 May, nevertheless, we know that he remained in town, presumably working, because his wife, Mixina Francisci Orandi, dictated her will on 9 July (in the same parish in which her husband was working). Mixina died within four days of making her will since Petrus drew up his own testament as a widower on 13 July.[38] That notaries remained in town though their siblings became ill is shown by the brother of a notary, Johannes fq

[36] Mem, vol. 228, fol. 168r (will of Becta fq Acharexii de Latezana).

[37] For about half of these testators the notaries redacting the act noted that they were the relatives of notaries, but the rest have been identified by cross-references with other names in the database. These number could be expanded with the relatives of notaries who appear only as witnesses, not redactors. For example, Morandius Bertholomei de Morandis was witness for the redaction of another notary's sister on 8 September: Mem, vol. 229, fol. 212r (Mina fq Bernardini Grassi). Morandius's own sister had already become ill of plague and made her will on 21 June: Mem, vol. 228, fol. 151r (Manina Bertholomei Morandi). The brother and sister of Ugutio Zanini appear as testators on 17 July and 3 August, but he appears only as witness to a will in San Biagio on 5 July. From information revealed in a bequest of property in his sister's will, we learn that Ugutio lived in San Tommaso della Braina, as did his brother, and thus he was serving a neighbor in the adjacent parish of San Biagio: Mem, vol. 229, fols. 6v, 9r, 22v.

[38] Mem, vol. 229, fol. 86r (Petrus fq Zangli olim Petri Martelli); vol. 230, fol. 155v (Mixina fq domini Francisci Orandi).

Nicholai de Manellis, who made his will on 20 July and was dead by 25 July (according to the will of his widow).[39] His brother Bertolomeus redacted ten wills in June and July, last appearing as a witness on 29 July.[40] Similarly, the widowed Montina fq Mondini Francholi made her will on 27 June, while her brother Francholus redacted and/or witnessed seven wills beginning on 9 July and continuing through August and September until 6 December.[41] The notary, Giullius Bernardini Grassi, served as witness to the will of his sister on 8 September. Thus his presence in town can be extended beyond 18 July, the third and last will he redacted.

As the last example demonstrates, in addition to redacting contracts for the ill, the notaries served as witnesses. In fact, theirs was the most common occupation listed for witnesses, with 59 notaries listed among the witnesses in a sample of 220 wills taken from the entire year, of whom 38 redacted wills both during the summer months and at different times during the year. Most (29) appeared as witnesses in July and August, but a few appear in the reduced number of wills for January through April and September and October. All but two of these identified notaries appear as witnesses only once—most likely due to the smaller sample of wills with witnesses entered into the database. This information expands the time they can be documented in town. For example, Matheus Phylippi de Muglio redacted wills on 20 June and 3 August, but appeared as witness on 15 February and 9 August. Mariscotus Petri Amodei, a notary who worked for the office of the *Memoriali*, was witness with 11 other men including another notary to a will in March. In May he joined a remarkably large gathering to hear the will of the wife of a noble from the Torelli family. The witnessing group included five notaries with seven other named men and who knows how many more unnamed—the redacting notary stated "et aliis pluribus testibus". We find him next with his son (who is not identified as a notary) aiding an ill testator at the end of June. We know that Mariscotus survived the worst of plague because his mother made her testament on 25 July naming him and his brothers as her executors and

[39] Mem, vol. 229, fols. 85v (domina Egidia fq Jacobini de Guidicagnis), 261r (Johannes fq Nicholai de Manellis).

[40] Five of these wills were for testators living in the parishes of Santa Cecilia, the parish of his brother, or San Donato, the adjacent parish. Most likely Bertolomeus lived in the same parish as his brother and his clients were primarily his neighbors.

[41] Mem, vol. 228, fol. 76v.

heirs. The redacting notary stated that these brothers were present before he went on to list nine witnesses, including three other notaries.[42]

We can examine the actions of other busy notary witnesses to gain further understanding of the movements of the notaries during the epidemic. Millionus Donati Federici redacted three wills (8 July, 27 July, and 4 August) and witnessed three others on 22 July, 29 July, and 6 August. Millionus, like Petrus above, worked as notary for the office of the *Memoriali* and is always noted as such when he appeared as witness. He chiefly worked in the peripheral area of town along the Strada Maggiore near the third sets of walls. We first see him in the parish of San Biagio where he was witness for an ill married woman. All of the witnesses for this will were parishioners of San Biagio including three smiths and a wool worker named Johannes Gerardi, who incidentally was witness for two other neighbors in Sant'Omobono and San Biagio in the following three days.[43] During the last week of July and first week of August, the notary Millionus redacted and witnessed wills in the adjacent parishes of Sant'Omobono, Santa Maria del Tempio and Santa Maria del Torleone—parishes that must have constituted his neighborhood. Millionus's duties may have included those of the good neighbor, since he was witness for a fellow parishioner, a butcher from Sant'Omobono, whose will was redacted outside their neighborhood, at the *Gabella* of the central market.

This butcher's testament presents yet another remarkable event at the height of plague. The testator, Mathiolus Johannis Bonaguide, was healthy and, since the will of his wife redacted on 4 November is extant, we know that Mathiolus survived the worst of the crisis. For the redaction of his will on 29 July there were seven notaries present along with two priests who were chaplains from the church of Santa Maria del Torleone. We do not know why these chaplains traveled to the central market to join a large group of seven notaries to aid Mathiolus, but this large gathering of professionals in the midst of epidemic disease is characteristic of the general evidence we have found for the experience of the Black Death.[44] Four of these notary witnesses also redacted wills

[42] Mem, vol. 228, fols. 101v, 140r, 347r; vol. 230, fol. 8v.

[43] Johannes Gerardi was witness for the wife of a jacketmaker in Sant'Omobono on 23 July and for a clothes dealer in San Biagio on 25 July: Mem, vol. 229, fols. 7r and 77r.

[44] A similar case of many notaries gathered in one spot to witness a will is documented in the testament of Jacobus Salvitti, a resident of the parish of Santa Maria Maddalena in the peripheral area of Strada San Donato by the third set of walls. The

during the time of plague. The busiest was Bencevenis Petri de Casola who redacted 15 wills in July, the only month in which he appears. Zacharias de Argelata may be the same Zacharias Lunardi de Argelata who had redacted a will two days before appearing as witness for Mathiolus. The other two notaries at Mathiolus's will worked in more months during the epidemic: Johannes Tomacis de Vinario redacted one will at the end of June, eight in July and another four in August; Bertholacius Nicolai de Manelis redacted six in June (from the first to the last week) and three others in July. Two notaries, however, do not appear anywhere else other than witnesses for Mathiolus. Thus the web of interactions traceable through the footsteps of Millionus is far-reaching.

The fact that there also are notaries traceable in the record only as witnesses, not as the redactors of contracts, confirms and extends the thesis that during the epidemic the notaries were present in large numbers and carried out their duties. In general such notaries usually appear only once as witnesses, but there is evidence to suggest that they remained in town at work, perhaps drawing up other kinds of contracts than wills, because several are members of families of notaries, including a few very busy redactors of wills. For example, Johannes Petri de Casola is revealed in the records only once, i.e. as a witness on 25 July. His brother, Bencevenis Petri de Casola, however, makes many appearances as noted above. Another example of a seemingly stray thread that can be tied to a much tighter, massive web of connections is Antonius Francisci de Castagnolo who served as witness during the epidemic on 6 August and after plague subsided on 22 November. He was a member of one of the most active families of notaries, and his presence as witness provides further evidence for the remarkable hard work of this family. His brother, Paulus Francisci de Castagnolo redacted 14 wills during the plague months and survived to redact a will in December.

Other examples can demonstrate how the numbers of notaries remaining in town and carrying out their duties during the Black

will was redacted at the work place of Johannes Francisci Johannis de Castagnolo at the *palatium vetus* on 19 August. Five notaries served as witnesses with the priest of the nearby cathedral of San Pietro as principal. The three other witnesses also did not come from his neighborhood area and may have instead been at the *palatium vetus* for their own purposes when they aided this testator. This will suggests that commercial and professional activity was continuing at the political and social center of town during the epidemic.

Death can be expanded beyond the numbers identified for June, July, and August and how they can be linked to other family members and other families. The two brothers, Matheus and Minus Chixini, both notaries, were witnesses at a will on 15 April. But while Matheus does not appear elsewhere as redactor or witness, his brother drew up 11 wills during the months of April, June, July, August, September, October, and November. Jacobus Dominici Rolandi was witness on 8 April. His brother worked throughout the crisis (redacting one will in June, eight in July, four in August, and one in September) and even into November when he redacted one will. Lastly, Andreas Arardi appears only as witness during the epidemic on August 17, when he was listed as a notary among the witnesses to a will of a smith in Santa Maria Maggiore on 17 August. The redactor of the will was Andreas's brother, Bonzaninus, one of the more active notaries during the Black Death who redacted nine wills in June, July, August, and October. Because the will of his wife, Braterxia fq Johannis de Donatis, dated on 24 July is extant, we know that Andreas's home was in Santa Maria Maggiore, and, thus, the smith was his neighbor. Braterxia named her brother-in-law, Bonzaninus, as *procurator* to go to the office of the *Memoriali* to register her will in her place.[45] Bonzaninus worked throughout the summer months of plague and into the fall, largely concentrating on testators in the area of Santa Maria Maggiore, where—we learn from his own will of 19 October—he lived.

An exceptional family group of notaries that worked through out the epidemic consisted of Andreas, Jullianus, Laurentius, Bondominicus, and their father, Johannis de Cento. The father redacted ten wills from the months of January through August (of which four were during July). Bondominicus was a witness with his father at a testament in July, Andreas wrote three wills in June and July, and Laurentius shows up as witness for a testament in May, but did not redact any testaments until 24 November. The fourth brother, Jullianus, while identified as notary

[45] She made her husband, the notary, universal heir and executor and left two other small bequests of 40 *solidi* each to her sisters. Her few pious bequests include 16 *lire* for the singing and celebrating of 1000 masses and 20 *solidi* to dopnus Jacobus, a chaplain for the altar of Santa Caterina in the church of San Pietro, most likely in recognition of his service as the principal witness to her will. Braterxia was originally from San Giovanni in Persiceto and it is interesting to note two out-of-towners, from Cento, at her bedside. The other two witnesses with identified parishes came from Santa Maria Maddalena and Santa Maria Mascarella in the northeastern part of the city, not in the neighborhood of Santa Maria Maggiore. See Mem, vol. 229, fol. 89v.

did not redact any extant testaments though he was witness with his brother Laurentius in May. Nevertheless, he provides the last glimpse of this family of notaries and may reflect the respect and appreciation that the townspeople felt for them—he was named heir and executor of a testator on 29 November.[46]

One would expect that the relatives of notaries might try to take advantage of their professional services. As noted above Braterxia was able to count on the notarial expertise of her husband, Andreas, and brother-in-law, Bonzaninus Arardi. In addition, two mothers of notaries, both widowed, named their sons as heirs and, in one case, executor during June.[47] Trust in notaries, actually, went beyond the family, evident by the fact that many townspeople turned to them for aid, often as executors. Antonius Petri Paponi was a notary who lived in the parish of San Giovanni in Monte. He redacted wills in June and August for two women living in neighboring Santo Stefano and San Damiano. On 10 June a wealthy spice dealer originally from Venice residing in San Biagio (just outside the second walls across from San Giovanni in Monte) came to his house to dictate his will and name Antonius as heir and executor.[48] Two days later a healthy woman of San Biagio met her parish rector and eight neighbors in her parish church to choose the notary Bologninus Rodulfi de Ripoli as her heir. Bologninus continued to aid his neighbors through the epidemic since he redacted wills for four other testators in San Biagio and neighboring San Leonardo in July and September. Bologninus had a brother, Salvestrus the butcher, who acted as witness in July. Bologninus obliged not only his neighbors, he also served Bologna's political elite, for we find him at the end of July and August drawing up the testaments of Ugolinus Zengali Pepoli and his wife who lived in the aristocratic center

[46] Mem, vol. 228, fols. 101v (Jullianus and Laurentius as witnesses), 196v (Johannes as redactor); vol. 229, fols. 92r (Johannes as redactor), 169v (Jullianus as heir and executor), 319r (Johannes and Bondominicus as witnesses with Andreas as redactor), 377r (Johannes as redactor); vol. 230, fols. 37r (Bondominicus as redactor), 195r (Johannes as redactor), 258r (Laurentius as redactor), 312r (Bondominicus as redactor); Dem, F. M. Camp. Rossi 339, 5082, 457 (Johannes as redactor), F.P. 193, 7527 and F. M. Camp. Rossi F, 340, 43 (Andreas as redactor), F. M. Instrumenti 89, 4221: 34 and F. M. Camp Rossi F, 340, 20 and 38 (Johannes as redactor).

[47] Mem, vol. 228, fols. 102r (mother of Jacobus Alberti Petri Massarii, her heir and executor, who went on to redact wills in July) and 103v (the mother of two notaries). These are the only mothers of notaries for whom I have entered data on heirs; the other mothers may well have named their notary sons as heirs.

[48] Mem, vol. 228, fol. 153v; vol. 229, fols. 263r, 365r.

of town.[49] A doctor of medicine who made his will in mid August had two notaries among his executors. He placed great faith in one of these men, Bertolomeus Bertonis Mansoris, since he also charged him to be guardian for his young son and heir. Bertolomeus was a good choice, as he can be located in the records as a survivor of the worst of the epidemic and redactor in October.[50] Similarly, Stefanus Corvolini of San Leonardo was witness for another notary of his parish on 30 July and executor for testators in July and October.[51] Lastly, on 20 July a bootmaker called Gerardinus Phylippini of San Biagio gave his lands in the contado over to the infirmaries of the Dominicans, Franciscans and Carmelites as well as three confraternity hospitals. He named the notary Petrus Johannis de Tavernolla as his executor along with Franciscan friar Gracianus and a butcher. The notary was made heir of the estate. Six days later Petrus himself lay ill and made a codicil in which he took care of Gerardinus's last wishes. He bequeathed "all and every land that he held in the village of Monte Renzio" that Gerardinus had willed to him to a confraternity hospital, he provided the servant (*famula*) of Gerardinus with a good dowry of 150 *lire*, and he left five *lire* to friar Gracianus, whom he chose as executor with his wife. What was left of the estate of Gerardinus—which amounted to the goodly sum of 500 *lire*—he had friar Gracianus distribute for the benefit of his and Gerardinus's soul.[52] The evidence suggests, then, that during the Black Death most notaries of Bologna acted in accordance with the public faith entrusted to their profession.

Notaries were inevitably endangering their lives when they served sick testators during the epidemic. Among the *Memoriali* and *Demaniale* wills are those of 27 notaries who dictated their last wishes during the Black Death, of which 12 also drew up testaments for the plague-stricken and stood among them as their witnesses before finally succumbing to plague themselves.[53] Table 4.1 lists their names, as well as the date, place, and capacity of their service. As demonstrated for the notaries discussed

[49] Mem, vol. 228, fol. 98r; vol. 229, fols. 7r, 201r; vol. 230, fols. 116v, 144v, 158v, 505r.

[50] Dem, F.P. 193, 7527: unnumbered page.

[51] Mem, vol. 229, fols. 8v, 73v; vol. 230, fol. 133r.

[52] Mem, vol. 230, fol. 159v and Dem, F. M. Camp. Rossi F, 340, 5083, I: 5.

[53] There are 14 more testators who declare their occupation as notary, but nevertheless did not redact any of the extant wills in the *Memoriali* or appear among individuals named in the sample of complete wills in the database. Their wills were redacted in March (1), June (2), July (3), August (4), September (1), and October (3).

Table 4.1 Notary Testators During the Black Death

Name	Date	Parish or Site	Capacity
Phylippus fq Boniohannis de Muglo	21 Mar.	S. Caterina de Sarag.	Testator
providus vir Bitinus fq Angelini	14 June	In a church	Testator
Egidius Auliverii fq Egidii de Scudellis	25 June	S. M. Maggiore	Testator
Dominicus Pauli Vitalis	1 June	In *scholis* F.M.	Redactor
	9 June	In *scholis* F.M.	Redactor
	12 July	In S. Lorenzo	Testator
Bertolomeus fq d. Dominici Zangli	5 July	S. Biagio	Redactor
	13 July	S. Biagio	Redactor
	13 July	S. Biagio	Redactor
	16 July	In a hospital	Testator
Petrus fq Zanzi Martelli	25 May	S. M. Maddalena	Redactor
	13 July	S. M. Maddalena	Testator
Johannes Benvenuti de Albirolis	15 July	S. Mamolo	Witness
	18 July	S. Mamolo	Testator
Bertolomeus fq Bernardini de Quarto	14 June	S. Sigismondo	Redactor
	4 July	In *guardia civitatis*	Redactor
	18 July	In *guardia civitatis*	Testator
Petrus fq d. Johannis de Tavernulla	27 July	S. Juliano	Testator
Bonvixinus Johannis Bonvixini	2 July	S. Sinesio	Redactor
	11 July	S. Martino dell'Aposa	Redactor
	25 July	S. Martino dell'Aposa	Redactor
	29 July	*In stationem*	Testator
Matheus fq Philippi de Guercino	7 July	S. Dalmasio	Witness
	11 July	S. Vitale	Redactor
	30 July	S. Leonardo	Testator
Nicolaus fq Upicini de Grimaldis	31 July	S. Mamolo	Testator
Bonucius fq d. Jacobi de Papazonibus	2 Aug.	S. Nicolo degli Albari	Testator
Albericus fq Michaelis olim Nicolai	No date	S. Mamolo	Redactor
	15 July	S. Mamolo	Redactor
	15 July	S. Giacomo dei Carb.	Redactor
	3 Aug.	S. Cristoforo di Sara.	Testator
	3 Aug.	S. Cristoforo di Sara.	Codicil
Jacobus Alberti Petri Massari	6 July	Cataldo dei Lambert.	Redactor
	10 July	S. Maria d. Uccelletti	Redactor
	20 July	S. Michele Mercato	Redactor
	5 Aug.	S. Maria d. Uccelleti	Testator

Table 4.1 (*cont.*)

Name	Date	Parish or Site	Capacity
Petrus fq Galixii	5 Aug.	S. Vito e S. Maria	Testator
Gerardinus fq Oddi Gerardini Oddi	22 June	S. Gervasio	Testator
	15 July	S. Maria d. Muratelle	Redactor
	28 July	S. Martino Caccian.	Redactor
	8 Aug.	S. Felice	Redactor
ser Nicolaus Francisci Manzavache	17 Aug.	S. Martino dell'Aposa	Testator
Johannes Anthonii Yvani	17 June	S. Alberto	Redactor
	7 July	S. Dalmasio	Witness
	11 Aug.	S. Alberto	Redactor
	13 Aug.	S. Alberto	Redactor
	18 Aug.	S. Leonardo	Testator
Franciscus fq Guaschoris Bonvixini	22 Aug.	S. Tommaso Mercato	Testator
Giullus Johannis Bonvixini	27 July	S. Tommaso Mercato	Redactor
	25 Aug.	S. Tommaso Mercato	Testator
Jacobus fq d. Alberti Pugni Zagnonis	5 Sep.	S. Maria Maggiore	Testator
Gulielmus fq Nicholai Jacobini Mathei	10 Oct.	S. Maria Mascarella	Testator
Gregorius Benedicti de Casi	8 Mar.	S. Marino	Redactor
	12 Oct.	S. Marino	Testator
Bonzaninus fq Arardi Bonzanini	15 June	S. Felice	Redactor
	23 June	S. Maria Maggiore	Redactor
	24 June	S. Maria Maggiore	Redactor
	27 June	S. Giorgio	Redactor
	12 July	S. Caterina Saragozza	Redactor
	24 July	S. Maria Maggiore	Procurator
	25 July	S. Lorenzo P.Stiera	Redactor
	25 July	S. Lorenzo P.Stiera	Redactor
	17 Aug.	S. Maria Maggiore	Redactor
	14 Oct.	S. Maria Maggiore	Redactor
	19 Oct.	S. Maria Maggiore	Testator
Guarentinus fq Francisci Ugolini Munsi	29 Oct.	S. Andrea d. Ansaldi	Testator
Bonbolognus fq Panichalis de Gato	31 Oct.	S. Andrea d. Pietesi	Testator

Source: ASB, Memoriali, vols. 228, 229, 230 and Dem: San Francesco and San Domenico: Campioni Rossi, Instrumenti

above, they chiefly worked in areas comprising two to three nearby or contiguous parishes. Because we have their testaments, we know that these work zones were their own neighborhoods. The notaries did not specialize by type of client, but by geographical area. Even though their activity is spread out over several days or weeks, it was generally focused on a circumscribed area of town. When the notary moved out of his neighborhood, it appears to have been for a special situation, such as the redaction of a nobleman's will in the center of town. We also learn from this group of notary testators that many notaries were working up till a few days before they became ill and had to make a will. Of this group of notaries only the busiest, Bonzaninus, survived the worst of the plague months to redact a will for a neighbor on 14 October. Five days later, he made his own will. For most the date of their testament is the last we hear of them, but for one the situation was reversed. Gerardinus fq Oddi Gerardini makes his documentary presence first when he went to the church of San Francesco on 22 June to dictate a secret will before the friars. He was healthy at that time and somehow managed to be free from infection during July and August when he redacted three wills.[54]

When notaries became ill testators they were able to turn for help to their colleagues and neighbors, whom they had served throughout the epidemic. As we have seen for the work pattern of notaries, neighbors came from the home parish or adjoining parishes to stand as witness. For example, three out of the seven witnesses at the will of the notary Johannes Anthonii Yvani were from his home parish of San Leonardo in the east near the third set of walls, while a fifth was from Sant'Alberto, adjacent but outside of the walls. The sixth witness came instead from Sant'Isaia in the west across town. The presiding cleric was an Augustinian Hermit friar from the convent of San Giacomo located in his home parish.[55] Similarly, Dominicus Pauli Vitalis, a notary living in San Lorenzo Porta Stiera, relied on three men from his parish and one from San Nicolò di Felice bordering his parish for his will on 12 July. In addition to neighbors, Dominicus relied on his colleagues, for he nominated a notary, Ansaldinus Ugolini Peregrini, as his executor.[56]

[54] His testament is in Demaniale, F. M. Camp. Rossi F, 340, 30.

[55] Mem, vol. 229, fol. 77r. Other examples include ser Nicolaus filius Francischi Manzavache whose will on 17 August includes two witnesses from his home parish of Santa Maria Mascarella in the north, three from adjacent parishes, with a last journeying from San Giuliano across town in the south.

[56] Mem, vol. 229, fol. 82v.

An excellent example of notaries helping their own took place at the redaction of the will of Bonvixinus Johannis Bonvixini on 29 July. The busiest notary of all, ser Franciscus de Castagnolo, served as principal witness in place of a priest in order to identify the testator, while another member of the Castagnolo family, Johannes Dominici de Castagnolo, wrote the will, and a third notary, Andreas Johannis de Crespellano, served as witness. Although Bonvixinus was ill, the redaction took place at the work place of Johannes de Castagnolo at the *palatium vetus*. A student of medicine, also present as witness, may have been tending to Bonvixinus's medical needs.[57]

In addition to enabling their wills, notaries also helped each other for the long-term well-being of their families. This is evident in the case of Gregorius Benedicti de Casi who redacted several wills in 1337 and one in March of 1348. When he made his testament on his sickbed at home on 12 October, Gregorius declared he wished it to be kept secret in the sacristy of the Franciscans. Surrounded by eight Franciscan friars, he named as executor and guardian for his two young daughters ser Dominicus fq Alberti de Lanceis who had redacted extant wills of June and July. Gregorius must have died within ten days because his testament, today found in the *Demaniale*, contains a note at the end dated 22 October 1348 declaring that the testament was "opened and heard" at the *palatium novum* before the Franciscan sacristy and a friar as well as a judge of the *podestà*.[58]

Notaries became ill and died because of their duties, but others survived and continued to serve their fellow townspeople in the following years. Several worked for the office of the *Provvisori* and, thus, we know that they were alive in the years following the Black Death. Nineteen

---

[57] The student was Petrus Jacobi from Genoa, "scolaris Bononie in medicinalibus". See Mem, vol. 229, fol. 210v. Other examples of medical students are: Mem, vol. 228, fol. 143r (will of Taurellus fq Gerardutii de Taurellis of 29 June) with two "scolares in medicinali scientia". A further example of notaries helping their own is Montanarius Jacobi Montanarii from the parish of San Leonardo who served as witness for the will of notary Johannes Anthonii Yvani, his neighbor, on 18 August. See Mem, vol. 229, fol. 76v.

[58] Dem, F. M. Camp. Rossi F, 340: 17. Several testaments in the *Demaniale* indicate the formal, public ceremonies when the content of these secret wills were made public. This is strong evidence that their contemporaries seriously considered and honored testators's declarations. The tendency among some modern observers to see these declarations as simply wishes that may or may not have been honored goes against the evidence. The rigorous and complicated procedures governing last wills and testaments and the high incidence of will-making both support the argument that these wishes were generally honored.

notaries who were active during the Black Death can be identified as survivors.[59] They range from notaries who wrote few to many wills during the epidemic, such as the following: Plevale Nicholai de Stupa who wrote six wills during 1348 and was working for the *Provvisori* in 1349 and 1350; Signorellus de Segnorelli who redacted 17 wills during the summer months of plague, one in September, and lastly two on one day in October, and was alive and working in 1354; and Johannes Laurentii Stephani, who was very active, redacting 33 wills during the epidemic, only two of which were in the fall months, and survived into 1349.[60] Only three notaries of 1348 can be found in the *Provvisori* during and after the second onslaught of plague in Bologna in 1362. These are Franciscus Aspetati de Cento who wrote nine wills in the plague year of 1348 and appears in 1350 and 1362 and Johannes Alberti Dominici, who wrote two wills in July and November of 1348 and does not appear again until the second outbreak had passed in 1363. The third is an example of astonishing resistance and endurance: Petrus Francisci Ugonis redacted one will during February, twenty-three during the plague months, and two in the fall of 1348. He was being a good neighbor to friends and clients since he redacted or witnessed wills in parishes adjacent to his home parish of San Leonardo.[61] He survived to work in 1350 continuing on until 1369, the last year for which a notary of the Black Death can be found in the *Provvisori* office.

Practitioners of Medicine

One of the notaries mentioned above had a medical student attending the declaration of his last will. There is, in fact, evidence of the presence of several medical practitioners attending the afflicted in the wills of the *Memoriali*. Apart from the negative comments from chroniclers, very

[59] See Appendix A for names and years of employment.

[60] This very active notary went into the homes of ill testators and even hosted one testator, the ill wife of a butcher of his parish, in his own home on 8 July: Mem, vol. 230, fol. 168v.

[61] In addition to witnessing in July the will of another notary who lived in his home parish of San Leonardo, Petrus fq Francisci Ugonis redacted five wills in his home parish in February, June, July, and August; he was in Santa Maria Maddalena, San Sigismondo, and Santa Maria del Torleone—parishes adjacent to his—in June and July; and he was in the neighboring parishes of San Vitale, San Tommaso della Braina, and Sant'Antonino in June, and San Egidio in July.

little evidence is available for the activity of doctors during the Black Death elsewhere in Italy. Cities such as Florence and Perugia requested doctors to carry out autopsies on plague victims during the epidemic.[62] And it is well known that physicians across Europe (from Italy, France, Spain, and Germany) responded to the Black Death by writing plague tractates or *consilia* detailing advice concerning prevention, cure, and recipes.[63] As John Henderson and Jon Arrizabalaga have shown, town councils in Italy and across Europe enacted legislation following the doctors's proposed *regimina*.[64] It would seem that the plague doctor was an active and dutiful public servant, just as we have discovered the notaries to be.[65] The wills allow us to go beyond the evidence of the physicians's *consilia* and legislative action to discern the movements and activities of a few more practitioners in Bologna.

Three professors of medicine (two *doctor medicine* and a *professor physice*) and three doctors (*medicus*) appear among plague testators in July, August, and September. [66] In addition there were various relatives of six deceased doctors (a widow, a son, and four daughters), but we do not know when these doctors had died.[67] Certainly the doctor testa-

---

[62] Park, *Doctors and Medicine*. In his plague tract of 1348, magister Jacme d'Agramont calls for physicians to conduct autopsies of plague victims "so that thousands, and more than thousands could benefit by preventive measures against those things which produce the maladies and deaths discussed". See Jacme d'Agramont "Regimen of Protection Against Epidemics or Pestilence and Mortality," trans. M. L. Duran-Reynals and C. E. A. Winslow, *Bulletin of the History of Medicine* 22 (1948), 57–89, especially, pp. 78–79.

[63] The fundamental works on plague tractates of the Black Death are: Campbell, *Black Death and Men of Learning*; Palazzotto, "The Black Death and Medicine"; Arrizabalaga, "Facing the Black Death".

[64] Arrizabalaga, "Facing the Black Death," p. 287; Henderson, "The Black Death in Florence," pp. 145–147. This view is challenged by Irma Naso who argues that the Italian doctors had little involvement on an official level because the authorities had little faith in their effectiveness and because the doctors themselves felt impotent and frustrated in the face of the disease. See Irma Naso, "Individuazione diagnostica della 'peste nera': Cultura medica e aspetti clinici," in *La peste nera*, pp. 355–357.

[65] For more on this argument see Wray, "Boccaccio and the Doctors".

[66] The three *medici* were: magister Thomaxinus fq magistri Lanzallocti of the parish of San Donato, who made his will in town on 28 July (Mem, vol. 229, fol. 2r); magister Gerus fq magistri Nerini who made his will on 8 September in his home in the parish of Sant'Antonino and whose brother, magister Madinus, was a professor of medicine (Mem, vol. 229, fol. 200v); and magister Phyllipus fq domini Henrici who was married to the daughter of a goldsmith and dictated his secret will on 8 August in the Franciscan sacristy (Dem, F. M. Camp. Rossi, F. 340, 53).

[67] Malgarita fq Corbellani of San Biagio, widow, on 5 July (Mem, vol. 230, fol. 135v); Johannes fq olim magistri Jacobi, on 21 July (Mem, vol. 229, fol. 207r); Johanna fq magistri Jacobi Bonbaroni, on 10 August (Mem, vol. 229, fol. 29r); discreta domina Francisca fq magistri Giulli, on 16 July (Mem, vol. 230, fol. 197v); Malgarita fq magistri

tors had not fled during the height of the Black Death, but remained in town and became ill of plague. It is likely (but impossible to prove) that they aided their fellow citizens and died as a result of their service.[68] Concern for Bologna's hospitals, at least, is evident in the will of one such doctor. Magister Phylippus fq Henrici Morreri went to the church of San Francesco to dictate his secret will on 8 August. In addition to pious bequests for masses for his soul he left money for two hospitals. His wealth is indicated by the large dowry of 500 *lire* he returned to his wife, the daughter of a goldsmith. She was to have usufruct of his goods, and his heirs would be any male children yet to be born. If they died, the money would go to building a chapel at San Francesco—his burial place—and to contribute to the dowries of several girls as well as to supplement his servant's salary by ten *lire*. He chose a professor of law as his executor, but added the cautionary note that should he die the executors would be two Franciscan friars. Although magister Phylippus declared he was healthy and may have believed that children would be born to be his heirs, he was being overly optimistic. His wife, Gardina, made her will at their home eight days later, already a widow. There were no children as heirs, but instead she named the children of an unrelated man, possibly a notary. She did not match her husband's generosity to hospitals but did continue his concern for undowered girls and for pious bequests to church of San Francesco (for cloth for an altar and for burial). The law professor may no longer have been able to help this family because Gardina asked a notary and the Franciscan sacristan to be her executors.[69]

There is positive evidence of doctors serving patients, since they were recorded in lists of witnesses to wills. Among the witnesses in the sample of 200 wills from June, July and August are four doctors or *medici* (of whom one is designated a surgeon, *medicus cerusicus*) and one professor of medicine (*professor fixice*), with another professor appearing at the bedside of the ill in October after the disease had died down. The first example is from 16 June when magister Petrus fq magistri Egidi, a surgeon, served as witness for a widowed noblewoman.[70] Then on

Ingiranis olim Zuntini on 29 November (Mem, vol. 230, fol. 158v); Lucia fq magistri Jacobi Baroni on 20 June (Mem, vol. 228, fol. 78r).

[68] These men, like the vast majority of testators in July and in normal times, declared they were sick as they dictated their wills.

[69] Mem, vol. 229, fol. 427r (will of Gardina fq Anthoni).

[70] Mem, vol. 228, fol. 109r (will of Mina fq domini Cavalerii de Cavaleriis).

24 June the wife of a farrier dictated her will in the home of magister Grandeus, a doctor living in her parish.[71] Magister Manfredinus traveled from his home parish of San Marino di Porta Nova in the western section of aristocratic center of town out to an eastern parish in an area of town heavily populated by artisans where he was present as witness in the home of the widow of a smith on 5 July.[72] On 17 July, magister Andreas Jacobi de Barberiis professor of *physica* was present as witness to the will of his niece.[73] On 24 July, an aristocratic widow left a bequest of eight *lire* in payment of fee for care by a doctor and his female assistant.[74] Lastly, on 27 July magister Johannes fq magistri Bertholomei *medicus* was witness at the will of a notary's wife. Earlier in the year, on 15 April before the worst of the epidemic, he had been named executor and witness by another notary's widow.[75]

It probably was not regular practice for doctors to stay and serve as witness to a will after they had examined a patient in the home. Instead, better evidence for continued medical attention during the epidemic comes from barber surgeons who appear in greater numbers among the witnesses of plague wills. Out of the sample, there are 21 wills from the plague months of June, July, and August that have barbers listed among the witnesses.[76] Five of these belonged to sick or ill testators who dictated secret wills inside the Franciscan convent—either in the church, the chapel, the sacristy, or in the house belonging to the servants (*in domo famulorum fratrum minorum*). The extraordinary figure of brother Franceschinus, specified as barber of the Franciscans, was tending to them all. In the city at large there were numerous other men who served members of the elite and non-elite classes alike: five of the testators using barbers had elite surnames and the other seven included market gardeners, the wife of a tailor, and the daughter of a deceased shoemaker. All but two barbers were treating patients who lived in their own or an adjacent parish. One barber, Francescus

[71] Mem, vol. 228, fol. 93v (will of Colla fq Bolognipti de Flagnano).

[72] Mem, vol. 229, fol. 9r (will of Benvenuta fq Boni).

[73] Mem, vol. 229, fol. 91v (will of Francesca Fellini de Barberiis).

[74] Mem, vol. 229, fol. 206r (will of domina Pellegrina de Bechadellis): "magistro Johanni de Barberiis qui curavit eam et quidam eius famula octo *lire* bon. pro ipsius mercede, salario, et labore". One servant received ten *lire* and the other a bed and usufruct of rents.

[75] Mem, vol. 228, fol. 104r and 230, fol. 200v.

[76] In Memoriali, vol. 229, fols. 2v (28 July), 17r (10 July), 20r (23 July), 73r (19 July), 74r (7 July), 78r (20 June), 86v (25 July), 203v (17 July), 207r, 210v (20 July), 222v (1 August), 256r (9 July); vol. 230, fol. 302v (20 July) vol. 228, fols. 154v, 317r.

Symonis, worked hard during the terrible month of July appearing at the wills of two parishioners, a man and a women bearing aristocratic names on 10 July and 23 July. A team of father and son also appear: Johannes filius Benzevenis of the parish of Sant'Omobono worked for an ill woman in his neighborhood on 7 July, while two weeks later, Benzevenis fq Bertolli, also of the parish of Sant'Omobono, and most likely Johannes's father, cared for an *ortolanus* of that parish. These barber surgeons would have been following the instructions of a doctor, carrying out phlebotomies, which were prescribed by all the plague doctors.[77] They were putting their lives in danger, and, in fact, there are two testators who were barbers, namely, Guidus fq Benasai of 1 July and friar Dominicus fq magistri Alberti tertiary of the Cistercians (*barberius fratrum penitencie tercii ordini sancti Bernardi*) of 6 August.[78] Guidus left to Mateus Benzevenis, a *laborator* or agricultural worker, his scissors, all his shaving cloths (*panellos rasuros*) as well as "half" a sharpening wheel, which they owned jointly. Perhaps this Mateus was brother of Johannes Benzevenis of Sant'Omobono (but without any indication of parish for Mateus, this is only a guess). Friar Dominicus relied on the assistance of a woman, perhaps for his trade. He left six *lire* to Maria fq Alberti (who is not named as servant) as salary "for the time she stayed with him" as well as his bed and bedding (a common bequest) and tools.

Students of medicine occasionally appear as witnesses: in June two *scolares in medicinali scientia* aided at the will of a man from the aristocratic Torelli family; in July a certain Petrus Jacobi of Genoa, a *scholaris Bononie in medicinalibus*, was present at the will of a notary; also in July magister Paulus Sozi of Gubbio, a *scholaris in scientia medicine* was present at the will of a widow of a Bolognese professor of logic and philosophy; and lastly, in August a Bolognese nobleman was aided by a magister Rosinus de Umbertis of Ancisa, a student of medicine.[79] The presence of these five students are reminders of the importance of Bologna's medical faculty at the time—the only other students found in the wills are a few students of the famous school of law who also appeared as witnesses and once as an executor. Judging

[77] Gentile da Foligno, in his *consilium* against pestilence directed to Genoa, states "[l]audo etiam flebotomias, et de salvatellis flebotomias opinor esse multum utile" in Sudhoff, "Pestschriften," p. 334.

[78] Mem, vol. 229, fol. 87v and Dem, F. M. Instrumenti, 90, 4222: 4.

[79] Mem, vol. 229, fol. 210; vol. 228, fol. 143r.

from the surnames of these men, some were well-off (as we know about students in general at Bologna). Most used the title Master or *magister* (as did all the *medici*, but not the barber surgeons), and thus they were probably medical practitioners as well or at least had their university degrees.

The testators of Bologna trusted medical practitioners during the epidemic, despite chroniclers's negative portrayals that have shaped so much modern opinion. Testators left bequests to their doctors in payment for services. Doctors administered to plague patients (*curare*) and prescribed medication (*medicinis et receptis*) in their time of need.[80] A certain sign of trust and confidence in her doctor during the crisis is displayed by the widow of a professor who named a doctor (*medicus*) as her executor on 27 July.[81] Bologna was proud of its doctors and had honored them highly during the thirteenth and fourteenth century. A few of them, such as Taddeo Alderotti, the famous physician memorialized by Dante in the *Divine Comedy*, and Mondino de Liuzzi, author of the first anatomy textbook, made it into the city chronicles that were otherwise focused on military and political men. This evidence of physicians and barber surgeons coming to the aid of the ill is corroborated by the recent work of Angela Montford who has demonstrated by means of mendicant convent records that the friars of Bologna received visits from their doctors and bought the required supplies for medication throughout the Black Death.[82]

The Clergy

Members of the governing offices, the law courts, the notariate, and the university whose professional capacities would have aided social order and health during the crisis stayed in town. Was there similar behavior

---

[80] Mem, vol. 228, fol. 143r (two florins bequeathed to a *doctor medicine* on 29 June) and vol. 229, fol. 206r (widow left eight *lire* on 24 July for the salary of magister Johannes de Barberiis *qui curavit eam* and his female assistant, *et quamdam eius famulam*); on 26 June a Garisendi man left five *lire* to the servant of a doctor *pro medicinis et aliis receptis* (Mem, vol. 229, fol. 309v).

[81] Mem, vol. 230, fol. 215r (Jacoba fq Bertolini de Orellis on 27 July 1348). Another example is earlier in the year when magister Johannes magistri Bertholomei de Granarolo was executor and witness for the widow of a notary on 15 April (Mem, vol. 228, fol. 104r).

[82] Angela M. Montford, *Health, Sickness, Medicine and the Friars in the Thirteenth and Fourteenth Centuries* (Aldershot, UK, 2004), pp. 164–167.

among the religious communities of Bologna? The city chronicles do not report an official response on the part of the church; there are no details on the types of processions or masses that took place in other towns. Bologna's confraternities may well have aided in plague burials as has been discovered for later plague epidemics in Italy, but we do not have the evidence.[83] The notarial record, however, does provide some information about religious houses and civic organizations acting as groups in the midst of the epidemic, but it is limited by the purposes of the notarial act. The *instrumentum syndici*, or *instrumentum sindicationis* as it is called in the *Memoriali*, was used by communities and associations such as convents, monasteries, hospitals, and guilds to enter into negotiations by means of a representative both for business transactions and legal action, such as dispute settlements.[84] When such groups congregated to choose a proxy, their meeting and decision was given legal force through the notarial act.

The *Memoriali* record three such meetings during the height of the epidemic. On 10 August, ten members of the confraternity of Santa Maria delle Laudi connected to the hospital of San Lorenzo dei Guarini met "as was their usual custom" in a house belonging to the Augustinian Hermits's church of San Giacomo to name a representative for future possible law suits.[85] Cross-reference with the testaments reveals that one of these confraternity brothers had been present as witness for a

---

[83] Henderson states in "Religious Confraternities and Death" in *Continuity and Change*, p. 388 that "Fraternities of the Misericordia and San Frediano in Florence, the Scuole Grandi of Venice, and companies such as the Compagnia del Crocifisso of Borgo San Sepolcro, gave free burials to the poor, especially during epidemics such as the Black Death." The evidence for these activities mainly comes from the repeated outbreaks of the 15th and 16th centuries. How widespread or officially organized this activity was during the first outbreak is not clear.

[84] For examples of *syndicus* contracts see Salatiele, *Ars Notarie*, 2:292 and Rolandino *Contractus*, pp. 258–266.

[85] This is the Laudesi confraternity that met, according to Mario Fanti, first in the Augustinian Hermits's church of San Giacomo in 1298 and then at the church of San Lorenzo dei Guarini where a hospital was founded in 1317. According to the notarial acts of 1348, the confraternity's identity was connected to both institutions. For example, in one testament there were bequests for the altar and for masses at San Giacomo, the principal witnesses were two Augustinian Hermits, and two executors were members of the society *Sancte Marie de Laudis hospitalis de Guarinis* (Mem, vol. 229, fol. 3v). Despite the presence of two other laudesi confraternities cited in Fanti, this is the only confraternity that refers to itself as Santa Maria delle Laudi. The laudesi confraternity connected with the church of Santa Maria dei Servi does not appear in the 1348 acts, nor is there reference to the third Compagnia delle Laudi founded in 1317 based at San Francesco that founded the hospital of Nosadella. The hospital of Nosadella, however, received several pious legacies and was the site for the redaction of two testaments in

will dictated at the beginning of the epidemic while another was made executor for a testator dying of plague at the end of July.[86] Another testament of 25 July nominated as executor a brother of the hospital of Nosadella connected to another Compagnia delle Laudi and asked that either the chief officer, *massarius*, or a *procurator* of the hospital choose the Poor of Christ who were to receive his patrimony.[87] We do not know if the men of these confraternities extended their civic duties of congregating for legal representation, witnessing, and executing wills also to providing for burials and prayers for relief from plague, but it is very possible since their community remained intact and in town.

We know that on 15 August nine nuns of the convent of Santa Maria delle Vergini met with their prioress in their parlatory at the sound of bells, as was their custom, to name a legal agent (*sindicum, procuratorem, factorem*). Again, we do not know what these nuns did during the epidemic, but at least a majority (*ultra quam tres partes*) of the nunnery could act cooperatively to make a community decision during the crisis.[88] Lastly, on 25 August, as plague was diminishing, the monks of Spirito Santo who according to their act of *sindicationis* sought alms for the deserving poor in Bologna, met at their house at the sound of a bell to name four of their brothers as agents for any future dealings with property or rights belonging to their monastery.[89] The long act makes no mention of plague nor its effect on their community and instead is filled with the legal formulae transferring representation to their chosen brothers. This pious community was collectively planning for the distribution of alms gained from property donated to them during the epidemic, but the documents are silent about what else

1348. See Mario Fanti, *Confraternite e città a Bologna nel medioevo e nell'età moderna* (Roma, 2001), pp. 179–188.

[86] Mem, vol. 229, fol. 3v. The men are noted by name, but only three record an occupation: a bootmaker (*chalegarius*), a weaver (*tessarius*), and their treasurer or *masserius*, whom they named as *sindicus*, was a clothes dealer (*strazarius*). The specific need for a *sindicus* is left unspecified: "in litibus controversiis que et quas predicti homines dicte societatis habunt vel habere possent".

[87] Mem, vol. 229, fol. 119v.

[88] Mem, vol. 229, fol. 15v.

[89] Mem, vol. 230, fol. 226v. These monks originated in Armenia with the rule of Saint Basil. They moved to Bologna in 1303 and were located outside the gate of San Mamolo. Their church was consecrated in 1342 with the name Santo Spirito. See Paolo Foschi, "Gli ordini religiosi medievali a Bologna e nel suo territorio," in *Storia della Chiesa di Bologna*, eds. Paolo Prodi and Lorenzo Paolini, 2 vols. (Bologna, 1997), 2:487.

they may have done as a result of the widespread disease and massive numbers of deaths.

Although we have no information about an official response on the part of the church, the notarial records make it abundantly clear that Bologna was well served by the clergy. The laws that instituted the *Memoriali* required the presence of clergy at the testament of an ill testator. This priest or friar had to confirm the identity and attest to the sanity of the testator (essentially corroborating at the end of the testament its initial declaration by the testator that he or she was "healthy in mind and body"). Naturally, they would also have heard confession and given last rites for the dying. Friars also assisted the men who came to their convent to make and deposit a secret will. Because nearly half of the secret wills were dictated within the sacristies of the Franciscan or, less frequently, the Dominican convent, with a smaller number in a home belonging to the convent or in a chapel of the mendicant church, these wills allow us to enter also the doors of the religious houses to see what the friars were doing during the epidemic.[90] As we have done for the notaries and doctors who appear among the sample of wills with witnesses taken from July and August, we can provide evidence for the activity of clergy during the Black Death. Again, the evidence from the wills tempers the claims of chroniclers that priests and friars fled from their duties, since many in Bologna stayed to provide spiritual succor to the dying.

From wills in both the *Memoriali* and *Demaniale* a remarkable picture of the friars during the Black Death can be reconstructed. I have found the names of 22 dedicated Franciscans and Dominicans and two Carmelites (listed in Appendix B) who came to support testators five or more times during the epidemic. Some of these friars exerted themselves intensely during the worst of the plague months and disappear from view after that. This was the case for the hardest-working friars Franciscan Gandolfinus from Parma who was witness to 15 wills between the end of May and the end of July and the Franciscan sacristan Jacobus de Nigrobonis who witnessed 14 times in June and July. Another Franciscan sacristan demonstrates how some friars labored over much of the year: Johannes de Aposa witnessed 13 wills between

[90] The rest of the testaments in the *Demaniale* archive, about a third, were written up in the home of the testator, with the specific instructions that the will was to be deposited in the sacristy, not the *Memoriali*, and to remain secret.

February and end of October. Similarly, Franciscan friar Jacobus de Guizardini appears in the record 11 times, once in February, then at the end of May and finally at the end of September. Many of these occasions were for testaments made within the convent, but the friars frequently went out into the city to enter the homes of the ill, traveling in pairs or even larger groups around the city.

The mendicants, especially Franciscans, were providing more than spiritual aid. The sacristan (*guardianus*) had the responsibility to preserve the secret wills. As the documents explain in a final added clause, before three or four mendicant witnesses the testament was placed in the hands of the sacristan who declared he would "guard and preserve it for all time" and then authenticated it with the convent's seal.[91] These bureaucratic duties can be added to their other public capacities, such as arbiters, sponsors of the university elections of professors, and supervisors of elections of civic officials.[92] All of these functions would have forged strong connections between the mendicants and the populace.[93] As will be discussed in Chapter Six, the friars were frequently appointed as executors during the plague months of June through August. A final example of their service is the friar Francescus, barber for the order, who

---

[91] This practice was done regardless of whether the secret will was made in the mendicant house or at the home of the testator—a much less frequent occurrence. If the will was dictated at home, its transfer to the mendicant sacristy followed within days. For example, a Cistercian tertiary dictated his will at home on 28 May. According to the clause added after the *actum* clause, this testator designated a Dominican friar as *procurator* who then deposited it in the hands of the sacristan on 1 June before two friar witnesses who declared they knew the sacristan, the proctor, and the testator. Dem, F.P., 193, 7527, unnumbered.

[92] For documents evidencing Dominicans as witnesses for the elections of the Faculty of Medicine and Arts see Celestino Piana, *Ricerche sulle università di Bologna e di Parma nel secolo XV* (Florence, 1963), pp. 32–33. Augustine Thompson, O.P., has emphasized the mendicants's political power, especially in Bologna, in his *Cities of God: The Religion of the Italian Communes 1125–1325* (University Park, Penn., 2005), pp. 422–425. Arguing on the basis of city statutes, Thompson claims that mendicants selected the 16 *ministrales* and supervised municipal elections in Bologna. The election lists for 1348, however, do not bear the imprint of mendicant involvement. The arenga states that the elections are made *per parrochianos*, and the notarial registry is the responsibility of the vicar's notary: Comune Governo, Riformagioni e Provvigioni, 273 (1348) register entitled "Ministrales dei quartieri, officiali, militi, etc.", no page numbers.

[93] Another connection is the fact that friars also lent money to the populace. Fr. Francescus de Chalanchis was a witness for testators who came to the Franciscan sacristy to dictate wills on 29 June and 3, 7, 15, 16 July. One testators left him three *lire* "pro suis necessitatibus" (a standard type of bequest), while another left seven *solidi* and six *denarii* in repayment for a loan "ex causa mutui": Dem, F. M., Camp. Rossi, F, 340, 46, n. 42; Dem, F. M. Camp. Rossi, 339, 5082, 456; Dem, F. M. Instrumenti, 89, 4221, 49; Dem, F. M. Camp. Rossi F, 340, 23, n. 20.

as noted above was witness during the epidemic and perhaps administered medically as well as spiritually in comforting the ill testators. For the populace all of these various functions taken on by the friars must have brought welcome relief during the crisis.

The community of the convent was a sanctuary for those who lived within, but it did allow outsiders to enter. Some testators came into the mendicant houses as healthy testators who declared their secret wishes and then returned to their homes. These testators named their family members as heirs, and so it appears they had turned to the Franciscans mainly for the surety and support they offered to their secular arrangements. For example, ser Baldus fq Bonacurxi of the parish of Caterina di Saragozza located behind San Francesco left five *lire* for masses in San Francesco and requested burial there, but named his wife as executor and his grandsons as heirs.[94] Others had a more intimate connection to the religious house. For example, an ill widower declared his secret will before nine friars in a house within the Franciscan complex. We do not know when he came there before making his will on 6 August, but the friars had let him into the heart of their community during the crisis: the *actum* clause states the will was made in "the room of brother Johannes de Aposa next to the cloister".[95] Johannes de Aposa attended also those outside the friary, because on 2 August he was the principal witness for a widowed Franciscan tertiary in the parish of San Lorenzo di Porta Stiera (in a house "near the ditch," i.e., the part of that large parish near the second walls and thus near San Francesco).[96] In fact, the intimate spiritual community spilled out beyond the convent walls to encompass the close neighborhood, especially the parish of Sant'Isaia. In that parish lived three men identified as *familiaris fratrum minorum*. Paulus fq Ugolini de Argele was named heir by six men and women who lived around the city, but also by his peer and fellow parishioner Darius fq Farolfini, another *familiaris*. Paulus appeared as witness for three wills dictated inside the Franciscan sacristy. Darius was made heir twice by testators, viz., by a third *familiaris*, Paulucius fq Boni also of Sant'Isaia, and a testator from the neighboring parish of Santa Cristina.

---

[94] Dem. F. M., Camp. Rossi F, 340, 20: testament of 27 August 1348.

[95] Dem, F. M. Camp. Rossi F. 340, 54, n. 50.

[96] This will of a female testator appears to have gone against the rules of the *Memoriali*. She did not declare that the will should be secret and there is no clause stating it was delivered to the sacristan. Yet, there is not the standard declaration that the testament was registered with the *Memoriali*.

Furthermore, all three of these men received legacies to distribute for the benefit of testators's souls. The formal relationship of these *familiares* to the Franciscans is not explicit, but clearly they were part of the spiritual community that formed the church and its monastery as well as the surrounding neighborhood.[97] The friars worked throughout the Black Death within this close spiritual community and throughout the wider urban community.

The Franciscans and Dominicans appear prominently in the record because of their bureaucratic functions surrounding secret wills, but the other mendicant orders also played important roles in civic life, especially during the crisis of plague. The Augustinian Hermits also had a major church and pious center during the fourteenth century. Although their church of San Giacomo Maggiore (see Map of Bologna) is known today mainly for its fifteenth-century architectural and artistic developments, especially the chapel celebrating the powerful Renaissance Bentivoglio family, the 1330s and 1340s were a significant period in the construction of this important civic and religious monument as well as for the expansion of the order's presence in town. At that time the main building had just been completed and was being expanded with chapels and a bell tower, and the order had also recently took over the nearby parish church of Santa Cecilia. During both 1337 and 1348, the Augustinian Hermits and their church provided significant spiritual support for a few testators who dictated their testaments inside these two churches, requested burial at San Giacomo, or asked a friar to serve as executor.

The sample of wills allows the reconstruction of the activity of a few Augustinian Hermit friars who worked before, during, and after the plague struck. On 19 March 1348 friar Matiolus de Corbelaris was made executor and principal witness for a widow living in the parish of San Vitale behind the Augustinians's church on San Donato. Declaring her wishes within the church of San Giacomo, she left bequests to them for masses and requested burial at their church. Of the eight other brothers with Matiolus on that day was friar Johannes de Castro Britorum who appeared with Matiolus at the next occasion we find the Augustinian Hermit frairs together. This was during the epidemic on 3 June when

[97] For a discussion on the more flexible and less restricted roles of the female *familiaris*, compared with the *conversa*, in confraternity hospitals in Bergamo see Roisin Cossar, *The Transformation of the Laity in Bergamo, 1265–c. 1400* (Leiden, 2006), pp. 78–81.

eight friars met within the church of Santa Cecilia with the parish priest to hear the last wishes of a widow who requested burial in San Giacomo and asked the prior of the Augustinian hermits, "whomever he was", to be her executor. We next find Matiolus on 26 June witnessing the will of a widow dictated inside the church of San Giacomo. She requested burial in their church and asked the prior, Johannes of San Giovanni in Monte, to be her executor "if he lives or if not whomever is prior". These three friars disappear, but we can trace the activity of another friar on that day, Tomas de Sancto Alberto who had first appeared on 12 and 14 June as witness for testaments dictated inside San Giacomo and then for the testaments of a mother and daughter also made within the church on 11 July. He did not always stay within the convent since he was present also in the homes of testators in the nearby parish of Santa Cecilia as well as that of Sant'Omobono that lay outside the third walls and was a significant distance away from San Giacomo.[98] Brother Tomas made it through the ordeal since his last appearance was on 29 October where he served a married woman of the parish of Santa Cecilia, standing with many of her neighbors, in her home. Although the order of the Augustinian Hermits did not offer the bureaucratic services of preservers of secret wills as the Franciscans and Dominicans did, its church and friars did play important roles for testamentary and spiritual support, in particular to the neighborhoods surrounding them.

The fourth principal mendicant order, the Carmelites, did not build their own monumental complex, but their presence in the parish church of San Martino dell'Aposa with the Augustinian Hermits nearby provided a northern balance to the major sites of the Franciscans and Dominicans to the south and southwest. Since 1293 the Carmelites had been housed in the early thirteenth-century parish church, located just inside the second set of walls next to the sprawling northern parish of Santa Maria della Mascarella. Again, these mendicants were vital to civic and neighborhood life throughout the epidemic. According to the sample of wills, their prior friar Calandrinus witnessed nine wills

[98] Another example of Augustinian friars traveling outside of the church of San Giacomo is friar Nicola who first appears on 5 July in the parish of San Nicolò dell'Aposa and then on 9 August in the adjacent parish of San Donato (at the end of the street from his convent). Another of his brothers, friar Paulus, went to the parishes of San Vitale and San Sigismondo along Strada San Vitale, just behind the convent, on 5, 10, and 29 July: Mem, vol. 229, fols. 3v, 19r, 24r, 27v, 73v.

between 18 June and 10 October. Five of the testators lived in the parish of San Martino dell'Aposa, two others lived in adjacent parishes of San Nicolo dei Albari and Santa Maria Mascarella, and only one lived outside of this neighborhood in San Michele dei Leprosetti. Except for one case in which a healthy merchant testator had entered the sacristy of the Carmelite church to dictate a secret will, Calandrinus went into the homes of his sick neighbors to hear their last wishes. Most of the testators were well-off citizens who expressed their gratitude with small bequests for masses in the Carmelite church with money directed to the prior himself (and smaller bequests made to the convent). Calandrinus's dedication was selfless: grants up to ten *lire* were the extent of the populace's generosity to the Carmelites. Calandrinus served as executor for an unmarried woman in their parish who while leaving 20 *solidi* to two Carmelites and a bed for their infirmary, left her patrimony to her three brothers and asked for burial in the church of the Servites. Calandrinus appeared with several different brothers, in twos or fours, among the other lay witnesses to testaments. A frequent companion was brother Maginardus who, like him, survived the worst of the epidemic. Maginardus appeared at the side of seven ill neighbors in July, August, September, and November.[99] Both aided the substantial men and women of the parish of San Martino dell'Aposa and the neighboring Santa Maria della Mascarella. Two testators rewarded Maginardus with small bequests of ten and 20 *solidi* "for his necessities".

Friars from other mendicant orders appear in fewer numbers and did not offer their churches as the sites for redaction, so we cannot follow as many of their footsteps. Although the Servite friars were the third mendicant order established in Bologna (arriving in 1265) and at the time of our investigation had graduated from being housed in various parish churches to be able to construct a major church of their own on the city's main street, the testamentary evidence for their presence in the mid fourteenth century is thin: their order is only seldom added as a fifth recipient in pious bequests to all mendicant houses and the friars themselves are infrequently named, none more than once.[100] No testaments were drawn up in their church of Santa Maria dei Servi on Strada Maggiore, perhaps because it had to wait completion until 1354. However, during the plague months of June, July, and August

[99] Mem, vol. 229, fols. 29v, 206v.
[100] Foschi, "Gli ordini religiosi," in *Storia della Chiesa*, 2:483.

and afterwards in November, Servite friars did occasionally travel to the homes of their neighbors (viz., two testators of Santa Maria del Torleone) as well as to homes located at fair distances in other quarters of the city.

Servite brothers based at the church of Santa Margarita in Barbiano outside of the city walls aided another family in several ways. At the end of June an unmarried woman, Missina filia Massigoli de Massigni, who was living in the parish of Santa Cecilia dictated her will as she lay ill in the home of her father in Barbiano in the *guardia civitatis* with his recorded consent. He was charged as executor to oversee her wishes including burial in the church of Santa Margarita in Barbiano and the devolution of her property to her sister with the cautionary note that he could not have the property that came from his deceased wife's dowry. Ten days later, the father's sister and aunt of Missina lay ill in the same house in Barbiano. She also asked for burial in Santa Margarita and made Massigolus her heir and executor, adding that he must not sell her house to cover the costs of her stated legacies. The principal witness for both of these wills was brother Benedictus, prior of church of Santa Margarita of the order of Servites.[101] This friar's presence at the bedsides of these dying testators did not simply facilitate the making of valid wills during this time of intense crisis, but his repeated visits to the same household meant that two unmarried women could call upon support in their uneasy property relations with a male family member.

The other orders in Bologna also had a small but significant presence. The Humiliati friars of San Giacomo di Savena who were based at the monastery of Santi Filippo e Giacomo (of a previous community that had been suppressed in 1315), located near the parishes of Santa Maria Maddalena and San Leonardo at the edge of the third set of walls, aided people living in those parishes. Their prior, brother Antonius, went out five times from 23 July to 8 September, usually with brother Gregorius to visit the ill. The populace asked burial at their church and, once, asked brother Antonius to be executor. The last group of friars in Bologna that appear in the record were hermits of the order of Santa Maria di Ripa di Sasso who were housed at the parish church of Santa Maria di Castel dei Britti. This church was surrounded by the

[101] Mem, vol. 228, fol. 274r and vol. 229, fol. 204v. These friars are *ordinis servorum ordinis ecclesie sancte Malgarite de Barbiano.*

parishes of San Biagio, Santa Lucia, and San Tommaso del Mercato. Five testators from these parishes asked the hermit friars to hear last wishes during July and August. Either in pairs or alone they stood as principal witnesses with the priests of these parish churches in the homes of their neighbors.

Although the evidence is impressive for the mendicant friars because of the preservation of secret wills, the majority of testaments named priests, not friars, as principal witnesses. Most people turned to their parish priest and church for assistance in formalizing their last wishes and preparing for burial. Here too we find stories of courageous, selfless priests who went from house to house throughout the crisis. After one appearance in the sample of wills on 24 June, dopnus Gerardus of San Biagio appeared 13 other times in July. Dopnus Nicolaus of Santa Caterina di Saragozza served as principal witness eight times in January, March, April, and June. He may have died, since a different parish priest is recorded for that parish in July. Dopnus Lucha of San Marco at the central area of Porta Ravegnana worked during the toughest period ministering to eight testators between 10 July and 30 September. Similarly, at the other end of Strada Maggiore in Santa Maria del Torleone, dopnus Raynerius aided seven people from 15 July to 11 August. The sample sheds light on these men and several others who appear in two or three testaments, but all of them may have served many more times during the epidemic, and there were certainly more priests than those identified in the sample.

The parish priests moved in either their own parish or the close neighborhood comprising their parish and one or two adjacent parishes. Dopnus Bertolomeus, chaplain for the parish of Santa Maria del Torleone, was by the side of five neighbors in the three parishes located next to each other along Strada Maggiore, viz., his own parish and those of Santa Maria in Tempio within the walls and Sant'Omobono without. Dopnus Gerardus, noted above, worked in all but one case for his parishioners of San Biagio. Dopnus Lucha was principal witness for four different parishes clustered together around Piazza di Porta Ravegnana, the location of his parish of San Marco.[102] Because of its central location,

[102] Mem, vol. 229, fols. 20r, 29r, 73v, 76v, 84v, 194v; vol. 230, fol. 128v. Similar examples include: dopnus Bertolomeus of Santa Maria del Torleone who aided three testators in his own parish and two next door in Santa Maria del Tempio between 12 July and 4 August, a day when he went to two homes; dopnus Mathiollus of San Mamolo who worked in his own and the adjoining San Procolo five times between

many of Lucha's flock were of the highest elite, such as the Garisendi, who left bequests for him to say masses for their soul or made him executor.[103] Hard-working Raynerius was in his parish of Santa Maria del Torleone and in Santa Maria del Tempio, next door along Strada Maggiore, four times between 23 July and 10 August. However, he traveled up Strada Maggiore to the center of town on 19 July to aid a member of the Pepoli household and on 29 July to help Mathiolus the butcher, who lived in Sant'Omobono (located a short distance along Strada Maggiore from Santa Maria del Torleone). This will, as noted above, was redacted not in the home parish of Mathiolus, but at the central market in the presence of no less than seven notaries.

Neighborhood Officials

The neighborhood, therefore, was a center of activity during the Black Death. Notaries, friars, and priests worked in neighborhoods variously characterized by two, three, or four adjacent parishes. At the center of these webs of activity and support stood the parish. The religious leaders of the parish, the parish priests, focused their attention on their parishioners during the crisis of plague. They were not alone, since the secular leaders of the parish, the *ministrales cappellarum*, also actively assisted the people of their parish. This office was held by usually one or two men, although sometimes four or five worked together, who were elected for a year's term in January. The officers were of varied social status with occupations of those named for 1348 ranging from a comb seller, wine carrier (*brentator*), porter, agricultural worker (*laborator*) and winnower (*mundator*) to several butchers, smiths, bakers, shoemakers, and leather workers. Men with aristocratic surnames were a minority, as were men of wealthy occupations such as goldsmith or apothecary. Also among the *ministrales* were men of public faith, such as notaries and a town crier (*nuncius comunis*). Their salaries were paid

9 July and 30 August; dopnus Graciollus of San Giovanni in Monte who worked in three neighboring parishes (but not his own) on 28 July, 30 July, and 21 August; and dopnus Jacobus of Sant'Omobono who appeared in his own parish four times between 8 July and 23 July.

[103] Other examples of active priests being called upon as executors include Graciollus, canon of San Giovanni in Monte, who was present at the bedside of three neighbors, and brother Zacharias, a chaplain of Santa Maria di Castel dei Britti nominated as executor on 1 August and as principal witness on 4 August.

from monies collected from parish residents, with renters and owners of homes allotted different amounts. Their first duty each January was to draw up the lists of *venticinquine*, or men-at-arms. However, their duties were more general as they were responsible for the supervision of hygiene, morality, public order, and fire prevention.[104] Many of these parish leaders did not flee the town, but remained to aid their neighbors as witnesses and executors, even opening their homes to ill testators for the redaction of their wills.

The records of the *ministrales cappellarum* registers their nominations, which took place at the beginning of each year either at the parish church or at a notary's station in front of the *palatium vetus*, with the outgoing *ministrales* naming their new counterparts. When the nomination was done in the parish church, parishioners and neighbors were gathered together at the sound of the bells and the nomination was formally witnessed by three men before the altar who vouched for the identity of the *ministrales*. When the naming took place at the *palatium vetus*, three men from the parish, sometimes including the parish priest, declared to a notary that they knew the *ministrales*. Each parish had its own notarized parchment registers, which were preserved by the notaries of the *Camera degli Atti*, i.e., the communal archive. The records are incomplete, but the names of *ministrales* from 74 parishes do remain for 1348 and these can be cross-checked with names recorded in the wills from that year.[105] The result shows that the leaders of the parishes were remaining in town during the epidemic continuing their duties and succumbing to plague.

A few of the *ministrales* were notaries, and it should not be surprising that we find these men acting with exceptional loyalty and service to their neighbors during the horror of the epidemic. Johannes Dominici de Castagnolo was the *ministralis* of the parish of San Vitale during 1348. He stayed in town throughout the epidemic to redact 19 wills (14 of which were written during the worst of the epidemic in July). This notary, unlike his colleagues noted above, moved around a lot, since each testator lived in a different parish. His duties as notary took him far beyond the parish for which he was *ministralis*, since he redacted wills for clients who lived beyond the vicinity of his parish

[104] Pini, "Le ripartizioni territoriali," pp. 21–23.

[105] The notaries did not record the fact that an individual was a *ministralis cappellarum*. I have been able to deduce this by locating for the *ministralis*, a man with the same name, occupation, and parish in the *Memoriali* or *Demaniale*. I thank Sarah Blanshei for assistance.

and neighboring parishes. He survived the worst and was still redacting wills and serving his parishioners as *ministralis* in October. The notary, Petrus Phylipi Ysnardi, who was elected as a *ministralis* of Santa Maria Maddalena, also appears both during and after the epidemic had waned, since he redacted a will in July for a widow and in September for an elite man, both from neighboring Santa Cecilia, and then in November served Juliana Pepoli when she dictated her will at her home in San Damiano.[106] Rolandinus Panigalis was elected *ministralis* of Sant'Andrea dei Piatesi in January, but only appears in the wills in September when he redacted a will for another notary who lived next door in Santa Maria Maggiore.[107] Rolandinus's brother was also a notary living in Sant'Andrea dei Piatesi and, although he does not appear to have redacted any wills during 1348, he had his own will drawn up on October.[108] It is very possible that both brothers were active notaries during the epidemic, since Bonbolognus's wife was clearly in town and affected by plague, as we have her will, which was redacted in the home noted as belonging to her husband on 17 July.[109]

Not all *ministrales*, however, were men of public standing such as notaries. Most, in fact, were rank and file citizens. These parish leaders played other important roles for their neighbors as they struggled to deal with the epidemic. Some were nominated as executors, others as heirs, but they appear in the records principally as witnesses.[110] Sometimes they were assisting the members of their parish, as did Petrus fq Jacobelli de Malavoltis, *ministralis* of the parish of Santa Maria di Mascarella, who appeared on 9 July as witness for a widow of a baker living in that parish, and Bertholomeus fq Ubertini Palmieri, *ministralis*

[106] Mem, vol. 229, fol. 262v (Romana fq domini Ricardini Lambertini); vol. 230, fols. 210r (Andreas fq domini Francisci de Bernardinis), 386r (Juliana de Peppolis).

[107] Mem, vol. 229, fol. 250v (Jacobus fq Alberti Pugni).

[108] Mem, vol. 230, fol. 19v (codicil of Bonbolognus Panichalis).

[109] Mem, vol. 229, fol. 91v (Francesca domini Fellini de Barberiis).

[110] The *ministralis* of San Leonardo was named as a *prudens vir* to be the executor for a notary, also of San Leonardo, who made his will during the plague-filled month of August: Mem, vol. 229, fol. 76v (Johannes Anthoni Yvani). The *ministralis* of San Martino dei Santi was named as executor by another testator in June: Mem, vol. 228, fol. 147r (Maghinardus fq Petri). An unmarried woman living in San Giovanni in Monte shared a home with the *ministralis* of that parish and named him her heir when she had her will written up in August: Mem, vol. 230, fol. 239r (Lucia fq Guidonis). A similar acknowledgement of personal importance to an individual testator dying from plague can be determined by another unmarried woman of the parish of Sant'Andrea dei Piatesi who lay ill in the home of the *ministralis* of San Leonardo when she made her will in August: Mem, vol. 229, fol. 192r (Chaterina fq Johannis Chambini).

of Santa Maria Maddalena, who was present on 29 July in the home of an ill man in his parish.[111] Other *ministrales* aided men who lived outside of their own parish, but within the neighborhood of adjacent parishes. Thus Jacobus fq Bonaventure Petri, *ministralis* of Sant'Andrea degli Ansaldi, went to aid a widow in San Procolo next door on August 7.[112] Guidus fq Cazaguere, a *merzarius* and *ministralis* of San Simone e Guida, however, traveled through several parishes on 21 July to serve as witness for the son of a deceased doctor in his home in Santa Maria Maggiore. The final example of *ministrales* serving as witnesses shows up in the record when one helped out his family: the *ministralis* of San Sigismondo, Chabriel Bertolomei de Muzolis, who was a merchant and son of a deceased notary, was at the side of his sister who lived in the adjacent parish of Santa Cecilia.[113]

We can infer the presence in town during the epidemic of seven other *ministrales* whose close relatives appear in the plague wills. *Ministrales* were the husbands of three plague testators, while others were either a brother, brother-in-law, or father-in-law of testators or a brother of a witness. The *ministrales* were staying in town, aiding the residents of their parish, and as a result they were becoming ill and dying of plague. Six *ministrales* were, in fact, testators whose wills appear in the *Memoriali* (although the notaries did not record their office as *ministralis*). They all were ill and dying in July. Bertus magistri Guarneri was a master carpenter and *ministralis* of Sant'Alberto who had his will written up on 9 July. He may have died immediately, since his brother Maxolinus of the same parish made his will on the following day and did not mention his name.[114] Similarly, Petrus fq Francisci Sanuti the leader of San Giuseppe di Borgo del Galliera made his will on 15 July and when his brother Jacobus, a notary of the same

---

[111] Mem, vol. 229, fols. 22v (Johannes fq Jacobi Johannis), 112r (Chaterina fq Jacobini). Another example of *ministrales* serving their close neighbors is Vicentius de Alle, one of the five *ministrales* of Santa Maria Maddalena, who was witness for a married women in his parish before plague struck Bologna: Mem, vol. 228, fol. 182r (Mixina fq Azollini de Seravale on 29 April 1348).

[112] Mem, vol. 229, fols. 94r (Jacoba fq ser Francisci Tencharari), 207r (Johannes filius olim magistri Jachobi medici). After plague subsided, Antonius fq magistri Guidonis, *ministralis* of Santa Maria dei Bulgari in the quarter of San Procolo was witness for an elite man from the San Cristoforo dei Geremei also in San Procolo: Mem, vol. 229, fol. 169v (Alidoxius olim domini Buvalelli de Buvalellis on 29 November 1348).

[113] Mem, vol. 229, fol. 180v (Mixina fq Bertolomeis de Muzolis).

[114] Mem, vol. 229, fols. 376v (Maxolinus fq magistri Guarneri), 377r (Bertus fq magistri Guarneri).

parish, went to dictate his secret will at San Francesco a week later he did not mention his brother.[115] Johannes fq Zonis de Gargognano, a butcher and *ministralis* of San Leonardo, made his will on 18 July as did his brother who lived in the same parish.[116] Matiolus fq Johannis Bonaguide, a butcher and *ministralis* of Sant'Omobono, made his will at the end of July, while his wife lasted a little longer to make her will in early November.[117] Thus the evidence of the *ministrales* corroborates what has been found already for families faced with plague.

The tiny tesserae of information about the whereabouts of the many individual notaries, physicians, priests, friars, and *ministrales* in Bologna during the Black Death can be fitted together to complete a mosaic with clear patterns and themes. These men were remaining at their posts throughout the awful summer months of the epidemic. They appeared in numerous capacities, all for the purpose of aiding the populace. Principally, they worked in neighborhoods, which appear to have served as structures of support and interaction. In the following chapter we will examine the webs of interactions among neighbors.

[115] Dem, F. M. Camp. Rossi F, 340, 39, n. 35 (Jacobus fq Francisci Sanuti); Mem, vol. 230, fol. 449r (Petrus fq Francisci Sanuti).

[116] Mem, vol. 229, fol. 375 (Johannes fq Zonis de Garganano).

[117] Mem, vol. 229, fol. 194v (Matiolus fq Johannis Bonaguide) and vol. 230, fol. 442r (Jacoba fq Donellis). The other *ministrales* who appear as testators are a jacketmaker from Santa Maria Maddalena and the noble Johannes fq Ugolini ser Bondi de Planellis of Sant'Andrea degli Ansaldi: Mem, vol. 229, fols. 6v, 109v.

CHAPTER FIVE

NEIGHBORHOOD ACTIVITY DURING THE BLACK DEATH

Neighborhood has long been recognized and studied as a fundamental aspect of late medieval and Renaissance urban life. Much of the attention has been focused on Renaissance Florence and Venice with thorough investigations of neighborhood life carried out by Monica Chojnacka, Samuel Kline Cohn, Jr., Nicholas Eckstein, Dale Kent, Francis W. Kent, Christiane Klapisch, Dennis Romano, and Ronald Weissman.[1] Neighborhoods were communities of individuals located in a particular area who were connected by webs of interactions involving the multifaceted social bonds of work, gender, kinship, and clientage. The close and frequent contacts of neighborhood life concentrated social networks. These bonds permeated the rituals and activities of daily life beyond the neighborhood and into the city at large, but they could be generated and/or strengthened by the neighborhood, that is, by the fact of living in proximity. Nearness enabled, but did not determine, the creation of the networks of social bonds—as Eckstein warns, one must avoid a "geographical determinism" in analysis.[2] Neighborhood could reinforce the social bonds of work, since one's neighbors might help one find contacts to procure employment or customers, to ensure credit or raw materials. Neighborhood bonds might dominate other social connections, as one may have felt a stronger affinity and connection for a peer tradesman in one's neighborhood than elsewhere.

---

[1] Christiane Klapisch explicated the overlapping layers of family, friendship, and neighborhood in her seminal article of 1976 translated as "'Kin, Friends, and Neighbors': The Urban Territory of a Merchant Family in 1400," in her *Women, Family, and Ritual*, pp. 68–93. On the Florentine neighborhood see Francis W. Kent and Dale V. Kent, *Neighbours and Neighbourhoods in Renaissance Florence: The District of the Red Lion in the Fifteenth Century* (Locust Valley, N.Y., 1982); Nicholas Eckstein, *The District of the Green Dragon: Neighbourhood Life and Social Change in Renaissance Florence* (Florence, 1995); Cohn, *Laboring Classes*. For Venice see Dennis Romano, *Patricians and Popolani: The Social Foundations of the Venetian Renaissance State* (Baltimore, 1987); Monica Chojnacka, *Working Women of Early Modern Venice* (Baltimore, 2001).

[2] Nicholas Eckstein, "The Neighborhood as Microcosm," in *Renaissance Florence: A Social History*, eds. Roger J. Crum and John T. Paoletti (New York, 2006), pp. 220–221.

Fundamental decisions made by individuals and families, such as the choice of marriage partners, were shaped and maintained by neighborhood bonds. Death and funerals encompassed and acknowledged the importance of the neighborhood ties. Neighbors took their place with friends and fellow guild members in funeral processions to demonstrate and continue to fulfill the social bonds that had functioned during the life of the deceased.[3] The identity of many families, especially among the elite, was linked to neighborhood.

While recognizing that many late medieval city-dwellers were a litigious bunch, often involved in on-going conflicts that were settled both by the sword and the courts through various processes of resolution, most scholars have seen social urban networks as constructive, creating a sense of solidarity in the political and commercial world that radiated beyond and encompassed the neighborhood.[4] Ronald Weissman, in his investigation of the social organization and ritual behavior of Renaissance Florentine confraternities, has instead characterized social relations in urban life as fraught with competition, suspicion, and animosity, in short, as "agonistic". They had to be continually managed and manipulated.[5] This study of Bolognese society during a time replete with danger is a good way to test the quality of social ties. Did individuals in late medieval towns face the horror of plague burdened by the necessity of navigating competing social relations or were they strengthened by the mutually supportive bonds of kinship, family, business, and neighborhood? If, as Weissman asserts, "[t]he agonistic character of social relations imbued all social contacts with potential danger" why would one go to the enormous effort of continuing social contact during an epidemic?[6]

---

[3] Sharon Strocchia, *Death and Ritual in Renaissance Florence* (Baltimore and London, 1992), Chapter 1.

[4] For the litigious character of late medieval Italian and French cities see Daniel Lord Smail, *The Consumption of Justice: Emotions, Publicity, and Legal Culture in Marseille, 1264–1423* (Ithaca and London, 2003), Introduction and ch. 1; Massimo Vallerani, *La giustizia pubblica medievale* (Bologna, 2005), Introduzione and ch. 1; Christopher Wickham, *Courts and Conflict in Twelfth-Century Lucca* (Oxford, 2003).

[5] The ritual space and heterogeneous membership of the confraternities, on the other hand, at least during the fourteenth and fifteenth centuries, acted as a foil to or temporary release from the conflicting and competitive bonds that functioned in the outside social world. See Ronald F. E. Weissman, *Ritual Brotherhood in Renaissance Florence* (New York, 1982), Chapters One, esp. pp. 26–35, and Chapter Two, and, by the same author, "The Importance of Being Ambiguous: Social Relations, Individualism, and Identity in Renaissance Florence," in *Urban Life in the Renaissance*, eds. Susan Zimmerman and Ronald F. E. Weissman (Newark, 1989), pp. 269–280.

[6] Weissman, *Ritual Brotherhood*, p. 41.

If social contacts were maintained during the Black Death—and we have already seen this to be the case for families and certain professionals and clerics—it would be better to argue, without abandoning the notion that competition and conflict did exist, that strength was the primary characteristic of social relations.

In their efforts to demonstrate the continued importance of social bonds of a corporate nature, the breakdown of which has been identified with the rise of modern society, historians of the early modern city have illuminated the day-to-day interactions of the neighborhood. Ironically, although the importance of neighborhood in the medieval city is clearly recognized and has been masterfully studied, for example, for Genoa by Diane Owen Hughes, such detailed studies of neighborhood life are harder to produce because of limited source material.[7] The testaments of Bologna during the Black Death provide an excellent means to examine the social bonds of hundreds of neighbors in action. As expressed in Chapter One, notarial law and communal statutes were concerned to make testaments the accurate wishes of individuals and as such they demanded that the will be corroborated by several impartial witnesses. Thus the making of a will drew upon the efforts of the wider community, not simply the individual testator and notary. The legal norms required the presence of many witnesses, and the circumstances of the Black Death, furthermore, brought many more individuals into the historical record, whose actions, because of the narrow time frame, can be traced and retraced in the record. The testament is a good source to examine the ties of a testator to the wider community of the neighborhood, because the request and service of witnesses were socially significant acts. While witnesses may have often worked in the service of a notary, the evidence below demonstrates when a man came to the side of a testator and allowed his name to be recorded as witness for the dictation of the will, he came because of the social bonds that connected him with the testator.[8] Serving as witness required one to enter into the household of a dying man or woman and to take part in an important social and religious ritual. Requesting a witness did not mean merely hailing the

[7] Diane Owen Hughes, "Kinsmen and Neighbors in Medieval Genoa," in *The Medieval City*, eds. Harry A. Miskimin, David Herlihy and A. L. Udovitch (New Haven, 1977), pp. 95–111.

[8] This is not the kind of legalistic formality that was, for example, the requirement of a *mundualdus* or male guardian for a woman engaging in a legal contract in medieval Florence. See Thomas Kuehn, "'Cum Consensu Mundualdi': Legal Guardianship of Women in Quattrocento Florence," in Kuehn, *Law, Family, and Women*, pp. 212–237.

closest available person off the street. People were asked and came to serve because of the social bonds of kinship, work, friendship, and neighborhood between testator and witnesses. The action of serving as witness was a demonstration of a social bond imbued with the kind of quality of human interaction that is both the product of and an ingredient for community.[9] The documents accurately reflect these actions in the lists of witnesses that came at the end of each testament, because the number of witnesses was not always the same and because distinct and reasonable patterns can be determined by analyzing those lists. In other words we are not dealing with fiction: notaries did not simply write down seven names of men who were not present. Of course there is no way to prove that what the notaries wrote was a faithful reproduction of what happened in the past, but neither is there evidence in the wills to suggest that notaries merely took down names provided by a testator who remained alone.[10] My method is to follow the record.

This study of medieval Bologna follows the approach advocated by Nicholas Eckstein for the neighborhoods of Renaissance Florence. In order to understand neighborhoods one must begin with the social relationships which can then be traced to specific locations.[11] Most researchers begin with an administrative division of the town, such

[9] On the multifaceted nature of neighborhood interactions, see David Garrioch, *Neighborhood and Community in Paris, 1740–1790* (Cambridge, 1986), pp. 1–6 and 55. On witnessing as a means to gain legal and business expertise, foster relationships, and promote civic roles such as officeholders and arbitrators, see Mary Lampe, "Survival and Profit: Witnessing Groups in Post-Vespers Palermo" (PhD diss., University of California at Santa Barbara, 2007), pp. 51–60.

[10] As Julius Kirshner rightly advised we should be aware of the fact that legal texts could mask rather than reveal reality, as for example dotal acts that falsely reported dowry amounts, dates, and exchanges. Dowry and loan acts served the purposes of clients who sometimes preferred to hide or fabricate certain information for their financial benefit, but testaments were not financial acts. A will was drawn up as part of a social ritual for which witnesses were an integral part. It is possible that a few testators did not wish to have seven witnesses, but those few had and took the option of making a secret will or noting secret instructions (see Chapter One). It is instead more likely that most testators wanted the presence of witnesses and correct notarial form in order to ensure their statements would have legal force in the future. Notaries—as their formularies attest—shared this view. Julius Kirshner, "Some problems in the interpretation of legal texts *re* the Italian city-state," *Archiv fur Begriffsgeschichte* 19 (1975), 17–27.

[11] According to Nicholas Eckstein, "[t]o speak in any meaningful sense of neighborhood, it is first necessary to ascertain people's membership in the networks of bonds by which we understand a community, and thereafter to establish the connection of these bonds to the charged landscape of the neighborhood itself". Eckstein, "Neighborhood as Microcosm," p. 230.

as the ward or *gonfalone* in Florence or district or *sestiere* in Venice, and then proceed to explore the social bonds of interaction within this area. Neighborhoods, however, were not determined administratively from the top down, but from the interactions of individuals linked in social bonds that gave meaning to their lives. As David Garrioch states, the local community, or for our purposes, the neighborhood, "[l]ike a living tissue... can be understood only when observed in operation, and not by stopping it and breaking it down into its different parts".[12] So, while historians of Renaissance Venice and Florence, including Eckstein himself, have traditionally chosen the district as the unit of analysis, I have let the evidence determine my unit of analysis by searching for patterns of association that emerge from the bonds revealed in the wills in order to define the neighborhood. This is partly because the administrative division of Bologna, the quarter, was too large to constitute a neighborhood and the other topographical division used for religious and administrative purposes, namely, the parish, was, I argue, too small to constitute a neighborhood. The terms that notaries used to identify the residence of testators or location of sites of the redaction of the will, similarly, are not helpful in determining neighborhood, since they used either the parish (*cappella*) or street. A few homes were described as located in a particular *contrata, androna, braida, burgus*, or *locus*, terms often considered to indicate neighborhood, but which by the fourteenth century had come to designate street.[13] Thus neighborhood cannot be determined by the terminology used in the historical record, but by the actions of individuals revealed in those records. As we have seen was the case for notaries, friars and priests, people worked in areas that did not always follow either the boundaries of parish or quarter, but instead in clusters of parishes that could cross quarter boundaries.

This chapter will investigate the social networks and interactions within the parishes and neighborhoods during the Black Death in Bologna. By means of the general database of testators from the *Memoriali* of 1337 and 1348 and the sample of 255 testaments from the plague months with data entered on witnesses, I will define some neighborhood areas

[12] Garrioch, p. 55.

[13] Pini, "Le ripartizioni territoriali," pp. 20–30. Wills were redacted "in cappella Sancti Blaxii in brayna Sancti Stephani" (in the parish of San Biagio on Via Santo Stefano), "in cappella Sancti Arcangeli in androna de Agrestis" (in the parish of Sant'Arcangelo on Via degli Agresti), "in cappella Sancti Leonardi in androna Sancti Leonardi" (in the parish of San Leonardo on Via San Leonardo).

by means of the location of testators's residences and by the actions of individuals, principally witnesses, during the epidemic.[14]

The Parish

Any discussion of neighborhood must begin with the parish. Since the early thirteenth century when many of their churches were built, the parish was the core of religious life for most individuals, and, for the administrators who drafted records, it served as the principal identifier of an individual's identity. Next to an individual's first name and that of his or her father, a resident of late medieval Bologna was known to notaries and thus to us by the parish.[15] The few individuals (5 per cent of testators) whose parish was not recorded by the notaries were either elites with noble family names whose identity was well known or members of the religious communities, such as three priests, a tertiary sister, and a servant of a convent.[16] For elites, notaries were more likely to omit the address for men, while they identified elite wives by means of a parish (along with fathers's and husbands's names).[17] The only individual in the testaments who did not bear an aristocratic surname or ecclesiastical connection and who was not assigned a parish was a woman identified as the *familiana* of a nobleman, her identity being subsumed under his.

The parish or *cappella* was the original topographical division of the city, which, after the establishment of the quarter system in 1219, had both civil and ecclesiastical purposes as it fit into the larger administrative organization of the town. As discussed in Chapter One, the quarters were used for the administrative purposes of military recruitment, taxation assessment, and imposition of public works, while the parish,

[14] See Chapter One, footnote 99 on this sample.

[15] This is different from the contemporary situation in southern France. Daniel Lord Smail found that notaries rarely used parish in mid fourteenth-century Marseille. See his *Imaginary Cartographies: Possession and Identity in Late Medieval Marseille* (Ithaca and London, 1999), pp. 17–18.

[16] This is similar to Smail's findings for fourteenth-century Marseille where laborers were more carefully identified than noblemen in notarial contracts. See Ibid., p. 26.

[17] For example, the will of Pax de Suricis does not record his parish, even in the *actum* phrase, while his widow, Ghexia fq Jacobini de Ripolli, is identified by their home parish of Santo Stefano. The same notary redacted both wills nearly a month apart (Mem, vol. 230, fol. 98v on 14 July for Pax and Mem, vol. 229, fol. 76r on 6 August for Ghexia).

as we saw in Chapter Four, also had its own political leaders called *ministrales cappellarum*.[18] The office of the *ministrales* was created after the imposition of the quarters, which meant that parishes that were cut in two, such as the parish of San Vitale which was divided by the boundary of the quarters of Porta Piera and Porta Ravennate that ran along its central road, had two sets of *ministrales*.[19] It is likely that the residents of the parish identified themselves more closely as belonging to the older ecclesiastical area of the entire parish, rather than the administratively determined area of the part of the parish lying within a particular quarter. This is borne out by the identification of individuals named in the wills: no one is recorded as living in, for example, San Vitale of Porta Piera, but as simply in San Vitale. Identification with the ecclesiastical division of the parish would have been the case even though the social composition of parishes were not always homogeneous, as roads and ancient walls could form social barriers within the parish.[20]

A further important element in the identity of the parish and the individual was the family, which, especially among the elite, was strongly associated with the parish. As the evidence of testator families in Chapter Three showed, members of a family usually made their homes in the same parish. The list of sibling testators includes many brothers who would most likely be heading up their own households, since their fathers were dead.[21] These brothers almost always lived in the same parish. Married sisters, too, often lived near their siblings, but they

[18] See Giorgio Tamba, "I documenti del governo del comune bolognese (1116–1512): Lineamenti della struttura istituzionale della città durante il Medioevo," *Quaderni Culturali Bolognesi* 2 (1978), p. 46.

[19] Only the locations of the parish churches, not the boundaries of the parishes, are known.

[20] For an investigation of the parish of San Vitale and its varied social composition, see Antonio Ivan Pini, "La chiesa, il monastero e la parrocchia di San Vitale a Bologna dalle origini alla fine del XIII secolo," reprinted in Pini, *Città, chiesa e culti civici in Bologna medievale* (Bologna, 1999), 91–118, especially pp. 109–114.

[21] Only seven homes described as belonging to pairs of brothers appear in the *actum* clause of the wills from 1337 and 1348. One was described as belonging to the sons of the widowed testator, another as belonging to the husband of the testator and his brother. In four other cases the testator was temporarily living in the home belonging to two brothers who were not related to the testator. It may be the case that many male testators owned the home with their brothers, and, although only the testator's name is ascribed to the ownership of the house, the brother's ownership is assumed. However, there is one example of a house described as belonging to both the testator and his brother, which would work against this assumption.

were much more likely to have left the parish of the natal family.[22] While a common trait, the familial identity with the parish is best recognized in Bologna's most elite families, as several parishes took their name from the nobles who dominated them. The noble towers and their family churches marked the center of their local power. Some of the ancient designations of parishes after an aristocratic lineage still had real social meaning in the mid fourteenth century. For example, the Galluzzi were still prominent in the parish of Santa Maria Rotunda dei Galluzzi since four testators of that family made their homes there: one male head of household, two wives, and a widow.[23] The Galluzzi daughters, however, had moved out of the parish as a result of marriage.[24] Other members of the Galluzzi line lived in different parishes.[25] Similarly, there are testators of the Lambertini line, such as the "generous and magnificent knight" Eganus fq Lambertini de Lambertinis and Giulius olim Azonis Petri de Lambertinis, who lived in the noble family parish, San Cataldo dei Lambertini, while their daughters and sisters can be found in other parishes.[26] The home of Eganus de Lambertinis had special social significance for the Bolognese elite, since three testaments were dictated there. These belonged to noble wives and a widow who resided in other parishes, but for some reason were "at present" living in the household of Eganus when they drew up their wills. This was the case both for the pre-plague evidence of 1337 and during the epidemic, when Eganus

---

[22] It is hard to judge the testators who are related as parent and child, because these mainly include widowed daughters who all lived in the same parish as their parents, and may in fact have moved back to their natal family's household after having left it at marriage.

[23] Burniollus fq domini Blanchi de Galuciis (Mem, vol. 230, fol. 249r); Jacobina fq domini Jacobi de Nucharellibus, wife of Soldanus de Galuciis; Agnesia Versi de Blanchuciis, the widow of Gerus Blanchi de Galuciis (Mem, vol. 229, fol. 127r); Bertolomea Ramberti de Ghissilieriis was wife of the noble knight Petrus fq Henrigiti de Galuciis (Mem, vol. 193, fol. 292r).

[24] Gexia fq domini Johannis de Galuciis married into the Bentivoglio family and lived in their parish of Santa Cecilia (Mem, vol. 230, fol. 150r), while the widowed Philippa Mathioli de Galuciis had moved to Santa Maria dei Guidoscalchi (Mem, vol. 192, fol. 256r).

[25] Simona fq ser Bonmerchati, wife of Gulielmus Magli Neri Galuciis, lived in Nicolò degli Albari.

[26] Bexia fq Azonis Petri de Lambertinis lived in San Tecle on the street of Santo Stefano (Mem, vol. 229, 336r) and Elena Ricardi de Lambertinis lived in Santa Maria dei Guidoscalchi (Mem, vol. 192, fol. 276r). Carocius Mathei de Lambertinis lived in Santa Maria Maddalena (Mem, vol. 230, fol. 235r). A further example of the principal Lambertini line still residing in San Cataldo dei Lambertini is in the will of Manfredus fq Guidonis de Canetulo which was redacted in San Cataldo in the home of the knight Franciscus de Lambertinis (Mem, vol. 230, fol. 497r).

died and passed the house to his heirs.[27] His house was also the first place where the town heralds, the *bannitores comunis*, made the *crida* or called out the public banns (*bannum cridare*).[28]

No single parish was characterized by one type of occupation. Similarly, no occupation is found in only one parish and nowhere else. The only craft that comes close to some kind of strict occupational zoning were the parchment makers (*cartolarii*), who were concentrated in the parish of San Biagio.[29] All but two of the 20 witnesses, testators, or legatees in the *Memoriali* of 1348 who named this occupation lived in San Biagio. Nevertheless, although parchment-making was the most common profession in San Biagio, second only to butchers, as Pini also found in his investigation of the guild matriculation list of 1294, the range of occupations of residents in this parish was very large: tailors, tanners, shoemakers, notaries, leather workers, weavers, woolmongers, smiths, an armorer and a mason also crowded into this parish along the Savena canal.[30] Many of these workers were taking advantage of the available water of the canal, necessary for their trades.

Occupational Zones

If we move beyond the individual parish to study areas of contiguous parishes, much more occupational grouping comes to light, and here we can determine areas with more neighbor-like bonds. For example, although butchers made their homes in 19 different parishes, the bulk of them were concentrated within a few parishes. Most of the butchers preferred to live in four parishes that ran along the Savena canal: Santa

---

[27] During the epidemic, the noble widow, Vilana fq fratris Simonis de Rodaldis who gave no original parish, lay ill "at the home of the heirs of Eganus" on 23 July (Mem, vol. 230, fol. 452v), as did Diana fq Zambini de Villa Nova of San Sinesio on 3 August (Mem, vol. 229, fol. 437r). Before the epidemic, the married Agnesia fq Bertolomei of Modena, residing in the parish of Santa Caterina di Saragozza and "presently staying in the house of Eganus," made her will there on 2 September 1337 (Mem, vol. 193, fol. 169r). Eganus may not have been at his home when Vilana and Diana testated there. He made his will on 18 July in the monastery of Santa Maria di Camaldoli outside of town (Mem, vol. 229, fol. 378r).

[28] Braidi, *Gli Statuti del Comune*, 2:945.

[29] Pini found that in 1294 most parchment makers lived in San Biagio (152 men who matriculated as parchment makers were located there). See Pini, "La ripartizione topografica," p. 200.

[30] Ibid.

Lucia, San Biagio, San Tomaso della Braina, and San Leonardo (see Map of Parishes of Bologna). We see that these neighborhoods do not follow the boundaries of the quarters, since three of these butcher-preferred parishes lay within the boundaries of the quarter of Porta Ravennate, while Santa Lucia was within Porta Procola. Another smaller group of butchers can be found in three parishes clustered along the Strada Maggiore near the southeastern edge of the third set of walls. The rest of the butchers were spread around town without any clear grouping of residences.

Butchers often lived near shoemakers and bootmakers (*calzarius, calegarius*), another leading occupation in mid fourteenth-century Bologna, who lived in 22 parishes, but were present in four roughly equal groups of numbers who tended to make their homes in clusters of parishes located in different parts of the town. About one quarter of the shoemakers lived in the parishes clustered on the western side of the town (opposite from the preferred neighborhoods of the butchers) near the Riva del Reno in the parishes of San Felice, San Nicolo del Borgo di San Felice, and San Lorenzo di Porta Stiera, while three other equally-sized groups lived in four contiguous parishes that stretched back from San Biagio to the walls and beyond to Sant'Omobono (not along the canal as did the neighborhoods of the butchers), in three parishes centered in the north on either side of the second set of walls (Santa Maria Maggiore, San Giuseppe del Borgo di Galliera, San Giorgio Poggiale), and in three parishes clustered in the northeastern corner of the walls (Santa Maria Mascarella, Santa Maria Maddalena, and Sant'Egidio).

Occupational zoning seems apparent also among the many smiths who appear in the wills. Again, we find them in the same general areas as butchers and shoemakers, but they form their own pattern of grouping, since more than half lived in four contiguous parishes stretching out from San Biagio towards the southeastern corner of the city (San Biagio, Santa Cristina della Fondazza, Santa Maria del Torleone and Sant'Omobono). Thus neighborhoods based on bonds of work can be identified. These took the form of clusters of two to four adjacent parishes, not individual parishes, and they followed the physical environment of the city, streets and, especially canals, not the administrative boundaries of the quarter.

The most common occupation listed by testators and witnesses in the wills is notary. Their documentary presence is not simply because they produced the evidence, but reflects their immense numbers in town. Pini's study of the guild matriculation lists of 1294 revealed 1308 notaries enrolled in that guild and that they lived in 90 of Bologna's 99 parishes, making them the most dispersed trade.[31] Brian Carniello further analyzed the lists to determine that the guild of notaries contained a larger number of families than other guilds—in contrast to the bankers's guild which contained many members of a few wealthy families—and that notaries were matriculated in many other guilds as well as their own.[32] The testamentary evidence from mid fourteenth century does not match the numbers of the end of the thirteenth century, but the residential patterns are similar. Notaries are found in all four quarters. Their dispersed nature highlights the very different residential preferences of the butchers, smiths, and shoemakers who tended to live in clusters of parishes near canals. Also unlike these artisans, most notaries lived between the first and second walls, a wealthier zone than the area between the second and third walls. Notaries can be found in the less wealthy areas nearer the third walls and two are even located beyond the walls. But only three lived within the aristocratic nucleus within the first set of walls. The notaries served people living all over the city, and there do not appear to have been clear neighborhoods which were characterized by notaries's residences, although we have seen that notaries worked in neighborhood regions. Nevertheless, one quarter of the notaries did live in nine parishes that encircled the central market area around the parish of San Tommaso del Mercato. This cluster of parishes included two of the parishes most populated with notaries, viz., Santa Maria Maggiore and San Martino dell'Aposa. Because the parishes within the second, and especially the first, set of walls were much smaller than those beyond the second set of walls, it is possible that these more numerous parishes did in fact form a neighborhood.

Neighborhoods During the Black Death

From an examination of the residence patterns of Bologna's workers we find that the parishes were the cells that together formed the organ of the neighborhood. How did these hold up when disease entered the body, i.e., the city of Bologna? When plague struck, the ill and dying

---

[31] Ibid., pp. 200 and 207.
[32] Carniello, "Notaries of Bologna," Chapter 3.

had to be taken care of and assisted within the family and within the neighborhood. The kind of social behavior found for the professionals and public persons during the Black Death can be expanded to include many more individuals when we turn to examine the witnesses who attended the redaction of the testaments. It took the courage of thousands of individual men and women to ensure the preservation of the last wishes of the dying testators. Linked by the social networks that functioned within the communities of parish and neighborhood, these people came to aid the dying during the crisis.

The *Memoriali* demonstrate that witnesses entered the homes of the ill, since the *actum* clause of the vast majority of testaments states that redaction took place in a home: 832 of the 915 wills from June, July, and August were *in domo*.[33] They were meeting inside the home and occasionally the room was specified. Only four wills were made either in the garden (*in orto*) or field (*in champa*) or under the portico of a home. The extant wills demonstrate that plague victims were usually dying in their own home: *in domo testatoris*. Testators, however, were also hosted in the homes of others during the epidemic. Occasionally these homes are noted as belonging to the heirs of a deceased man, an indication of the frequent change of ownership due to plague deaths. It is interesting to note that a married woman could be described as a "guest" in her own home, a condition that Christiane Klapisch has argued was the case for women of the Florentine merchant elite in the Renaissance.[34] A small minority (6 per cent) of the redaction sites of married female testators was described as belonging to the husband alone (*in domo mariti*), with a smaller number stating that the home belonged to both spouses (*in domo mariti et testatricis*).[35] Widows, in fact, were more likely than married women to be living in homes that were specified as theirs.[36] It must be noted, however, that overall the majority of widows and wives stated

[33] Fourteen of these were "in domibus" of a church or monastery. The secret wills of the *Demaniale* are not included in this analysis because they were examples of exceptional practice, usually redacted in the religious houses.

[34] See Klapisch-Zuber, "The Cruel Mother," p. 118.

[35] Of 39 married women in June, one lived in her husband's home, for two the home belonged to both spouses; of 109 married women in July, the home of eight belonged to the husband alone, while six shared ownership; and of 22 married women in August, two homes belonged to the husband and one was owned by wife, husband and his brother.

[36] In June the homes of 70 per cent of widows, compared to 59 per cent of married women, were described as their own. In July, the numbers are about equal with 63 per cent of widows and 64 per cent of married women in their own homes. In August, 62 per cent of widows, compared to 50 per cent of wives, were in their own homes.

they were in their own homes. Although the declaration in the *actum* clause of a will may not always have indicated who was the owner of the home, it does show that, at least in the context of legal language, most women were not merely viewed as passing guests in their husbands's or fathers's home—these houses were considered to be their homes.

While the typical situation was a testator surrounded by his family and neighbors in his own home, 46 *Memoriali* testators from the summer months made their wills in a church, with the spot sometime specified as in a chapel, the sacristy, cloister, before an altar or the door. Most, but not all, of these testators were healthy, and the majority were widows or unmarried women. (Men who chose to dictate their wills in a church, as we have seen, usually chose to make secret wills with the mendicants.) Although within a church, these redactions could have also been carried out in the presence of family members: as was the case for two sisters who made their wills together before the altar of Saint Catherine in the church of San Giacomo of the Augustinian Hermits on 19 June; for a widowed mother and her daughter who dictated their wills at the same spot a month later on 11 July; and for a husband and wife, both ill, from Borgo Panigale who met in a church in the *guardia civitatis* on 3 August.[37] Six individuals, including a mother and daughter, met *in scolis* of the Franciscans and Dominicans. In these cases friars usually comprised all of the witnesses (as was the case for the secret wills of men discussed in Chapter Four). Eight healthy and ill men and women chose a more public forum for the redaction of their wills since they met notaries at their workplaces in front of the *palatium notariorum* and the *palatium vetus* to draw up their wills. These testators were assisted by several notaries and other men who came from parishes spread around town. Of the testators found in a hospital, two men may have had no family left, since one made the hospital his heir and the other designated the Poor of Christ, whom the hospital was to select. They both charged hospital officials to be their executors.[38] Thus the home was the principal choice for making a will during the crisis of plague, but this intimate, domestic option was supplemented by the religious houses (for men's secret wills and for women's publicly registered testaments) or lay institutions such as hospitals and notaries's workplaces.

---

[37] Mem, vol. 228, fols. 25r (Beleza fq Bertholuci de Manticis and Bitixia fq domini Felloni de Baxacomatribus), 273r–v (Chatellina and Zanna fq Francisci de Artenixiis); vol. 230, fol. 216v (Bertolomea fq Ture Padulis Salis and Michaele fq Pirolli).

[38] Mem, vol. 228, fols. 140r (Jacobus Johannis), 119v (Johannes fq Petri Gerardi).

Witnessing During the Black Death

Whether they were in a hospital, church, or home, all of the testators were surrounded by at least seven men, whom the notary listed as witnesses, and probably more family members who were not listed. Who were these men? In the previous chapter we noted the presence of several men of public faith, such as notaries, doctors and *ministrales*, who served as witnesses. Table 5.1, listing the occupations reported for witnesses in a sample of 200 testaments redacted during the summer months, demonstrates that government officials also appeared as witnesses: seven town criers of the commune (*nuntius comunis, bannitor*) and two soldiers (*stipendarius ad stipendium dominorum civitatum*). In addition, many priors, friars, priests and rectors of Bologna's churches acted beyond the capacity of principal witness, standing with their fellow clerics. The university body, however, does not have a large showing among the witnesses. Apart from the five medical students named in the previous chapter, there appear four other students (twice noted as studying civil law). Connected to the university economy were eight parchment makers and two copiers or *scriptores*. Most of the witnesses came from the general populace and from lower-level occupations.

Table 5.1 confirms the evidence from testators presented in Chapter Two that Bologna was dominated by men in the butchering and leather or pelt trades, with the many familiar shoemakers, tanners, and a leather worker.[39] However, the list of witnesses may be more revealing of the types of occupations in town, since we see more men from the textile industry, which was growing in Bologna at that time, including ten woolmongers, seven weavers, seven jacketmakers, five dyers, four linen sellers, four cloth shearers, a cotton worker, and three cloth agents, in addition to the many tailors and clothes dealers already noted among the testators. Men of lower-paid trades were more likely to appear as witnesses than as testators. In fact, the poor make a strong showing with eight agricultural workers, eleven wine carriers, three carters, and five porters. A few men with humble occupations not found among the testators include three

[39] This information can be compared with the smaller numbers of witnesses recorded in the 1337 database. Again, the notaries (14), butchers (4), shoemakers (8), and tanners (6) dominate the trades. There is one professor of grammar, two physicians (*medici*), and four barbers. Common occupations also revealed by testators and witnesses of 1348 can be deduced from the fact that two each of clothes dealers, parchment makers, bakers, farriers, and *brentatores* appear as witnesses.

Table 5.1 Occupations of Witnesses During the Black Death

Occupation	Group Total	Occupation	Group Total
Textile Workers & Retailers:	76	Medical and Health Practitioners:	26
tailor (*sartor*), 19		barber (*barberius*), 16	
clothes dealer (*strazarius*), 16		doctor (*medicus*), 5	
woolmonger (*lanarius*, *lanarolus*), 10		druggist (*spetiarius*, *spezialis*), 3	
		professor (*professor physice*), 2	
weaver (*tessarius*), 7			
jacketmaker (*zubonerius*), 7		University: Students & Book Trade:	21
dyer (*tintor*), 5		parchment maker (*cartolarius*), 8	
cloth shearer (*cimator*), 4		student (*scolaris*), 10	
linen seller (*linarolus*), 4		copyist (*scriptor*), 3	
broker (*sensalereus*), 3		book-seller (*stationarius*), 1	
cotton worker (*bambaxarius*), 1		[also professor of medicine above]	
Leather/Fur Artisans & Retailers:	71	Wood or Stone Workers:	12
shoemaker (*calzarius*), 45		carpenter (*magister legnaminis*), 6	
tanners (*pelacanus, peliparius*), 24		mason (*murator*), 6	
leatherworker (*galegarius*), 1			
furrier (*pelizarius*), 1		Miscellaneous Artisans & Retailers:	11
		mercer (*merzarius*), 6	
Legal Professionals:	63	innkeeper (*hospitator*), 3	
notary (*notarius*), 62		painter (*pictor*), 2	
judge (*iudex*), 1		wine seller (*tavernarius vini*), 1	
Metal Workers:	34	Merchants and Goldsmiths:	10
smith (*faber*), 30		goldsmith (*aurifex*), 7	
farrier (*mariscalcus*), 2		merchant (*mercator*), 3	
armorer (*armarolus*), 1			
shield-maker (*scudarius*), 1		Government Employees:	9
		town crier (*banditor, nuntius*), 7	
Food Preparers and Retailers:	32	mercenary (*stipendarius*), 2	
baker (*fornarius*), 22			
fishmonger (*piscator*), 5		Miscellaneous Artisans:	5
saltseller (*salarolus*), 4		pot maker (*parolarius*), 3	
market gardener (*ortolanus*), 3		basket maker (*corbellarius*), 1	
		tub maker (*mastelarius*), 1	
Agriculture/Manual Laborers:	30		
wine carrier (*brentator*), 11		Total number of occupations listed:	428
carter (*caraterius, victurallis*), 3			
agricultural worker (*laborator*), 8			
porter (*portator*), 5			
winnower (*mundator*), 1			
sifter (*aburatator*), 1			
Butchers:	28		
butcher (*beccarius*), 26			
pork butcher (*lardarolus*), 2			

Source: ASB, Memoriali, vols. 227, 229, 230

copper pot makers, a tub maker, and a basket maker.[40] As was the case for testators, we see that Bolognese from the middling to lower social levels could and did serve their fellow townspeople during the Black Death.

Unfortunately for the researcher, many witnesses did not have their occupations listed. Among these are men with aristocratic surnames, many of whom are not provided with noble titles.[41] The list of surnames of aristocratic origin is very long, but it is worthwhile noting the appearance among the witnesses of more than one member of the following aristocratic lineages: Albergati, Armi, Bandi, Basacomari, Cavaleri, Codagnelli, Garisendi, Ghisilieri, Guastavillani, Leoni, Libri, Magnani, de Manzolino, Omoboni, Plantavigni, and Recepti. Often these elite brothers would appear together to hear the same will—a subject discussed below—and do not appear again, but all were around during some part of the summer months of plague.

Most witnesses were unrelated to the testator, but a few relatives came to serve. Only 15 wills of the sample have witnesses who were clearly related by kin to the testator: five contain brothers, two have several cousins, two have nephews, and three with other more distant relatives. Men and women were equally as likely to call upon relatives, but all but one of the brothers came to the side of their sisters. Since a person under the legal authority of the testator could not stand as witness, there were no sons of testators among the witnesses.[42] The inclusion of brothers and other male relatives was not exceptional to the epidemic, since the same kinds of relatives can be found as witnesses in 1337. Moreover, the reason for their inclusion was not because a testator needed to ensure the minimum number of witnesses during a time of panic and flight, since they appear in wills with more than the required number of witnesses. For example, Mixina fq Bertholomei de Muzolis was the daughter of a deceased notary and a widow living in the parish of Santa Cecilia.

[40] One abbreviated occupation for a witness may be *somarolus* or muleteer.

[41] Only a small minority of witnesses with noble last names are given a title, and, occasionally, a nobleman would be listed as witness "domino" in one will, but without such title in another.

[42] There is only one exception to this rule: a son who appeared as witness for his mother (Mem, vol. 228, fol. 109r). Similarly, witnesses were not supposed to be beneficiaries. Apart from a handful of testators who left a few *solidi* to all witnesses, I have found only one instance of a witness receiving a substantial bequest: ser Datus de Ugolinellis, originally from Lucca, left a piece of land in Pietro Santo to Puzinellus Cursi of that town who served as witness (Mem, vol. 229, fol. 9v).

She had her will drawn up on 8 September with 12 witnesses. One was her brother, Gabrielle, who was a merchant (*mercator*) and the *ministralis* of the parish of San Sigismondo. He had made the trip to her home for reasons other than a concern over lack of witnesses—most likely his social stature as merchant and parish official as well as familial duties or affection. Similarly, Mina fq Bernardini Grassi of Santa Cristina della Fondazza was the sister of a notary who also acted as witness to her will along with eight other men.[43] When the "noble and prudent man" Johannes, son of the late noble knight Lanza de Garisendis, made his will on 15 August in his home in San Donato, it was an important event for a leading noble family. No less than five of the eight witnesses (apart from the presiding priest) were members of the Garisendi line.[44] These men were not granted bequests—as this was not proper for a witness—and came to witness for reasons of family ties. Other relatives, who were beneficiaries but not witnesses, were most likely present. These included Johannes's brother, known as Tannus, whom he named as principal heir and two cousins, Aldrovandinus and Ghettus fq Guroni de Garisendis, who were the substitute heirs. Thus the social and familial function of the ritual of making a powerful nobleman's will was maintained during the time of plague.

Instead of relating to the testator, it was much more likely that the witnesses related to each other. Several sets of fathers and sons and brothers came together as witnesses at the redaction of wills. The dictation of a will by a man or woman of the elite, in particular, were important social events, which plague did not prevent. Sometimes elite served as witnesses for their peers as, for example, two Codagnelli brothers and three members of the Leoni family who came to aid an elite widow of the Pegoloti family in their parish on 23 July, and a father and son of the Aqualti family who came to an ill elite man in their quarter.[45] Multiple members of a family did not appear together at the same time even if witnessing was common among its members. For example, the four sons of magister Petrus, smith of the parish of San Biagio, were witnesses for their neighbors in their parish but never all at once: two brothers appeared together on 8 July for a *strazarius*, while another witnessed at the home of an unmarried woman the next day, and the

[43] Mem, vol. 229, fol. 212r.
[44] Mem, vol. 229, fol. 24v.
[45] Mem, vol. 229, fols. 20r (Zanbrassina fq Francisci olim domini Bonbollogni de Pegollotis) and 77r (Veclus fq Bertolomei ser Vecli de Oleo).

fourth showed up on 25 July for the brother of the *strazarius* of 8 July who had by then passed away.[46]

At other times the relatives that came together to honor the social bonds they had with an elite were not themselves elite, as was the case for a salt seller and his brother who came to the side of noble Bella de Prendipartibus who was dying in their parish on 27 July, or for the two sets of father and son who came across two quarters to aid an ill elite widow on 7 July.[47] Elite status and compatriot bonds may have helped a resident of San Procolo, originally from Lucca, with an elite surname who had as witnesses a porter and his brother who lived in a different parish in Bologna but were originally from Lucca. Although it was more likely that relatives would come in groups to the redaction of an elite person's will, it was not unknown for such social gatherings at the will-making of non-elites. For example, in July a *lanarolus* and his brother from the parish of San Biagio came together for the widow of a jacketmaker from the adjacent parish of Sant'Omobono, and a tanner and his two sons aided an unmarried woman in their parish, while in November three brothers traveled beyond the city walls to the *guardia civitatis* to act as witnesses together.[48] These brothers, sons, and fathers were at the redaction of these wills because their family shared some social bond with the testator.

The types of individuals who served as witness was broad, and the number of different people who came to the sides of their fellow townspeople was very large during the epidemic. Many people agreed to serve and usually did so once. It was a widespread and common activity during the crisis. Almost all of the parishes from all zones were represented by witnesses in the sample. As we saw with the notaries, friars and priests, the dying did not have to rely on the efforts of a select group of exceptional individuals. Some men, however, were more active in helping out their friends and neighbors. From the sample, I have been able to identify 68 men who were witnesses for two different testators, and a further 13 who were at the sides of three or more testators. These 81 men came from 30 different parishes, demonstrating, again, that

[46] Mem, vol. 229, fol. 77r (Petrobellus fq Fratris Ugolini); vol. 230, fols. 97v (Mengonus fq Fratris Ugolini on 8 July), 135v (Malgarita fq Petri Gerardi).

[47] Mem, vol. 229, fols. 113r (Bella olim nobilis viri domini Tani de Prendipartibus) and 204r (Lixia fq Mixini de Masignis).

[48] Mem, vol. 229, fols. 7r (Bitina fq Francisci, called Checha), 10r (Jacobus fq ser Amodei), 19r (Margarita fq Petri Thomacis).

serving as a witness was a common experience for men from all over the town.

We can follow some artisans of the parish of San Biagio as examples of individuals in the context of neighborhood. Bertone fq Jacobi was an armorer (*armarolus*) who appeared in the sample initially on 8 July at the home of Figliocarius (the parchment maker discussed in Chapter Three), with eight other parishioners, most *cartolarii*, and their parish priest, dopnus Gerardus. Among the witnesses was the tailor Johannes fq Albertini, who joined Bertone the next day at the home of an unmarried woman of their parish, and Andriolus the smith who went on to witness two other wills in July. We last see Bertone on 30 July at the home of Mattheus, a well-off butcher (whose wife's dowry amounted to 525 *lire*), with seven other men of his parish including the parish priest Gerardus (whose frequent dedication to his parishioners was noted in the last chapter), but not Johannes the tailor or Andriolus the smith, who on that day had gone instead to hear the son of Figliocarius dictate his will. Bertone agreed to serve as the Mattheus's *procurator*, so he went with the redacting notary to register the testament at the office of the *Memoriali*.[49]

This dense web of interactions went beyond the single parish. For example, Pasquale fq Jacobi, a *lanarius* or wool worker of San Biagio, was witness at a testament redacted in February before plague arrived and during the epidemic can be found at the sides of testators from his parish and nearby San Leonardo. He assisted a married woman of San Biagio who made her will on 24 June. On 10 July a man of San Leonardo came to the house of a shoemaker of San Biagio, Gerardinus, to meet with Pasquale and six other men of that parish including the parish priest dopnus Gerardus as well as a notary from neighboring San Giuliano.[50] Twelve days after hosting an ill man, Gerardinus the shoemaker himself dictated a will before his neighbors (although Pasquale was not among them), the priest Gerardus and the same redacting notary.[51] This shoemaker asked his neighbor the butcher Mattheus to be one of his executors—but that man had little time to manage the estate of another since, as just mentioned, he was testator on 30 July.

Neighbors of the adjoining parishes of Santa Maria in Tempio, Santa

---

[49] Mem, vol. 229, fol. 77v (Mattheus fq Phylippini Crescenci).

[50] Mem, vol. 228, fols. 187v (Padoanus fq nobilis militis domini Liazarii de Liazariis), 76v (Dana fq domini Pini); vol. 229, fol. 7r (Tomas fq Dominici Egidii).

[51] Mem, vol. 230, fol. 356v (Gerardinus fq Phylippini).

Maria del Torleone, and Sant'Omobono regularly associated with each other despite the fact that they were divided by the city walls. Testators from the two parishes within the walls commonly had witnesses from those parishes with frequent visits from men of Sant'Omobono and occasional representation from San Biagio, San Leonardo, and even farther off San Vitale. Residents of Sant'Omobono outside of the walls, on the other hand, were more likely to have men of their own parish with frequent additions by other residents of parishes farther away in the *guardia civitatis* such as Santa Maria degli Alemanni, Sant'Antonino and Sant'Egidio.[52] Occasionally, however, neighbors from Santa Maria in Tempio or Santa Maria del Torleone did show up beyond the city walls.

We can see how this neighborhood's core of Santa Maria del Torleone, Santa Maria in Tempio, and Sant'Omobono functioned by following a few witnesses. Jacobus Petrisegni was witness with the parish priest and nine men from his parish of Sant'Omobono for magister Stefanus de Tempestis, a professor of medicine, who made his will on 8 July in that parish "near Bologna and next to the walls of Strada Maggiore".[53] On 16 July Jacobus was present at the will of a widow of the same parish who had called on men of Sant'Omobono as well as a neighbor from Santa Maria del Tempio. On that day inside the walls, another good neighbor Siverinus Bonzanini of Santa Maria del Tempio aided the wife of a miller of that parish. These two men (Jacobus and Siverinus) came together on 27 July with another neighbor, Baldinus Benvenuti of Sant'Omobono, at the will of a shoemaker's daughter who lived in Santa Maria del Tempio. From there we can pick up the trail of Baldinus who, like the men of his neighborhood, went in and out of the city walls to hear testators's wishes. We last find him on 10 August inside the walls standing with prominent men of Santa Maria del Torleone (including a man of the Bentivoglio family) to hear the last wishes of a doctor's daughter.[54] The men of this neighborhood acted for the health of their community and not for themselves, but there would have been exceptions. One such possible

[52] The parish of Sant'Egidio is in the quarter of Porta Piera, while the others noted are in that of Porta Ravennate. This is further evidence that the topographical features of the city, such as walls, canals, and parish churches were more important for neighborhood identity than the administrative category of quarter.

[53] Mem, vol. 230, fol. 176v. See Chapter Two for a discussion of his will in the context of other professors.

[54] Mem, vol. 229, fols. 3r (Ghixia fq ser Berti), 29r (Johana fq magistri Jacobi Bonbaroni), 206v (Chaterina fq Mathioli Alferi); vol. 230, fol. 126v (Agnexia fq Andree).

case is the *ministralis* of Sant'Omobono, a butcher named Mathiolus, who went into the center of town on 27 July, accompanied by two priests from the parish of Santa Maria del Torleone, to declare his last wishes while still healthy. As an owner of land in the *guardia civitatis* and in the village of Medicina, he could have left town after that in order to escape plague. In any case, he was still alive when his wife made her will on 4 November at their home.[55]

Only two men in the sample carried on the unhealthy activity of attending different ill testators on the same day. Albertus Johannis de Receptis of San Biagio was at the home of a wealthy widow in his own parish on 21 August, but also traveled on that day to Santo Stefano (located on the same street but outside the second set of walls) to be at the side of an ill man lying in the home of the parish *ministralis* there. Philippus Guidonis de Thomacis of Santa Maria del Torleone was a witness on 19 July for Gexia, the aristocratic widow of Johannes de Cavaleriis, and when her in-law, Bonbollognus Cavaleri de Cavaleriis made his will on 4 August in the same parish, he served again as witness, being able to also aid on the same day Adelaxia, an elite but unrelated widow of the same parish.[56] Seven other men appear as witnesses in the short span of two or three consecutive days, but the vast majority of those making multiple appearances did so over the span of the epidemic and into the fall months. This information stands in contrast to some chroniclers's accounts of rapid death among individuals exposed to other plague victims and poses problems for Cohn's recent attempts at revising the epidemiology of plague outbreaks.[57] For the purposes of this book, it offers the social evidence that many individuals endured the difficult experience of aiding people who were dying of an awful disease and that epidemic disease and fear did not stop them from repeating their efforts and aiding others as plague continued to infect the populace throughout the summer. It is important to remember the stalwart actions of these men when we read the familiar words of the

[55] Mem, vol. 229, fol. 194v (Mathiolus fq Johannis Bonaguide); vol. 230, fol. 442 (Jacoba fq Donellis).

[56] Mem, vol. 229, fols. 21r (Bonbollognus fq Chavalleri de Chavalleris on 4 August 1348), 74v (Gexia fq Alberti de Picigotis on 19 July 1348), 97v (Adelexia fq Thomacis on 4 August 1348).

[57] Studying epidemics in early modern Italy, Cohn argues that the principal characteristics of plague were rapidity and virulence and that plague deaths were clustered within households with no or short time intervals between deaths. See Cohn and Alfani, "Households and Plague," 180–181.

chroniclers who highlighted how fear prevented many from aiding their friends and neighbors.

We can see how social bonds connected several individuals in a parish and endured throughout the epidemic by further tracking the activities of witnesses who showed up together at the homes of different testators over time.[58] Two *cartolarii* of San Biagio, Jacobus Picini and Petrus Rumioli, were witnesses for Ursollina, the widow of a parchment maker from their parish, on 23 July and a week later they both were at the side of Johannes Carini, the son of a parchment maker of San Biagio.[59] For these parchment makers the bonds of work and neighborhood overlapped. Similar bonds of work and neighborhood were at play for Gerardus fq Gerardi de Lana of San Bartolo who was partner in trade with Zunta Loti, an apothecary or spice dealer, living in the adjacent parish of Santa Maria di Porta Ravennate. On 20 July Zunta left bequests to Gerardus, who shows up later in August as witness for Zunta's wife.[60] Johannes Carini also had ties to two other men of his parish, not named as parchment makers, Zaninus fq magistri Yvani and Zenanus fq Petri of San Biagio, so that both men showed up for his will on 30 July as well as for the will of his brother-in-law, a clothes dealer in San Biagio.[61] Franciscus Jacobi and Bonaventura fq Johannis Bargelini of San Vitale traveled to Santa Maria Maddalena for Petrus Zangi olim Petri Martelli on 13 July and later on 1 August to the parish of San Leonardo where Chaterina fq Johannis Cambini of the parish of Sant'Andrea dei Piatesi lay ill in the home of another. Although we cannot determine the bonds of work or parish, a web of social connections was functioning that caused Franciscus and Bonaventura to go around the city during the crisis and aid the ill.

Despite the survival of some men there is no doubt that serving as witness to your ill neighbors meant putting your life in danger. The residents of Bologna knew this yet continued to remain faithful to their social ties. Many died as a result. There are in fact witnesses who

---

[58] I am not including here the examples of related testators who had their wills drawn up on the same day, in the same place, and had the same witnesses. See, for example, the wills of Lipa Francischi Guidocheri de Galuciis and her daughter, Soldana fq Mathei de Mallavoltis, which were redacted in the home of a member of the Malavolti line and at which were present the same seven witnesses: Mem, vol. 229, fol. 183r.

[59] Mem, vol. 229, fols. 9r (Ursollina fq Thomacis Ursii) and 77v (Johannes fq Carini).

[60] Mem, vol. 229, fols. 79r (Nicholeta fq ser Zani) and 199v (Zunta fq Locti).

[61] Mem, vol. 229, fol. 77r (Petrobellus fq Fratris Ugollini).

turn up again in the historical record as dying testators. Having aided their fellow neighbors when they were healthy, other neighbors come to their side soon afterwards when they became ill. This happened to men who were witnesses for others in their own neighborhood. For example, Salamon fq Johannis de Chavaleriis, a wealthy citizen of Santa Maria del Torleone was witness for a neighbor in the adjacent parish of Santa Maria in Tempio on 19 July. Three days later he made his own will. We know that Salamon was dead by 4 August because his cousin, Bonbollognus Cavaleri de Cavaleriis, had his will redacted on that day in "domo heredis olim Sallamonis Cavalleris". Salamon's mother, who was living in the same parish, had already made her will on 17 July, and the sister of Bonbolognus had made hers in June.[62] Another prominent noble, Albertus, known as Berthus fq Thomacis de Baxacomatribus of San Tommaso della Braina was witness for Phylippus fq Johannis de Flagnano of his parish on 25 July. We next find him making his own will on 5 August.[63] Johannes fq Johannis magistri Donis of San Biagio, was witness for an elite widow of his parish on 7 July. It is interesting that Johannes's own wife (who bears a noble title) had made her will only five days before. He stayed in town through the epidemic, perhaps aiding others in his family and neighborhood, after his wife died. We last find him dictating his last will to his neighbors and family on 18 August.[64]

There are also examples of more humble folk acting in solidarity with their neighbors and dying as a result. Sometimes it is within the narrow confines of the parish that we find them, such as magister Zambonis fq Pacis, a smith of Sant'Egidio, who was witness for a married woman in his own parish on 17 July, but later fell ill and made his own will on 17 August.[65] Dominicus, known as Menghus fq Johannis, a baker of San Vitale, was witness for an unmarried woman in the adjacent parish of

[62] Mem, vol. 228, fol. 109r (Mina fq domini Cavaleri de Cavaleris); vol. 229, fols. 21r (Bonbollognus fq Chavalleri de Chavalleris), 74v (Gexia fq Alberti de Picigotis); vol. 230, fol. 365v (Salamon fq Johannis de Chavaleris).

[63] Mem, vol. 229, fols. 110v (Phylippus fq domini Johannis de Flagnano), 322v (Albertus fq domini Thomacis de Baxacomatribus). Incidentally, in the parish next door on the next day, 6 August, the sister of Berthus's wife made her will. Several of her relatives also appear as testators in July and August. So often when light is shed on one set of social ties, another set comes into view as well.

[64] Mem, vol. 230, fols. 80r (Bertholomea fq Petri olim domini Benzevenis de Salliceto), 230v (Johannes fq Johannis magistri Amadoris), 372v (discreta domina domina Ursollina fq Lanfranchi de Muzollis).

[65] Mem, vol. 229, fols. 28r (Zepta fq Petri Zogolli), 209r (magister Zanbonis fq Pacis).

San Sigismondo on 10 July and less than two weeks later lay dying as he made his will on 23 July.[66] Johannes fq Venture Zanelli, a parchment maker of San Biagio, went into his parish church to hear the last wishes of an unmarried woman of his parish on 12 June, then on 5 July entered the home of a doctor's widow and on 20 July was named heir of another man of his parish, only to have his own will made in his home on the next day. In addition to being so conscientious of his neighbors's plight, Johannes was a family man, a widower with three unmarried daughters and a son, all of whom he named as heirs in equal division. If all of his children were to die, he arranged that 25 *lire* be distributed for his soul—directing his money from the family back to the neighborhood.[67] Another good neighbor, Rodulfus fq Johannis de Roseno was a painter (*pictor*) of San Mamolo who had hosted a testator from Sant'Egidio in the *guardia civitatis* in June, gone to a home of a notary living in San Mamolo to hear the wishes of a widow of that parish at the end of July, and then on 12 August lay in his own home dictating his will.[68] Two weeks after Zenaninus fq Philippi the cloth shearer (*cimator*) had gone into the home (in the room with the great fireplace) of an elite citizen who lived in the central parish of San Dalmasio, he lay ill in his own home in San Leonardo near the second set of walls.[69]

A further example of neighbors serving neighbors through the community-building act of witnessing is Antonius magistri Alberti, a spice dealer of Santa Maria in Tempio, who lay ill in the house of a shoemaker located in Santa Maria del Torleone, the parish next door. The shoemaker and another man from neighboring San Leonardo were to be his executors and guardians, with his wife and sister, for his small daughter whom he designated as heir. In addition Antonius asked his neighbors to distribute 50 *lire* for clothing the poor and dowering poor girls. He made these requests surrounded by the parish priest of Santa Maria del Torleone and nine other neighbors including a smith, two weavers, and the son of a notary. Doubtless the neighbors who met together for this testament all knew that nine days earlier the testator Antonius had been witness with one of the weavers, Balzarinus fq Petri of Santa Maria in Tempio, at the will of a neighbor. They did not

[66] Mem, vol. 229, fol. 19r (Azzolina fq Jacobi); vol. 230, fol. 500r (Dominicus fq Johannis).

[67] Mem, vol. 228, fol. 98r; vol. 230, fols. 103r, 110r (Johannes fq Venture Zanelli), 135r.

[68] Mem, vol. 229, fols. 115r, 408v, 440r (Rodulfus fq Johannis de Roffeno).

[69] Mem, vol. 229, fol. 77r; 230, fol. 111v (Zenaninus fq Philippi).

know the following: that among them Salamon de Chavaleriis would make his will only three days later and die shortly thereafter, as noted above; that the notary's son, Jacobus Angelelli de Manzolino would go to the deceased Salamon's house on 4 August to hear the last wishes of another Cavaleri man of Santa Maria del Torleone; and that on 5 August Jacobus Angelelli and Balzarinus would again meet up in Santa Maria del Torleone to aid another dying neighbor.[70]

At this 5 August meeting was introduced in the record another neighbor, Bonazunte fq Sanuti de Manzolino, who lived at least until 18 November when he made a codicil. He highlights the fact that some men managed to survive the worst and held out until the end of the year even though they had been helping the sick during the height of the epidemic.[71] This was the case, again, for both elite and non-elite who helped residents in their own parish, in their wider neighborhood, or even beyond. For example, Zacharias fq Petri of Santo Stefano had been witness for a widow of that parish on 6 July and survived until at least the redaction of his will on 19 November.[72] A member of the noble Galluzzi family left his home in the aristocratic central parish of Santa Maria dei Galluzzi to visit a wealthy resident of San Felice beyond the second set of walls. After the plague had subsided in October, he made his will lying ill in his home parish.[73] Lencius fq Nicholai de Columbis who lived on the *contrata* or street of San Vitale in the same-named parish, went up his street and far outside the city walls on 25 July to witness the will of an *ortolanus* living in the parish of Sant'Antolini. Lencius survived the worst of the epidemic, but did become ill, so we find him dying in his home parish on 1 October.[74] A final example of the actions of witnesses during the epidemic is the very dedicated neighbor Philipus Guidonis de Tomaciis of Santa Maria del Torleone who was present at the wills of testators in his parish four times during July and August (on 15 July, 24 July when he was named a substitute heir, 4 August, and 6 August) and yet made it through the epidemic to serve as witness outside of his

[70] Mem, vol. 229, fols. 17r, 21r, 75v; vol. 230, fols. 117v , 157v.
[71] Mem, vol. 230, fol. 144v.
[72] Mem, vol. 229, fol. 76r (Ghixia fq Jacobini de Ripolli); vol. 230, fol. 200r (Zacharias fq Petri).
[73] Mem, vol. 229, fol. 268v (magister Migletus fq Mediglatri Andree); vol. 230, fol. 249r (Burniollus fq domini Blanchi de Galucis).
[74] Mem, vol. 229, fol. 86v (Johannes Petri); vol. 230, fol. 136v (Lencius fq Nicholai de Cholunbis).

neighborhood on 4 October.[75] Philippus's example is not unique. With a larger sample and more names entered, it would have been possible to restore to view many more individuals's actions during the Black Death and reveal deeper and wider levels of neighborhood connections, but the general picture would have remained the same: neighborhood communities functioned during the crisis.

If we shift the focus on to the testators to see who they chose to rely on for support, the same general picture is revealed with some shades of difference by class. An analysis of the residence of each witness in the 200 groups of witnesses from the plague months reveals that testators chose groups of witnesses with the following characteristics: either all came from their neighborhood, which was generally comprised of two to three parishes contiguous with the home parish; all came from one parish or mainly from the testator's parish with one outsider joining the group; all came from numerous parishes spread around the city; all were friars, in which case the will was redacted in a religious house; or the group was mixed with neighbors and some men who were foreigners living in Bologna.[76] A minority of testators relied on groups of witnesses who came only from their parish. Elites were somewhat less likely than non-elite testators to do this: seven men and women, or nine per cent of the 75 elite testators chose witnesses from their parish alone, while 17, or 13.6 per cent, of the 125 non-elite testators did so. This situation is revealed in the will of a man living in the parish of Santa Maria Maddalena, who called upon eight men of his parish, two of whom are identified as fishermen, as well as his parish priest.[77] If we include those testators for whom the parish was the principal core area of support

---

[75] Mem, vol. 229, fol. 21r (Bonbollognus fq domini Chavalleri de Chavalleris); vol. 230, fols. 126r (Romaninus fq domini Philippi Dessiderii), 127r (Ugo fq Gerardi olim domini Mafei de Luteriis), 140r (Laxia fq domini Alberti de Malavoltis); Dem, F. M. Instrumenti, 90, 4222:4 (fr. Dominicus fq magistri Alberti).

[76] In her study of the registers of notarial families of thirteenth-century Palermo, Mary Lampe identifies and emphasizes the importance of "witnessing groups" or informal partnerships of witnesses who met with notaries to authenticate acts. She traces the habitual association of these groups over time, noting that witnesses and the notaries for whom they served could act also as guardians, executors, and guarantors for each other and often shared business enterprises. Since this investigation of the immediate experience of the Black Death in Bologna has also demonstrated some social and occupational links between notaries, clients, and witnesses, it is likely that many were involved in the types of long-term witnessing groups that Lampe stressed. See Lampe, "Survival and Profit," Chapter Three.

[77] Mem, vol. 229, fol. 214v (Franciscus fq Benvenuti).

with the addition of one witness who arrived from an outside, usually adjacent, parish, we find that 18 per cent of the elite testators versus 30 per cent of the non-elites drew principally on the parish. For example, seven men from the parish of Santa Maria Maddalena, including a tailor, shoemaker, and smith, joined their parish priest, and a neighbor who came along the Strada San Donato from the parish of Santa Cecilia, to be at the bedside of a tailor of Santa Maria Maddalena in the middle of July.[78]

Neighbors from parishes adjacent to the testator's home comprised the other prominent type of witness group: 32 per cent of the less well-off testators turned to contacts in their neighborhood, which behavior was similar for the elites, since 25 per cent of them had witnesses coming from a cluster of two or three adjacent parishes to their own. A typical example of this type of testator is a married woman who lived in San Nicolò del Borgo di San Felice just west of the second set of walls, at whose will came three men from her parish with four neighbors from adjacent parishes that lay to the west of the second set of walls and along the Riva di Reno. The priest that served as principal witness was the chaplain of San Felice, next to her parish.[79] The parish and neighborhood, then, formed the principal area of support for the majority of testators in Bologna.

Both elites and less well-off testators were also able, however, to appeal for help from individuals beyond their neighborhood: 25 per cent of elite and 23 per cent of non-elite testators in the sample had people arriving at their sides from locations all over the town. The difference between elite and non-elite dependence on close parish or wider neighborhood ties is due to the fact that elite testators were more likely than non-elites to be within a mendicant convent and thus surrounded by friars (8.0 per cent versus 0.8 per cent) and they were slightly more likely to have foreigners from outside Bologna attending their wills. An example of the ability to draw on wide-ranging social networks is found in the will of a merchant with the title of *providus discretus vir,* who lived in the parish of San Michele del Mercato, in the aristocratic center of town near the central market. He called upon contacts from the parish of San Colombo also within the first walls, from the parish of San Lorenzo Porta Stiera lying

[78] Mem, vol. 228, fol. 26r (ser Jacobus fq Jacobi Passiti).
[79] Mem, vol. 229, fol. 92r (Benvenuta fq Mathioli).

to the west outside the second set of walls, from San Leonardo to the west in the quarter of Porta Piera, and from Lucca.[80]

This last example indicates that people traveled some distance to aid their friends during the epidemic. People whose residences were outside of Bologna or new immigrants had networks of support that stretched beyond a parish or neighborhood in Bologna. It is hard to imagine that there was much travel into the city during the summer of plague, but it is certain that foreigners living within the walls came to the aid of their compatriots. For example, at the will of an elite widow of San Michele dei Leprosetti who was originally from Varignana in the contado of Bologna, the only witness who had an identifiable address in Bologna was her parish priest. The other eight men included elites, for whom the recording of a parish may have been seen as unnecessary, and three men from villages in the contado.[81] Another example of an immigrant is a widow from Linari in the contado of Florence, who "was at present living in Bologna" in the parish of San Marco. Three of her neighbors from San Marco, San Donato, and San Vitale arrived at her house in July, along with three men from Lucca, Pistoia, and Florence, for whom no Bolognese parish is recorded.[82] Foreigners who did not have permanent residence in Bologna had to face the epidemic far from their home and normal social networks, but they also managed to find support from their compatriots in town. Thus a married woman from the contado of Lucca for whom no parish in Bologna is recorded was guest in the home of a certain ser Landucius in the parish of Sant'Andrea degli Ansaldi "who was from Lucca". All of the witnesses at her will are identified as being from Lucca.[83] Whatever one's situation was in Bologna during the Black Death one was able to turn to either the members of one's parish, one's neighbors, or one's compatriots to write a will, the essential preparation at the end of life for the body, soul, and family.

The evidence for activities of witnesses that can be teased out of the remaining wills constructs a model picture of citizen solidarity during an extraordinary crisis. In the Introduction to the *Decameron*, Boccaccio reminded people that what mattered most was how you behaved to others when you were healthy, so that you would be treated as such when you were ill: *in ogni luogo, avendo essi stessi, quando sani erano,*

[80] Mem, vol. 229, fol. 217v (Gerardus fq Civitini de Sera).
[81] Mem, vol. 229, fol. 1v (Guida domini Bitini de Soldaderiis).
[82] Mem, vol. 229, fol. 5v (Zanobia fq Michaelis).
[83] Mem, vol. 230, fol. 325r (Dina fq Gerardi de Sabluni de Plano).

esempio data a coloro che sani rimanevano, quasi abbandonati per tutto languieno. The foundation of human society was compassion for one's citizens, neighbors, and family, and if this compassion was lacking, then society would dissolve. In Boccaccio's hands, plague in Florence was a parable for social disaster. In the actions of individuals revealed in the wills of Bologna, we see that compassion and solidarity remained. The social networks of work, neighborhood, and family operated during the epidemic from the level of the parish out to the clusters of parishes forming neighborhoods. Priests and notaries had to be at the dictation of each will, and, as we have seen, a great many did their job with much attention to duty in the face of plague. Friars traveled throughout the town to the homes of the populace and also allowed the Bolognese to enter their convents to seek solace and a safe place for the preservation of their last wishes. Medical practitioners and parish leaders were at the sides of testators at the height of the epidemic. The requirements of a valid testament required the aid of huge numbers of townspeople, beyond men with public roles such as clerics or notaries—all of whom received little or no remuneration for their efforts. Even though the daily contacts and business dealings that went on between these neighbors would not always have been free of antagonism and competition, the interactions of the populace of Bologna during the Black Death have demonstrated that neighborhoods provided a source of cohesion and strength for medieval society.

CHAPTER SIX

THE INDIVIDUAL AND THE FAMILY

During the crisis of the Black Death the townspeople of Bologna were able to turn to strong networks of support operating within the communities of the parish and neighborhood. The original, closest, and, usually, the continuous and final source of support for the testator was the family. While notaries, clergy, and neighbors—the subjects of Chapters Four and Five—came to assist the testator in writing up the will, it was usually up to the family to carry out the dictated instructions. Chapter Three demonstrated that there was no widespread abandonment of family members in Bologna and, thus, we can assume that the testators dictated their last wishes with the knowledge that their families and kin would make the effort to put them into effect.

As noted in Chapter One, the will is the best instrument to study the decisions of a testator, because it came at the end of life for most men and women who had few opportunities—or need—to make changes by means of codicils, and because they were rarely repudiated. The testament represents the last important set of instructions for an individual's intentions in terms of piety and family. A testator may have made many previous pious donations in his or her life before having a testament drawn up, and, thus, pious or charitable legacies in the testament may only inaccurately reflect a life of piety. On the contrary, the testament is an excellent record of decisions concerning the family, for it is here that the heir is nominated and the devolution of the patrimony is arranged. The Bolognese notarial authorities, Rolandino Passaggeri and Salatiele, following Roman law, stressed the characteristic of the testament as a document designed with the explicit purpose of nominating an heir. This chapter will examine the decisions of testators that closely involved reliance on the family for aid, namely, instructions for burial, the nomination of executor, the guardianship of children, and the naming of heirs. I will first set out typical testamentary decisions using a sample of 100 wills from the plague-free year of 1337 and then compare them to the experience of the Black Death using the sample of 225 wills redacted after plague entered Bologna (June to December, 1348).[1]

Burials

We begin with burial, the testator's decision concerning his or her last worldly presence. Before the Black Death the great majority of testators simply stated that they wished to be buried *apud ecclesiam* and instructed their executors to pay for the funeral expenses in the amount that they saw fit. It was rare to request burial in a tomb: only four per cent specified an *archa*, either in a parish or mendicant church. Most testators simply entrusted to their executors the choice of how much was to be spent on a funeral, since only about 40 per cent provided for a certain amount. Sixty-five per cent of testators chose a parish church, while the remaining selected burial at the mendicant convent of the Franciscans, Dominicans, or Augustinian Hermits, with the one exception of burial in a church belonging to a hospital.[2] Two thirds of all testators were buried in their own parish church, again, usually letting the executor determine the amount spent on the funeral. Women were more likely to choose a mendicant burial place (over half of them did so), whereas men were more equally divided between a parish church and a mendicant or other location. The Franciscans were by far the most popular of these mendicant burial sites, followed by the Hermit friars, but the highest sums were set aside for burials at the Franciscan and Dominican churches. Thus, burials were regularly a matter of one's

[1] The wills from the Black Death discussed here are drawn from the sample used in Chapters One, Four, and Five to examine the activities of witnesses (see Chapter One, footnote 99). Not all wills in the sample had data entered on bequests, thus the smaller number of wills here. Those from the database of wills redacted in 1337 represent about one third of the total wills that year and, as is the case for the sample from 1348, more come from the first registers than the final registers in the volumes. I have excluded the secret wills of the *Demaniale* from this analysis—except for the occasional comparison—because, unlike the publicly registered wills in the *Memoriali*, most of them were dictated within the mendicant houses before the friars. Testators could have been influenced differently than the typical testator at home before a notary, family, and friends.

[2] Another unusual request was to make arrangements for burial outside of the city. On 3 April, 1337 a widow, originally from the contado of Bologna, requested burial at the churches of the nuns of Saint Francis or of Saint Clare if she were to die in Bologna. If she died in the contado, she wanted to be buried in a Franciscan church in the contado. Mem, vol. 191, fol. 63r (Grecha fq domini Adami).

parish church with frequent burial at mendicant churches, of which the elite preferred San Francesco and San Domenico.

Burials During the Black Death

Did the epidemic change the normal course of instructions for burial? We learn from other sources that burial during the Black Death became a major issue for secular and religious leaders alike. Bishops had to consecrate new ground for the huge number of corpses needing burial, and town councils issued legislation regulating the procedures for expedited burial.[3] Chroniclers, such as Agnolo di Tura del Grasso and Gabriele de' Mussis, noted the truncated funeral rituals.[4] Boccaccio described mass graves in Florence "into which new arrivals were placed in their hundreds, stowed tier upon tier like ships's cargo, each layer of corpses being covered over with a thin layer of soil till the trench was filled to the top" and this was repeated by Marchionne di Coppo Stefani in his famous description of bodies layered like lasagna.[5] All of these arrangements, while necessary in a time of crisis, must have been deeply upsetting for the living, since they did away with the healing qualities that burial provided for the communities left behind. The disruption of funeral rites and the unnatural circumstances of anonymous burial in a pit would have served to intensify the stress on the social fabric rent by so many deaths at once. Boccaccio expressed this frustration and disgust when he charged "there were no tears or candles or mourners to honour the dead; in fact, no more respect was accorded to dead people than would nowadays be shown towards dead goats".[6] Nevertheless, the digging of mass graves and shortened liturgy for funerals that were devoid of the normal crowds of participants, no matter how distressing, were a part of the religious and ruling groups's

[3] Chiappelli, "Ordinamenti sanitari". Horrox provides English sources that detail bishops's efforts to consecrate new burial grounds. See Horrox, *Black Death*, pp. 266–271.

[4] Gabriele de' Mussis describes the shortened burials: "No prayer, trumpet or bell summoned friends and neighbours to the funeral, nor was mass performed... Men were borne to burial by day and night, since needs must, and only with a short service," translated in Horrox, *Black Death*, pp. 22–23. According to Agnolo di Tura "[m]embers of a household brought their dead to a ditch as best they could, without priest, without divine offices," translated in Bowksy, *Black Death*, p. 13, original in *Cronica Senese*, p. 555.

[5] Boccaccio, *Decameron*, trans. McWilliam, p. 12.

[6] Ibid., p. 11.

active efforts to deal with a catastrophic situation. How were testators to deal with this new situation? Samuel Cohn found that in Florence during 1348 an unusually high number of testators provided for the construction of new tombs, chapels, and other means of demarcating individual graves. He suggests that threat of mass burial coupled with fear of abandonment were the causes for this heightened concern for burials among Florentine testators.[7] Such concern over burial was not present in the wills of testators from the other five Tuscan and Umbrian towns he examined, and it is worth knowing what was the case in Bologna, where the death rate was probably not as high as Florence.

Testators dictating their wills at the height of the epidemic in Bologna behaved, in fact, very much like their counterparts before the crisis of plague. Sixty per cent of testators wanted to be buried in a parish church, which for most was their own parish.[8] Some, however, had ties to other churches in town for reasons of family or personal preference. This was not always a matter of gender—for example, that women were being drawn back to burial preferences of their birth families contrary to those of their husbands—since women were equally as likely as men to be buried in a parish church that was not in their home parish.

We can estimate the forces at work behind some of the decisions of such testators. Returning to the birth family may have been the factor behind the choices of the following two widows. Lixia de Masignis of the parish of San Vitale (presumably her deceased husband's) had gone to her brother's home in the *guardia civitatis*, outside of the town walls, to dictate her will. She asked to be buried in the church of Santa Margarita in Barbiano (in the *guardia civitatis*), and attending her will was the sacristan from that church.[9] Margarita Ugutionis was a widow living "at present" in the parish of San Bartolo in Porta Ravennate. She left five *solidi* to a chaplain of that church for masses and orations for her soul and another of its chaplains was present at her side. Nevertheless her connections to the parish of her brother, San Tommaso della Braina, were strong, since she requested burial in that church to which she left the larger sum of 20 *solidi*. She also had a house there next to her

[7] Samuel Kline Cohn, Jr. *The Cult of Remembrance and the Black Death: Six Renaissance Cities in Central Italy* (Baltimore, 1992), pp. 140–141.

[8] Only 25 per cent of the secret wills in the *Demaniale* specified burial in a parish church. These testators instead chose the Franciscan and Dominican churches (with 85 per cent of such requests for San Francesco).

[9] Mem, vol. 229, fol. 204v.

brother's house, and this she left to her son and daughter.[10] Margarita's brother made his will two weeks later and requested burial in the same parish church as his sister.[11] An unusual case of ties to burial places through marriage appears in the will of Guidus fq Benasai, a barber of Santa Maria Maggiore, who wanted to be buried in the parish church of Santa Maria Mascarella, in the tomb of his deceased brother-in-law, a shoemaker.[12] A personal, but unclear, reason was at work in the case of a clothes dealer from Santa Maria Mascarella who asked to be buried in the church of San Martino dell'Aposa in the tomb of another man, whose only apparent ties to the testator is a bequest of seven *lire* made from the will of the deceased friend, which the testator was distributing for the benefit of his soul.[13] Thus, natal family ties to a parish church often influenced choice of burial, but newer bonds created through marriage or friendship could have the same effect.

For others the local parish church may not have been as attractive as a nearby church with greater prestige. The Benedictine monastery of San Procolo, long associated with the law school, was the place to go, if you lived in its vicinity. This was the choice of the *ministralis* of Sant'Andrea degli Ansaldi and another from San Mamolo (parishes adjacent to San Procolo in the south; see Map of Parishes of Bologna).[14] San Vitale, one of the oldest churches of the city, held similar religious clout in its neighborhood. This may have been at work for Pelegrina of neighboring San Leonardo or Antonius of the parish of Santa Maria del Tempio further away.[15] Both of these wills demonstrate strong connections to the testator's immediate neighborhood, since the presiding priests and witnesses came from either the home parish or next door, but San Vitale was the burial choice. Long-term family ties to this esteemed church are apparent in a will drawn up after plague had subsided, i.e., in September, when one doctor who lived in the parish of Sant'Antolini beyond the walls requested that he be buried "in the tomb of his ancestors" in San Vitale.[16] This doctor was following the fourteenth-century trends

[10] Mem, vol. 229, fol. 6r.
[11] Mem, vol. 229, fol. 22v.
[12] Mem, vol. 229, fol. 87v.
[13] Mem, vol. 229, fol. 78v (Phyllipus fq Fratris Pauli).
[14] Mem, vol. 229, fol. 109v (Johannes fq Ugolini ser Bondi de Planellis), fol. 110r (Franciscus olim Bonazunte).
[15] Mem, vol. 229, fol. 75b (Antonius fq magistri Alberti), fol. 204v (Pelegrina fq Albucii de Sancto Petro).
[16] Mem, vol. 229, fol. 200v (magister Gerus fq magistri Nerini).

of the distinguished tradition of Bologna's physicians and professors of medicine: the famous anatomist, Mondino de Liuzzi, and his uncle Liuzzo dei Liuzzi were buried in S. Vitale in 1326 and 1318.[17]

Those who did not request burial in a parish church, i.e., over one third, specified a mendicant church—following pre-plague traditions exactly. During 1348, the Dominicans were the most popular choice for burials at a mendicant institution, since they drew nearly 60 per cent of such requests, followed by the Augustinian Hermits and the Franciscans (who had been the top choice before the Black Death). The church of San Giacomo of the Augustinian Hermits served as a neighborhood burial ground for many, since half of the testators requesting burial there lived in nearby parishes. Those preferring burial in the Franciscan and Dominican churches, however, were more likely to live outside of their immediate vicinity. Burial in these churches appears to have been a matter of prestige, since the largest sums spent on a tomb and/or funeral during the plague months were given to either the church of San Francesco or San Domenico. Thus, the distinguished doctor of civil law, Jacopo Bottrigari, expected to rest in the chapel of his ancestors in San Francesco. For the immigrants of Bologna, the mendicant churches, and above all, San Domenico, were the preferred burial spot. A few of these were wealthy men, as we saw in Chapter Two, who lavished unusually high sums on funerals or a tomb. For example, a spice dealer from the Venetian *contrata* of the Santi Apostoli left 38 ducats for masses and a tomb at San Domenico. Other well-off Tuscans did not name a sum, but left it up to the executors, as most testators did. Interestingly, a few did not make arrangements for burial at all. This included all but one of the immigrants from the nearby contado, who, as noted in Chapter Two, tended to be less wealthy than their Tuscan counterparts.

The only comparable amount left for burial in a parish church was a three *lire* bequest for "funeral rites and burial" by an unmarried woman, originally from the contado and "now staying in Bologna", who was being hosted in a house in the parish of San Giovanni in Monte. During the crisis, she was dependent on her host whom she asked to distribute ten *lire* for masses for her soul and then remunerated as her heir.[18] As a newcomer she may have felt it better to allot specific monies for her

[17] Tabarroni, "Notizie biografiche su alcuni maestri di arti e medicina," pp. 614–615.
[18] Mem, vol. 229, fol. 75v (Gasdia fq Guidonis).

funeral expenses. Apart from two bequests of 20 *solidi* for funerals at San Vitale and Santa Caterina di Saragozza, testators in the plague sample did not set aside specific money for the funeral at a parish church.[19]

Most testators (over 90 per cent of the sample) entrusted to their executors the decision of how much would be spent on their funerals or even their tombs. And, as we saw was the case in pre-plague times, the vast majority—this time over 80 per cent—stated that they wished simply to be buried at the church and did not specify a tomb. These numbers do not indicate an increased concern for mass burial during the Black Death. One testator, the *ministralis* of the parish of Santa Maria Maddalena, left to his executor the decision of cost for his burial, "whether it was a public or private burial".[20] Here might be an indication of possible mass burial, but it is unique in the sample. Such public mass burials must have taken place—a mortality rate such as Bologna's would have resulted in drastic changes from normal burial practices—but the populace appears to have resigned themselves to this reality.

The percentage of those requesting a tomb did, however, increase to triple what had been the case before the Black Death, i.e., twelve per cent of the burial site instructions included the request for a tomb (*archa* or *sepulcrum* or *monumentum*). Two thirds of these tombs were in a parish church, though usually not in one's home parish, while the others were in either the Franciscan or Dominican church. It was not necessary to leave money along with the instructions for a tomb, since the executor was usually asked to decide the final cost. It would be wrong to single out these bequests as indicators of a general panic or excessive anxiety about burials. For most, the money for burial came out of monies remaining from the devolution of property that executors could use as they saw fit. Burials were not singled out in monetary bequests. Instead testators made small pious bequests to their parish church for prayers for the benefit of their soul. In Bologna, the funeral was part of a larger religious package, as exemplified in the will of a certain Martinus Alexii, which included burial as part of a larger bequest for seven *lire* distributed for the poor and to pious places in town.[21]

There are almost no descriptions in the wills of how testators wanted their funerals to be carried out during the epidemic. Besides one testator

---

[19] Mem, vol. 229, fols. 73v (Bertonus fq Gerardi), 119v (Johannes fq Petri Gerardi).
[20] Mem, vol. 229, fol. 6v (Andreas fq Fatii on 22 July 1348).
[21] Mem, vol. 229, fol. 75r.

who left two *solidi* for each porter, the only testator who provided details on his burial was a wealthy spice dealer from Pistoia who wanted his body to be carried to the church of San Francesco on a *sestorio* (bier) and then buried in a tomb.[22] For most, and perhaps for this spice dealer, their tombs already existed and were described as belonging to their ancestors, their fathers or associates. Nevertheless, one testator, a professor of medicine, did believe that a tomb would be constructed for him during the epidemic. He has left a remarkable expectation of distinguished remembrance during the crisis, as he called for a tomb to be built on the outside of his parish church of San Martino dei Caccianemici in the center of town (later demolished in order to build San Petronio), which was to be similar to the tomb of a member of the noble Garisendi family placed at the church of San Marco at Piazza di Porta Ravegnana. We do not know how much he expected to spend on this monument or "for the honoring of his body" at his funeral, since this was left up to his executors, but this wealthy professor did set aside the very large sum of 400 *lire* in order to endow the altar to the Virgin Mary in this parish church, the proceeds for which were to come from the administration by his executors of his properties in the contado of Bologna.[23] As we saw in Chapter Two, the professors's residences and bequests indicated wealth, and as we see here, for some, their burial choices expressed a desire to emulate the example of power and authority that was held by a leading family. They expected this prestige to be honored with the building of a suitable tomb, despite the difficult circumstances of the epidemic.

This professor and the spice dealer were exceptional in their details, but the expectation that some kind of burial would take place and that the dead would be administered by clergy was widespread. Small pious bequests to parish and mendicant churches, to their priests, friars and altars, were common during the epidemic. In July, one man left the exceptionally large sum of 250 *lire* for the construction and ornamentation of a new altar at San Francesco at which masses and orations were to be said and celebrated for his soul and the souls of his deceased relatives.[24] He left a further 50 *lire* for his burial at San Francesco. His large bequest should not be interpreted as a sign of increased anxiety that his burial

---

[22] Magister Matheus fq Petroboni left money "portatori qui ipsum testatorem portabit ad funus et sepulturam": Dem, F.M. Camp. Rossi F, 340, 28, num. 24; Mem, vol. 229, fol. 199v (Zunta fq Locti).

[23] Mem, vol. 229, fol. 319r (Saraconus fq magistri Doni on 11 July 1348).

[24] Mem, vol. 229, fol. 95r (Paulus olim domini Petri de Ziziis on 3 July 1348).

might not happen the way he would like or that prayers for his soul would not be said. He was wealthy and could make such pious bequests, and he expected them to be fulfilled, just as did magister Tardicius, a professor of grammar, who wanted to be buried in the cathedral of San Pietro (the only such request in the sample) and designated 200 *lire* to be used for a silver chalice and a missal for the altar as well as for the appointment of a "good and honest priest" to pray daily for his soul at the altar.[25] Most of the Bolognese populace could not leave such large bequests. The majority of pious bequests range from five to ten or 20 *solidi* and are to one's parish church or to the mendicant churches for the chanting and saying of masses. This was similar to pre-plague behavior.

Thus, the expectation that one's parish would administer to the spiritual needs of its parishioners was strong during the epidemic, and, as we have been able to determine, a good number of parish priests were complying. Similarly, testators depended heavily on their families and executors. Indeed, many testators did not name a burial place at all—presumably one's family and executors would see to it as best they could. The change, if it really was one, from the pre-plague to the plague wills is the appearance of the phrase that the testator wished to be buried wherever the executors chose (*ubicumque vellent et elligerent commissarii*). Even the wealthy Johannes de Garisendis, in his will of 15 August, wished his burial would be "where and in which site his executors preferred" (*ibi et in eo loco quo placuerit eius commissariis*), although his brother who had made his will six days before had requested burial in San Domenico.[26] Beleza de Manticis explicitly left the decision of burial place up to her mother, whom she named as executor with her sister.[27] Bertholanus, the emancipated son of Santus of the parish of San Bartolo, may have had only his father left to turn to when he dictated his last wishes on 25 July. His mother had made her will on 6 July, followed by his brother, Johannes, on 11 July. Bertholanus left his property to his father, set aside 30 *solidi* for masses to benefit his soul "according to the wishes of his father" and asked for burial in his parish church, the expenses for which were "as pleased his father".[28] This was the

[25] Mem, vol. 229, fol. 266r (magister Tarducius fq Bonavogle de Piro on 7 July 1348).
[26] Mem, vol. 229, fol. 24v.
[27] Mem, vol. 229, fol. 25r (on 11 July 1348).
[28] Mem, vol. 229, fol. 87r.

reality of the epidemic, which we can find in the chronicles despite the expressions of horror at the mass graves and truncated funerals. People turned to their families for the disposal of their bodies as the chronicler Gabriele de' Mussis wrote of the Black Death in Pistoia: "And when the victim had breathed his last, it was often the mother who shrouded her son and placed him in the coffin, or the husband who did the same for his wife, for everybody else refused to touch the dead body."[29] Agnolo di Tura del Grasso, the chronicler of Siena, wrote that he buried his five children with his own hands. Executors, who arranged burials, were often family members. We will next examine the role and identities of these important individuals.

Executors

The executor (*commissarius*) carried out several important tasks. In addition to ensuring the distribution of the bequests that the testator specified in the will, he or she would act as the testator's substitute after death and make decisions for the deceased. For example, many testators made the executor responsible for nominating the poor people and religious places that were the beneficiaries of charitable requests, and, as we have seen, the choice of burial place was often left up to the executor.

In the non-plague year, 1337, there was a wide variety of executors chosen, most of whom were of the testators's kin. In general, an executor did not serve alone, but acted in a group of two, three, or even four people. The larger groups tended to include people who were unrelated to the testator and who acted in tandem with family members. Women tended to display the widest range of choice among their executors, since they included female relatives, such as sisters and daughters, that men did not. Two thirds of the married female testators included their husbands among their choices, whom they usually expected to act with the advice of a cleric. If they did not turn to their husband, it was their sisters or daughters or son-in-law who aided them. Widows relied most heavily on their sons, followed by their brothers. Most of the male testators were married, but unlike their wives they chose their spouse as executors only

[29] Horrox, *Black Death*, pp. 22–23.

about a third of the time. These wives were aided by either a cleric or by a professional, such as a notary. Clerics, in general, however, had a larger role as executors for women. Some even appear as the sole executor of female testators, although this was only for widows. Male testators, on the other hand, were much more likely than women to turn outside of the family to nominate unrelated men, who were not clergy. Over half of the male testators named such individuals, among whom included notaries or members of their trade (mimicking the pattern we saw for witnesses). Only one third of women named unrelated individuals (who were not clergy), and unlike the male testators, these could be women (even a female servant appears). Despite these differences, most testators (i.e., 80 per cent) whether male or female, married or not, chose someone related to them by blood or marriage as their executors, although often they were not expected to stand alone. Only 20 per cent of testators made use only of individuals who were not related to them. It was men who turned more often either for extra or exclusive assistance to unrelated men, not clerics; while women, especially, turned for extra help, or even for sole counsel, to clerics.

Executors During the Black Death

During the crisis of plague, testators faced the difficult situation of loss of family members who were the primary source for executors. After plague arrived the vast majority (94 per cent) still named an executor, but within a diminished population some traditional choices had to be modified. A significant change in the nomination of executors that may reflect the mortality of family members is that the proportion of testators who sought help without any aid of their families rose to 32 per cent. There were three groups that testators could turn to beyond the family: professionals especially notaries, but also *ministrales* and doctors; clerics including parish priests and friars; and men and women linked to the testators through the social bonds of neighborhood, work, and friendship. We will examine these choices separately.

Notaries and clerics stepped in to act as executors more frequently during the plague. Only two per cent of the pre-plague testators nominated a notary as executor, but seven per cent did so during 1348. When notaries were the sole executors, they usually managed the estates of family members, especially their mothers, or foreign residents of Bologna.[30] It was more common for them to be appointed alongside clerics and/or the testators's kin.[31] Twenty per cent of the plague testators asked a cleric—either a mendicant friar and/or their parish priest—to serve as executor. While it was very rare for a testator to ask a cleric and no one else to serve as executor before the Black Death (only one person in the sample did so), once plague arrived more took this option (remaining, nonetheless, a small minority of five per cent of testators).[32] This was an almost exclusively female trait—with seven per cent of women and only one man naming a cleric only—and characteristic of either widows or unmarried females. While parish priests were asked to serve as executors together with kin or friends, the friars (Franciscan, Augustinian Hermits, or Dominicans in descending order of number of requests) were the only clerics to be called upon to serve alone. The testators who made these choices were rather unusual and their wills demonstrate strong ties to the mendicant establishments, since they wished either to be buried in a mendicant church or had their will redacted in a mendicant church. Most named religious heirs, either the mendicant convent or the Poor of Christ. As we have seen in the discussion of redaction sites and as we will see in the discussion of heirs, these testators were unusual. The high mortality due to plague brought to light those testators with especially close ties to the mendicants.

The other choice outside of the family were one's friends, neighbors, and co-workers. Men were more much more likely than women to turn to this group exclusively. Only 16 per cent of female testators, but 28 per cent of males, named executors who were neither clerics nor family. It was rare to name a woman as executor who was not kin, but three men relied on female executors, whom they nominated to serve alone. Female testators named four female executors, but they were expected

[30] Antonius Ugollini Bellondi a spice dealer of Venice living in San Biagio had his will made up in a neighboring parish in the home of a notary, whom he made heir and executor (Mem, vol. 228, fol. 153v). One example of a widowed mother of a notary who turned to her son as executor is Becta fq Acharixii de Latezana (Mem, vol. 228, fol. 168r).

[31] Even when not made sole executors, notaries often managed the estates of other notarial families. For example, the notary, Dominicus fq Paulli Vitalis, named a notary and his brother (not identified as a notary) as executors (Mem, vol. 229, fol. 82v) and Unghina fq Lappi Philippi, widow of a notary, named a notary, a doctor, and a third man with no identifiable trade or relation to her (Mem, vol. 228, fol. 104r).

[32] There is only one example in the pre-plague sample of sole reliance on a cleric, in this case an Augustinian Hermit: Mem, vol. 193, fol. 49v (Agnes fq Megli de Tagliavinis on 3 November 1337).

to act with the aid of other men or a relative. Instead, these executors from outside of the family were men connected to the testators because they lived in the same parish or practiced the same trade, or because they were of high social status. An example of turning to one's parish for aid is furnished by Johannes fq Ugolini ser Bondi de Planellis, the *ministralis* of Sant'Andrea degli Ansaldi, who named a certain Nicolaus magistri Ture of his parish as executor. It was not lack of family members that caused Johannes to seek out his neighbor for aid, since his three brothers were alive—he named them as his heirs.[33] Bertolomea Guidonis Lixignoli, Johanna Amodei, and Maria Raymondi Guidonis, on the other hand, were all unmarried women who named no family members in their wills. They too could rely on their neighbors, since each asked men of their parish to be executors and appointed them or their sons as heirs.[34]

Plague robbed many testators of family members whom they would normally have asked. As we saw was the case for the witnesses, prominent citizens or men of public faith, such as notaries and the *ministrales*, stepped in to fill the gap. This may have been the situation of the widower, Johannes fq Petri Gerardi, who made his will as he lay ill in a hospital. He sought out men with important social and professional status, since he named as executors an official of the hospital and a notary, whom he rewarded with a 20 *solidi* bequest.[35] Others with family still available turned to notaries or doctors, such as the widow of a professor of logic whose will records the presence of sons, daughters and a sister, but names a *medicus* as executor.[36]

Others with no family turned to the prominent families of the town. Judging from her will, the elite widowed Pelegrina fq Albucii de Sancto Petro was survived only by the daughter of her deceased husband. She left this daughter furniture and gave some money to the servant of her deceased sister, but she named a cloth merchant as her heir. To distribute her property she called on two noblemen, including one from the famous Garisendi family. She rewarded four other Garisendi women with bequests of ten *lire* each.[37] Similar connections to social

[33] Mem, vol. 229, fol. 109v.
[34] Mem, vol. 228, fol. 103r; vol. 229, fols. 1r, 3r.
[35] Mem, vol. 229, fol. 119v.
[36] Mem, vol. 230, fol. 215r.
[37] Mem, vol. 229, fol. 204v. A nobleman of the de Boitis family named as executors and guardians for his children another Garisendi nobleman who was to serve with his wife and a relative: Mem, vol. 229, fol. 89v.

and political power may have been at work for the noble unmarried Bertholomea de Tenchårariis who named a female member of the ruling Pepoli family as executor and heir.[38]

Lastly, one could make use of connections forged through work. For example, Johannes, a clothes dealer and widower, made use of the bonds of occupation, since he relied on another clothes dealer and a mercer to act as his executor.[39] Work was also important for carpenter Sylverius who appears not to have married, since the only relative he mentioned in his will was his dead brother. Sylverius sought as executors the sons of another deceased master carpenter as well as a furrier.[40] Although we do not know the trades of any female testators, we can see the bonds of work functioning in the wills of widows of a deceased parchment maker and furrier who named as executors men from their husbands's trades.[41]

Newcomers to Bologna could rely on their compatriots both as witnesses, as we saw in the last chapter, and as executors. Some drew upon fellow residents of their home town, such as ser Datus, originally from Lucca, who appointed as executors his sisters and another man of Lucca. Others drew from immigrants coming from the same region, such as Zanobia, originally from Linari in the contado of Florence, who nominated a Florentine. Or, lastly, one immigrant could turn to another irregardless of regional ties. For example, a widow, Nicholeta, originally from Poggi Bonsi, asked her mother and a citizen of Venice for aid.[42]

Although we have seen that women, like men, sought outside help, the examples noted above suggest that this was not common to all women—marriage status made a difference. In fact, the women who sought help beyond the family most often were widows, like Pelegrina de Sancto Petro, or unmarried women, like Bertholomea de Tenchårariis. Married women were the least likely to look beyond the family. Their choices among their relatives were limited, since the majority, not surprisingly, named their husbands. One elite woman named her brothers, another her mother and father, and two others named sisters. For the most part, wives's arenas of support stayed within these smaller family circles. The

[38] Mem, vol. 229, fol. 267r.
[39] Mem, vol. 229, fol. 205r.
[40] Mem, vol. 229, fol. 256r.
[41] Mem, vol. 228, fol. 145r; vol. 229, fol. 87r.
[42] Mem, vol. 229, fols. 5v (Zanobia fq Michaelis), 9v (ser Datus fq Puzini de Ugollinellis), 79r (Nicholeta fq ser Zanis de Podio Bonici).

one exception was a noble woman, whose will demonstrated strong social personal ties to the women she chose as executors. Zanbraxina Bonbollogni de Pegollotis named her husband as heir, but chose as executors two noble, widowed sisters, to whom she left sizeable bequests. The sons of one of these executors appeared among the witnesses.[43] Thus, the choices of married women do not appear to have been greatly transformed by plague.

Married women were not unusual in their reliance on family, because most testators did this to some degree. The principal choices of family members remained the same for men and women before and during the Black Death: men turned to their brothers or wives, while the top choices for women were their brothers and husbands (in both cases these testators made up fifteen per cent of women who named family members as executors). As before, women included more of their female relatives than men: twelve per cent asked sisters (compared to eight per cent of the male testators naming family members after plague arrived); seven per cent named mothers (against five per cent of men). This marks, however, a big change for men from before the epidemic, since not one male testator named a sister before the Black Death. In fact, no man named a woman (whether a relative or not), other than his mother, as executor in 1337. After plague struck, men did turn to women more often, including their blood kin, relatives by marriage, or women unrelated to them. Some of these men are atypical, i.e., they were unmarried or widowed with few male relatives alive. One was an unmarried man of the aristocratic Malavolti family who left several bequests of land and money to women, including a wet nurse, a female servant, a nurse and two female cousins, who were made executors.[44] Another was a elite widower who had lost his wife and mother but still had an unmarried daughter and two male cousins. He made his daughter his heir, to be substituted in the case of her death by his cousins. All three were to be his executors.[45] Sisters were important for unmarried men, such as an unmarried professor of medicine who named his mother and sister as heirs and executors, and a rector who named his sister. As we will see such testators also nominated sisters as their heirs in greater numbers after plague devastated the town.

---

[43] Mem, vol. 229, fol. 20r.
[44] Mem, vol. 229, fol. 186v (Zandonatus fq Manfredi de Malavoltis).
[45] Mem, vol. 229, fol. 179v (Ugolinus fq Bertholomei de Bernardinis).

As before the Black Death, the least preferred executors for testators during the epidemic were fathers, because so many were dead by the time a testator made a will, and daughters, who were either married out of the family or were minors without full legal authority of their own. Sons, however, did act as executors, but rarely for their fathers, and instead, for their widowed mothers. As before the period of plague, widows tended to rely on their children, but during the epidemic they included their siblings more often. Thus, to summarize, after plague arrived testators had to rely on men and women outside of the family more than they had done before. Notaries and clerics showed up as executors more than before, however, sole reliance on them was characteristic of a minority of the population. People were able to turn to their neighbors or colleagues in work or others who possessed social significance. Immigrants to Bologna could rely on their own communities of newcomers to tackle some of the difficulties of the epidemic. Yet the family was still the main arena of support. Married women continued to rely on their immediate families. Widows also looked to their children, as they had done before, but with the crisis of plague they, along with single women, were forced to look beyond the family more often. Faced with the depletion of members of the immediate family, men turned to more relatives, especially siblings and their female kin. Similarly, women who were unrelated to the testator, stepped into the limelight more than before to serve as executors for male testators.

Inheritance

According to notarial law, the primary purpose of the testament was to name an heir to the patrimony. We will now turn to this important topic, investigating firstly regular patterns of inheritance and secondly changes that occurred in inheritance choices during the epidemic. The subject of inheritance in late medieval urban society is complicated and one of long debate, especially on the hereditary rights of women.[46]

[46] See introduction to Gianna Lumia-Ostinelli, "'Ut cippus domus magis conservetur': La successione a Siena tra statuti e testamenti (secoli XII–XVII)," *Archivio Storico Italiano* 161 (2003), 3–51 with references to Jack Goody, Diane Owen Hughes, Christiane Klapisch-Zuber, Stanley Chojnacki, Isabelle Chabot, Thomas Kuehn and others. For the debate on dowry that is intimately related to the discussion of inheritance, see articles in the issue, "Femmes, Dots, et Patrimoines," *CLIO, Histoire, Femmes Sociétés* 7 (1998). For a survey of inheritance practices see Christine Meek, "Women, Dowries and the

Complicating the examination of inheritance practices is the fact that individual testators made choices depending on their own wishes and on the survival of various family members who were able to inherit. One cannot simply count up heirs to fully understand the practice, but must take into consideration the real circumstances of each testator. While general norms that followed statutes put into place in the Italian towns from the thirteenth century onwards did have an effect on testators's choices, the particularities of marriage status and the presence of children and other family members were also important. This investigation of inheritance in the wills of fourteenth-century Bologna will take into consideration the factors of gender, marital and social status, and will note where possible the particular situation of extant family members. This nuanced picture of late medieval inheritance will serve as comparison for the analysis below of inheritance practices during the Black Death.

The best place to begin the discussion of inheritance is with the theoretical realm of law before we enter the study of actual testamentary practices as evidenced in the wills. As is well known, succession in late medieval Italy was preferential to sons and the patrilineal line. Indeed, the laws of intestate inheritance formalized the strong preference for male patrilineal interests to the detriment of women.[47] According to the laws of intestacy, there were very few instances in which a woman could inherit property. As long as there existed male relatives along the patriline, those males would inherit. Wives could not inherit from their husbands if he had any living male relatives. The customary patterns of inheritance, accepted by scholars, is that women were usually excluded from inheriting. In general, the patrimony was divided among the sons, while daughters received only their dowries, with which they had to remain "quiet and content".[48]

Family in Late Medieval Italian Cities," in *"The Fragility of Her Sex"?: Medieval Irishwomen in Their European Context*, eds. Christine Meek and Katharine Simms (Dublin, 1996), pp. 142–146. See Chabot and Bellavitis, "A proposito di 'Men and Women in Renaissance Venice' di Stanley Chojnacki," pp. 203–238.

[47] Florentine laws have received the most attention. See Isabelle Chabot, "Le Loi du lignage: Notes sur le système successoral florentin (XIVe/X[ve]–XIIe siècles)," *CLIO* 7 (1998), pp. 51–72 and Crabb, *Strozzi*, pp. 35–36.

[48] The common phrase is that the testator "iubens eam de hiis esse contentam". For a discussion of the development of "exclusio propter dotem" see Manlio Bellomo, *Ricerche sui rapporti patrimoniali tra coniugi: Contributo alla storia della famiglia medievale* (Milan, 1961), pp. 163–185; Diane Owen Hughes, "From Brideprice to Dowry in Mediterranean Europe," *Journal of Family History* 3 (1978), pp. 262–296;

This regime of *exclusio propter dotem* also functioned in late medieval Bologna. The thirteenth-century communal statutes declared that daughters who were dowered had to be content with what their fathers left them in a testament and could seek nothing else from his goods than the dowry.[49] There are two ways to understand the application of this rule. In the case that her father had made a will, the daughter could make no further legal claim to property other than what she received in that testament: the law stated "that daughters must be content with that which their father left to them in his will and that they cannot seek anything else from his goods".[50] She was at an equal disadvantage in the second way in which the law could be applied, i.e., when no will was extant and her father died intestate, since in that case the law allowed her to claim only her dowry from her father's property, stating "that if

---

and Christiane Klapisch-Zuber who argued that "the dowry was not considered a female share in inheritance; to the contrary, it worked to exclude its beneficiary from inheritance" in Christiane Klapisch-Zuber, "The Griselda Complex: Dowry and Marriage Gifts in the Quattrocento," in her *Women, Family, and Ritual*, p. 216. A fascinating example of the ways that practice can flaunt the legal theory is in the will made on 24 May, 1337 of Nicolaus fq Johannis olim Petrizani de Calzina who named his mother and two brothers as heirs. The brothers, however, were granted only 20 *solidi* each, with which they were to be "contentos et tacitos". Nicolaus was not married and was living in his mother's house: Mem, vol. 191, fol. 148v.

[49] This was first spelled out in a statute of 1222 that declared that daughters could not make any claim or protest from the property of surviving or succeeding males even if their father's will assigned them less than the *falcidia*, i.e, the legitimate portion, typically the *quarta*, of the paternal estate reserved for heirs under Roman law. See Luigi Frati, ed. *Statuti del comune di Bologna dall'anno 1245 all'anno 1267* (Bologna, 1869), 1:413–414: "In filiabus omnibus et neptibus natis ex filia vel nepte dicimus adversus fratres vel sorores per virilem sexum descendentes quod defuncto vel defuncta masculo vel masculis tam existentibus et succedentibus de replectione non agatur etiam si minus falcidia eis relictum fuerit a parente a qualibetcumque voluntate vel iure restitutionis, vel per legatum vel fideicommissum vel donationem causa mortis et alia voluntate." Then in 1223, it was established that daughters had to be content with their dowry and that if their father died intestate, or if they were undowered, this would be the only thing they could claim. See Frati, *Statuti*, 1:414–415: "Statuimus quod si quis moriretur intestatus relictis vel filiabus feminis, si filia nupta fuerit sit illa contenta de dote qui fuit data quod ea in bonis paternis amplius non petat. Si autem non fuerit nupta, vel dos pro ea constituta non fuerit, si pro aliqua earum dos esset constituta alia pro qua dos non esset constituta tantum habeat quantum pro alia fuit in dotem constitutam, si facultates que fuerunt patris non sunt diminute."

[50] Fasoli and Sella, *Statuti*, 2:85: "quod filie femine debeant esse contempte de eo quod pater relinquerit eis quocumque relicti titulo in testamento suo et quod non possint aliquid ultra petere in bonis patris". Equally, a daughter had no claim against her brothers and had to be satisfied with what her mother left her in a testament. Ibid.: "dicimus in matre ex testamento decedente, relictis filia una vel pluribus et filiis masculis uno vel pluribus, scilicet quod filia etiam in minus legiptima instituta adversus fratres masculos unum vel plures institutos universales heredes ad repletionem non agatur."

anyone died intestate...his dowered daughters must be content with their dowries and cannot seek anything else from their father's goods".[51] Furthermore, in the laws of 1288/1289 daughters and their offspring were prohibited from inheriting as long as there remained any sons or the children of sons or "any successive descendents along the masculine line".[52] This does not mean, however, that a father could not name his daughter or other female relative as heir in his testament. In the cases of intestacy, the law stepped in, but one could make a different choice in the will.[53] As historians of Renaissance Tuscan cities have found, there was not always strict correspondence between the law and practice.[54] Many testators followed the laws of intestacy in passing the patrimony down to sons, but others made their own choices, which would have been affected by the presence or lack of male and female relatives and by their own personal affections.

The wills of late medieval Bologna reveal this disconnection between theory and practice. The sample of wills from 1337, the pre-plague year, demonstrates that sons were the top choice among testators: 36 per cent of all testators named only sons as heirs. Nonetheless, daughters did commonly inherit, since they were named by 17 per cent of the testators, either alone (from eight per cent of testators) or with their brothers (nine per cent of testators). These were unmarried daughters who would then use their share of the patrimony for a dowry, but nevertheless, their fathers were not following intestacy laws of succession. But the raw numbers explain little. It is useful to break down the sample by

[51] Ibid.: "quod si quis intestatus decesserit...filia seu filie que dotate sunt, sint contente de ipsa dote sue dotibus, et in bonis paternis amplius non petant". According to Giulia Serenadori, the unpublished statutes from 1335 through the fourteenth century added that the daughter's dowry must be provided from the paternal goods only so that the maternal inheritance devolved to sons. See her "*De re uxoris*: Dote e successione negli Statuti bolognesi (1250–1454)," *Archivio Storico Italiano* 606 (2005), 661–664.

[52] Ibid., p. 86: "Item quod dictum est in filiabus et filiis remanentibus patre vel matre decedentibus ab intestato, obtineat per omnia in nepte seu neptibus ex filio vel filiis masculis natis superstitibus filiis defuncti vel nepote vel nepotibus ex filio vel filiis masculis. Nepotes autem vel neptes ex filia remanentibus filio vel filiis masculis vel nepote vel nepotibus ex filio vel filiis ex defuncto vel defuncta ab intestato a successione paterna vel materna et avita penitus excludantur. Si vero supersint filia vel filie et neptes ex filio vel filia premortuis non extantibus filiis masculis vel nepotibus vel deinceps ex linea masculina tunc successio ipsarum procedat de iure comuni."

[53] As the statutes of Padova state "pater possit relinquere filie quicquid vult in ultima voluntate". Quoted in Bellomo, *Rapporti*, pp. 179–180.

[54] See Crabb, *Strozzi*, Lumia-Ostinelli, "Successione a Siena," pp. 33–51, and Elena Brizio, "La dote nella normativa statuaria e nella pratica testamentaria senese (fine sec. XII-metà sec. XIV)," *Bullettino senese di storia patria* 111 (2004), 9–39.

gender, marriage status, and class because these factors appear to have affected conformity to the laws of intestate succession. It must be noted, however, that because of the small sample size (100 wills), the groups become quite small and any conclusions could be reversed with larger numbers.

Those who most closely followed the law were elite, married men, since 77 per cent of them named only sons and none named a daughter.[55] Men from the more modest social levels named daughters as heirs 20 per cent of the time.[56] Half of these nominations (i.e. ten per cent of non-elite fathers) were of daughters standing alone, and in these cases, either there were no sons or the son was a cleric.[57] However, the other half of these nominations were daughters who shared the inheritance with their brothers. These were unmarried daughters, who would presumably take their share to use as a dowry, but, it is important to note that they were sharing equally with their brothers. Nevertheless, the general preference was for sons, since 45 per cent of these non-elite married men preferred only sons, and another ten per cent allowed them to inherit alongside their sisters, which makes the frequency of appointment of sons more than twice that of daughters.

The husbands belonging to modest social levels also stood out as different from their wealthier peers and as departing from the intestacy laws because they were much more likely to appoint their wives as their heirs (25 per cent versus 11 per cent of elite husbands, actually only one man). In late medieval Italy, a husband used his will to return his wife's dowry, the fruits of which he had been able to enjoy during the marriage for the purposes of supporting the burden of matrimony, and to give her a further legacy of money if he so wished. Typically, the husband further granted her authority and usufruct of his goods (*domina et usufructuaria omnium suorum bonorum*) as long as she remained a widow in the home of the children (*donec visserit et vitam vidualem servaverit*) and did not ask for her dowry to be returned to her.[58] If "she did not want to live with

[55] There are nine elite married men in the sample. The other relatives they named were a wife, brother, and nephew.

[56] There are 20 non-elite married men in the sample.

[57] A shoemaker of San Procolo left his money to his two daughters and gave only 20 *solidi* to his son who was a friar. This shoemaker was of very modest social status, since his wife's dowry was only 50 *lire*: Mem, vol. 192, fol. 298r (Dondus fq Juliani).

[58] An expanded phrase would be: "donec visserit et vitam honestam et chastam condusserit et servaverit et voluerit stare mori et habitare in domo et cum herede sua infrascripta habitare." Whether or not it was legally possible to have both "dominion"

the heirs" or if "she chose another life", she would only receive her dowry and any legacy of money that her husband might choose to add.[59] This clause in the testament that granted usufruct of the husband's goods is not part of the nomination of the heir, but appears in the section discussing the return of the dowry (including the statement of its receipt and its amount). These instructions correspond to the Bolognese law on intestate succession that states that mothers could not inherit the goods of their sons or daughters who died intestate as long as there remained any of the father's (her husband's) brothers and sisters, whether uterine, i.e., from a different father, or consanguine, i.e., from the same father, or any of his uncles or sons of his brothers (all agnates to the father). If any of these relatives were alive she was allowed to receive only the usufruct of her deceased husband's goods.[60] This meant that she had the right to use the property and enjoy its benefits during her life, as long as she did not impair its substance, and that the patrimony did not belong to her, but would be passed on to the male heirs of her husband at her death. The reasoning here is that the children's property came from the husband and must be kept in the patriline and not passed to an outsider, such as the mother.[61] The result, according to intestacy, is that women could inherit from men only as their daughters (not as their wives or mothers), i.e., as the agnate offspring of their fathers, but this, of course, they did only in terms of their dowry, which we can best understand as a means to exclude them from inheritance.[62] Wives who were mothers

and "usufruct" at the same time was a matter of debate in notarial law, with some arguing that the dominion was reserved for the heir. See Renzo Villata, "Il volto della famiglia medievale," pp. 450–454.

[59] Notarial manuals emphasized that sons must honor, venerate, and obey their mother, and consider her as *domina*, but also recognize that she may leave. The wills, however, are not explicitly cautionary in this regards towards sons, although they do accept the possibility that the widow may chose to live elsewhere.

[60] Fasoli and Sella, *Statuti*, 2:87: "quod filio vel filia decedente ab intestato sine liberis, fratribus vel sororibus consanguineis et uterinis vel consanguineis tantum, vel patruis vel filiis fratrum vel consanguineis ex latere patris defuncti existentibus, matre superstite, mater succedat in usufructu eius partis que sibi a iure defertur".

[61] Here Bolognese laws on intestate succession correspond perfectly to the Florentine situation presented by Klapisch in "Cruel Mother," p. 118, that women were passing guests in the *case* of men.

[62] Also part the instructions on dowry and usufruct was a husband's typical bequest to his wife of her clothes "omnes pannos lineos et laneos ad usum dicte N", "omnes suos pannos quos ipsa utebatur tempore vite sue" or, if wealthy, her jewelry "perlas zoaglas et ornamenta ipsius dicte N" or "omnia sua jochalia". Such legal phrases are akin to those sometimes used for bequests to servants from their employers. When husbands made gifts to their wives at marriage or during marriage of clothes and goods

of children, then, should not have been named heirs by their husbands. Accordingly, the wealthy husband who did make his wife his heir added the "condition and agreement" that after her death his property would pass to his two sons. Essentially she was granted only usufruct, in conformity with the laws of succession, while the proper heirs were his sons.[63] But wives were made heirs by husbands of lower social levels, and such clauses specifying usufruct were not included in the nomination of their wives as heirs.[64] The laws of intestate succession were designed with the interests and exigencies of the upper classes in mind.

Wives were more likely to name their spouse as heir than their husbands did, but, again, it was the moderately well-off wives who turned to their husbands most often (54 per cent of them did so versus 30 per cent of the elite wives).[65] Elite wives were more likely to appoint their children (50 per cent did this), with sons alone making up forty per cent of those heirs. Wives of modest income nominated their children 36 per cent of the time and instead gave their money to more mature men, viz., their husbands and brothers. Elite widows left their wealth overwhelmingly to their children (93 per cent of elite widows), while non-elite widows only did so in 63 per cent of the cases, preferring to also leave their patrimony to their siblings and grandchildren.[66] Elite widows behaved much like elite married men, since they displayed the second highest frequency of naming sons alone (64 per cent of them did). However, they did name daughters as their sole heirs in a proportion equal to that of married women. Thus, among people who had a family, children formed the bulk of heirs, but this tendency was heightened with the elite parents who preferred sons over daughters and children over their spouse or any other relatives. The less well-off Bolognese considered spouses more often and, after their spouses, they chose siblings and grandchildren.

---

they retained ownership of the gifts and, thus, bequeathed the items to their wives by means of a testament.

[63] Mem, vol. 191, fol. 58v (Bertalinus fq Albertini de Malavoltis on 5 April, 1337).

[64] Examples of commoners of 1337 who named wives are: ser Albertinus fq ser Petri, identified as *laborator* (Mem, vol. 192, fol. 7r); Jacobinus fq Guarini, a tailor (vol. 192, fol. 60v); Petrus fq Nicholai Bolognipti who returned a dowry of ten *lire* to his wife (vol. 192, fol. 428v); Nerbona fq Gucii whose wife's dowry was 75 *lire* (vol. 193, fol. 9v).

[65] There are 11 non-elite and 10 elite wives in the sample.

[66] There are 19 non-elite and 14 elite widows in the sample.

The chosen relatives for testators who had not married and did not have children were siblings and mothers.[67] This choice was not repeated among any of the other groups of testators. Single women behaved very differently from wives and widows, and even from single men, because two thirds of them left their patrimony to individuals who were unrelated to them. Again it was the non-elite women who were more likely to go beyond the family, since 80 per cent of them chose people not related to them, while half that percentage of the elite single women did so. Less wealthy single women chose to leave their money to women (five cases) rather than men (three cases). Some of these women were closely involved in giving and receiving support from their parish. For example, Johanna fq Alberti relied on her neighbors in nominating as heir a widow, legating five *lire* and 40 *solidi* to a man and woman respectively, and naming as executor a shoemaker—all of whom were from her parish.[68] Elite single women did not leave wealth to outsiders as frequently, nor to any who were women. Nevertheless, they were unusual in passing their wealth beyond the family, as did Francisca fq Gerardi de Zachullis who left small bequests of 20 *solidi* to her married sister and nephew (her sister's son), but gave most of her wealth to an unrelated man from her parish.[69]

The other way to leave one's money beyond the family was to name a pious heir, such as a religious institution or the "Poor of Christ". This was a very rare choice for any testator before the Black Death. Only one man, a widower, gave his wealth to the poor, and two women, a widow and a wife, named religious institutions. The case of one of the women, an elite wife, shows how unusual such a situation was. Although married, she had no children, and chose the Augustinian Hermit convent of San Giacomo in Bologna as heir, instructing the friars to give all the revenue to her deaf and dumb sister and to allow her to live at the infirmary there.[70] After her sister's death, the revenues of the patrimony were to go to the infirmary "for the needs of its ill". The sister could not be made an heir because of her condition, so giving her usufruct was the closest she could come to inheriting. Indicative of the general schema of succession in the minds of testators, i.e., the primacy of the family, especially of sons, the secondary place enjoyed by collateral relatives and the marginal, but

[67] There are three single unmarried men and 15 single women in the sample.
[68] Mem, vol. 191, fol. 149r.
[69] Mem, vol. 193, fol. 54v.
[70] Mem, vol. 193, fol. 24r (Phyllipa fq Matei olim Pellegrini).

sometimes necessary, use of religious heirs is the example of a member of the aristocratic Basacomari family who was not yet married when he made his will as a healthy man. He called upon two cousins (sons of his father's brother) to be executors and nominated his mother as heir. He stated, however, that if he were to marry and have children, he would leave his daughters each a dowry of 500 *lire* and make his sons his heirs. If, however, he died before leaving children, then his property would pass to the Poor of Christ, whom he wished his mother to name before she died.[71]

Although the last wishes of the Basacomari nobleman are a fine example of *exclusio propter dotem* and the typical elite preference for sons, he was atypical in naming secondary and tertiary heirs, a practice carried out by about a third of testators. Moreover, the ranks of his primary and secondary heirs would have been switched by the typical testator, that is, normally, one's children would rank before one's mother. In fact, testators tended to use substitute heirs to nominate their wider kin, especially sisters, but also mothers or nieces (the children of sisters). The final layer of heirs—either tertiary or for some even a fourth choice—was generally reserved for pious causes. This could consist of a religious establishment or the Poor of Christ, as noted above, or the poor and "needy" or "miserable" persons. Only when testators considered the exhaustion of possible heirs of their kin did they wish to leave their patrimony beyond the family. Instead, most testators chose to make their pious donations in the form of legacies to hospitals, churches, or to poor and needy clerics or laymen in town. These might be fairly large gifts, involving money, grain, even all of one's furniture and, very rarely, perhaps a house or a piece of land, but most were small bequests of 5, 10, 20, or 40 *solidi* and thus, would not have come close to the protected portion of the estate reserved for the heirs, i.e., that of the *lex Falcidia* of Roman law.

In summary, in testamentary practice, the restriction of daughters, wives, and mothers that is so strongly emphasized in intestate law is present, but not across the board. In my judgement of the Bolognese wills, it seems that testators saw the lines of transmission of inheritance as radiating from oneself to initially descend to one's offspring (and for elites that meant sons), to then move laterally to one's siblings and their offspring, or ascending to one's mother or the siblings of one's mother

[71] Mem, vol. 193, fol. 55r (Johannes fq Burnioli olim domini Petri de Baxacomatribus).

or father.[72] The path does not travel simply from agnate as preferred to cognate relatives as secondary choice, since testators would rank higher in the nomination of heirs the children of a sister (who would be cognate, although the sister is agnate) then they would rank the siblings of a father (an aunt or uncle, who would be agnate) or their paternal uncles's children (agnate cousins). Focus seems to be on the immediate household and its descendents, which for married people included the children and spouse, but for unmarried people, would be the mother and siblings. Beyond the immediate family, agnate or cognate relatives would be named, and beyond them, there was the possibility of a religious heir. The testament of Dotta Natalis Pasqualis of 4 March, 1337 demonstrates these attitudes at work. Her marriage status was either new or being arranged and she was healthy. She named her mother as primary heir, her sister as secondary heir with that sister's children as her substitute. If all those substitutes died, then her wealth was to be distributed to "poor and piteous persons" for the purpose of dotal subsidies or "any other use or for works of piety and mercy". If Dotta, however, were to give birth to children "from the present or any other marriage" all of the previous heirs were annulled and her children would take their place.[73]

Inheritance During the Black Death

How was this complicated picture of succession affected by the catastrophic mortality of the Black Death? The largest change in terms of difference in percentage is for pious heirs, since the percentage of testators making this choice more than doubled during the Black Death. Married men and women named such heirs during the epidemic, whereas before it was only the widowed or unmarried. Class may have also entered the picture, since, in all cases except one married elite man, it was the non-elites who named pious heirs. Again, the wealthy display a greater concern to reserve the patrimony for their immediate family and the patriline, while non-elites would transmit what goods they had easily to siblings and unrelated individuals. The elite husband who named a pious heir stipulated that the Poor of Christ would share with any of

[72] Fathers appear as heirs so infrequently because a testator had to be *sui iuris*, i.e. independent of their father's *potestas*, which normally occurred through his death, or else they had been emancipated.

[73] Mem, vol. 191, fol. 14v.

his sons that might be born.[74] However, it is important to note that despite the doubling in percentage and the greater variety of types of testators making religious causes their heirs, this kind of decision was taken by a small minority of testators (4.5 per cent of testators in the sample). The Black Death did not bring on a large transfer of property to the church nor a wave of demonstrations of piety in charitable giving to the poor.[75] Regardless of whether or not the end of the world was at hand, the family came first in inheritance.

Families, however, did suffer during the crisis, for, as we saw in Chapter Three, husbands and wives and their children were dying. Wives and husbands were less frequently nominated after plague entered the town than before: wives drop from six to one per cent of testators's choices and husbands from nine to six per cent. While 36 per cent of testators named only sons in 1337, 25 per cent did so after epidemic disease set in. Plague affected households, as the chroniclers related, and thus there were fewer spouses and children to name. Disease may have carried off more parents, infrequent heirs in more stable times, since their presence is diminished among testators's choices after plague moved in. Daughters, however, were slightly more visible as heirs during the epidemic, since the percentage of testators making this choices rose from nine to eleven per cent. In their efforts to benefit the immediate family, testators now turned to daughters more than before.

Under the frequent, immediate, threat of the dissolution of the household, testators had to search further along the lines of kin to find family members to whom they could direct wealth. Thus, married men and women for the first time nominated relatives, viz., siblings, grandsons, nephews and nieces, to whom wealth would not previously have been given. In fact, before the Black Death no testator named a nephew, niece or cousin as primary heir, but six per cent of testators named them during 1348. This trend was most evident in the presence of many more widowed or unmarried men in the sample, who formed one third of all testators after plague arrived. The mortality made men prepare their wills in a state most would not normally have expected or

---

[74] Mem, vol. 229, fol. 95r (Paulus olim Petri de Ziziis).

[75] Even the *Demaniale* testators—who dictated their wishes before mendicants and asked them to preserve their wills and bury their bodies—also overwhelmingly left their patrimony to family during the Black Death. Seventy-four per cent named family members as heirs, 11 per cent named unrelated men, including three *familiares* connected to the mendicants, and nine per cent designated pious heirs, viz., hospitals, the Poor of Christ, and in one instance, a Carthusian monastery.

preferred, i.e., either as a widower or the unmarried son of a deceased father. Of this group, once again, it turns out that the lower social levels were more likely to extend their choices further along the lines of kin, to include parents, siblings, cousins, nephews, nieces, and an aunt and uncle, while the elite widowed or single males named siblings (mainly brothers) and a mother in addition to their children. The less well-off named pious heirs, either a hospital or the Poor of Christ, while the wealthy did not. For example, two brothers of the noble Garisendi family made their wills within a week of each other during August. The first brother, a widower, named his unmarried brother as heir with two cousins (sons of a paternal uncle) to stand as substitutes. The second brother named a third brother, and again listed the cousins as substitutes.[76]

As the Garisendi brothers indicate, siblings became very important in inheritance during the Black Death. Before plague, men did not leave their wealth to their brothers, unless they (the testators) were unmarried. After plague, not only men, but all testators, were more likely to transmit their property to their siblings. The frequency of nominating siblings went from nine to eighteen per cent of testators during the Black Death. Brothers were thought of more often (six compared to ten per cent of the time), but sisters appear to have benefited the most as receivers of property in 1348 (going from three per cent to seven per cent of all testators's choices). Sometimes sisters passed over their brothers. For example, Soldana de Mallavoltis named as heirs her three sisters, Mia, Jacoba, and Clara. Soldana wrote her will while she was still healthy at the same time as her widowed mother, Lipa de Galuciis, who also was healthy. Interestingly, Soldana's three sisters were their mother's heirs, but Soldana was given only 20 *solidi*. Also cut out from the considerable wealth of this family was Soldana's brother. He received only 25 *lire* from his mother, which he could have only when his sisters married or entered a convent. Soldana passed her wealth to her three sisters (Mia, Jacoba, and Clara). She had a son, to whom she legated only ten *lire*. Lipa's connections with her deceased husband's family were strong, since she named a female cousin of his line (Mia) as executor and she, along with her daughter, redacted her will in the home of a male cousin

[76] Mem, vol. 229, fols. 24r–v (Nicolaus olim nobilis militis domini Lanze de Garisendis on 9 August 1348 and Johannes olim nobilis militis domini Lanze de Garisendis on 15 August 1348).

(Zandonatus) of her husband. Zandonatus had written his will nine days earlier and, although sick, was still alive to host Lipa and Soldana. He also relied on Mia as executor.[77] Although they were members of Bologna's elite class, the men in Lipa and Soldana's family were not privileged in inheritance over the women. This was highly unusual and may have been the result of the special circumstances of the epidemic. Although no sons appear to have been passed over, a similar case of sisters and daughters benefiting during the epidemic appear in the wills of dopnus Thomas, the rector of the parish church of San Tommaso della Braina, who named his married sister, Agnexia, his heir and executor. She made her will only five days later when she had already fallen ill. Both she and her brother had their wills drawn up by the same notary in a house that belonged to the parish church. Her wealth went to her daughter who was also to be executor.[78] She did not name her husband—perhaps he too had quickly fallen ill from plague.

As noted above and in the previous examples, daughters also benefited from the unusual circumstances of plague, sometimes even to the detriment of their brothers as did Soldana's sisters. The biggest change came from those men who had considered them the least. While no wealthy father named a daughter as heir in the pre-plague sample, nine per cent of the fathers in the plague sample allowed them to share equally with their brothers and another 14 per cent nominated them alone, in which case there were no sons. This means that the presence of daughters as heirs of the elite went from non-existent (at least in the sample) to the choice of 24 per cent of their fathers. The less-well-off fathers also nominated their daughters much more often after plague set in. The frequency of daughters being able to share with their brothers doubled among these fathers in the sample (from 10 per cent in 1337 to 20 per cent in 1348), and nearly doubled for daughters standing alone (from 10 per cent to 17 per cent). The expectation would have been that these daughters were to use their father's wealth for their dowries, but they were not being excluded from an equal share in the patrimony because of the dowry, i.e., *exclusio propter dotem* was not working here.

There are, in fact, examples from the plague sample of dowered

[77] Mem, vol. 229, fols. 183r-186v (Lipa fq Francischi Guidocheri de Galuciis on 17 November; Soldana fq Mathei de Mallavoltis on 17 November; Zandonatus fq Manfredi de Mallavoltis on 8 November 1337).

[78] Mem, vol. 229, fols. 264v (Agnexia fq Jacobi Bonandi on 18 July 1348), 265v (dopnus Thomas fq Jacobi Bonandi on 13 August 1348).

daughters who were allowed to inherit. Bitinus fq Dominici, a shoemaker of the parish of San Giulliano, nominated as heir his only child, Chatellina, who was married to a smith, magister Petrus. He left to his wife her modest dowry of 60 *lire* without any conditions. Chatellina was to act as executor for his estate, which involved the duties of arranging his burial and distributing the few, small pious bequests of five *solidi* to his parish church and two hospitals.[79] Similarly, Bertolinus fq Dominici, a butcher of modest status—his wife's dowry was only 50 *lire*—living in the parish of San Nicolò del Borgo di San Felice, provided dowries for his two daughters *and* named them as his heirs.[80] Did these men choose to pass along their patrimony to dowered daughters because plague had killed their relatives and the situation was now the scenario permitted by intestacy law, i.e., "with no sons or grandsons or successive relatives along the masculine line surviving" and thus dowered daughters were able to succeed?[81] We do not know in these cases, but the noble widow Bitixia de Baxacomatribus did provide dowries for her two daughters, Beleza and Sina, and, furthermore, allowed them to inherit the patrimony thereby excluding her son, Blaxius, to whom she legated 50 *lire*, the dowry of her mother, and some furniture. Beleza's will is also extant, so we can learn that Blaxius was passed over again, for Sina was to inherit from her sister.[82] Bitixia appears to have gone against intestate succession; for Bitinus the shoemaker and Bertolinus the butcher we are unsure. But it is also possible that none of these testators was concerned about the laws of intestacy. They may have made purely personal choices, perhaps seeing their daughters as competent individuals who could manage their estate and were the best chance for the future of the family. We cannot know what motivated them, but the decisions of Bitinus, Bertolinus, and Bitixia confirm one or the other of the hypotheses suggested by the wills of Bologna, i.e., that testamentary practice did not always follow the rigidly patrilineal and anti-female bias of the intestacy laws and that daughters benefited in the transmission of wealth as a result of the Black Death.

---

[79] Mem, vol. 229, fol. 12v.

[80] Mem, vol. 228, fol. 317r. One daughter received 140 *lire* as dowry, while the other daughter who was already engaged to marry received an addition of 40 *lire* to her unstated dowry. The testament records no other children, nor does it specify an executor.

[81] Fasoli and Sella, *Statuti*, 2:86.

[82] Mem, vol. 228, fol. 25r (Bitixia fq Felloni de Baxacomatribus and Beleza fq Bertholuci de Manticis).

Isabelle Chabot has argued that after the Black Death the exclusion of women in intestate succession increased. The intestate laws of later fourteenth- and early fifteenth-century Florence called for more rigidly patrilineal succession to the point that even a mother's dowry had to pass to her sons and could not be devolved between daughters and sons.[83] The evidence from Bologna during the Black Death would support the view that the elite men of late medieval and Renaissance Italy were reacting against a betterment for women in the acquisition of wealth that they found threatening. We see here a possible first improvement in transmission of property to daughters and female relatives that may have continued with the recurrent outbreaks of plague, threatening the male property interests. It is important to note, however, that the Black Death did not introduce the strong preference from males in hereditary succession. Bologna was legislating against female inheritance in 1222/3 and 1288/89, well in advance of Florence. It is very possible, however, that the repeated mortality of plague resulted in more of the kinds of exceptional behavior benefiting women that we have discovered in Bologna, thus provoking a backlash by the elite legislators in Florence and elsewhere.

Guardianship

After the testator had named the executor and heirs, the next task was the nomination of guardian or *tutor*, if needed. For children who inherited the patrimony as minors, the parents, usually the father, had to arrange for a guardian to manage the finances. One could name a guardian in a will or make a separate contract, which was often done.[84] Roughly ten per cent of testators used their wills to nominate guardians, both before and during the Black Death.

Before the epidemic, the wife was the principal choice, with only one exceptional elite man who named his two brothers as guardians. This man's wife was alive and was granted usufruct of three pieces of land in the contado and residency anywhere in his house as long as she remained a widow and stayed with her three sons. The sons were

[83] Chabot, "Le loi du lignage," pp. 53–62.

[84] On guardianship contracts see Gigliola di Renzo Villata, "Il volta della famiglia medievale," pp. 423–438.

named heirs and his brothers were to substitute if they all died.[85] It is not clear why the wife was not nominated as guardian, since she was clearly carrying out the duties of their caretaker, but the husband may have wished for her to have male assistance and simply named only the men. A master carpenter followed the same practice by asking a notary living in his parish to be guardian with his wife, to whom he did assign *tutela*. He gave his wife *alimenta* suitable for her widowed state for as long as she remained a widow in the house with their two minor sons, whom he named as heirs. In case his wife was pregnant, any new sons could inherit, but his daughters were to only receive their "legitimate portion" by law. The wife could substitute for the sons after they died only in usufruct, and, at her death, his wealth was to be distributed for the benefit of his soul to poor and needy persons.[86] While it was unusual to distribute one's wealth to the poor for the purposes of piety, it was standard practice to grant the wife, as *tutrix*, usufruct of either some land, the house or part of it, or even all of the husband's goods, while making the sons heirs—the wife did not inherit.[87]

The men who named their wives as guardians had land and/or noble heritage. The husbands of lower social levels who made their wives heirs were probably doing this with the same idea in mind as these elite husbands, i.e., that the wife would use the money to support the children. The elite husbands, however, were more concerned that their wealth descend along the agnate lines only, so they used the legal institution of guardianship to accomplish what their non-elite counterparts did through inheritance. Another explanation could be Chabot's, i.e., that a husband empowered his wife as guardian with usufruct over his property in order to prevent her from remarrying and taking her property away from his family.[88]

---

[85] Mem, vol. 191, fol. 44v (Janes fq domini Boni de Raxuriis).

[86] Mem, vol. 193, fol. 69r (Guarentius fq Albertucii).

[87] This is similar to later fourteenth-century Florence. See Isabelle Chabot, "Lineage strategies and the control of widows in Renaissance Florence," in *Widowhood in Medieval and Early Modern Europe*, eds. Sandra Cavallo and Lyndan Warner (New York, 1999), pp. 137–139.

[88] Ibid., p. 138.

Guardianship During the Black Death

After plague arrived, much of the general practice of guardianship remained the same. Most testators naming guardians in 1348 were wealthy husbands who named their wives (76 per cent) and made them *domina* of their goods as long as they stayed a widow in the home with the ward. The ward was the heir, with a substitute sometimes being a male relative, such as a nephew on the paternal side. One man appointed his sisters as guardian for his small daughter—perhaps he was newly widowed due to plague. There does appear, however, the unusual figure of a widow who called on her sister as guardian for her daughter. The sister was granted no special legacy to assist in carrying out her duty. In the case that her daughter died, this widow wanted her wealth to be distributed to the "poor, needy, sick, and those begging for bread for the benefit of her soul and her deceased husband and his two sisters".[89] It is unusual to find a widow arranging for guardianship of her children—this may been the result of the epidemic.

Also likely to have been the result of plague mortality is the appointment of many more individuals to assist the wives (or in one case, the sister) than before. These extra people could be female relatives of the ward's mother: two wives served as guardians along with their mothers and another with her sister. However, more than relatives of the wives, unrelated men appear and with much higher frequency than before. These men also served as the executors of the testators, and as we saw was the case for executors, they were tied to the testators with social bonds: those guardians coming from outside of the family included two partners in trade, a notary, a neighbor, a member of the powerful Garisendi family, and a *familiaris* or retainer of an elite citizen. In a few cases these men were remunerated for their troubles: the *familiaris* was granted use of a house; two men, unrelated to the testator, were made the substitutes of their ward (the heir) in inheriting the patrimony; and a spice dealer stated that he wished the capital that he had invested in a spice shop near the market be given "as quickly as can suitably be done" to the ward and guardians.[90] Thus, to sum up, during the Black Death testators who needed to appoint guardians continued to depend on

[89] Mem, vol. 228, fol. 9r (Ursolina fq Thomacis Ursiis).

[90] Mem, vol. 229, fols. 10r (Jacobus fq ser Amodei originally from Castel dei Britti appointed two men from the contado as guardians), 83v (Dominicus fq Thome Phylipi), 199v (Zunta fq Locti, *speciarius*).

their families, but were forced to seek additional help making use of ties of work, neighborhood, and friendship or patronage (as in the case of the Garisendi man and the retainer).

Legacies During the Black Death

The family and social communities of city and neighborhood were important sources of support for aid in burial and distribution of property, through the role of executor, and as wards of children, through the role of guardian. Most property of the testators went as a transfer of patrimony to their immediate or wider family, and during the epidemic, sometimes even to daughters and sisters. But testators acknowledged the importance of friends and people of their trade through many smaller bequests. These gifts also had the important function of creating and confirming their own social roles in the parish and neighborhood. Most of the legatees are identified by name only, but among the identified occupations are many with special significance to testators whether they were of the same trade or associated with that trade, such as the *bidellus* (beadle) of a law professor.[91] As we noted above, some executors were not part of the testator's family and they, and sometimes their children, were rewarded with bequests. Wet nurses, although unrelated, would have had special significance for testators and were often acknowledged with bequests ranging from 10 *solidi* to 10 *lire*.[92]

The largest category of types of individuals who received small bequests from testators were servants, and especially female servants who were rewarded four times as often as male servants (simply because most servants were female). During the crisis, people may have had to rely heavily on their servants's services to aid the ill or to help manage the household while the ill were tended to by family members. Boccaccio stated that in Florence during the Black Death those servants who stayed to aid their masters demanded high wages and often died from

[91] The *bidellus* was responsible for opening and closing classrooms and bringing professors's books.

[92] Zandonatus de Malavoltis left 10 *solidi* to his sister's wet nurse (*nuptrici Zanne sue sororis*) (Mem, vol. 229, fol. 186v); Jacopo Bottrigari left 3 *lire* to a nurse (Mem, vol. 229, 7v); Francisca fq Jacobi olim Andree from Venice left 10 *lire* to Dena, *nutricula* (Mem, vol. 229, fol. 201r); Juliana Pepoli left 10 *lire* to the son of her nurse (*Bertolio filio Banille nutricis dicte testatricis*) (Mem, vol. 230, fol. 386r).

their services.[93] The many bequests to servants suggest, once again, that the testators were attended within the household during the frightening months of the epidemic. Most of these bequests were supplements to their salaries for the benefit of the testator's soul, commonly in the amount of 20 *solidi*. A few pledged the larger sums, *pro anima*, of five or ten *lire*, and one nobleman left 25 *lire* as a dowry to his servant. Others left money designated as the servant's salary (*pro salario* or *pro mercede*), which was commonly ten *lire* or under. A baker, Landus, left his servant (*famulus)* his baking business.[94] Although a business deal, this bequest made in mid-July indicates options were found within the household during the epidemic.

Bequests to servants that took the form of gifts to a subservient were more likely to come from the wealthy elite, and again indicate that at least some households were served by their hired help. Three such bequests to female servants stand out for their size. A widow of the noble Galluzzi family granted her female servant 25 *lire* as salary along with the ownership (not usufruct) of land, a bed (i.e., blanket (*cultra*), pillow (*capizale*) and sheets (*lentiamina*)), and all of the testator's clothes (*omnes eius testatricis pannos lineos et laneos*). Another noble widow made sure that her female servant was provided with six *lire* and six measures of grain every year as long as she lived. Lastly, a third noble widow, gave her female servant ten *lire*, a bed, and the "use and usufruct" of revenue from a rental property. This widow also left money for a doctor and his female assistant who took care of her (*qui eam curavit... pro salario, mercede et labore*).[95] The doctor was surely there because she was ill of plague, and it is equally likely that the servants were nursing their sick masters, but the wills do not tell us so. The notaries only used the legal phrases *pro anima* or *pro salario*—unfortunately for us there was no legal formula such as *pro cura in tempore mortalitatis magne*. Common sense would indicate that that is what servants were doing and that these bequests were in recognition of such aid.

[93] Boccaccio, *Decameron*, trans. McWilliam, p. 9.

[94] In addition to providing his servant with the bed and linens "on which he lies" and all the wood in the house *pro mercede et labore*, Landus instructed his brother and heir that he must rent his house (where he had his shop) to Bertolomeus at a yearly rent of seven *lire* as long as he maintained the business. Mem, vol. 230, fol. 97v: "si Bertolomeus eius famulus volet conducere domum ipsius testatoris cum omnibus massaricis deputatis ad usum furni".

[95] Mem, vol. 229, fols. 127r (Agnesia fq Versi de Blanchuciis), 206r (Pellegrina fq domini Bonii de Bechadellis), 318v (honesta domina Chaterina fq domini Petri de Blanchuciis).

In addition to cash and beds, masters left their servants clothes: fur coats (*pilizonus* and *guarnacchia*), woolen cloaks (*clamis, clamidem de panno bisello*), a kind of shirt (*diplois, diploidem*), and dresses (*indutum*). None of these types of bequests to servants was unusual; also before the plague, masters left beds, clothes, even land and annual bequests of grain to their servants. But we must remember that there was an epidemic of plague going on, and the clothing and linens were viewed by magistrates as possible reservoirs of miasma (the fibers could trap the bad air). As noted in Chapter Four, the "Ordinances against the pestilence" of Pistoia promulgated during 1348 prohibited the importation into the city or its district of "any old cloth of linen or wool to be used by men or women or for their beds". Violators were fined 200 *lire* and the cloth was burned in the central square.[96] Nevertheless, it was common among all testators to pass along such potentially dangerous items during the epidemic. Men left their wives the traditional widow's dress, and those deprived of their wives because of plague asked that spouses's clothes be sold for charity or be distributed to the poor in hospitals in Bologna for the benefit of their souls. Women left cloaks, fur coats, and skirts (*gonella*) of a variety of colors and qualities of cloth to their sisters, servants, or unrelated women. Testators had always done this and would continue to do so, despite the danger of plague and infection.

Even testators connected to the university, whom we would expect to be fully informed on the miasmic qualities of plague and medical recommendations, passed along their clothes as they lay dying from plague. A professor of civil law provided a *roba* to his beadle and the widow of a professor of logic and philosophy left one of her silk shirts "half green and half violet colored" as a hanging for an altar.[97] It must be said, however, that the professor of medicine bequeathed no clothes, but instead left lots of money for the endowment of an altar. He had the money, but most people had much less. All considered clothes and bedding as part of their wealth to be bequeathed. Testators gave away what they had. People passed along tools of their trade: a barber gave away his razors, scissors, and clothes; a law professor his many books; and, at the height of the epidemic in July, an innkeeper left five beds

---

[96] Chiappelli, "Ordinamenti sanitari," pp. 8–9.

[97] In bequeathing her clothes with instructions for their use in church, this widow was behaving similarly to women studied elsewhere in Europe who, as Katherine French has stated, "merged their notions of home economy and domesticity with their piety." See Katherine L. French, *The Good Women of the Parish: Gender and Religion after the Black Death* (Philadelphia, 2008), p. 43.

(i.e. pillows and bedding) to a hospital and three female acquaintances.[98] It is hard to imagine extensive, panicked abandonment of the plague-stricken happening in a place where ill testators were giving away their bedding and clothing as gifts of gratitude and charity.

The last wishes of testators during the Black Death reveal their efforts to live through the extremely difficult circumstances of a massive epidemic. People had to trust in their families, friends, and neighbors to help them out as they had always done. The family had normally made burial arrangements, and this continued after the onslaught of plague. Although there is no evidence for its dissolution on a wide scale, choices regarding the family were changed as a result of the epidemic that robbed so many of their immediate family, their first choice for support. Other kin and acquaintances stepped in to aid the stricken and become executors of the estates. For some women, clerics became the sole person they could turn to, but many testators chose neighbors, people connected to their work, or socially significant individuals, such as leading noble families or notaries and officials. For those who continued to choose family members, they were more likely to name female relatives after plague had arrived than before. In a similar way, inheritance practices were forced to change as a result of the epidemic. Testators chose more pious heirs than they had done before, but there was no large transformation in charitable giving, no wholesale shift by testators to turn their property over to the church in expiation for humankind's sins that had brought on the plague. This is not to say that testaments during the Black Death did not display intense religious devotion. Less well-off testators used their testaments for the principal purpose of naming an heir but would often include small donations to their parish church or priest, while wealthy testators also included long lists of substantial bequests for masses, for the endowment of altars, and for the distribution of philanthropy to the poor. There is no lack of religiosity in the face of plague. Nevertheless, the family came first, and because the traditional choices had narrowed due to the mortality from plague, testators had to make unusual choices. Women, especially daughters and siblings, benefited from this situation.

[98] Mem, vol. 228, fols. 5r (Petrutius fq Alberti, *hospitator* on 10 July 1348), 7v (egregius doctor dominus Jacobus fq recollende memorie domini Jacobi Butrigariis), 87v (Guidus fq Benasai, *barberius*).

The testamentary choices of one couple during the Black Death tie together many of the elements highlighted in this book. Philippinus fq Lencii was a butcher living in the parish of San Felice. On 22 June, while plague was raging, he entered the Franciscan sacristy as a healthy man to dictate his last wishes "which he wanted to remain secret" before a notary and ten friars. His connections to the mendicants is further demonstrated by the fact that he dedicated a fourth of the revenues from his butcher's shop for candles at an altar in San Francesco and asked his wife to distribute 200 *lire* in the form of rents for the poor, dowry for his servant Sante, and as well as funds for the Franciscans, Augustinian Hermits, and Carmelites. While his wife was alive she would have usufruct of the proceeds of two houses and some land, which would then pass to "poor and needy people" after her death. Phylippinus named his daughter, Cadiana, and wife as executors. Cadiana was to share usufruct of various household items with her sister Agnexia, while the heir of the patrimony—following elite custom—was their brother Lencius. One month later, on 29 July, Philippinus's wife, Phylippa fq Arardi, fell ill and dictated her will in their home. She left three *lire* to her parish priest, who served as principal witness as well as 20 *lire* for her female servant. Most of her attention went to her daughter Cadiana, who was to receive 25 *lire* after her father died, and to the children of her now-deceased daughter, Agnexia. She named her husband as heir and presumably also as executor. She was surrounded by seven neighbors from the parishes of San Felice and San Nicolò del Borgo di Felice. By the time he dictated a new will in his home on 9 August, Phylippinus had lost his wife and son (and his grandchildren had lost their father). Phylippinus continued his philanthropy by using the proceeds of sale of land in Borgo Panigale outside Bologna to endow an altar in the parish church of San Lorenzo di Porta Stiera (next door to that of San Felice) and to provide clothing for the poor and money for a pilgrim to go to the shrine of Saint James of Campostella. Sante, his servant, was still by his side and was rewarded with clothes and bedding that had belonged to his wife. He still relied on his daughter, Cadiana, as executor but asked that she be assisted in managing his estate by the rector of the parish church of San Lorenzo di Porta Stiera and a civic official, the prior for the worthy poor. She was also to be guardian for the four grandchildren, now orphaned. For added help in the guardianship, Phylippinus turned to a notary, Paulus son of the very active notary ser Francescus de Castagnolo. He left a bequest of ten *lire* to each of the notary's daughters. His concern for the future of his family and kin is further exemplified in this second will with legacies for the children of his brother (who perhaps had died in the interim). The burden was now on his daughter Cadiana to distribute his wealth and safeguard his family—although she was to be assisted in this by a notary and clergy—but she also gained, since she now was made the heir. Philippinus dictated his will surrounded by seven neighbors and associates, consisting of men from the parishes of San Felice, San Nicolò del Borgo Felice and San Lorenzo di Porta Stiera—one of whom had been witness for his wife—with two men from Borgo Panigale where Philippinus owned land.[99] This family stayed together during the terrifying experience of the Black Death. They had to confront the problem of deceased family members and make new decisions concerning succession, legacies, and guardianship in order to protect the future of the family. Throughout, the family was supported by its servants within the domestic household and their communities of the parish and neighborhood beyond.

[99] Mem, vol. 229, fol. 117v (Phylippa fq Arardi); vol. 230, fol. 1r (Phylippinus fq Laurentii olim Fratris Phylippi); Dem, FM., Camp. Rossi F, 340–5083, n. 19 (Philippinus fq Lencii). Phylippa left her two granddaughters 40 *lire*, but her two grandsons only got 40 *solidi* presumably because their father was still alive and would nominate them as his heirs.

CONCLUSION

The notarial acts of the *Libri Memoriali* and *Demaniale* are a magnificent memorial to the hard-working notaries, clerics, and townspeople of Bologna. Their monumental efforts have left a detailed record of how late medieval society faced an unprecedented disaster. Through this record we are able to watch the epidemic of plague take hold in Bologna. The shock of the Black Death in Bologna is clear. Daily life was radically changed as more and more people fell ill, were unable to carry on their usual commercial transactions, and instead made their wills. Although the testators used their testaments to nominate heirs to the patrimony and arrange for the future of their families and souls, we can use these documents to build a picture of their daily actions, of the social experience of communities undergoing a crisis. The testaments allow us to track the individual during the epidemic, to follow some people as they become sick and die, and to discern the overlapping communities within which these men and women lived their daily lives.

The neighborhood was one such community. It comprised three to four contiguous parishes and was built upon individuals and families living there linked together by social networks. Indeed, the neighborhood formed the core of late medieval urban activity: notaries worked within neighborhoods and people practicing the same trade or trades with similar work requirements lived in neighborhoods. The parishes were the cells making up the neighborhood, and one did not exist without the other. The religious and public leaders of the parish—the parish priests and *ministrales cappellarum*—carried out their ecclesiastical and civic duties within the parish, but also served their neighbors in the adjoining parishes. We have seen these men serving as witnesses and executors for dying testators who were their neighbors. Neighborhoods proved to be strong sources of support for the townspeople during the epidemic of plague. Neighbors relied on each other to serve as witnesses to the dictation of their last wishes and to the arrangement of their burial and estate after death. Neighborhoods remained intact and functioning during the plague. They do not appear to have suffered from extensive flight. The testaments record the presence of neighbors who remained in town to aid each other and the results of this service. Through them we see neighbors acting out the common plight of the plague victim, from faithful witness to dying testator.

Also serving as a strong community of support during the plague was the family. Parents, siblings, and children stayed together and died together during the epidemic. When they were healthy, many traveled with their family members to listen to the last wishes of neighbors or others of their kin. Family members remained in town as their loved ones became ill and died. At the last moments of life the ultimate hopes for the future still remained with the family. Testators during the Black Death appear resigned to the presence of massive death. They had to trust their families to continue the tasks that they had always done, i.e., to arrange for burial of their remains and to distribute their wealth for the purposes of charity and the family's future. The notarial records demonstrate that parents and siblings worked hard during the epidemic to make arrangements for their loved ones: they nominated guardians for young children, they stood as *curatores* or financial advisors, they arranged for marriages, and they nominated the heirs to their patrimony. Nevertheless, because of the death of so many loved ones, some changes had to be made. Testators sometimes had to look beyond the family, to their neighbors or men of public faith such as clerics, notaries, and physicians, for added assistance in managing these tasks. They also called upon their more distant kin in this difficult time. They considered new options for the devolution of their property. The traditional practice of passing wealth down to sons alone was not as practical in a time of heavy mortality. Thus, testators widened their choices of heirs as they considered their daughters and sisters in greater numbers than before.

The notaries of Bologna made possible this examination of the experience of plague. The processes of registration and preservation of contracts and testaments in the *Provvisori* and *Memoriali* and of the deposit of wills in the *Demaniale* were complicated and very demanding. Despite the presence of epidemic disease, the notaries continued their efforts to record the last wishes of the townspeople. The strain was sometimes too much, and many testaments that were registered in the *Provvisori* were not copied out into the *Memoriali*. But the notaries did not give up and abandon their work. They kept at it both during and after the epidemic had subsided, and spent the next decade dutifully inserting into their *memoriali* testaments of 1348 that they eventually managed to reproduce in full. The story of how this remarkable primary source endured the Black Death mirrors that of the townspeople. People persevered at what they had always done: their work, their family, and their civic duties. They were supported in their efforts by the strong communities of the parish, neighborhood, and the family.

This picture of resilience, stability, and determination to carry on in a time of crisis is strikingly different from the general impression one gets from the more familiar literary sources. No single view gives us the entire picture. The *Memoriali* and *Demaniale* contain the last wishes of a small percentage of the men and women who died in 1348. Not all of the testaments were preserved and not everyone wrote a will. But the record that does remain should not be ignored. It represents a greater effort on the part of the townspeople and, especially, the notaries than ever before. The chronicles have their share of problems, but within these sometimes sensational and moralistic accounts one can catch some glimpses of the grim reality of individuals and families dealing with disaster as best they could. The literary and notarial record each tells some part of the truth and judging them together enables us to better understand the medieval past.

The argument of this book that society did not break down, but remained intact and functioning during the Black Death has been posited before for France and other Italian cities. Nevertheless, the assumption that panic was everywhere and social chaos reigned has been perpetuated by textbooks and recent general works, such as Norman Cantor's *In the Wake of Plague*. Even Samuel Cohn who, in his *The Black Death Transformed*, used a wide array of masses of evidence that could not have been created in a time of general social dissolution assumed there was widespread panic and abandonment in 1348. Cohn argued that stability and optimism came only after the return of plague in 1363. We should recognize the efforts of the people living during 1348. Governments passed legislation to tackle the crisis in ways very similar to their counterparts in the Renaissance. Physicians wrote and publicized tracts to individuals and communities on the identity of the disease and on the best ways to prevent infection. Men of public faith, such as notaries, parish leaders, and clerics, came to the aid of their fellow townspeople as did neighbors and kin.

In a way all of these communities, from the communal governments to the medical community and notarial workforce and the neighborhoods, were doing what they had always done. They had powerful resources to draw upon to combat the crisis. In all towns, the institutions of public health such as the guilds of doctors and apothecaries and hospitals, were already in place, since most were established during the century before the Black Death. Communal doctors provided free service for the poor. Physicians turned to the classical texts of Hippocratic and Galenic medicine, and their authorities provided the answers they needed. They did not view the disease as something completely new, but rather a much more serious form of pestilence than the past had known.[1] The communes were able to draw on these precedents to act at the time of crisis. Governments reissued sanitary laws that were designed and promulgated in the thirteenth century. The notaries also had a long tradition from which to base their actions during the Black Death. Their guild statutes emphasized their civic role as men of *fides publica*, and this ideal matched reality in the case of the Black Death. Their actions cannot be explained by the desire to profit from disaster, since so many others who were not paid for their services joined them in their efforts.

Although they were faced with a new disease, medieval people were not completely unprepared. This is the key to understanding medieval society's resilience in the face of the Black Death. For many it was one in a long chain of disasters, of wars, famines, and disease. William Chester Jordan argued similarly for the experience of the Great Famine of 1315–1319.[2] Disaster was not new, and people had the means to resist. In addition to the intellectual and legal traditions on which the political and medical communities relied, the social structure of the late medieval city came into play. People lived out their lives in communities, webs of social interactions, that continued to function during the epidemic. This book has tried to reveal the workings of these networks through the myriad examples of connections of individuals in the town of Bologna. All of the information presented here could be expanded with more data entry and sleuthing. There are many more stories to tell, but the picture portrayed thus far should be convincingly clear. The communities of late medieval Bologna remained intact during the crisis of the Black Death.

[1] Arrizabalaga, "Facing the Black Death," pp. 237–288. This view concurs with Ann Carmichael and others who see the roots of early modern plague administration going back to the Middle Ages. Ann Carmichael, *Plague and the Poor in Renaissance Florence* (Cambridge, 1986), p. 128.

[2] Jordan, *The Great Famine.*

MAP OF BOLOGNA

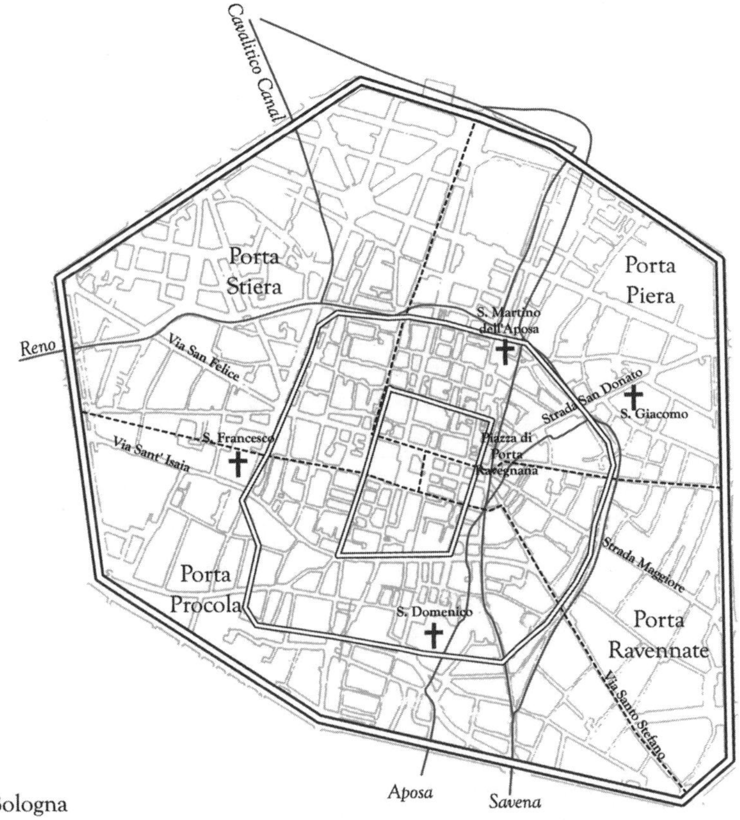

Map of Bologna

City Walls
Quarter Boundaries
Streams and Canals

MAP OF PARISHES OF BOLOGNA

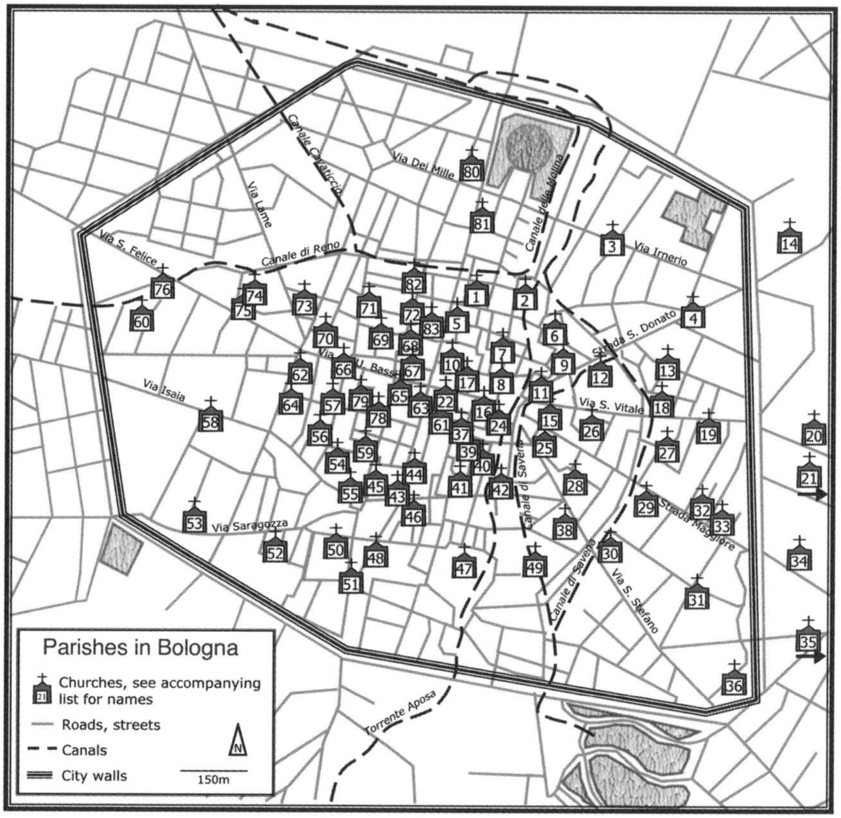

LIST OF PARISHES FOR MAP OF PARISHES OF BOLOGNA

(Number on Map) Name of Parish	Quarter
1) San Tommaso del Mercato	Porta Piera
2) San Martino dell'Aposa	Porta Piera
3) Santa Maria della Mascarella	Porta Piera
4) Santa Maria Maddalena	Porta Piera
5) Santi Giacomo e Filippo dei Piatesi	Porta Piera
6) Santi Simone e Giuda	Porta Piera
7) San Nicolò degli Albari	Porta Piera
8) San Lorenzo dei Guarini	Porta Piera
9) San Donato	Porta Piera
10) San Pietro	Porta Piera
11) San Marco	Porta Piera
12) Santa Cecilia	Porta Piera
13) San Sigismondo	Porta Piera
14) Sant'Egidio	Porta Piera
15) San Bartolomeo di Porta Ravegnana	Porta Piera and Porta Ravennate
16) San Cataldo dei Lambertini	Porta Piera and Porta Ravennate
17) San Michele del Mercato di Mezzo	Porta Piera and Porta Ravennate
18) San Vitale	Porta Piera and Porta Ravennate
19) San Leonardo	Porta Piera and Porta Ravennate
20) Sant'Alberto	Porta Piera and Porta Ravennate
21) Sant'Antonino or Sant'Antolino	Porta Piera and Porta Ravennate
22) San Giusta	Porta Ravennate
23) Santa Maria in Solario	Porta Ravennate
24) San Matteo degli Accarisi	Porta Ravennate
25) Santa Maria di Porta Ravegnana	Porta Ravennate
26) San Michele dei Leprosetti	Porta Ravennate
27) San Damiano	Porta Ravennate
28) Santo Stefano	Porta Ravennate
29) San Tommaso della Braina	Porta Ravennate
30) San Biagio	Porta Ravennate
31) Santa Cristina della Fondazza	Porta Ravennate
32) Santa Maria del Torleone	Porta Ravennate
33) Santa Maria del Tempio	Porta Ravennate
34) Sant'Omobono	Porta Ravennate
35) Santa Maria degli Alemanni	Porta Ravennate
36) San Giuliano	Porta Ravennate
37) San Tecla dei Lambertazzi	Porta Procola and Porta Ravennate

Table (*cont.*)

(Number on Map) Name of Parish	Quarter
38) San Giovanni in Monte	Porta Procola and Porta Ravennate
39) San Cristoforo dei Geremei	Porta Procola
40) Santa Maria della Chiavica	Porta Procola
41) Santa Maria dei Bulgari	Porta Procola
42) Sant'Agata	Porta Procola
43) Santa Maria Rotonda dei Galluzzi	Porta Procola
44) San Simone dei Maccagnani	Porta Procola
45) Santa Maria dei Guidoscalchi	Porta Procola
46) Sant'Andrea degli Ansaldi	Porta Procola
47) San Domenico	Porta Procola
48) San Procolo	Porta Procola
49) Santa Lucia	Porta Procola
50) San Cristoforo di Saragozza	Porta Procola
51) San Mamolo	Porta Procola
52) Santa Maria delle Muratelle	Porta Procola
53) Santa Caterina di Saragozza	Porta Procola
54) Santa Margherita	Porta Procola
55) San Martino della Croce dei Santi	Porta Procola
56) San Barbaziano	Porta Procola
57) Santi Pietro e Marcellino	Porta Procola
58) Sant'Isaia	Porta Procola and Porta Stiera
59) Sant'Arcangelo	Porta Procola and Porta Stiera
60) Santa Cristina	Porta Stiera
61) Santa Maria dei Rustigani	Porta Stiera
62) San Benedetto di Porta Nuova	Porta Stiera
63) San Martino de' Caccianemici	Porta Stiera
64) San Tecla di Porta Nuova	Porta Stiera
65) San Bartolomeo in Palazzo	Porta Stiera
66) San Prospero	Porta Stiera
67) Santi Fabiano e Sebastiano	Porta Stiera
68) San Luca di Castello	Porta Stiera
69) San Siro	Porta Stiera
70) Santi Gervasio e Protasio	Porta Stiera
71) San Giorgio in Poggiale	Porta Stiera
72) San Colombano	Porta Stiera
73) San Lorenzo di Porta Stiera	Porta Stiera
74) San Felice	Porta Stiera
75) San Nicolò del Borgo di San Felice	Porta Stiera
76) Santa Maria della Carità	Porta Stiera
77) Santa Croce	Porta Stiera
78) San Salvatore	Porta Stiera
79) San Marino di Porta Nuova	Porta Stiera
80) San Benedetto del Borgo di Galliera	Porta Stiera

Table (*cont.*)

(Number on Map) Name of Parish	Quarter
81) San Giuseppe del Borgo di Galliera	Porta Stiera
82) Santa Maria Maggiore	Porta Piera and Porta Stiera
83) Sant'Andrea dei Piatesi	Porta Piera and Porta Stiera
The following parishes are not located on the Map of Parishes:	
84) Sant'Ambrogio	Porta Procola
85) Sant'Antonio	Porta Stiera and Porta Procola
86) San Dalmasio	Porta Ravennate
87) San Geminiano	Porta Procola
88) San Giacomo dei Carbonesi	Porta Procola
89) Sant'Ippolito	Porta Stiera and Porta Procola
90) Santa Maria della Baroncella	Porta Procola
91) Santa Maria dei Carrari	Porta Procola
92) Santa Maria del Castello	Porta Stiera
93) Santa Maria dei Castel dei Britti	Porta Ravennate
94) Santa Maria degli Oselitti	Porta Procola
95) San Remedio	Porta Ravennate
96) San Simone e Giuda	Porta Piera
97) San Sinesio	Porta Procola
98) San Tecla di Santo Stefano	Porta Ravennate
99) San Vito	Porta Ravennate

The names and locations of parish churches are derived from lists and maps in: Aldo Berselli, ed., *Storia della Emilia Romagna* (Bologna, 1975), pp. ccxxxi–ccxxxii; Francesca Bocchi, *Bologna, II: Il Duecento*, Atlante Storico delle Città Italiane, Emilia-Romagna (Bologna, 1995); Antonio Ivan Pini, "La ripartizione topografica degli artigiani a Bologna nel 1294: Un esempio di demografia sociale," in *Artigiani e salariati: Il mondo del lavoro nell'Italia dei secoli XII–XV* (Pistoia, 1984), pp. 218–221.

APPENDIX A

List of notaries working for the Office of the *Memoriali* in 1348 who were later employed as *Provvisori* notaries (with years of employment noted):

Bertolomeus Iacobini de Sassuno: 1352
Bolognictus Francisci de Flagnano: 1350
Franciscus Aspetati de Cento: 1349, 1350, 1362
Gratianus Dominici Lambertini de Castrofranco: 1350
Guillielmus Bernardini Grassis: 1351
Iohannes Jacobi Benlafaremo: 1355
Iohannes Laurentii Stephani: 1349
Iohannes q. Alberti Dominici: 1363
Iohannes q. Iacobi Perini: 1356
Montanarius q. Bertolotti Guidonis: 1353
Nicolaus Egidii de Sabluni: 1349
Nicolaus Francisci de Libris: 1352
Petrus Francisci Ugonis: 1350, 1369
Petrus Romei de Lambordinis: 1352
Philippus q. Iacobi de Alberghis: 1353, 1354
Plevale Nicholai de Stupa: 1349, 1350
Sanutus Iacobi Sanuti: 1349, 1350
Scardouinus q. Bertholomei de Scardovis: 1358
Signorellus q. Allamani de Signorellis: 1354

APPENDIX B

List of friars who appear as witnesses in wills five or more times during 1348: (ASB, Memoriali vols. 228, 229, 230; ASB, Demaniale, Instrumenti, Campioni Rossi)

Fr. Albertus de Castro Sancti Petri, FM:
20 June (twice), 22 June (three times), 28 June, 3 July

Fr. Antonius de Ariminio, FH:
11 July (twice), 23 July, 30 July, 6 August, 18 August, 8 September (twice)

Fr. Azo de Ubaldinis, FM:
16 (twice), 22 July, 23 July, 31 July, 5 August, 8 August, 21 August, 25 September

Fr. Calandrinus, FP:
18 June, 22 June, 25 June (twice), 27 July, 31 July, 10 August, 8 October, 10 October

Fr. Francisus, barberius, FM:
13 February, 7 June, 3 July, 4 July, 27 August

Fr. Franciscus de Burgo Galerie, FM:
9 June, 15 July, 22 July, 29 July, 31 July, 5 August, 6 August, 21 August, 25 September, 4 December

Fr. Franciscus de Calanchis, FM:
29 June, 3 July, 7 July, 9 July, 15 July

Fr. Francisus de Ungaria, FM:
28 June, 15 July, 29 July, 31 July, 8 August, 19 September

Fr. Gandolfinus de Parma, FM:
27 May, 1 June, 2 June, 7 June, 20 June (twice), 21 June, 22 June, 3 July, 7 July, 12 July, 22 July, 23 July, 27 August

Fr. Jacobus de Guizardinis, FM:
13 February, 30 May, 20 June (twice), 3 July, 9 July, 11 July, 12 July, 18 July, 23 July, 25 September

Fr. Jacobus de Negrobonis, FM:
1 June, 20 June (twice), 21 June, 22 June (three times), 28 June, 3 July (twice), 4 July, 7 July, 14 July, 27 August

Fr. Jacobus de Sancto Johanne in Persiceto, FM:
30 May, 22 June, 3 July, 4 July, 11 July, 12 July, 23 July, 29 July, 6 August, 8 August

Fr. Jacobus Magnano, FM:
2 June, 20 June (twice), 22 June, 3 July, 9 July, 27 August

Fr. Johannes de Aposa, FM:
15 February, 27 May, 1 June, 9 June, 21 June, 28 June, 22 July, 5 August (twice), 6 August, 7 September, 19 September, 29 October

Fr. Johannes de Buzanigris, FH:
3 June, 26 June, 11 July (twice)

Fr. Johannes de Dataris, FM:
11 January, 2 June, 21 June, 9 July, 11 July

Fr. Johannes de Plebe Centi, FM:
22 June (three times), 7 July, 23 July, 12 October

Fr. Maghinardus, FC:
20 June, 24 July (twice), 31 July, 22 August, 3 September, 22 November

Fr. Michaelis de Nosadella, FM:
3 July, 9 July, 11 July, 14 July, 18 July, 20 July, 5 August, 6 August, 25 September

Fr. Michaelis de Tenchararis, FM:
7 June, 3 July, 7 July, 9 July, 11 July, 12 July

Fr. Nascimbenis de S. Proculo, FM:
11 January, 7 June, 9 June, 4 July, 14 July, 18 July, 23 July, 29 July, 31 July, 5 August, 21 August, 27 August, 25 September

Fr. Petrus de Sancta Elena, FM:
27 May, 1 June, 2 June, 20 June (twice), 22 June

Fr. Rolandus de Sancto Johanne, FM:
22 June, 22 July, 23 July, 29 July, 5 August, 6 August, 7 September

Fr. Thomas de Burgo Lamarum, FM:
13 February, 28 June, 11 July, 15 July, 16 July, 5 August, 6 August, 8 August, 19 September

Fr. Torinus, sartor, FM:
29 July, 31 July, 5 August (twice), 6 August, 21 August, 19 September, 12 October

Fr. Ugolinus de Aposa, FM:
11 January, 13 February, 9 June, 20 June (twice), 21 June

BIBLIOGRAPHY

Primary Sources in Manuscript

Archivio di Stato di Bologna, Comune, *Memoriali*, vols. 191, 192, 193 (1337); 228, 229, 230 (1348).

Archivio di Stato di Bologna, Comune, *Provvisori*, ser. cartacei, vols. 152, 153, 154, 155 (1348).

Archivio di Stato di Bologna, Comune, *Provvisori*, ser. pergamenei, vol. 16 (1348) and vol. 30 (1362).

Archivio di Stato di Bologna, Comune, Archivio di Stato di Bologna, *Provvigioni cartacee*, Signoria Pepoli, reg. 36 (1348).

Archivio di Stato di Bologna, Demaniale, San Francesco, Instrumenti.

Archivio di Stato di Bologna, Demaniale, San Francesco, Campioni Rossi.

Archivio di Stato di Bologna, Demaniale, San Domenico, Instrumenti.

Archivio di Stato di Bologna, Demaniale, Miscellanea delle corporazioni religiose.

Printed Primary Sources

"Annales Forolivienses." Edited by G. Mazzatinti in *Rerum Italicarum Scriptores*, n.s., vol. 22, pt. 2. Città di Castello: S. Lapi, 1903.

Boccaccio, Giovanni. *Decameron*. Edited by Vittore Branca. Torino: Einaudi 1980, 1987.

Braidi, Valeria. *Gli Statuti del Comune di Bologna degli anni 1352, 1357, 1376, 1389: Libri I–III*. 2 vols. Bologna: Deputazione di storia patria per le provincie di Romagna, 2002.

"Chronica de Novitatibus Padue et Lombardie Guilielmi de Cortusis." Edited by B. Pagnin in *RIS*, n.s. vol. 12, pt. 5. Città di Castello: S. Lapi, 1941.

"Chronica Raphayni de Caresinis Cancellarii Venetiarum." Edited by E. Pastorello in *RIS*, n.s. vol. 12, pt 2. Città di Castello: S. Lapi, 1922.

"Chronicon de Rebus in Apulia Gestis." Edited by A. Sorbelli in *RIS*, n.s. vol. 12, pt. 3. Città di Castello: S. Lapi, 1903.

"Chronicon Parvum Ripaltae." Edited by F. Gabotto in *RIS*, n.s. vol. 17, pt. 3. Città di Castello: S. Lapi, 1911–1912.

"Chronicon Sublacense." Edited by R. Morghen in *RIS*, n.s. 24, pt. 6. Città di Castello: S. Lapi, 1927.

"Cronaca Carrarese." Edited by R. Cessi in *RIS*, n.s. vol. 17, pt. 1. Bologna: Zanichelli, 1931.

"Cronaca Malatestiana del secolo XIV." Edited by A. F. Massèra in *RIS*, n.s. vol. 15, pt. 2. Città di Castello: S. Lapi, 1922–1924.

"Cronaca senese di Agnolo di Tura del Grasso." Edited by A. Lisini and F. Iacometti in *RIS*, n.s. vol. 15, pt. 6. Bologna: Zanichelli, 1935.

"Cronaca Senese." Edited by A. Lisini and F. Iacometti in *RIS*, n.s. vol. 15, pt. 6. Bologna: Zanichelli, 1935.

Cronica di Matteo Villani a miglior lezione ridotta coll'aiuto de' testi a penna. Edited by Ignazio Moutier, 1. Florence: Magheri, 1825.

"Cronica Fiorentina di Marchionne di Coppo Stefani." Edited by N. Rodolico in *RIS*, n.s. vol. 30, pt. 1. Città di Castello: S. Lapi, 1903.

"Cronica gestorum ac factorum memorabilium civitatis Bononie edita a fratre Hyeronimo de Bursellis ab urbe condita ad a. 1497." A. Sorbelli, ed, *RIS*, vol. 23, pt. 2. Città di Castello: S. Lapi, 1911–1929.

d'Agramont, Jacme. "Regimen of Protection Against Epidemics or Pestilence and Mortality." Translated by M. L. Duran-Reynals and C.-E. A. Winslow, *Bulletin of the History of Medicine* 22 (1948): 57–89.

"Ephemerides Urbevetanae" or "Discorso Historico con Molti Accidenti Occorsi in Orvieto." Edited by L. Fumi in *RIS*, n.s. vol. 15, pt. 5. Città di Castello: S. Lapi, 1920.

Fasoli, Gina and Pietro Sella, eds. *Statuti di Bologna dell'anno 1288*, 2 vols. Vatican City: Biblioteca Apostolica Vaticana, 1937 and 1939.

Frati, Luigi, ed. *Statuti di Bologna dall'anno 1245 all'anno 1267*. 3 vols. Bologna: Regia Topografia, 1869–1880.

"Liber Gestorum in Lombardia Petri Azarii." in *RIS*, n.s. vol. 16, pt. 4. Bologna: Zanichelli, 1925–1939.

"Marcha di Marco Battagli da Rimini." Edited by A. F. Massèra in *RIS*, n.s. vol. 16, pt. 3. Città di Castello: S. Lapi, 1912.

Mattheo dei Griffoni. "Memoriale Historicum." In *RIS*, n.s. vol. 18, pt. 2. Città del Castello: S. Lapi, 1902.

"Memoriale historicum de rebus Bononiensium." Edited by L. Frati and A. Sorbelli in *RIS*, n.s. vol. 18, pt. 2. Città di Castello: S. Lapi, 1902.

Montanari, Paolo, ed. *Documenti su la popolazione di Bologna all fine del Trecento*, Fonti per la storia di Bologna, 1. Bologna: Istituto per la storia di Bologna, 1966.

Passaggeri, Rolandino. *Contractus*. Edited by Roberto Ferrara. Rome: Consiglio Nazionale del Notariato, 1983.

——. *Summa totius artis notariae*. Venice: Iuntas, 1546. Reprint, Bologna: Arnaldo Forni, 1977.

Salatiele, *Ars Notarie*, edited by Gianfranco Orlandelli. 2 vols. Milan: Giuffrè, 1961.

"Storie Pistoresi." Edited S. A. Barbi in *RIS*, n.s. vol. 11, pt. 5. Città di Castello: S. Lapi, 1906.

Secondary Sources

Aberth, John. *The Black Death 1348–1350: A Brief History with Documents*. Boston, Mass.: Bedford, 2005.

Amundsen, Darrel W. "Medical Deontology and Pestilential Disease in the Late Middle Ages." In *Medicine, Society, and Faith in the Ancient and Medieval Worlds*, 289–309. Baltimore: Johns Hopkins University Press, 1996.

Antonioli, Guido. *Conservator pacis et iustitie: la signoria di Taddeo Pepoli a Bologna (1337–1347)*. Bologna: Clueb, 2004.

Arrizabalaga, Jon. "Facing the Black Death: Perceptions and reactions of university medical practitioners." In *Practical Medicine from Salerno to the Black Death*, 237–288. Cambridge: Cambridge University Press, 1994.

Bagliani, Agostino Paravicini and Francesco Santi, eds. *The Regulation of Evil: Social and Cultural Attitudes to Epidemics in the late Middle Ages*. Florence: Sismel, 1998.

Banchi, Luciano. "Alcuni documenti che concernono la venuta in Siena nell'anno 1321 dei lettori e degli scolari dello studio bolognese." *Giornale storico degli archivi toscani* 5 (1861): 237–247, 309–331.

Banker, James. *Death in the Community: Memorialization and Confraternities in an Italian Commune in the Late Middle Ages*. Athens: University of Georgia Press, 1988.

Bellomo, Manlio. *Ricerche sui rapporti patrimoniali tra coniugi: contributo alla storia della famiglia medievale*. Milan: Giuffrè, 1961.

Benadusi, Giovanna. "Investing the Riches of the Poor: Servant Women and Their Last Wills." *American Historical Review* 109 (2004): 805–826.

Benedictow, Ole. *The Black Death 1346–1353: The Complete History*. Rochester, NY: Boydell & Brewer, 2004.

Benevolo, Giancarlo. "Espansione urbana e suburbi di Bologna nel medioevo: la 'Guardia Civitatis'." *Ricerche storiche* 22 (1992): 455–81.

Bertram, Martin. "Testamenti medievali bolognesi: Una miniera documentaria tutta da esplorare." *Rassegna degli Archivi di Stato* 52 (1992): 307–323.

——. "'Renaissance Mentality' in Italian Testaments?" Review of *The Black Death and the Cult of Remembrance* by Samuel Kline Cohn, Jr. *Journal of Modern History* 67 (1995): 358–369.

——. "Bologneser Testamente: Erster Teil: Die urkundliche Uberlieferung." *Quellen und Forschungen aus italienischen Archiven und Bibliotheken* 70 (1990): 153–233.

——. "Bologneser Testamente: Zweiter Teil: Sondierungen in den *Libri Memoriali.*" *Quellen und Forschungen aus italienischen Archiven und Bibliotheken* 71 (1991): 195–240.

——. "Mittelalterliche Testamente: Zur entedeckung einer Quellengattung in Italien." *Quellen und Forschungen aus italienischen Archiven und Bibliotheken* 68 (1988): 509–545.

Besta, Enrico. *La famiglia nella storia del diritto italiano*. Milan: Giuffrè, 1962.

Biraben, Jean-Noël. *Les hommes et la peste en France et dans les pays européens et méditerranéens*. Civilisations et Sociétés, 35. Mouton, Paris, La Haye: Mouton & Co and École des Hautes Études en Sciences Sociales, 1975. Tome 1: La peste dans l'histoire.

Blanshei, Sarah Rubin. "Criminal Law and Politics in Medieval Bologna." *Criminal Justice History* 2 (1981): 1–30.

Bocchi, Francesca. "Dalla grande crisi all'età comunale (secoli IV–XII)." In *Da Felsina a Bologna dalle origini al XII secolo*, eds. Giuseppe Sassatelli, Cristiana Morigi Govi, Jacopo Ortalli, Francesca Bocchi, 50–114. Bologna: Grafis Edizioni, 1996.

——. "Suburbi e fasce suburbane." *Storia della città* 5 (1977): 15–33.

——. "Trasferimenti di lavoratori e studenti a Bologna nel basso Medioevo." In *Forestieri e stranieri nelle città basso-medievali*. Atti del Seminario Internazionale di Studio Bagno a Ripoli (Firenze), 4–8 giugno 1984, 249–261. Florence: Libreria editrice Salimbeni, 1988.

——. *Bologna, II: Il Duecento*. Atlante Storico delle Città Italiane, Emilia-Romagna. Bologna: Grafis Edizioni, 1995.

Bonanno, Claudio, Metello Bonanno and Luciana Pellegrini. "I legati "pro anima" ed il problema della salvezza nei testamenti fiorentini della seconda meta del Trecento." *Ricerche storiche* 6 (1976): 183–220.

Bongi, Salvatore. *I bandi lucchesi del secolo decimoquarto*. Bologna: Tipografia del Progresso, 1863.

Bowsky, William. "The Impact of the Black Death upon Sienese Government and Society." *Speculum*, 39 (1964): 1–34.

——. *The Black Death: A Turning Point in History?*. New York: Holt, Rinehart, and Winston, 1971.

Branca, Vittorio. *Boccaccio medievale*. Florence: L'Impronta, 1956.

Brentano, Robert. "Death in Gualdo Tadino and in Rome (1340, 1296)." *Studia gratiana* 19 (1976): 79–100.

——. *A New World in a Small Place: Church and Religion in the Diocese of Rieti, 1088–1378*. Berkeley and Los Angeles: University of California Press, 1994.

——. *Rome Before Avignon: A Social History of Thirteenth-Century Rome*. New York: Basic Books, 1974.

Brizio, Elena. "La dote nella normativa statuaria e nella pratica testamentaria senese (fine sec. XII–metà sec. XIV)". *Bullettino senese di storia patria* 111 (2004): 9–39.

Brucker, Gene. "Florence and the Black Death." In *Boccaccio: Secoli di vita: atti del Congresso internazionale Boccaccio 1975*, eds. Marga Cottino-Jones and Edward Tuttle, 21–30. Ravenna: Longo, 1977.

Brunetti, Mario. "Venezia durante la peste del 1348." *Ateneo Veneto* 22, n. 1 (1909): 290–311 and 22, n. 2 (1909): 5–42.

Campbell, Anna Montgomery. *The Black Death and Men of Learning*. New York: Columbia University Press, 1931.

Carabellese, Francesco. *La peste del 1348 e le condizioni della sanità pubblica in Toscana*. Rocca San Casciano: L. Cappelli, 1897.

Carmichael, Ann. *Plague and the Poor in Renaissance Florence*. Cambridge and London: Cambridge University Press, 1986.

Carniello, Brian. "The Notaries of Bologna: Family, Profession and Popular Politics in a Medieval Italian City-State". PhD diss., University of California at Santa Barbara, 2005.

Carpentier, Élisabeth. "Autour de la Peste Noire: Famine et epidemies dans l'histoire du XIVe siecle." *Annales: Economies, Societes, Civilisations* 17 (1962): 1062–1092.

——. *Une Ville Devant la Peste: Orvieto et la Peste Noire de 1348*. Paris: S.E.V.P.E.N.: 1962.

Castiglioni, Arturo. "I libri italiani della pestilenza." In *Il volto di Ippocrate: Istorie di Medici e Medicine d'altri tempi*, 147–169. Milano: Unitas, 1925.

Chabot, Isabelle. "Le Loi du lignage: Notes sur le système successoral florentin (XIVe/XVe–XIIe siècles)." *CLIO* 7 (1998): 51–72.

——. "Lineage strategies and the control of widows in Renaissance Florence." In *Widowhood in Medieval and Early Modern Europe*, eds. Sandra Cavallo and Lyndan Warner, 127–144. New York: Pearson Education Limited, 1999.

Chabot, Isabelle and Anna Bellavitis. "A proposito di 'Men and Women in Renaissance Venice' Stanley Chojnacki." *Quaderni Storici* 118 (2005): 203–238.

Chiappelli, A. "Gli ordinamenti sanitari del comune di Pistoia contro la pestilenza del 1348." *Archivio Storico Italiano* s. 4, 20 (1887): 3–21.

Chiffoleau, Jacques. *La comptabilité de l'au-delà: Les hommes, la mort et la religion dans la région d'Avignon à la fin due moyen âge (vers 1320–vers 1480)*. Rome: École Française de Rome, 1980.

Chiodi, Giovanni. "Rolandino e il testamento." In *Rolandino e l'ars notaria da Bologna all'Europa*, ed. Giorgio Tamba, 461–582. Milano: Giuffrè Editore, 2002.

Chojnacka, Monica. *Working Women of Early Modern Venice*. Baltimore: Johns Hopkins University Press, 2001.

Chojnacki, Stanley. *Women and Men in Renaissance Venice: Twelve Essays on Patrician Society*. Baltimore: Johns Hopkins University Press, 2000.

Cipolla, Carlo. "A Plague Doctor." In *The Medieval City*, edited by Harry A. Miskimin, David Herlihy, and A.L. Udovitch, 65–72. New Haven and London: Yale University Press, 1977.

——. Carlo. *Faith, Reason and the Plague in Seventeenth-Century Tuscany*. New York: Norton, 1979.

——. *Fighting the Plague in Seventeenth-Century Italy*. Madison, WI: University of Wisconsin Press, 1981.

Cohn, Samuel Kline, Jr. *Death and Property in Siena, 1205–1800: Strategies for the Afterlife*. Baltimore: Johns Hopkins University Press, 1988.

——. "Last Wills: Family, Women, and the Black Death in Central Italy." In *Women in the Streets: Essays on Sex and Power in Renaissance Italy*, 39–56. Baltimore: Johns Hopkins University Press, 1996.

——. "Le ultime voluntà: Famiglia, donne e peste nera nell'Italia centrale." *Politica ed economia* 2 (1992): 859–875.

——. "The Black Death: End of a Paradigm." *American Historical Review* 107 (2002): 703–38.

——. *The Black Death Transformed: Disease and Culture in Early Renaissance Europe*. New York: Arnold, 2002.

——. *The Cult of Remembrance and the Black Death: Six Renaissance Cities in Central Italy*. Baltimore: Johns Hopkins University Press, 1992.
——. *The Laboring Classes of Renaissance Florence*. New York: Free Press, 1980.
Continelli, Luisa, ed. *L'Archivio dell'Ufficio dei Memoriali: Inventario: Vol. I Memoriali, 1265–1436, Tomo I, 1265–1333*. Bologna: L'Istituto per la Storia dell'Università, 1988.
——, ed. *L'Archivio dell'Ufficio dei Memoriali: Inventario: Vol. I Memoriali, 1265–1436, Tomo II, 1334–1436*. Bologna: Bononia University Press, 2008.
Cossar, Roisin. *The Transformation of the Laity in Bergamo, 1265–c. 1400*. Leiden and Boston: Brill, 2006.
Crabb, Ann. *The Strozzi of Florence: Widowhood and Family Solidarity in the Renaissance*. Ann Arbor: University of Michigan Press, 2000.
D'Amato, Alfonso. "I Domenicani a Bologna nel '200." In *Archeologia medievale a Bologna: Gli scavi nel Convento di San Domenico*, eds. Sauro Gelichi and Riccardo Merlo, 91–97. Bologna: Grafis Edizioni, 1987.
——. *I Domenicani e l'Università di Bologna*. Bologna: Edizioni Domenicani, 1988.
Dal Pane, Luigi. "Lo 'Studio' e l'economia della città." In *Atti del convegno internazionale di Studi Accursiani*, 1: 48–53. Milan: Giuffrè, 1968.
Del Panta, Lorenzo. *Le epidemie nella storia demografica italiana*. Turin: Loescher, 1980.
Dolcini, Carlo and Girolamo Arnaldi. *Università e studenti a Bologna nei secoli XIII e XIV*. Torino: UTET, 1988.
Dondarini, Rolando. *Bologna medievale nella storia delle città*. Bologna: Patron Editore, 2000.
——. *La 'Descriptio civitatis Bononie eiusque comitatus' del cardinale Anglico (1371). Introduzione ed edizione critica*. Deputazione di Storia patria per le province di Romagna, Documenti e Studi, 24. Bologna: Pàtron, 1990.
——. "La populazione del territorio bolognese fra XIII e XIV secolo: Stato e prospettive delle ricerche." In *Demografia e società nell'Italia medievale*, eds. Rinaldo Comba and Irma Naso. Società per gli Studi e Storici della Provincia di Cuneo, 203–230. Cuneo: Boves, 1994.
Dowd, Douglas F. "Power and Economic Development: The Rise and Decline of Medieval Bologna." *Journal of European Economic History* 3 (1974): 424–452.
Eckstein, Nicholas. *The District of the Green Dragon: Neighbourhood Life and Social Change in Renaissance Florence*. Florence: L.S. Olschki, 1995.
——. "The Neighborhood as Microcosm" in *Renaissance Florence: A Social History*, eds. Roger J. Crum and John T. Paoletti, 219–239. New York: Cambridge University Press, 2006.
Emery, Richard. "The Black Death in 1348 in Perpignan." *Speculum* 42 (1967): 611–23.
Epstein, Steven A. *Wills and Wealth in Medieval Genoa, 1150–1250*. Cambridge, MA and London: Harvard University Press, 1984.
Falsini, Aliberto Benigno. "Firenze dopo il 1348: Le conseguenze della peste nera." *Archivio Storico Italiano* 129 (1971): 425–503.
Fanti, Mario. *Confraternite e città a Bologna nel medioevo e nell'età moderna*. Roma: Herder, 2001.
——. *I Macellai Bolognesi – mestiere, politica e vita civile nella storia di una categoria attraverso i secoli*. Bologna, 1980.
Farina, Sandra. "I conventi mendicanti nel tessuto urbanistico di Bologna." *Storia della città* 9 (1978): 56–61.
Farmer, Sharon. *Surviving Poverty in Medieval Paris: Gender, Ideology, and the Daily Lives of the Poor*. Ithaca: Cornell University Press, 2002.
Fasoli, Gina. "Bologna nell'età medievale (1115–1506)." In *Storia di Bologna*, edited by Amadeo Benati, Antonio Ferri, and Giancarlo Roversi, 129–196. Bologna: ALFA, 1984.

——. "Il notaio nella vita cittadina bolognese." In *Notariato medievale bolognese*, 2: 134–141. Studi Storici sul Notariato Italiano, 3. Roma: Consiglio Nazionale del Notariato, 1977.

——. "Le Compagnie delle Arti in Bologna fino al principio del sec. XV." *L'Archiginnasio* 30 (1935): 237–280 and 31 (1936): 46–79.

Favoro, Antonio. "Ancora del tentativo di procurare una nuova emigrazione di scolari dallo studio di Bologna a quello di Padova intorno all metà del secolo XIV." *Atti e memorie della Deputazione di storia patria per le provincie di Romagna* 4th ser., 7 (1917): 195–202.

——. "Di un tentativo per procurare una nuova emigrazione di scolari dallo studio di Bologna a quello di Padova intorno alla metà del secolo XIV." *Nuovo Archivio Veneto* 31 (1916): 254–259.

——. "Nuovi documenti intorno all'emigrazione dei professori e degli scolari dallo Studio di Bologna, avvenuta nel 1321." *Atti e memorie della Deputazione di storia patria per le provincie di Romagna* 3rd ser., 10 (1893): 313–323.

Filippini, F. "L'Esodo degli Studenti da Bologna nel 1321 e il 'Polifemo' dantesco." *Studi e memorie per la storia dell'Università di Bologna* 6 (1921): 107–157.

Frati, Ludovico. "Gli stazionari bolognesi nel Medio Evo." *Archivio Storico Italiano* 5th ser., 15 (1910): 380–390.

French, Katherine L. *The Good Women of the Parish: Gender and Religion after the Black Death.* Philadephia: University of Pennsylvania Press, 2008.

Garrioch, David. *Neighborhood and Community in Paris, 1740–1790.* Cambridge: Cambridge University Press, 1986.

Gasquet, Francis Aiden, D.D. *The Black Death of 1348 and 1349.* London: George Bell and Sons, 1908.

Gaudenzi, A. "Statuti dei mercanti fiorentini dimoranti in Bologna negli anni 1279–1289." *Archivio Storico Italiano*, s. 5, 1 (1881): 1–19.

Getz, Faye Marie. "Black Death and the Silver Lining: Meaning, Continuity, and Revolutionary Change in Histories of Medieval Plague." *Journal of the History of Biology* 24 (1991): 265–89.

Giansante, Massimo and Giorgio Marcon, *Giudici e poeti toscani a Bologna: Tracce archivistiche fra tardo stilnovismo e preumanesimo.* Bologna: Archivio di Stato di Bologna, 1994.

Giansante, Massimo. "Il quartiere bolognese di Porta Procola alla fine del Duecento Aspetti economici e sociali nell'estimo del 1296–97." *Il Carrobbio* 11 (1985): 123–141.

——."L'età comunale a Bologna: Strutture sociali, vita economica e temi urbanistico-demografici: orientamenti e problemi." *Bullettino dell'Istituto Storico Italiano per il Medio Evo e Archivio Muratoriano* 92 (1985/1986): 103–222.

——. *Patrimonio familiare e potere nel periodo tardo-comunale: Il progetto signorile di Romeo Pepoli banchiere bolognese (1250 c. – 1322).* Università degli Studi di Bologna, Dipartimento di Paleografia e Medievistica, Fonti e saggi di storia regionale, 1. Bologna: La Fotocromo Emiliana, 1991.

——. *Retorica e politica nel Duecento: I notai bolognesi e l'ideologia comunale.* Istituto Storico Italiano per il Medio Evo, Nuovi Studi Storici, 48. Roma: Istituto Storico Italiano per il Medio Evo, 1999.

Gigliola di Renzo Villata, Maria. "Il volta della famiglia medievale tra practica e teoria nella *Summa totius artis notariae.*" In *Rolandino e l'ars notaria da Bologna all'Europa*, ed. Giorgio Tamba, 380–458. Milano: Giuffrè, 2002.

Ginatempo, Maria and Lucia Sandri. *L'Italia delle città: il popolamento urbano tra Medioevo e Rinascimento (secoli XIII–XVI.* Florence: Le Lettere, 1990.

Giuliodori, Serena. "*De re uxoris*: Dote e successione negli Statuti bolognesi (1250–1454)." *Archivio Storico Italiano* 606 (2005): 651–685.

Gottfried, Robert. *The Black Death: Natural and Human Disaster in Medieval Europe.* New York: Free Press, 1983.

Greci, Roberto. "La tariffa daziaria bolognese del 1351." *Il Carrobbio* 4 (1978): 265–289.
Grubb, James S. *Provincial Families of the Renaissance: Private and Public Life in the Veneto*. Baltimore: Johns Hopkins University Press, 1996.
Guidoni, Enrico and Angelica Zolla. *Progetti per una città: Bologna nei secoli XIII e XIV*. Rome: Bonsignori Editore, 2000.
Guzzetti, Linda. "Testamentsforschung in Europa seit den 1970er Jahren: Bibliographischer Überblick." In *Seelenheil und irdischer Besitz: Testamente als Quellen für den Umgang mit den 'letzten Dingen'*, eds. Markwart Herzog and Cecilie Hollberg, 17–33. Constance, 2007.
——. "Le donne a Venezia nel XIV secolo: Uno studio sulla loro presenza nella società e nella famiglia." *Studi Veneziani*, n.s. 35 (1998): 15–87.
Henderson, John. "The Black Death in Florence: medical and communal responses." In *Death in Towns: Urban Responses to the Dying and Dead, 100–1600*, ed. S. Bassett, 136–150. Leicester: Leicester University Press, 1992.
Herlihy, David and Christiane Klapisch-Zuber. *Les Toscans et leurs familles: Une étude du catasto florentin de 1427*. Paris: Fondation Nationale des Sciences Politiques, 1978.
Herlihy, David. *Opera Muliebria: Women and Work in Medieval Europe*. New York: McGraw-Hill, 1990.
——. "The Black Death: Shock and Social Fissures." *The Maine Scholar* 5 (1992): 33–42.
——. *The Black Death and the Transformation of the West*. Edited by Samuel Kline Cohn, Jr. Cambridge, MA and London: Harvard University Press, 1997.
Hessel, Alfred. *Storia della città di Bologna dal 1116 al 1280*. Edited and translated by Gina Fasoli. Bologna: ALFA, 1975.
Horrox, Rosemary, trans. and ed. *The Black Death*. Manchester: Manchester University Press, 1994.
Hughes, Diane Owen. "Domestic Ideals and Social Behavior: Evidence from Medieval-Genoa." In *The Family in History*, eds. Charles Rosenburg and Stephen Allen Kaplan, 115–143. Philadephia: University of Pennsylvania Press, 1975.
——. "Urban Growth and Family Structure in Medieval Genoa." *Past and Present* 66 (1975): 3–28.
——. "From Brideprice to Dowry in Mediterranean Europe." *Journal of Family History* 3 (1978): 262–296.
——. "Kinsmen and Neighbors in Medieval Genoa." In *The Medieval City*, eds. Harry A. Miskimin, David Herlihy, and A. L. Udovitch, 95–111. New Haven and London: Yale University Press, 1977.
——. "Toward Historical Ethnography: Notarial Records and Family History in the Middle Ages." *Historical Methods Newsletter* 7 (1974): 61–71.
Hyde, J. K. *Society and Politics in Medieval Italy: The Evolution of the Civil Life, 1000–1350*. New York: St. Martin's Press, 1973.
Jansen, Katherine L. "Peacemaking in the Oltrarno, 1287–1297." In *Pope, Church, and Society: Essays in Honour of Brenda M. Bolton*. Edited by Frances Andrews, Christoph Egger and Constance M. Rousseau, 327–344. Leiden: Brill, 2004.
Jordan, William Chester. *The Great Famine*. Princeton: Princeton University Press, 1997.
Kedar, Benjamin Z. "The Genoese Notaries of 1382: The Anatomy of an Urban Occupational Group." In *The Medieval City*, edited by Harry A. Miskimin, David Herlihy, and A. L. Udovitch. New Haven and London: Yale University Press, 1977.
Kelly, John. *The Great Mortality: An Intimate History of the Black Death, the Most Devastating Plauge of All Time*. New York: HarperCollins, 2005.
Kent, Francis W. and Dale V. Kent, *Neighbours and Neighbourhoods in Renaissance Florence: The District of the Red Lion in the Fifteenth Century*. Locust Valley, N.Y.: J. J. Augustin, 1982.
Kibre, Pearl. *Scholarly Privileges in the Middle Ages: The Rights, Privileges, and Immunities, of Scholars and Universities at Bologna, Padua, Paris, and Oxford*. Cambridge, MA: Mediaeval Academy of America, 1962.

——. *The Nations in the Medieval Universities*. Cambridge, MA: Mediaeval Academy of America, 1948.

Kirshner, Julius. "Some problems in the interpretation of legal texts re the Italian city-State." *Archiv fur Begriffsgeschichte* 19 (1975): 17–27.

——. "*Civitas sibi faciat civem*: Bartolus of Sassoferato's Doctrine on the Making of a Citizen" *Speculum* 48 (1973).

——. "Made Exiles for the Love of Knowledge: Students in Late Medieval Italy" forthcoming in *Atti del Convegno su Bartolomeo Cipolla: un giurista veronese del Quattrocento tra cattedra, foro e luoghi del potere (Verona, 15–16 ottobre 2004)*.

Klapisch-Zuber, Christiane. *Women, Family, and Ritual in Renaissance Italy*. Translated by Lydia Cochrane. Chicago and London: University of Chicago, 1985.

Kohl, Benjamin. *Major Problems in the History of the Italian Renaissance*. Lexington, Mass. and Toronto: Heath, 1995.

Kuehn, Thomas. *Heirs, Kin, and Creditors in Renaissance Florence*. Cambridge: Cambridge University Press, 2008.

——. "Law, Death, and Heirs in the Renaissance: Repudiation of Inheritance in Florence." *Renaissance Quarterly* 15 (1992): 484–516.

——. *Law, Family, and Women: Toward a Legal Anthropology of Renaissance Italy*. Chicago and London: University of Chicago Press, 1991.

——. Review of Steven Epstein, *Wills and Wealth in Medieval Genoa, 1150–1250. Speculum* 61 (1986): 145.

——. *Emancipation in Late Medieval Florence*. New Brunswick, N.J.: Rutgers University Press, 1982.

Kumhera, Glenn. "Making Peace in Medieval Siena: Instruments of Peace, 1280–1400." PhD diss., University of Chicago, 2005.

Lampe, Mary. "Survival and Profit: Witnessing Groups in Post-Vespers Palermo". PhD diss., University of California at Santa Barbara, 2007.

La peste nera: dati di una realtà ed elementi di una interpretazione. Spoleto: Centro italiano di studi sull'alto medioevo, 1994.

Larner, John. *The lords of Romagna: Romagnol society and the origins of the signorie*. Ithaca, NY: Cornell University Press, 1965.

Lazzari, Tiziana. *Comitato senza città: Bologna e l'aristocrazia del territorio, secoli IX–XI*. Torino: Paravia Scriptorium, 1998.

Lee, Frederic S. "Theory foundation and the methodological foundations of Post Keynesian economics." In *Applied Economics and the Critical Realist Critique*, ed. Paul Downward, 170–193. London and New York: Routledge, 2003.

Livi, G. "I mercanti di seta lucchesi in Bologna nei secoli XIII e XIV. Notizie e documenti." *Archivio Storico Italiano*, s. IV, 7 (1881): 29–55.

Lumia-Ostinelli, Gianna. "'Ut cippus domus magis conservetur': La sucessione a Siena tra statuti e testamenti (secoli XII–XVII)." *Archivio Storico Italiano* 161, 595 (2003): 3–51.

Maire Vigueur, Jean-Claude. "Révolution documentaire et révolution scripturaire: le cas de l'Italie médiévale" *Bibliothèque de l'École des chartes* 153 (1995): 177–185.

Mazzaoui, Maureen Fennell. "The Emigration of Veronese Textile Artisans to Bologna in the Thirteenth Century." *Atti e memorie dell'Accademia di Agricoltura, Scienze e Lettere di Verona*, s. 6, 18–19 (1967–68): 275–322.

McKee, Sally. "Households in Fourteenth-Century Venetian Crete." *Speculum* 70 (1995): 27–67.

Meek, Christine. "Women, Dowries and the Family in Late Medieval Italian Cities." In *"The Fragility of Her Sex"?: Medieval Irishwomen in Their European Context*, eds. Christine Meek and Katharine Simms. Dublin: Four Courts Press, 1996.

Milani, Giuliano. *L'esclusione dal comune: Conflitti e bandi politici a Bologna e in altre città italiane tra XII e XIV secolo*. Istituto Storico Italiano per il Medio Evo, Nuovi Studi Storici, 63. Rome: Istituto Storico Italiano per il Medio Evo, 2003.

Molho, Anthony. *Marriage alliance in late Medieval Florence*. Cambridge, MA: Harvard University Press, 1994.

Montford, Angela M. *Health, Sickness, Medicine and the Friars in the Thirteenth and Fourteenth Centuries*. Aldershot, UK and Burlington, VT: Ashgate, 2004.

Mueller, Reinhold. "Aspetti sociali ed economici della pesta a Venezia nel Medioevo." In *Venezia e la peste 1348/1797*, 71–76. Venice: Marsilio, 1979.

——. "Peste e demografia: Medioevo e Rinascimento." In *Venezia e la Peste 1348/1797*, 93–96. Venice: Marsilio, 1979.

Naphy, William and Andrew Spicer, *The Black Death and the History of Plagues 1345–1730*. Stroud, Gloucestershire: Tempus, 2000.

Naso, Irma. "Individuazione diagnostica della 'peste nera'. Cultura medica e aspetti clinici." In *La peste nera: Dati di una realtà ed elementi di una interpretazione*, 349–381. Spoleto: Centro italiano per studi sull'alto medioevo, 1994.

Nolens intestatus decedere: Il testamento come fonte della storia religiosa e sociale. Atti dell'incontro di studio (Perugia, 3 maggio 1983). Regione di Umbria: Editrice Umbra Cooperative, 1985.

Orlandelli, Gianfranco. *Il libro a Bologna dal 1300 al 1330: Documenti con uno studio su il contratto di scrittura nella dottrina notarile bolognese*. Bologna: Zanichelli, 1959.

——. "I Memoriali bolognesi come fonte per la storia dei tempi di Dante." In *Dante e Bologna nei tempi di Dante*, 193–205. Bologna: Facoltà di Lettere e Filosofia, University of Bologna, 1967.

Palazzotto, Dominick. "The Black Death and Medicine: A Report and Analysis of the Tractates written between 1348 and 1350." PhD diss, University of Kansas, 1973.

Paolini, Lorenzo. "Domus e zona degli eretici: L'esempio di Bologna nel XIII secolo." *Rivista di storia della chiesa in Italia* 35 (1981): 371–387.

Park, Katharine. *Doctors and Medicine in Early Renaissance Florence*. Princeton: Princeton University Press, 1985.

Piana, Celestino. *Ricerche sulle università di Bologna e di Parma nel secolo XV*. Florence: Typographia Collegii S. Bonaventurae, 1963.

——. *Nuovi documenti sull'Università di Bologna e sul Collegio di Spagna*. Studia Albornotiana, n.26. Bologna: Publicaciones del Real Colegio de España, 1976.

Pini, Antonio Ivan and Roberto Greci, "Una fonte per la demografia storica medievale: le 'venticinquine' bolognesi (1247–1404)." *Rassegna degli Archivi di Stato*, 26 (1976): 337–417.

Pini, Antonio Ivan. "Bologna nel suo secolo d'oro: Da 'comune aristocratico' a 'repubblica di notai'." In *Rolandino e l'Ars Notaria da Bologna all'Europa: Atti del convegno internazionale di studi storici sulla figura e l'opera di Rolandino*, ed. Giorgio Tamba, 3–20. Milano: Giuffrè, 2002.

——. *Campagne bolognesi: Le radici agrarie di una metropoli medievale*. Firenze: Le lettere, 1993.

——. "Circoscrizioni urbane e indici d'affollamento demografico a Bologna nel Due e Trecento." In *Misure umane: Un dibattito internazionale su borgo, citta, quartiere, comprensorio*, eds. C. Doglio, G. Fasoli, P. Guidicini, 49–53. Milan: Angeli, 1978.

——. *Città medievali e demografia storica: Bologna, Romagna, Italia (secc. XIII–XV)*. Bologna: CLUEB, 1996.

——. "Energia e industria tra Sàvena e Reno: I mulini idraulici bolognesi tra XI e XV secolo." In *Tecnica e società nell'Italia dei secoli XII–XVI*, 1–25. Pistoia: Centro italiano Studi di storia e d'arte, 1987. Reprinted in Pini, *Campagne bolognesi: Le radici agrarie di una metropoli medievale*. Firenze: Le Lettere, 1993.

——. "Famiglie, insediamenti e banchi ebraici a Bologna e nel bolognese nella seconda metà del Trecento." *Quaderni Storici* 18 (1983): 783–814.

——. "Forme di conduzione, rendita fondiaria e rese cerealicole nel Bolognese dopo la peste del 1348: l'azienda del convento di San Domenico." In *Medioevo rurale: Sulle*

tracce della civiltà contadina, eds. Vito Fumagalli and Gabriella Rossetti, 259–297. Bologna: Mulino, 1980.
——. "Gli estimi cittadini di Bologna dal 1296 al 1329: Un esempio di utilizzazione: il patrimonio fondiario del beccaio Giacomo Casella." *Studi Medievali*, ser. 3, 18 (1977): 111–59.
——. "L'arte del cambio a Bologna nel XIII secolo." *Archiginnasio* 57 (1962): 20–81.
——. "La chiesa, il monastero e la parrocchia di San Vitale a Bologna dalle origini alla fine del XIII secolo." Reprinted in Pini, *Città, chiesa e culti civici in Bologna medievale*, 91–118. Bologna: CLUEB, 1999.
——. "La ripartizione topografica degli artigiani a Bologna nel 1294: Un esempio di demografia sociale." In *Artigiani e salariati: Il mondo del lavoro nell'Italia dei secoli XII–XV*, 189–224. Pistoia: Centro italiano di studi di storia e d'arte, 1984.
——. "Le piazze medievali di Bologna." *Annali di architettura* 4–5 (1992–1993): 122–133.
——. "Le ripartizioni territoriali urbane di Bologna medievale: Quartiere, contrada, borgo, morello e quartirolo." *Quaderni Culturali Bolognesi* 1 (1977): 4–49.
——. "Mura e porte di Bologna medievale: la piazza di Porta Ravegnana." In *Fortifications, portes de villes, places publiques dans le monde méditerranéen*, ed. Jacques Heers, 197–235. Paris: Presses de l'Université de Paris-Sorbonne, 1985.
——. "Origine e testimonianze del sentimento civico bolognese." In *La coscienza cittadina nei comuni italiani del Duecento*, 139–193. Todi: Convegni del Centro di Studi sulla Spiritualità Medievale, 1972.
——. "Pesce, pescivendoli e mercanti di pesce in Bologna medievale." *Carrobbio* I (1975): 327–349.
——. "Potere pubblico e addetti ai trasporti e al vettovagliamento cittadino nel medioevo: Il caso di Bologna." *Nuova Rivista Storica* 66 (1982): 253–281.
——. "Problemi di demografia bolognese del Duecento." *Atti e Memorie della Deputazione di Storia Patria per le Provincie di Romagna*, n.s. 16–17, (1969): 147–222.
——. "Produzione artigianato e commercio a Bologna e in Romagna nel Medio Evo." In *Storia della Emilia Romagna*, ed. Aldo Berselli, 1:519–547. Bologna: University Press, 1975.
——. "Un principe dei notai in una "Repubblica di Notai": Rolandino Passaggeri nella Bologna del Duecento." *Nuova Rivista Storica* 84 (2000): 51–72.
——. "Una fonte per la demografia storica medievale: le 'venticinquinne' bolognesi (1247–1404)." *Rassegna degli Archivi di Stato* 36 (1976): 337–417.
——. *La società italiana prima e dopo la 'peste nera'*. Incontri Pistoesi di Storia Arte Cultura, 8. Pistoia: Società pistoiese di storia patria, 1981.
Platt, Colin. *King Death*. Toronto: University of Toronto Press, 1997.
Prodi, Paolo and Lorenzo Paolini, eds. *Storia della Chiesa di Bologna*. 2 vols. Bologna: Bolis, 1997.
Rawski, Conrad H. "Notes on the Rhetoric in Petrarch's *Invective contra medicum*." In *Francis Petrarch, Six Centuries Later: A Symposium*, edited by Aldo Scaglione, 249–277. Chapel Hill and The Newberry Library, Chicago: NCSRLL, 1975.
Ricci, Giovanni. *Le città nella storia d'Italia: Bologna*. Roma: Editori Laterza, 1985.
Ricci, Simona. *"De hac vita transire": La practica testimentaria nel Valdarno superiore all'indomani della Peste Nera*. Fonti e studi di storia locale, 11. Figline, Italy: Opus Libri, 1998.
Rashdall, Hastings. *The Universities of Europe in the Middle Ages*, 3 vols. Oxford: Oxford University Press, new ed. 1936.
Rodolico, Niccolò. *Dal comune alla signoria: Saggio sul governo di Taddeo Pepoli in Bologna*. Bologna: Zanichelli, 1898.
Rollo-Koster, Joelle. "The Women of Papal Avignon. A New Source: The *Liber Divisionis* of 1371." *Journal of Women's History* 8 (1996): 36–59.
Romano, Dennis. "Charity and Community in Early Renaissance Venice." *Journal of Urban History* 11 (1984): 63–82.

——. *Patricians and Popolani: The Social Foundations of the Venetian Renaissance State.* Baltimore: Johns Hopkins University Press, 1987.

Roversi, Giancarlo. "Le arti per l'arte. Le sedi e il patrimonio artistico delle antiche corporazioni di mestiere bolognesi." In *La Mercanzia di Bologna*, with contributions by Maurizio Armaroli, Pier Luigi Cervellati, Rolando Dondarini, Andrea Emiliani, Massimo Guagnini, Giancarlo Roversi, and Angelo Tantazzi, 149–154. Bologna: Nuova Alfa Editoriale, 1995.

Samaritani, Antonio. "Mentalità religiosa specie nell'ora del testamento in un castello bolognese: Cento nel sec. XIV." *Analecta pomposiana: studi di storia religiosa delle diocesi di Ferrara e Comacchio* 12 (1987): 5–36.

——. *Una pieve bolognese nel tardo medioevo: la pieve "de Cento" (secc. XIII–XV).* Cento: Cassa di Risparmio, 1992.

Schwarz, Brigide. "Das Notariat in Bologna im 13. Jahrhundert." *Quellen und Forschungen aus italienischen Archiven und Bibliotheken* 53 (1973): 49–92.

Scott, Susan and Christopher J. Duncan, *Biology of Plagues: Evidence from Historical Populations.* Cambridge: Cambridge University Press, 2001.

Siraisi, Nancy G. "The Physician's Task: Medical Reputations in humanist collective biographies." Reprinted in *Medicine and the Italian Universities 1250–1600.* Leiden, Boston, and Köln: Brill, 2001.

Smail, Daniel Lord. "Accommodating Plague in Medieval Marseille." *Continuity and Change* 11 (1996): 11–41.

——. *Imaginary Cartographies: Possession and Identity in Late Medieval Marseille.* Ithaca and London: Cornell University Press, 1999.

——. *The Consumption of Justice: Emotions, Publicity, and Legal Culture in Marseille, 1264–1423.* Ithaca and London: Cornell University Press, 2003.

Sorbelli, Albano. *Storia della Università di Bologna.* Bologna: Zanichelli, 1944. vol. I: Il Medioevo (sec. XI–XV).

——. "Gli stipendi dei professori dell'Università di Bologna nel secolo XIV." *L'Archiginnasio* 7 (1912): 1–10.

——. *Le croniche bolognesi del secolo XIV.* Bologna: Zanichelli, 1900.

Stelling-Michaud, Sven. *L'Université de Bologne et la pénétration des droits romain et canonique en Suisse au XIIIe et XIV siècles.* Geneva: Librairie E. Droz, 1955.

Storey, Wayne. *Transcription and Visual Poetics in the Early Italian Lyric.* New York: Garland, 1993.

Strocchia, Sharon. *Death and Ritual in Renaissance Florence.* Baltimore and London: Johns Hopkins University Press, 1992.

Tabarroni, Andrea. "Notizie biografiche su alcuni maestri di arti e medicina attivi nello *Studium* bolognese nel XIV secolo" in *L'insegnamento della logica a Bologna nel XIV secolo*, eds. Dino Buzzetti, Maurizio Ferriani, and Andrea Tabarroni. Bologna: L'Istituto per la storia universitaria, 1992.

Tamba, Giorgio, ed. *Rolandino (1215–1300). Alle origini del notariato moderno.* Bologna: Consiglio Nazionale del Notariato, 2000.

Tamba, Giorgio. "I documenti del governo del comune bolognese (1116–1512): Lineamenti della struttura istituzionale della città durante il Medioevo." *Quaderni Culturali Bolognesi* II (1978).

——. "I Memoriali del comune di Bologna nel secolo XIII: note di diplomatica." *Rassegna degli Archivi di Stato* 47 (1987): 235–290.

——. *Teorie e pratica della "commissione notarile" a Bologna nell'età comunale.* Bologna: Archivio di Stato di Bologna, 1991.

——. "Un archivio notarile? No, tuttavia..." *Archivi per la Storia* 3 (1990): 41–96.

Tenenti, Alberto. "La rappresentazione della morte collettiva nel 'Decameron'." *Intersezioni* 12, 2 (1992): 235–246.

Thompson, Augustine. *Cities of God: The Religion of the Italian Communes 1125–1325.* University Park: Pennsylvania State University Press, 2005.

Vallerani, Massimo. *La giustizia pubblica medievale*. Bologna: Il Mulino, 2005.

——. "The Generation of the 'Moderni' at Work: Jurists Between School and Politics in Medieval Bologna (1270–1305)" in *Europa und seine Regionen: 2000 Jahre Rechtsgeschichte*, eds. Andreas Bauer and Karl H.L. Welker, 139–156. Cologne: Böhlau, 2007.

Venezia e la peste 1348/1797. Venice: Marsilio Editore, 1979.

Volpi, Jacopo. "Mercanti e setaioli a Bologna intorno a 1400." *Archivio Storico Italiano* 570 (1996): 583–614.

Wandruszka, Nikolai. "The family origins of Christine de Pizan: Noble Lineage between city and contado in the thirteenth and fourteenth centuries." In *Au Champ des Escriptures. IIIe Colloque international sur Christine de Pizan*, ed. Eric Hicks, 111–129. Paris: Honoré Champion Éditeur, 2000.

Weissman, Ronald F. E. "The Importance of Being Ambiguous: Social Relations, Individualism, and Identity in Renaissance Florence." In *Urban Life in the Renaissance*, eds. Susan Zimmerman and Ronald F. E. Weissman, 269–280. Newark: University of Delaware Press, 1989.

——. *Ritual Brotherhood in Renaissance Florence*. New York: Academic Press, 1982.

Wickham, Christopher. *Courts and Conflict in Twelfth-Century Lucca*. Oxford: Oxford University Press, 2003.

Williman, Daniel, ed. *The Black Death : the Impact of the Fourteenth-Century Plague: Papers of the Eleventh Annual Conference of the Center for Medieval & Early Renaissance Studies*. Binghamton, NY: Center for Medieval & Early Renaissance Studies, 1982.

Wray, Shona Kelly [and Kelly Wray, Shona]. "Tracking Families and Flight in Bologna during the Black Death." *Medieval Prosopograpy: History and Collective Biography* 25 (2004, published 2008): 145–160.

——. "Boccaccio and the Doctors: Medicine and Compassion in the Face of Plague." *Journal of Medieval History* 30 (2004): 301–322.

——. "Women, Family, and Inheritance in Bologna during the Black Death." In *Love, Marriage, and Family Ties in the Middle Ages*, eds. Miriam Muller and Isabel Davis, 205–215. Belgium: Brepols, 2003.

——. "*Speculum et Exemplar*: The Notaries of Bologna during the Black Death." *Quellen und Forschungen aus italienischen Archiven und Bibliotheken* 81 (2001): 200–227.

Zanella, Gabrielle. "Italia, Francia e Germania: una storiografia a confronto." In *La peste nera: dati di una realtà ed elementi di una interpretazione*, 49–135. Spoleto: Centro italiano di studi sull'alto medioevo, 1994.

Ziegler, Philip. *The Black Death*. New York: Harper & Row, 1969; reprint, London: Sutton, 1997.

GENERAL INDEX

Note: Bolognese families, with italianized names, are included in this general index. For archival references for Bolognese testators, see the Index of Bolognese Individuals with the Latin names.

INDEX OF MEDIEVAL BOLOGNESE INDIVIDUALS (1348)

Note: This index can be used to find Bolognese testators and individuals who are noted in the testaments and contracts of the *Memoriali* and *Demaniale* of 1337 and, especially, 1348. Following the index format employed in Luisa Continelli, ed., *L'archivio dell'Ufficio dei Memoriali: Inventario: Vol. I Memoriali, 1265–1436, Tomo II, 1334–1436* (Bologna: Bononia University Press, 2008), the terms *quondam, olim, fratris, magister, ser, domini,* and titles have been removed, but can be found in the text and footnotes along with archival references. Individuals are listed by patronymic or surname, not first name (thus, they are listed only once in this index). Friars, priests, and officials, who are named in the Bolognese notarial records only by their first name (e.g. *dopnus* Gerardus) or by first name and place of origin (e.g. *frater* Johannes de Castro Britorum, Johannes de Feltro *iudex*) are not included here. This index also does not include names in the tables or appendices, as they can searched easily and the archival citations are not provided therein. In order to research groups of family members in the testaments of the *Memoriali* and *Demaniale* of 1348, find the name of person of interest below, then check Tables 3.1 (spouses), 3.2 (parents and children), 3.3 (siblings) to find the names of their family members and return to this index to find the reference to the archival citation of the relevant testament. The famous Bolognese individuals, such as jurists and rulers, as well as the elite families, cited in the text according to their italianized names, can be found in the General Index. For further names and archival references of the notarial record of 1337 and 1348, contact the author.